Instructor's Manual

MICROECONOMICS

Instructor's Manual

MICROECONOMICS

Sixth Edition

Robert S. Pindyck
Daniel L. Rubinfeld

Nora Underwood
University of Central Florida

PEARSON

Prentice
Hall

Upper Saddle River, New Jersey 07458

VP/Editorial Director: Jeff Shelstad
Executive Editor: David Alexander
Project Manager: Marie McHale
Manager, Print Production: Christy Mahon
Production Editor & Buyer: Wanda Rockwell
Printer/Binder: Courier, Bookmart Press

Pearson Prentice Hall^TM is a trademark of Pearson Education, Inc.

10 9 8 7 6 5 4 3 2 1
ISBN 0-13-008462-X

CONTENTS

PART I

INTRODUCTION: MARKETS AND PRICES

CHAPTER 1

PRELIMINARIES

TEACHING NOTES

The first two chapters reacquaint students with the microeconomics that they learned in their introductory course: Chapter 1 focuses on the general subject of economics, while Chapter 2 develops supply and demand analysis. The use of examples in Chapter 1 facilitates students' complete understanding of abstract economic concepts. Examples in this chapter discuss markets for prescription drugs (Section 1.2), introduction of a new automobile (Section 1.4), design of automobile emission standards (Section 1.4), the minimum wage (Section 1.3), the market for sweeteners (Section 1.3), and real and nominal prices of eggs and education (Section 1.3). Discussing some of these, or another, example is a useful way to review some important economic concepts such as scarcity, making tradeoffs, building economic models to explain how consumers and firms make decisions, and the distinction between competitive and non-competitive markets. Parts I and II of the text assume competitive markets, market power is discussed in Part III, and some consequences of market power are discussed in Part IV of the text.

Review Question (2) illustrates the difference between positive and normative economics and provides for a productive class discussion. Other examples for discussion are available in Kearl, Pope, Whiting, and Wimmer, "A Confusion of Economists," *American Economic Review* (May 1979).

The chapter concludes with a discussion of real and nominal prices. Given our reliance on dollar prices in the chapters that follow, students should understand that we are concerned with prices relative to a standard, which in this case is dollars for a particular year.

QUESTIONS FOR REVIEW

1. It is often said that a good theory is one that can be refuted by an empirical, data-oriented study. Explain why a theory that cannot be evaluated empirically is not a good theory.

There are two steps to consider when evaluating a theory: first, you should examine the reasonability of the theory's assumptions; second, you should test the theory's predictions by comparing them with facts. If a theory cannot be tested, it cannot be accepted or rejected. Therefore, it contributes little to our understanding of reality.

2. Which of the following two statements involves positive economic analysis and which normative? How do the two kinds of analysis differ?

a. Gasoline rationing (allocating to each individual a maximum amount of gasoline that can be purchased each year) is a poor social policy because it interferes with the workings of the competitive market system.

Positive economic analysis describes *what is*. Normative economic analysis describes *what ought to be*. Statement (a) merges both types of analysis. First, statement (a) makes a positive statement that gasoline rationing "interferes with the workings of the competitive market system." We know from economic analysis that a constraint placed on supply will change the market equilibrium. Second, statement (a) makes the normative statement (i.e., a value judgment) that gasoline rationing is a "poor social policy." Thus, statement (a) makes a normative comment based on a conclusion derived from positive economic analysis of the policy.

1

b. **Gasoline rationing is a policy under which more people are made worse off than are made better off.** → positive

Statement (b) is positive because it states what the effect of gasoline rationing is without making a value judgment about the desirability of the rationing policy.

3. Suppose the price of unleaded regular octane gasoline were 20 cents per gallon higher in New Jersey than in Oklahoma. Do you think there would be an opportunity for arbitrage (i.e., that firms could buy gas in Oklahoma and then sell it at a profit in New Jersey)? Why or why not?

Oklahoma and New Jersey represent separate geographic markets for gasoline because of high transportation costs. If transportation costs were zero, a price increase in New Jersey would prompt arbitrageurs to buy gasoline in Oklahoma and sell it in New Jersey. It is unlikely in this case that the 20 cents per gallon difference in costs would be high enough to create a profitable opportunity for arbitrage, given both transactions costs and transportation costs.

4. In Example 1.3, what economic forces explain why the real price of eggs has fallen while the real price of a college education has increased? How have these changes affected consumer choices?

The price and quantity of goods (e.g., eggs) and services (e.g., a college education) are determined by the interaction of supply and demand. The real price of eggs fell from 1970 to 1985 because of either a reduction in demand (consumers switched to lower-cholesterol food), a reduction in production costs (improvements in egg production technology), or both. In response, the price of eggs relative to other foods decreased. The real price of a college education rose because of either an increase in demand (e.g., more people recognized the value of an education), an increase in the cost of education (e.g., increase in staff salaries), or both.

5. Suppose that the Japanese yen rises against the U.S. dollar- that is, it will take more dollars to buy any given amount of Japanese yen. Explain why this increase simultaneously increases the real price of Japanese cars for U.S. consumers and lowers the real price of U.S. automobiles for Japanese consumers.

As the value of the yen grows relative to the dollar, more dollars exchange for fewer yen. Assume that the costs of production for both Japanese and U.S. automobiles remain unchanged. Then using the new exchange rate, the purchase of a Japanese automobile priced in yen requires more dollars. Similarly, the purchase of a U.S. automobile priced in dollars requires fewer yen.

6. The price of long-distance telephone service fell from 40 cents per minute in 1996 to 22 cents per minute in 1999, a 45-percent (18 cents/40 cents) decrease. The Consumer Price Index increased by 10-percent over this period. What happened to the real price of telephone service?

Let the CPI for 1996 equal 1 and the CPI for 1999 equal 1.1, which reflects a 10% increase in the overall price level. To find the real price of telephone service in each period, divide the nominal price by the CPI for that year. For 1996, we have 40/1 or 40 cents, and for 1999, we have 22/1.1 or 20 cents. The real price therefore fell from 40 to 20 cents, a 50% decline.

EXERCISES

1. Decide whether each of the following statements is true or false and explain why:

a. Fast food chains like McDonald's, Burger King, and Wendy's operate all over the United States. Therefore the market for fast food is a national market.

> This statement is false. People generally buy fast food within their current location and do not travel large distances across the United States just to buy a cheaper fast food meal. Given there is little potential for arbitrage between fast food restaurants that are located some distance from each other, there are likely to be multiple fast food markets across the country.

b. People generally buy clothing in the city in which they live. Therefore there is a clothing market in, say, Atlanta that is distinct from the clothing market in Los Angeles.

> This statement is false. Although consumers are unlikely to travel across the country to buy clothing, suppliers can easily move clothing from one part of the country to another. Thus, if clothing is more expensive in Atlanta than Los Angeles, clothing companies could shift supplies to Atlanta, which would reduce the price in Atlanta. Occasionally, there may be a market for a specific clothing item in a faraway market that results in a great opportunity for arbitrage, such as the market for blue jeans in the old Soviet Union.

c. Some consumers strongly prefer Pepsi and some strongly prefer Coke. Therefore there is no single market for colas.

> This statement is false. Although some people have strong preferences for a particular brand of cola, the different brands are similar enough that they constitute one market. There are consumers who do not have strong preferences for one type of cola, and there are consumers who may have a preference, but who will also be influenced by price. Given these possibilities, the price of cola drinks will not tend to differ by very much, particularly for Coke and Pepsi.

2. The following table shows the average retail price of butter and the Consumer Price Index from 1980 to 2001.

	1980	1985	1990	1995	2000	2001
CPI	100	130.58	158.62	184.95	208.98	214.93
Retail Price of butter (salted, grade AA, per lb.)	$1.88	$2.12	$1.99	$1.61	$2.52	$3.30

a.   Calculate the real price of butter in 1980 dollars. Has the real price increased/decreased/stayed the same since 1980?

> Real price of butter in year X $= \dfrac{CPI_{1980}}{CPI_{year\,X}} * nominal\ price\ in\ year\ X$.

1980	1985	1990	1995	2000	2001
$1.88	$1.62	$1.25	$0.87	$1.21	$1.54

> Since 1980 the real price of butter has decreased.

b. What is the percentage change in the real price (1980 dollars) from 1980 to 2001?

Percentage change in real price from 1980 to 2001 $= \dfrac{1.54 - 1.88}{1.88} = -0.18 = -18\%$.

c. Convert the CPI into 1990 = 100 and determine the real price of butter in 1990 dollars.

To convert the CPI into 1990=100, divide the CPI for each year by the CPI for 1990. Use the formula from part (a) and the new CPI numbers below to find the real price of milk. butter

New CPI			Real price of milk butter		
	1980	63.1		1980	$2.98
	1985	82.3		1985	$2.58
	1990	100		1990	$1.99
	1995	116.6		1995	$1.38
	2000	131.8		2000	$1.91
	2001	135.6		2001	$2.43

d. What is the percentage change in the real price (1990 dollars) from 1980 to 2001? Compare this with your answer in (b). What do you notice? Explain.

Percentage change in real price from 1980 to 2001 $= \dfrac{2.43 - 2.98}{2.98} = -0.18 = -18\%$. This answer is almost identical (except for rounding error) to the answer received for part b. It does not matter which year is chosen as the base year.

3. At the time this book went to print, the minimum wage was $5.15. To find the current minimum wage, go to http://www.bls.gov/cpi/home.htm

Click on: Consumer Price Index- All Urban Consumers (Current Series)

Select: U.S. All items

This will give you the CPI from 1913 to the present.

a. With these values, calculate the current real minimum wage in 1990 dollars.

real minimum wage 2003 $= \dfrac{CPI_{1990}}{CPI_{1998}} * 5.15 = \dfrac{130.7}{163} * 5.15 = \$4.13$.

b. What is the percentage change in the real minimum wage from 1985 to the present, stated in real 1990 dollars?

Assume the minimum wage in 1985 was $3.35. Then,

real minimum wage 1985 $= \dfrac{CPI_{1990}}{CPI_{1985}} * 3.35 = \dfrac{130.7}{107.6} * 3.35 = \$4.07$.

The percentage change in the real minimum wage is therefore

$$\dfrac{4.13 - 4.07}{4.07} = 0.0147, \text{ or about } 1.5\%.$$

CHAPTER 2
THE BASICS OF SUPPLY AND DEMAND

TEACHING NOTES

This chapter reviews the basics of supply and demand that students should be familiar with from their introductory economics class. The instructor can choose to spend more or less time on this chapter depending on how much of a review the students require. This chapter departs from the standard treatment of supply and demand basics found in most other intermediate microeconomics textbooks by discussing some of the world's most important markets (wheat, gasoline, and automobiles) and teaching students how to analyze these markets with the tools of supply and demand. The real-world applications of this theory can be enlightening for students.

Some problems plague the understanding of supply and demand analysis. One of the most common sources of confusion is between *movements along the demand curve* and *shifts in demand*. Through a discussion of the *ceteris paribus* assumption, stress that when representing a demand function (either with a graph or an equation), all other variables are held constant. Movements along the demand curve occur *only with changes in price*. As the omitted factors change, the entire demand function shifts. It may also be helpful to present an example of a demand function that depends not only on the price of the good, but also on income and the price of other goods directly. This helps students understand that these other variables are actually in the demand function, and are merely lumped into the intercept term of the simple linear demand function. Example 2.9 includes an example of a demand and supply function which each depend on the price of a substitute good. Students may also find a review of how to solve two equations with two unknowns helpful. In general, it is a good idea at this point to decide on the level of math that you will use in the class. If you plan to use a lot of algebra and calculus it is a good idea to introduce and review it early on.

To stress the quantitative aspects of the demand curve to students, make the distinction between quantity demanded as a function of price, $Q = D(P)$, and the inverse demand function, where price is a function of the quantity demanded, $P = D^{-1}(Q)$. This may clarify the positioning of price on the Y-axis and quantity on the X-axis.

Students may also question how the market adjusts to a new equilibrium. One simple mechanism is the partial-adjustment cobweb model. A discussion of the cobweb model (based on traditional corn-hog cycle or any other example) adds a certain realism to the discussion and is much appreciated by students. If you decide to write down the demand function so that income and other prices are visible variables in the demand function, you can also do some interesting examples, which explore the linkages between markets and how changes in one market affect price and quantity in other markets.

Although this chapter introduces demand, income, and cross-price elasticities, you may find it more appropriate to return to income and cross-price elasticity after demand elasticity is reintroduced in Chapter 4. Students invariably have a difficult time with the concept of elasticity. It is helpful to explain clearly why a firm may be interested in estimating elasticity. Use concrete examples. For example, a Wall Street Journal article back in the spring of 1998 discussed how elasticity could be used by the movie industry so that different movies could have different ticket prices. This example tends to go over well as college students watch a lot of movies. This type of discussion can also be postponed until revenue is discussed.

5

QUESTIONS FOR REVIEW

1. Suppose that unusually hot weather causes the demand curve for ice cream to shift to the right. Why will the price of ice cream rise to a new market-clearing level?

Assume the supply curve is fixed. The unusually hot weather will cause a rightward shift in the demand curve, creating short-run excess demand at the current price. Consumers will begin to bid against each other for the ice cream, putting upward pressure on the price. The price of ice cream will rise until the quantity demanded and the quantity supplied are equal.

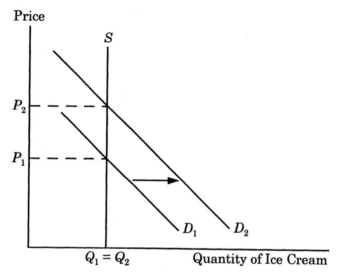

Figure 2.1

2. Use supply and demand curves to illustrate how each of the following events would affect the price of butter and the quantity of butter bought and sold:

a.   An increase in the price of margarine.

Most people consider butter and margarine to be substitute goods. An increase in the price of margarine will cause people to increase their consumption of butter, thereby shifting the demand curve for butter out from D_1 to D_2 in Figure 2.2.a. This shift in demand will cause the equilibrium price to rise from P_1 to P_2 and the equilibrium quantity to increase from Q_1 to Q_2.

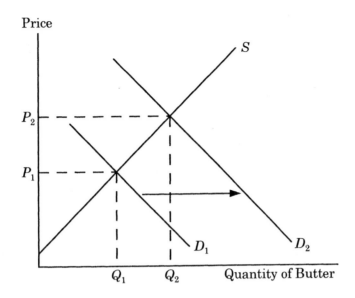

Figure 2.2.a

b. **An increase in the price of milk.**

Milk is the main ingredient in butter. An increase in the price of milk will increase the cost of producing butter. The supply curve for butter will shift from S_1 to S_2 in Figure 2.2.b, resulting in a higher equilibrium price, P_2, covering the higher production costs, and a lower equilibrium quantity, Q_2.

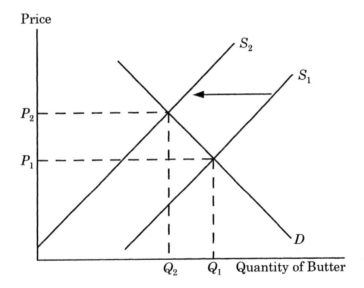

Figure 2.2.b

Note: Given that butter is in fact made from the fat that is skimmed off of the milk, butter and milk are joint products. If you are aware of this relationship, then your answer will change. In this case, as the price of milk increases, so does the quantity supplied. As the quantity supplied of milk increases, there is a larger supply of fat available to make butter. This will shift the supply of butter curve to the right and the price of butter will fall.

c.   A decrease in average income levels.

Assume that butter is a normal good. A decrease in the average income level will cause the demand curve for butter to shift from D_1 to D_2. This will result in a decline in the equilibrium price from P_1 to P_2, and a decline in the equilibrium quantity from Q_1 to Q_2. See Figure 2.2.c.

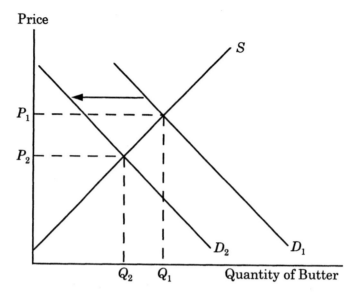

Figure 2.2.c

3. If a 3-percent increase in the price of corn flakes causes a 6-percent decline in the quantity demanded, what is the elasticity of demand?

The elasticity of demand is the percentage change in the quantity demanded divided by the percentage change in the price. The elasticity of demand for corn flakes is $\dfrac{-6}{+3} = -2$.

This is equivalent to saying that a 1% increase in price leads to a 2% decrease in quantity demanded. This is in the elastic region of the demand curve, where the elasticity of demand exceeds -1.0.

4. Explain the difference between a shift in the supply curve and a movement along the supply curve.

A movement along the supply curve is caused by a change in the price or the quantity of the good, since these are the variables on the axes. A shift of the supply curve is caused by any other relevant variable that causes a change in the quantity supplied at any given price. Some examples are changes in production costs and an increase in the number of firms supplying the product.

5. Explain why for many goods, the long-run price elasticity of supply is larger than the short-run elasticity.

The elasticity of supply is the percentage change in the quantity supplied divided by the percentage change in price. An increase in price induces an increase in the quantity supplied by firms. Some firms in some markets may respond quickly and cheaply to price changes. However, other firms may be constrained by their production capacity in the short run. The firms with short-run capacity constraints will have a short-run supply elasticity that is less elastic. However, in the long run all firms can increase their scale of production and thus have a larger long-run price elasticity.

6. Why do long-run elasticities of demand differ from short-run elasticities? Consider two goods: paper towels and televisions. Which is a durable good? Would you expect the price elasticity of demand for paper towels to be larger in the short-run or in the long-run? Why? What about the price elasticity of demand for televisions?

Long-run and short-run elasticities differ based on how rapidly consumers respond to price changes and how many substitutes are available. If the price of paper towels, a non-durable good, were to increase, consumers might react only minimally in the short run. In the long run, however, demand for paper towels would be more elastic as new substitutes entered the market (such as sponges or kitchen towels). In contrast, the quantity demanded of durable goods, such as televisions, might change dramatically in the short run following a price change. For example, the initial result of a price increase for televisions would cause consumers to delay purchases because durable goods are built to last longer. Eventually consumers must replace their televisions as they wear out or become obsolete, and therefore, we expect the demand for durables to be more inelastic in the long run.

7. Are the following statements true or false? Explain your answer.

a.   The elasticity of demand is the same as the slope of the demand curve.

False. Elasticity of demand is the percentage change in quantity demanded for a given percentage change in the price of the product. The slope of the demand curve is the change in price for a given change in quantity demanded, measured in units of output. Though similar in definition, the units for each measure are different.

b.   The cross price elasticity will always be positive.

False. The cross price elasticity measures the percentage change in the quantity demanded of one product for a given percentage change in the price of another product. This elasticity will be positive for substitutes (an increase in the price of hot dogs is likely to cause an increase in the quantity demanded of hamburgers) and negative for complements (an increase in the price of hot dogs is likely to cause a decrease in the quantity demanded of hot dog buns).

c.   The supply of apartments is more inelastic in the short run than the long run.

True. In the short run it is difficult to change the supply of apartments in response to a change in price. Increasing the supply requires constructing new apartment buildings, which can take a year or more. Since apartments are a durable good, in the long run a change in price will induce suppliers to create more apartments (if price increases) or delay construction (if price decreases).

8. Suppose the government regulates the prices of beef and chicken and sets them below their market-clearing levels. Explain why shortages of these goods will develop and what factors will determine the sizes of the shortages. What will happen to the price of pork? Explain briefly.

If the price of a commodity is set below its market-clearing level, the quantity that firms are willing to supply is less than the quantity that consumers wish to purchase. The extent of the excess demand implied by this response will depend on the relative elasticities of demand and supply. For instance, if both supply and demand are elastic, the shortage is larger than if both are inelastic. Factors such as the willingness of consumers to eat less meat and the ability of farmers to change the size of their herds and hence produce less will determine these elasticities and influence the size of excess demand. Customers whose demands are not met will attempt to purchase substitutes, thus increasing the demand for substitutes and raising their prices. If the prices of beef and chicken are set below market-clearing levels, the price of pork will rise, assuming that pork is a substitute for beef and chicken.

9. **The city council of a small college town decides to regulate rents in order to reduce student living expenses. Suppose the average annual market-clearing rent for a two-bedroom apartment had been $700 per month, and rents are expected to increase to $900 within a year. The city council limits rents to their current $700 per month level.**

a. **Draw a supply and demand graph to illustrate what will happen to the rental price of an apartment after the imposition of rent controls.**

The rental price will stay at the old equilibrium level of $700 per month. The expected increase to $900 per month may have been caused by an increase in demand. Given this is true, the price of $700 will be below the new equilibrium and there will be a shortage of apartments.

b. **Do you think this policy will benefit all students? Why or why not.**

It will benefit those students who get an apartment, though these students may also find that the costs of searching for an apartment are higher given the shortage of apartments. Those students who do not get an apartment may face higher costs as a result of having to live outside of the college town. Their rent may be higher and the transportation costs will be higher.

10. **In a discussion of tuition rates, a university official argues that the demand for admission is completely price inelastic. As evidence she notes that while the university has doubled its tuition (in real terms) over the past 15 years, neither the number nor quality of students applying has decreased. Would you accept this argument? Explain briefly. (Hint: The official makes an assertion about the demand for admission, but does she actually observe a demand curve? What else could be going on?)**

If demand is fixed, the individual firm (a university) may determine the shape of the demand curve it faces by raising the price and observing the change in quantity sold. The university official is not observing the entire demand curve, but rather only the equilibrium price and quantity over the last 15 years. If demand is shifting upward, as supply shifts upward, demand could have any elasticity. (See Figure 2.7, for example.) Demand could be shifting upward because the value of a college education has increased and students are willing to pay a high price for each opening. More market research would be required to support the conclusion that demand is completely price inelastic.

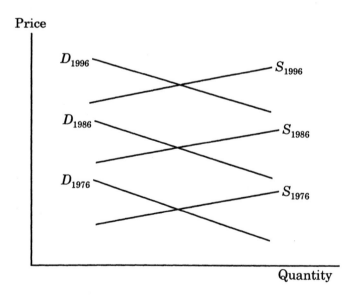

Figure 2.10

11. Suppose the demand curve for a product is given by Q=10-2P+P$_s$, where P is the price of the product and P$_s$ is the price of a substitute good. The price of the substitute good is $2.00.

a.   Suppose P=$1.00. What is the price elasticity of demand? What is the cross-price elasticity of demand?

First you need to find the quantity demanded at the price of $1.00. Q=10-2(1)+2=10.

$$\text{Price elasticity of demand} = \frac{P}{Q}\frac{\Delta Q}{\Delta P} = \frac{1}{10}(-2) = -\frac{2}{10} = -0.2.$$

$$\text{Cross-price elasticity of demand} = \frac{P_s}{Q}\frac{\Delta Q}{\Delta P_s} = \frac{2}{10}(1) = 0.2.$$

b.   Suppose the price of the good, P, goes to $2.00. Now what is the price elasticity of demand? What is the cross-price elasticity of demand?

First you need to find the quantity demanded at the price of $2.00. Q=10-2(2)+2=8.

$$\text{Price elasticity of demand} = \frac{P}{Q}\frac{\Delta Q}{\Delta P} = \frac{2}{8}(-2) = -\frac{4}{8} = -0.5.$$

$$\text{Cross-price elasticity of demand} = \frac{P_s}{Q}\frac{\Delta Q}{\Delta P_s} = \frac{2}{8}(1) = 0.25.$$

12. Suppose that rather than the declining demand assumed in Example 2.8, a decrease in the cost of copper production causes the supply curve to shift to the right by 40 percent. How will the price of copper change?

If the supply curve shifts to the right by 40% then the new quantity supplied will be 140 percent of the old quantity supplied at every price. The new supply curve is therefore

Q' = 1.4*(-4.5+16P) = -6.3+22.4P. To find the new equilibrium price of copper, set the new supply equal to demand so that –6.3+22.4P=13.5-8P. Solving for price results in P=65 cents per pound for the new equilibrium price. The price decreased by 10 cents per pound, or 13.3%.

13. Suppose the demand for natural gas is perfectly inelastic. What would be the effect, if any, of natural gas price controls?

If the demand for natural gas is perfectly inelastic, then the demand curve is vertical. Consumers will demand a certain quantity and will pay any price for this quantity. In this case, a price control will have no effect on the quantity demanded.

EXERCISES

1. **Suppose the demand curve for a product is given by Q=300-2P+4I, where I is average income measured in thousands of dollars. The supply curve is Q=3P-50.**

a. **If I=25, find the market clearing price and quantity for the product.**

Given I=25, the demand curve becomes Q=300-2P+4*25, or Q=400-2P. Setting demand equal to supply we can solve for P and then Q:

$$400-2P=3P-50$$

$$P=90$$

$$Q=220.$$

b. **If I=50, find the market clearing price and quantity for the product.**

Given I=50, the demand curve becomes Q=300-2P+4*50, or Q=500-2P. Setting demand equal to supply we can solve for P and then Q:

$$500-2P=3P-50$$

$$P=110$$

$$Q=280.$$

c. **Draw a graph to illustrate your answers.**

Equilibrium price and quantity are found at the intersection of the demand and supply curves. When the income level increases in part b, the demand curve will shift up and to the right. The intersection of the new demand curve and the supply curve is the new equilibrium point.

2. **Consider a competitive market for which the quantities demanded and supplied (per year) at various prices are given as follows:**

Price ($)	Demand (millions)	Supply (millions)
60	22	14
80	20	16
100	18	18
120	16	20

a. **Calculate the price elasticity of demand when the price is $80 and when the price is $100.**

We know that the price elasticity of demand may be calculated using equation 2.1 from the text:

$$E_D = \frac{\frac{\Delta Q_D}{Q_D}}{\frac{\Delta P}{P}} = \frac{P}{Q_D}\frac{\Delta Q_D}{\Delta P}.$$

With each price increase of $20, the quantity demanded decreases by 2. Therefore,

$$\left(\frac{\Delta Q_D}{\Delta P}\right) = \frac{-2}{20} = -0.1.$$

At $P = 80$, quantity demanded equals 20 and

$$E_D = \left(\frac{80}{20}\right)(-0.1) = -0.40.$$

Similarly, at $P = 100$, quantity demanded equals 18 and

$$E_D = \left(\frac{100}{18}\right)(-0.1) = -0.56.$$

b. **Calculate the price elasticity of supply when the price is $80 and when the price is $100.**

The elasticity of supply is given by:

$$E_S = \frac{\frac{\Delta Q_S}{Q_S}}{\frac{\Delta P}{P}} = \frac{P}{Q_S}\frac{\Delta Q_S}{\Delta P}.$$

With each price increase of $20, quantity supplied increases by 2. Therefore,

$$\left(\frac{\Delta Q_S}{\Delta P}\right) = \frac{2}{20} = 0.1.$$

At $P = 80$, quantity supplied equals 16 and

$$E_S = \left(\frac{80}{16}\right)(0.1) = 0.5.$$

Similarly, at $P = 100$, quantity supplied equals 18 and

$$E_S = \left(\frac{100}{18}\right)(0.1) = 0.56.$$

c. **What are the equilibrium price and quantity?**

The equilibrium price and quantity are found where the quantity supplied equals the quantity demanded at the same price. As we see from the table, the equilibrium price is $100 and the equilibrium quantity is 18 million.

d. **Suppose the government sets a price ceiling of $80. Will there be a shortage, and if so, how large will it be?**

With a price ceiling of $80, consumers would like to buy 20 million, but producers will supply only 16 million. This will result in a shortage of 4 million.

3. Refer to Example 2.5 on the market for wheat. At the end of 1998, both Brazil and Indonesia opened their wheat markets to U.S. farmers. Suppose that these new markets add 200 million bushels to U.S. wheat demand. What will be the free market price of wheat and what quantity will be produced and sold by U.S. farmers in this case?

The following equations describe the market for wheat in 1998:

$$Q_S = 1944 + 207P$$

and

$$Q_D = 3244 - 283P.$$

If Brazil and Indonesia add an additional 200 million bushels of wheat to U.S. wheat demand, the new demand curve would be equal to $Q_D + 200$, or

$$Q_D = (3244 - 283P) + 200 = 3444 - 283P.$$

Equating supply and the new demand, we may determine the new equilibrium price,

$$1944 + 207P = 3444 - 283P, \text{ or}$$

$$490P = 1500, \text{ or } P^* = \$3.06122 \text{ per bushel.}$$

To find the equilibrium quantity, substitute the price into either the supply or demand equation, e.g.,

$$Q_S = 1944 + (207)(3.06122) = 2{,}577.67$$

and

$$Q_D = 3444 - (283)(3.06122) = 2{,}577.67$$

4. A vegetable fiber is traded in a competitive world market, and the world price is $9 per pound. Unlimited quantities are available for import into the United States at this price. The U.S. domestic supply and demand for various price levels are shown below.

Price	U.S. Supply (million lbs.)	U.S. Demand (million lbs.)
3	2	34
6	4	28
9	6	22
12	8	16
15	10	10
18	12	4

a. What is the equation for demand? What is the equation for supply?

The equation for demand is of the form Q=a-bP. First find the slope, which is

$$\frac{\Delta Q}{\Delta P} = \frac{-6}{3} = -2 = -b.$$ You can figure this out by noticing that every time price increases by 3, quantity demanded falls by 6 million pounds. Demand is now Q=a-2P. To find a, plug in any of the price quantity demanded points from the table: Q=34=a-2*3 so that a=40 and demand is Q=40-2P.

The equation for supply is of the form $Q = c + dP$. First find the slope, which is

$$\frac{\Delta Q}{\Delta P} = \frac{2}{3} = d.$$ You can figure this out by noticing that every time price increases by 3,

quantity supplied increases by 2 million pounds. Supply is now $Q = c + \frac{2}{3}P.$ To find c

plug in any of the price quantity supplied points from the table: $Q = 2 = c + \frac{2}{3}(3)$ so

that c=0 and supply is $Q = \frac{2}{3}P.$

b. At a price of $9, what is the price elasticity of demand? What is it at price of $12?

Elasticity of demand at P=9 is $\dfrac{P}{Q}\dfrac{\Delta Q}{\Delta P} = \dfrac{9}{22}(-2) = \dfrac{-18}{22} = -0.82.$

Elasticity of demand at P=12 is $\dfrac{P}{Q}\dfrac{\Delta Q}{\Delta P} = \dfrac{12}{16}(-2) = \dfrac{-24}{16} = -1.5.$

c. What is the price elasticity of supply at $9? At $12?

Elasticity of supply at P=9 is $\dfrac{P}{Q}\dfrac{\Delta Q}{\Delta P} = \dfrac{9}{6}\left(\dfrac{2}{3}\right) = \dfrac{18}{18} = 1.0.$

14

Elasticity of supply at P=12 is $\dfrac{P}{Q}\dfrac{\Delta Q}{\Delta P}=\dfrac{12}{8}\left(\dfrac{2}{3}\right)=\dfrac{24}{24}=1.0.$

d. In a free market, what will be the U.S. price and level of fiber imports?

With no restrictions on trade, world price will be the price in the United States, so that P=\$9. At this price, the domestic supply is 6 million lbs., while the domestic demand is 22 million lbs. Imports make up the difference and are 16 million lbs.

5. Much of the demand for U.S. agricultural output has come from other countries. In 1998, the total demand for wheat was $Q = 3244 - 283P$. Of this, domestic demand was $Q_D = 1700 - 107P$. Domestic supply was $Q_S = 1944 + 207P$. Suppose the export demand for wheat falls by 40 percent.

a.   U.S. farmers are concerned about this drop in export demand. What happens to the free market price of wheat in the United States? Do the farmers have much reason to worry?

Given total demand, $Q = 3244 - 283P$, and domestic demand, $Q_d = 1700 - 107P$, we may subtract and determine export demand, $Q_e = 1544 - 176P$.

The initial market equilibrium price is found by setting total demand equal to supply:

$$3244 - 283P = 1944 + 207P,\text{ or}$$

$$P = \$2.65.$$

The best way to handle the 40 percent drop in export demand is to assume that the export demand curve pivots down and to the left around the vertical intercept so that at all prices demand decreases by 40 percent, and the reservation price (the maximum price that the foreign country is willing to pay) does not change. If you instead shifted the demand curve down to the left in a parallel fashion the effect on price and quantity will be qualitatively the same, but will differ quantitatively.

The new export demand is $0.6Q_e = 0.6(1544 - 176P) = 926.4 - 105.6P$. Graphically, export demand has pivoted inwards as illustrated in figure 2.5a below.

Total demand becomes

$$Q_D = Q_d + 0.6Q_e = 1700 - 107P + 926.4 - 105.6P = 2626.4 - 212.6P.$$

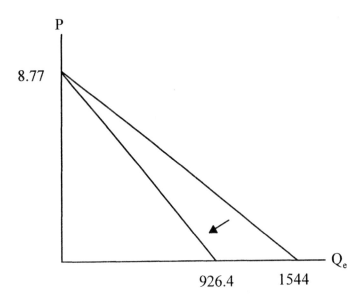

Figure 2.5a

15

Equating total supply and total demand,

$$1944 + 207P = 2626.4 - 212.6P, \text{ or}$$

$$P = \$1.63,$$

which is a significant drop from the market-clearing price of $2.65 per bushel. At this price, the market-clearing quantity is 2280.65 million bushels. Total revenue has decreased from $6614.6 million to $3709.0 million. Most farmers would worry.

b. **Now suppose the U.S. government wants to buy enough wheat each year to raise the price to $3.50 per bushel. With this drop in export demand, how much wheat would the government have to buy? How much would this cost the government?**

With a price of $3.50, the market is not in equilibrium. Quantity demanded and supplied are

$$Q_D = 2626.4 - 212.6(3.5) = 1882.3, \text{ and}$$

$$Q_S = 1944 + 207(3.5) = 2668.5.$$

Excess supply is therefore 2668.5 - 1882.3 = 786.2 million bushels. The government must purchase this amount to support a price of $3.5, and will spend

$3.5(786.2 \text{ million}) = \$2751.7$ million per year.

6. The rent control agency of New York City has found that aggregate demand is

$Q_D = 160 - 8P$. **Quantity is measured in tens of thousands of apartments. Price, the average monthly rental rate, is measured in hundreds of dollars. The agency also noted that the increase in Q at lower P results from more three-person families coming into the city from Long Island and demanding apartments. The city's board of realtors acknowledges that this is a good demand estimate and has shown that supply is $Q_S = 70 + 7P$.**

a. **If both the agency and the board are right about demand and supply, what is the free market price? What is the change in city population if the agency sets a maximum average monthly rental of $300, and all those who cannot find an apartment leave the city?**

To find the free market price for apartments, set supply equal to demand:

$$160 - 8P = 70 + 7P, \text{ or } P = \$600,$$

since price is measured in hundreds of dollars. Substituting the equilibrium price into either the demand or supply equation to determine the equilibrium quantity:

$$Q_D = 160 - (8)(6) = 112$$

and

$$Q_S = 70 + (7)(6) = 112.$$

We find that at the rental rate of $600, the quantity of apartments rented is 1,120,000. If the rent control agency sets the rental rate at $300, the quantity supplied would then be 910,000 ($Q_S = 70 + (7)(3) = 91$), a decrease of 210,000 apartments from the free market equilibrium. (Assuming three people per family per apartment, this would imply a loss of 630,000 people.) At the $300 rental rate, the demand for apartments is 1,360,000 units, and the resulting shortage is 450,000 units (1,360,000-910,000). However, excess demand (supply shortages) and lower quantity demanded are not the same concepts. The supply shortage means that the market cannot accommodate the new people who would have been willing to move into the city at the new lower price. Therefore, the city population will only fall by 630,000, which is represented by the drop in the number of actual apartments from 1,120,000 (the old equilibrium value) to 910,000, or 210,000 apartments with 3 people each.

b. **Suppose the agency bows to the wishes of the board and sets a rental of $900 per month on all apartments to allow landlords a "fair" rate of return. If 50 percent of any long-run increases in apartment offerings come from new construction, how many apartments are constructed?**

At a rental rate of $900, the supply of apartments would be $70 + 7(9) = 133$, or 1,330,000 units, which is an increase of 210,000 units over the free market equilibrium. Therefore, $(0.5)(210,000) = 105,000$ units would be constructed. Note, however, that since demand is only 880,000 units, 450,000 units would go unrented.

7. In 1998, Americans smoked 470 billion cigarettes, or 23.5 billion packs of cigarettes. The average retail price was $2 per pack. Statistical studies have shown that the price elasticity of demand is -0.4, and the price elasticity of supply is 0.5. Using this information, derive linear demand and supply curves for the cigarette market.

Let the demand curve be of the general form Q=a-bP and the supply curve be of the general form Q=c + dP, where a, b, c, and d are the constants that you have to find from the information given above. To begin, recall the formula for the price elasticity of demand

$$E_P^D = \frac{P}{Q}\frac{\Delta Q}{\Delta P}.$$

You are given information about the value of the elasticity, P, and Q, which means that you can solve for the slope, which is b in the above formula for the demand curve.

$$-0.4 = \frac{2}{23.5}\frac{\Delta Q}{\Delta P}$$

$$\frac{\Delta Q}{\Delta P} = -0.4\left(\frac{23.5}{2}\right) = -4.7 = -b.$$

To find the constant a, substitute for Q, P, and b into the above formula so that 23.5=a-4.7*2 and a=32.9. The equation for demand is therefore Q=32.9-4.7P. To find the supply curve, recall the formula for the elasticity of supply and follow the same method as above:

$$E_P^S = \frac{P}{Q}\frac{\Delta Q}{\Delta P}$$

$$0.5 = \frac{2}{23.5}\frac{\Delta Q}{\Delta P}$$

$$\frac{\Delta Q}{\Delta P} = 0.5\left(\frac{23.5}{2}\right) = 5.875 = d.$$

To find the constant c, substitute for Q, P, and d into the above formula so that 23.5=c+5.875*2 and c=11.75. The equation for supply is therefore Q=11.75+5.875P.

8. In Example 2.8 we examined the effect of a 20 percent decline in copper demand on the price of copper, using the linear supply and demand curves developed in Section 2.4. Suppose the long-run price elasticity of copper demand were -0.4 instead of -0.8.

a. **Assuming, as before, that the equilibrium price and quantity are *P** = 75 cents per pound and *Q** = 7.5 million metric tons per year, derive the linear demand curve consistent with the smaller elasticity.**

Following the method outlined in Section 2.6, we solve for *a* and *b* in the demand equation $Q_D = a - bP$. First, we know that for a linear demand function

$E_D = -b\left(\dfrac{P*}{Q*}\right)$. Here E_D = -0.4 (the long-run price elasticity), $P*$ = 0.75 (the equilibrium price), and $Q*$ = 7.5 (the equilibrium quantity). Solving for b,

$$-0.4 = -b\left(\frac{0.75}{7.5}\right), \text{ or } b = 4.$$

To find the intercept, we substitute for b, Q_D (= $Q*$), and P (= $P*$) in the demand equation:

$$7.5 = a - (4)(0.75), \text{ or } a = 10.5.$$

The linear demand equation consistent with a long-run price elasticity of -0.4 is therefore

$$Q_D = 10.5 - 4P.$$

b. **Using this demand curve, recalculate the effect of a 20 percent decline in copper demand on the price of copper.**

The new demand is 20 percent below the original (using our convention that quantity demanded is reduced by 20% at every price):

$$Q'_D = (0.8)(10.5 - 4P) = 8.4 - 3.2P.$$

Equating this to supply,

$$8.4 - 3.2P = -4.5 + 16P, \text{ or}$$

$$P = 0.672.$$

With the 20 percent decline in the demand, the price of copper falls to 67.2 cents per pound.

9. **Example 2.9 analyzes the world oil market. Using the data given in that example:**

a. **Show that the short-run demand and competitive supply curves are indeed given by**

$$D = 24.08 - 0.06P$$

$$S_C = 11.74 + 0.07P.$$

First, considering non-OPEC supply:

$$S_c = Q* = 13.$$

With E_S = 0.10 and $P*$ = \$18, $E_S = d(P*/Q*)$ implies d = 0.07.

Substituting for d, S_c, and P in the supply equation, c = 11.74 and S_c = 11.74 + 0.07P.

Similarly, since Q_D = 23, $E_D = -b(P*/Q*)$ = -0.05, and b = 0.06. Substituting for b, Q_D = 23, and P = 18 in the demand equation gives 23 = a - 0.06(18), so that a = 24.08.

Hence Q_D = 24.08 - 0.06P.

b. **Show that the long-run demand and competitive supply curves are indeed given by**

$$D = 32.18 - 0.51P$$

$$S_C = 7.78 + 0.29P.$$

As above, E_S = 0.4 and E_D = -0.4: $E_S = d(P*/Q*)$ and $E_D = -b(P*/Q*)$, implying 0.4 = d(18/13) and -0.4 = -b(18/23). So d = 0.29 and b = 0.51.

Next solve for c and a:

$$S_c = c + dP \text{ and } Q_D = a - bP, \text{ implying } 13 = c + (0.29)(18) \text{ and } 23 = a - (0.51)(18).$$

So $c = 7.78$ and $a = 32.18$.

c. **In 2002, Saudi Arabia accounted for 3 billion barrels per year of OPEC's production. Suppose that war or revolution caused Saudi Arabia to stop producing oil. Use the model above to calculate what would happen to the price of oil in the short run and the long run if OPEC's production were to drop by 3 billion barrels per year.**

With OPEC's supply reduced from 10 bb/yr to 7 bb/yr, add this lower supply of 7 bb/yr to the short-run and long-run supply equations:

$$S_c' = 7 + S_c = 11.74 + 7 + 0.07P = 18.74 + 0.07P \text{ and } S'' = 7 + S_c = 14.78 + 0.29P.$$

These are equated with short-run and long-run demand, so that:

$$18.74 + 0.07P = 24.08 - 0.06P,$$

implying that $P = \$41.08$ in the short run; and

$$14.78 + 0.29P = 32.18 - 0.51P,$$

implying that $P = \$21.75$ in the long run.

10. **Refer to Example 2.10, which analyzes the effects of price controls on natural gas.**

a. **Using the data in the example, show that the following supply and demand curves did indeed describe the market in 1975:**

$$\text{Supply: } Q = 14 + 2P_G + 0.25P_O$$

$$\text{Demand: } Q = -5P_G + 3.75P_O$$

where P_G and P_O are the prices of natural gas and oil, respectively. Also, verify that if the price of oil is \$8.00, these curves imply a free market price of \$2.00 for natural gas.

To solve this problem, we apply the analysis of Section 2.6 to the definition of cross-price elasticity of demand given in Section 2.4. For example, the cross-price-elasticity of demand for natural gas with respect to the price of oil is:

$$E_{GO} = \left(\frac{\Delta Q_G}{\Delta P_O}\right)\left(\frac{P_O}{Q_G}\right).$$

$\left(\frac{\Delta Q_G}{\Delta P_O}\right)$ is the change in the quantity of natural gas demanded, because of a small change in the price of oil. For linear demand equations, $\left(\frac{\Delta Q_G}{\Delta P_O}\right)$ is constant. If we represent demand as:

$$Q_G = a - bP_G + eP_O$$

(notice that income is held constant), then $\left(\frac{\Delta Q_G}{\Delta P_O}\right) = e$. Substituting this into the cross-price elasticity, $E_{PO} = e\left(\frac{P_O^*}{Q_G^*}\right)$, where P_O^* and Q_G^* are the equilibrium price and quantity.

We know that $P_O^* = \$8$ and $Q_G^* = 20$ trillion cubic feet (Tcf). Solving for e,

$$1.5 = e\left(\frac{8}{20}\right), \text{ or } e = 3.75.$$

Similarly, if the general form of the supply equation is represented as:

$$Q_G = c + dP_G + gP_O,$$

the cross-price elasticity of supply is $g\left(\dfrac{P_O^*}{Q_G^*}\right)$, which we know to be 0.1. Solving for g,

$$0.1 = g\left(\frac{8}{20}\right), \text{ or } g = 0.25.$$

The values for d and b may be found with equations 2.5a and 2.5b in Section 2.6. We know that $E_S = 0.2$, $P^* = 2$, and $Q^* = 20$. Therefore,

$$0.2 = d\left(\frac{2}{20}\right), \text{ or } d = 2.$$

Also, $E_D = -0.5$, so

$$-0.5 = b\left(\frac{2}{20}\right), \text{ or } b = -5.$$

By substituting these values for d, g, b, and e into our linear supply and demand equations, we may solve for c and a:

$$20 = c + (2)(2) + (0.25)(8), \text{ or } c = 14,$$

and

$$20 = a - (5)(2) + (3.75)(8), \text{ or } a = 0.$$

If the price of oil is $8.00, these curves imply a free market price of $2.00 for natural gas. Substitute the price of oil in the supply and demand curves to verify these equations. Then set the curves equal to each other and solve for the price of gas.

$$14 + 2P_G + (0.25)(8) = -5P_G + (3.75)(8)$$

$$7P_G = 14$$

$$P_G = \$2.00.$$

b. **Suppose the regulated price of gas in 1975 had been $1.50 per thousand cubic feet, instead of $1.00. How much excess demand would there have been?**

With a regulated price of $1.50 for natural gas and a price of oil equal to $8.00 per barrel,

$$\text{Demand: } Q_D = (-5)(1.50) + (3.75)(8) = 22.5, \text{ and}$$
$$\text{Supply: } Q_S = 14 + (2)(1.5) + (0.25)(8) = 19.$$

With a supply of 19 Tcf and a demand of 22.5 Tcf, there would be an excess demand of 3.5 Tcf.

c. **Suppose that the market for natural gas had *not* been regulated. If the price of oil had increased from $8 to $16, what would have happened to the free market price of natural gas?**

If the price of natural gas had not been regulated and the price of oil had increased from $8 to $16, then

$$\text{Demand: } Q_D = -5P_G + (3.75)(16) = 60 - 5P_G, \text{ and}$$
$$\text{Supply: } Q_S = 14 + 2P_G + (0.25)(16) = 18 + 2P_G.$$

Equating supply and demand and solving for the equilibrium price,

$$18 + 2P_G = 60 - 5P_G, \text{ or } P_G = \$6.$$

The price of natural gas would have tripled from $2 to $6.

11. The table below shows the retail price and sales for instant coffee and roasted coffee for 1997 and 1998.

Year	Retail Price of Instant Coffee ($/lb)	Sales of Instant Coffee (million lbs)	Retail Price of Roasted Coffee ($/lb)	Sales of Roasted Coffee (million lbs)
1997	10.35	75	4.11	820
1998	10.48	70	3.76	850

a. Using this data alone, estimate the short-run price elasticity of demand for roasted coffee. Derive a linear demand curve for roasted coffee.

To find elasticity, you must first estimate the slope of the demand curve:

$$\frac{\Delta Q}{\Delta P} = \frac{820-850}{4.11-3.76} = -\frac{30}{0.35} = -85.7.$$

Given the slope, we can now estimate elasticity using the price and quantity data from the above table. Since the demand curve is assumed to be linear, the elasticity will differ in 1997 and 1998 because price and quantity are different. You can calculate the elasticity at both points and at the average point between the two years:

$$E_p^{97} = \frac{P}{Q}\frac{\Delta Q}{\Delta P} = \frac{4.11}{820}(-85.7) = -0.43$$

$$E_p^{98} = \frac{P}{Q}\frac{\Delta Q}{\Delta P} = \frac{3.76}{850}(-85.7) = -0.38$$

$$E_p^{AVE} = \frac{\frac{P_{97}+P_{98}}{2}}{\frac{Q_{97}+Q_{98}}{2}}\frac{\Delta Q}{\Delta P} = \frac{3.935}{835}(-85.7) = -0.40.$$

To derive the demand curve for roasted coffee Q=a-bP, note that the slope of the demand curve is -85.7=-b. To find the coefficient a, use either of the data points from the table above so that a=830+85.7*4.11=1172.3 or a=850+85.7*3.76=1172.3. The equation for the demand curve is therefore

Q=1172.3-85.7P.

b. Now estimate the short-run price elasticity of demand for instant coffee. Derive a linear demand curve for instant coffee.

To find elasticity, you must first estimate the slope of the demand curve:

$$\frac{\Delta Q}{\Delta P} = \frac{75-70}{10.35-10.48} = -\frac{5}{0.13} = -38.5.$$

Given the slope, we can now estimate elasticity using the price and quantity data from the above table. Since the demand curve Q=a-bP is assumed to be linear, the elasticity will differ in 1997 and 1998 because price and quantity are different. You can calculate the elasticity at both points and at the average point between the two years:

$$E_p^{97} = \frac{P}{Q}\frac{\Delta Q}{\Delta P} = \frac{10.35}{75}(-38.5) = -5.31$$

$$E_p^{98} = \frac{P}{Q}\frac{\Delta Q}{\Delta P} = \frac{10.48}{70}(-38.5) = -5.76$$

$$E_p^{AVE} = \frac{\dfrac{P_{97}+P_{98}}{2}}{\dfrac{Q_{97}+Q_{98}}{2}}\frac{\Delta Q}{\Delta P} = \frac{10.415}{72.5}(-38.5) = -5.53.$$

To derive the demand curve for instant coffee, note that the slope of the demand curve is -38.5=-b. To find the coefficient a, use either of the data points from the table above so that a=75+38.5*10.35=473.5 or a=70+38.5*10.48=473.5. The equation for the demand curve is therefore

Q=473.5-38.5P.

c.   **Which coffee has the higher short-run price elasticity of demand?   Why do you think this is the case?**

Instant coffee is significantly more elastic than roasted coffee. In fact, the demand for roasted coffee is inelastic and the demand for instant coffee is elastic. Roasted coffee may have an inelastic demand in the short-run as many people think of coffee as a necessary good.   Changes in the price of roasted coffee will not drastically affect demand because people must have this good. Many people, on the other hand, may view instant coffee, as a convenient, though imperfect, substitute for roasted coffee. For example, if the price rises a little, the quantity demanded will fall by a large percentage because people would rather drink roasted coffee instead of paying more for a low quality substitute.

PART II
PRODUCERS, CONSUMERS, AND COMPETITIVE MARKETS
CHAPTER 3
CONSUMER BEHAVIOR

TEACHING NOTES

Chapter 3 builds the foundation for deriving the demand curve in Chapter 4. In order to understand demand theory, students must have a firm grasp of indifference curves, the marginal rate of substitution, the budget line, and optimal consumer choice. It is possible to discuss consumer choice without going into extensive detail on utility theory. Many students find utility functions to be a more abstract concept than preference relationships. However, if you plan to discuss uncertainty in Chapter 5, you will need to cover marginal utility (section 3.5). Even if you cover utility theory only briefly, make sure students are comfortable with the term utility because it appears frequently in Chapter 4.

When introducing indifference curves, stress that physical quantities are represented on the two axes. After discussing supply and demand, students may think that price should be on the vertical axis. To illustrate the indifference curves, pick an initial bundle on the graph and ask which other bundles are likely to be more preferred and less preferred to the initial bundle. This will divide the graph into four quadrants, and it is then easier for students to figure out the set of bundles between which the consumer is indifferent. It is helpful to present a lot of examples with different types of goods and see if the class can figure out how to draw the indifference curves. The examples are also useful for explaining the significance of the assumptions made about preferences. In presenting different examples, you can ask which assumption would be violated.

Explaining utility follows naturally from the discussion of indifference curves. Though an abstract concept, it is possible to get students to understand the basic idea without spending too much time on the topic. You might point out that we as consumers have a goal in life, which is to maximize our utility subject to our budget constraint. When we go to the store we pick the basket that we like best and that stays within our budget. From this we derive demand curves. Emphasize that it is the ranking that is important and not the utility number, and point out that if we can graph an indifference curve we can certainly find an equation to represent it. Finally, what is most important is the rate at which consumers are willing to exchange goods (the marginal rate of substitution) and this is based on the relative satisfaction that they derive from each good at any particular time.

The marginal rate of substitution, *MRS*, can be confusing to students. Some confuse the *MRS* with the ratio of the two quantities. If this is the case, point out that the slope is equal to the ratio of the rise, *ΔY*, and the run, *ΔX*. This ratio is equal to the ratio of the intercepts of a line just tangent to the indifference curve. As we move along a convex indifference curve, these intercepts and the *MRS* change. Another problem is the terminology "of *X* for *Y*." This is confusing because we are not substituting "*X* for *Y*," but *Y* for one unit of *X*. You may want to present a variety of examples in class to explain this important concept.

QUESTIONS FOR REVIEW

1. What are the four basic assumptions about individual preferences? Explain the significance or meaning of each.

(1) Preferences are complete: this means that the consumer is able to compare and rank all possible baskets; (2) Preferences are transitive: this means that preferences are consistent, in that if bundle A is preferred to bundle B and bundle B is preferred to bundle C, then we should be able to conclude that bundle A is preferred to bundle C; (3) More is preferred to less: this means that all goods are desirable, and that the consumer will always prefer to have more of a good; (4) Diminishing marginal rate of substitution: this means that indifference curves are convex, and that the slope of the indifference curve increases (becomes less negative) as we move down along the curve. As a consumer moves down along her indifference curve she is willing to give

up fewer units of the good on the vertical axis in exchange for one more unit of the good on the horizontal axis. This assumption also means that balanced market baskets are preferred to baskets that have a lot of one good and very little of the other good.

2. Can a set of indifference curves be upward sloping? If so, what would this tell you about the two goods?

A set of indifference curves can be upward sloping if we violate assumption number three; more is preferred to less. When a set of indifference curves is upward sloping, it means one of the goods is a "bad" in that the consumer prefers less of the good rather than more of the good. The positive slope means that the consumer will accept more of the bad good only if she also receives more of the other good in return. As we move up along the indifference curve the consumer has more of the good she likes, and also more of the good she does not like.

3. Explain why two indifference curves cannot intersect.

The explanation is most easily achieved with the aid of a graph such as Figure 3.3, which shows two indifference curves intersecting at point A. We know from the definition of an indifference curve that a consumer has the same level of utility along any given curve. In this case, the consumer is indifferent between bundles A and B because they both lie on indifference curve U_1. Similarly, the consumer is indifferent between bundles A and C because they both lie on indifference curve U_2. By the transitivity of preferences this consumer should also be indifferent between C and B. However, we see from the graph that C lies above B, so C must be preferred to B. Thus, the fact that indifference curves cannot intersect is proven.

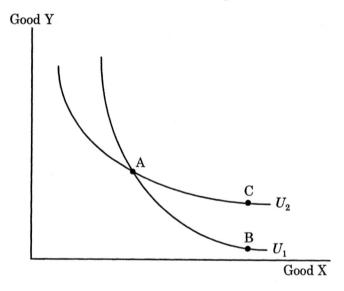

Figure 3.3

4. Jon is always willing to trade one can of coke for one can of sprite, or one can of sprite for one can of coke.

a.   What can you say about Jon's marginal rate of substitution?

Jon's marginal rate of substitution can be defined as the number of cans of coke he would be willing to give up in exchange for a can of sprite. Since he is always willing to trade one for one, his MRS is equal to 1.

b.   Draw a set of indifference curves for Jon.

Since Jon is always willing to trade one can of coke for one can of sprite, his indifference curves are linear with a slope of –1.

c.   Draw two budget lines with different slopes and illustrate the satisfaction-maximizing choice. What conclusion can you draw?

Jon's indifference curves are linear with a slope of –1. Jon's budget line is also linear, and will have a slope that reflects the ratio of the two prices. If Jon's budget line is steeper than his indifference curves then he will choose to consume only the good on the vertical axis. If Jon's budget line is flatter than his indifference curves then he will choose to consumer only the good on the horizontal axis. Jon will always choose a corner solution, unless his budget line has the same slope as his indifference curves. In this case any combination of Sprite and Coke that uses up his entire income with maximize his satisfaction.

5.   What happens to the marginal rate of substitution as you move along a convex indifference curve? A linear indifference curve?

The MRS measures how much of a good you are willing to give up in exchange for one more unit of the other good, keeping utility constant. The MRS diminishes along a convex indifference curve in that as you move down along the indifference curve, you are willing to give up less and less of the one good in exchange for the other. The MRS is also the slope of the indifference curve, which increases (becomes less negative) as you move down along the indifference curve. The MRS is constant along a linear indifference curve, since in this case the slope does not change. The consumer is always willing to trade the same number of units of one good in exchange for the other.

6. Explain why an MRS between two goods must equal the ratio of the price of the goods for the consumer to achieve maximum satisfaction.

The MRS describes the rate at which the consumer is willing to trade one good for another to maintain the same level of satisfaction. The ratio of prices describes the trade-off that the market is willing to make between the same two goods. The tangency of the indifference curve with the budget line represents the point at which the trade-offs are equal and consumer satisfaction is maximized. If the MRS between two goods is not equal to the ratio of prices, then the consumer could trade one good for another at market prices to obtain higher levels of satisfaction. For example, if the slope of the budget line (the ratio of the prices) is –4 then the consumer can trade 4 units of good 2 for one unit of good 1. If the MRS at the current bundle is –6, then the consumer is willing to trade 6 units of good 2 for one unit of good 1. Since the two slopes are not equal the consumer is not maximizing her satisfaction. The consumer is willing to trade 6 but only has to trade 4, so she should make the trade. This trading continues until the highest level of satisfaction is achieved. As trades are made, the MRS will change and become equal to the price ratio.

7.   Describe the indifference curves associated with two goods that are perfect substitutes. What if they are perfect complements?

Two goods are perfect substitutes if the MRS of one for another is a constant number. Given the MRS is a constant number, the slope of the indifference curves will be constant, and the indifference curves are therefore linear. If two goods are perfect complements, the indifference curves are L-shaped. In this case the consumer wants to consume the two goods in a fixed proportion, say one unit of good 1 for every 1 unit of good 2. If she has more of one good but not more of the other then she does not get any extra satisfaction.

8. What is the difference between ordinal utility and cardinal utility? Explain why the assumption of cardinal utility is not needed in order to rank consumer choices.

Ordinal utility implies an ordering among alternatives without regard for intensity of preference. For example, if the consumer's first choice is preferred to their second choice, then utility from the first choice will be higher than utility from the second choice. How much higher is not important. An ordinal utility function generates a ranking of bundles and no meaning is given to the utility number itself. Cardinal utility implies that the intensity of preferences may be quantified, and that the utility number itself has meaning. An ordinal ranking is all that is needed to rank consumer choices. It is not necessary to know how intensely a consumer prefers basket *A* over basket *B*; it is enough to know that *A* is preferred to *B*.

9. Upon merging with the West German economy, East German consumers indicated a preference for Mercedes-Benz automobiles over Volkswagens. However, when they converted their savings into deutsche marks, they flocked to Volkswagen dealerships. How can you explain this apparent paradox?

Three assumptions are required to address this question: 1) that a Mercedes costs more than a Volkswagen; 2) that the East German consumers' utility function comprises two goods, automobiles and all other goods evaluated in deutsche marks; and 3) that East Germans have incomes. Based on these assumptions, we can surmise that while East German consumers may prefer a Mercedes to a Volkswagen, they either cannot afford a Mercedes or they prefer a bundle of other goods plus a Volkswagen to a Mercedes alone. While the marginal utility of consuming a Mercedes exceeds the marginal utility of consuming a Volkswagen, the consumer will consider marginal utility per dollar for each good. This means the marginal utility per dollar must have been higher for the Volkswagen since consumers flocked to the Volkswagen dealerships and not the Mercedes dealerships.

10. Draw a budget line and then draw an indifference curve to illustrate the satisfaction maximizing choice associated with two products. Use your graph to answer the following questions.

a.   Suppose that one of the products is rationed. Explain why the consumer is likely to be worse off.

When goods are not rationed, the consumer is able to choose the satisfaction-maximizing bundle where the slope of the budget line is equal to the slope of the indifference curve, or the price ratio is equal to the MRS. This is point A in the graph below. If good 1 is now rationed the consumer will not be able to attain the utility maximizing point. He or she will have to consume more of the other good instead. This is point B below.

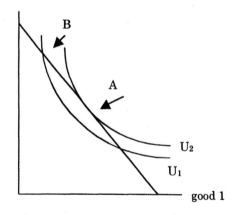

b. **Suppose now that the price of one of the products is fixed at a level below the current price. As a result, the consumer is not able to purchase as much as she would like of the product. Can you tell if the consumer is better off or worse off?**

When the price of the good is fixed at a level below the current (equilibrium) price, there will be a shortage of the good and the good will have to be effectively rationed. As in the question above, the consumer is worse off because she is not able to attain her utility maximizing point.

11. Based on his preferences, Bill is willing to trade 4 movie tickets for 1 ticket to a basketball game. If movie tickets cost $8 each and a ticket to the basketball game costs $40, should Bill make the trade? Why or why not?

No Bill should not make the trade. If he gives up the 4 movie tickets then he will save $8 per ticket for a total of $32. However, this is not enough for a basketball ticket. He would in fact have to give up 5 movie tickets if he wanted to buy another basketball ticket. Notice also, that the marginal utility per dollar is higher for movie tickets so Bill will be better off if he consumes more movie tickets and fewer basketball tickets. To figure this out recall that what Bill is willing to do defines his MRS. His MRS is 4 so this means that the marginal utility of a basketball game is 4 and the marginal utility of a movie is 1:

$$MRS = -4 = -\frac{MU_{ball}}{MU_{movie}} = -\frac{4}{1}.$$

Now the marginal utility per dollar can be computed:

$$\frac{MU_{ball}}{P_{ball}} = \frac{4}{40} = \frac{1}{10}$$

$$\frac{MU_{movie}}{P_{movie}} = \frac{1}{8}.$$

12. Describe the equal marginal principle. Explain why this principle may not hold if increasing marginal utility is associated with the consumption of one or both goods.

The equal marginal principle states that the ratio of the marginal utility to price must be equal across all goods to obtain maximum satisfaction. In other words, utility maximization is achieved when the budget is allocated so that the marginal utility per dollar of expenditure is the same for each good. If the marginal utility per dollar is not equal then utility can be increased by allocating more dollars to the good with the higher marginal utility per dollar. The consumer will obtain more "bang for the buck" if they reallocate their dollars.

If marginal utility is increasing, the consumer maximizes satisfaction by consuming ever larger amounts of the good. Thus, the consumer would spend all income on one good, assuming a constant price, resulting in a corner solution. With a corner solution, the equal marginal principle *cannot* hold.

13. The price of computers has fallen substantially over the past two decades. Use this drop in price to explain why the Consumer Price Index is likely to overstate substantially the cost-of-living index for individuals who use computers intensively.

The consumer price index measures the cost of a typical basket of goods purchased by the consumer in the current year relative to the cost of the basket in the base year. Each good in the basket is assigned a weight, which reflects the importance of the good to the consumer, and the weights are kept fixed from year to year. The problem with fixing the weights is that consumers will shift their purchases from year to year to give more weight to goods whose prices have fallen, and less weight to goods whose prices have risen. The CPI will therefore give too much weight to goods whose prices have risen, and too little weight to goods whose prices have fallen. For the individual who uses computers intensively, the fixed weight for computers in the basket will understate the importance of this good, and will hence understate the effect of the fall in the price of computers. The CPI will overstate the rise in the cost of living for this type of individual.

14. Explain why the Paasche index will generally understate the ideal cost-of-living index.

The Paasche index measures the current cost of the current bundle of goods relative to the base year cost of the current bundle of goods. The Paasche index will understate the ideal cost of living because it assumes the individual will buy the current year bundle in the base period. In reality, at base year prices the consumer would have been able to attain the same level of utility at a lower cost by altering their consumption bundle. Since the base year cost is overstated, the denominator will be larger and the index will be lower, or understated.

EXERCISES

1. In this chapter, consumer preferences for various commodities did not change during the analysis. Yet in some situations, preferences do change as consumption occurs. Discuss why and how preferences might change over time with consumption of these two commodities:

a.   cigarettes

The assumption that preferences do not change is a reasonable one if choices are independent across time. It does not hold, however, when "habit-forming" or addictive behavior is involved, as in the case of cigarettes: the consumption of cigarettes in one period influences their consumption in the next period.

b.   dinner for the first time at a restaurant with a special cuisine

This example is parallel to examples of adventure seeking. For some, a new dining experience creates enthusiasm to seek out more exciting and different cuisines and dishes. For others, they develop a fondness for regularity and consistency or fear of the new and unknown. In either of these cases, choices change as consumption occurs.

2. Draw indifference curves that represent the following individuals' preferences for hamburgers and soft drinks. Indicate the direction in which the individuals' satisfaction (or utility) is increasing.

a.   Joe has convex preferences and dislikes both hamburgers and soft drinks.
Since Joe dislikes both goods, his set of indifference curves will be bowed inwards towards the origin instead of outwards, as in the normal case where more is preferred to less. Given he dislikes both goods, his satisfaction is increasing in the direction of the origin. Convexity of preferences implies his indifference curves will have the normal shape in that they are bowed towards the direction of increasing satisfaction. Convexity also implies that given any two bundles between which the consumer is indifferent, the "average" of the two bundles will be in the preferred set, or will leave him at least as well off.

hamburger

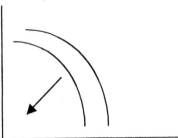

soft drink

b. **Jane loves hamburgers and dislikes soft drinks. If she is served a soft drink, she will pour it down the drain rather than drink it.**

Since Jane can freely dispose of the soft drink if it is given to her, she considers it to be a neutral good. This means she does not care about soft drinks one way or the other. With hamburgers on the vertical axis, her indifference curves are horizontal lines. Her satisfaction increases in the upward direction.

hamburger

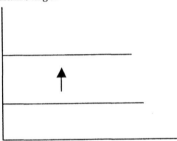

soft drink

c. **Bob loves hamburgers and dislikes soft drinks. If he is served a soft drink, he will drink it to be polite.**

Since Bob will drink the soft drink in order to be polite, it can be thought of as a "bad". When served another soft drink, he will require more hamburgers at the same time in order to keep his satisfaction constant. More soft drinks without more hamburgers will worsen his utility. More hamburgers and fewer soft drinks will increase his utility.

hamburger

soft drink

d. **Molly loves hamburgers and soft drinks, but insists on consuming exactly one soft drink for every two hamburgers that she eats.**

Molly wants to consume the two goods in a fixed proportion so her indifference curves are L-shaped. For any given amount of one good, she gets no extra satisfaction from having more of the other good. She will only increase her satisfaction if she has more of both goods.

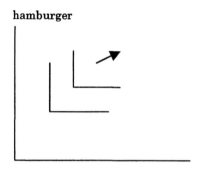

e.   Bill likes hamburgers, but neither likes nor dislikes soft drinks.
Like Jane, Bill considers soft drinks to be a neutral good. Since he does not care about soft drinks one way or the other we can assume that no matter how many he has, his utility will be the same. His level of satisfaction depends entirely on how many hamburgers he has.

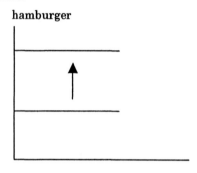

f.   Mary always gets twice as much satisfaction from an extra hamburger as she does from an extra soft drink.
How much extra satisfaction Mary gains from an extra hamburger or soft drink tells us something about the marginal utilities of the two goods, or about her MRS. If she always receives twice the satisfaction from an extra hamburger then her marginal utility from consuming an extra hamburger is twice her marginal utility from consuming an extra soft drink. Her MRS, with hamburgers on the vertical axis, is 1/2. Her indifference curves are straight lines with a slope of 1/2.

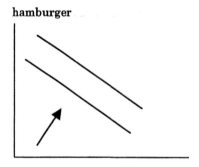

3. If Jane is currently willing to trade 4 movie tickets for 1 basketball ticket then she must like basketball better than movies. True or false? Explain.

This statement is not necessarily true. If she is always willing to trade 4 movie tickets for 1 basketball ticket then yes she likes basketball better because she will always gain the same satisfaction from 4 movie tickets as she does from 1 basketball ticket. However, it could be that she has convex preferences (diminishing marginal rate of substitution) and is at a bundle where she has a lot of movie tickets relative to basketball tickets. This would make her willing to give up more movie tickets to get another basketball ticket. It would not mean though that she liked basketball better. Her willingness to give up a good would in this case depend on the quantity of each good in her current basket.

4. Janelle and Brian each plan to spend $20,000 on the styling and gas mileage features of a new car. They can each choose all styling, all gas mileage, or some combination of the two. Janelle does not care at all about styling and wants the best gas mileage possible. Brian likes both equally and wants to spend an equal amount on the two features. Using indifference curves and budget lines, illustrate the choice that each person will make.

Assume styling is on the vertical axis and gas mileage is on the horizontal axis. Janelle has indifference curves that are vertical. If the styling is there she will take it, but she otherwise does not care about it. As her indifference curves move over to the right, she gains more gas mileage and more satisfaction. She will spend all $20,000 on gas mileage. Brian has indifference curves that are L-shaped. He will not spend more on one feature than on the other feature. He will spend $10,000 on styling and $10,000 on gas mileage.

5. Suppose that Bridget and Erin spend their income on two goods, food (F) and clothing (C). Bridget's preferences are represented by the utility function $U(F,C) = 10FC$, while Erin's preferences are represented by the utility function $U(F,C) = .20F^2C^2$.

a. **On a graph, with food on the horizontal axis and clothing on the vertical axis, identify the set of points that give Bridget the same level of utility as the bundle (10,5). Do the same for Erin on a separate graph.**

Bridget receives a utility of 10*10*5=500 from this bundle. The indifference curve is represented by the equation 10FC=500 or FC=50. Some bundles on this indifference curve are (5,10), (10,5), (25,2), and (2,25). Erin receives a utility of .2*10*10*5*5=500 from the bundle (10,5). Her indifference curve is represented by the equation $500 = .2F^2C^2$, or 50=FC. This is the same indifference curve as Bridget. Both indifference curves have the normal, convex shape.

b. **On the same two graphs, identify the set of bundles that give Bridget and Erin the same level of utility as the bundle (15,8).**

For each person, plug in F=15 and C=8 into their respective utility functions. For Bridget, this gives her a utility of 1200, so her indifference curve is given by the equation 10FC=1200, or FC=120. Some bundles on this indifference curve are (12,10), (10,12), (3,40), and (40,3). For Erin, this bundle gives her a utility of 2880, so her indifference curve is given by the equation $2880 = .2F^2C^2$, or FC=120. This is the same indifference curve as Bridget.

c. **Do you think Bridget and Erin have the same preferences or different preferences? Explain.**

They have the same preferences because for any given bundle they have the same level of utility. This means that they will rank all bundles in the same order. Note however, that it is not necessary that they receive the same level of utility to have the same set of preferences. All that is necessary is that they rank the bundles in the same order.

6. Suppose that Jones and Smith have each decided to allocate $1,000 per year to an entertainment budget in the form of hockey games or rock concerts. They both like hockey games and rock concerts and will choose to consume positive quantities of both goods. However, they differ substantially in their preferences for these two forms of entertainment. Jones prefers hockey games to rock concerts, while Smith prefers rock concerts to hockey games.

a. Draw a set of indifference curves for Jones and a second set for Smith.

Given they each like both goods and they will each choose to consume positive quantities of both goods, we can assume their indifference curves have the normal convex shape. However since Jones has an overall preference for hockey and Smith has an overall preference for rock concerts, their two sets of indifference curves will have different slopes. Suppose that we place rock concerts on the vertical axis and hockey games on the horizontal axis, Jones will have a larger MRS than Smith. Jones is willing to give up more rock concerts in exchange for a hockey game since he prefers hockey games. The indifference curves for Jones will be steeper.

b. Using the concept of marginal rate of substitution, explain why the two sets of curves are different from each other.

At any combination of hockey games and rock concerts, Jones is willing to give up more rock concerts for an additional hockey game, whereas, Smith is willing to give up fewer rock concerts for an additional hockey game. Since the MRS is a measure of how many of one good (rock concerts) an individual is willing to give up for an additional unit of the other good (hockey games), then the MRS, and hence the slope of the indifference curves, will be different for the two individuals.

7. The price of DVDs (D) is $20 and the price of CDs (C) is $10. Philip has a budget of $100 to spend on the two goods. Suppose that he has already bought one DVD and one CD. In addition there are 3 more DVDs and 5 more CDs that he would really like to buy.

a. Given the above prices and income, draw his budget line on a graph with CDs on the horizontal axis.
His budget line is $P_D D + P_C C = I$, or 20D+10C=100. If he spends his entire income on DVD's he could afford to buy 5. If he spends his entire income on CD's he could afford to buy 10.

b. Considering what he has already purchased, and what he still wants to purchase, identify the three different bundles of CDs and DVDs that he could choose. Assume that he cannot purchase fractional units for this part of the question.
Given he has already purchased one of each, for a total of $30, he has $70 left. Since he wants 3 more DVD's he can buy these for $60 and spend his remaining $10 on 1 CD. This is the first bundle below. He could also choose to buy only 2 DVD's for $40 and spend the remaining $30 on 3 CD's. He can choose the following bundles:

Purchased Quantities		Total Quantities	
D	C	D	C
3	1	2	6
2	3	3	4
1	5	4	2

8. **Anne has a job that requires her to travel three out of every four weeks. She has an annual travel budget and can either travel by train or by plane. The airline she typically flies with has a frequent traveler program that reduces the cost of her tickets depending on the number of miles she has flown in a given year. When she reaches 25,000 miles the airline will reduce the price of her tickets by 25% for the remainder of the year. When she reached 50,000 miles, the airline will reduce the price of her tickets by 50% for the remainder of the year. Graph Anne's budget line, with train miles on the vertical axis and plane miles on the horizontal axis.**

The typical budget line is linear (with a constant slope) because the prices of the two goods do not change as the consumer buys more or less of a particular good. In this case, the price of airline miles will change depending on how many miles she purchases. As the price changes, the slope of the budget line will change. Since there are three prices, there will be three slopes, or two kinks, to the budget line. Since the price falls as she flies more miles, the budget line will become flatter with every price change. See the graph in the problem below.

9. **Debra usually buys a soft drink when she goes to a movie theater, where she has a choice of three sizes: the 8 ounce drink costs $1.50, the 12 ounce drink, $2.00, and the 16 ounce drink, $2.25. Describe the budget constraint that Debra faces when deciding how many ounces of the drink to purchase. (Assume that Debra can costlessly dispose of any of the soft drink that she does not want.**

First notice that as the size of the drink increases, the price per ounce decreases. When she buys the 8-ounce soft drink she pays $\dfrac{\$1.50}{8\ oz} = \$0.19$ per *oz*. When she buys the 12-ounce size she pays $0.17 per ounce, and when she buys the 16-ounce size, she pays $0.14 per ounce. Given that there are three different prices per ounce of soft drink, the budget line will have two kinks in it, as illustrated below. Notice that at each kink, the slope of the budget line gets flatter (due to the decreasing cost per ounce relative to the "other good" on the vertical axis).

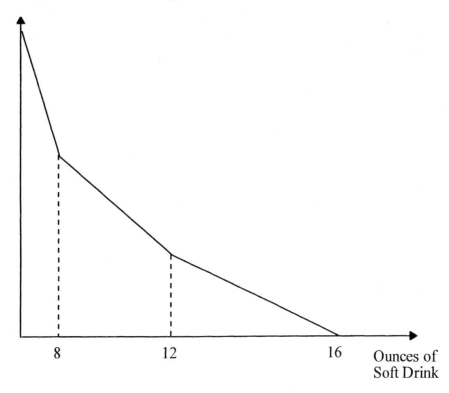

8	12	16 Ounces of Soft Drink

10. Antonio buys 5 new college textbooks during his first year at school at a cost of $80 each. Used books cost only $50 each. When the bookstore announces that there will be a 10% increase in the price of new books and a 5% increase in the price of used books, Antonio's father offers him $40 extra.

a. What happens to Antonio's budget line? Illustrate the change with new books on the vertical axis.

In the first year he spends $80 each on 5 new books for a total of $400. For the same amount of money he could have bought 8 used textbooks. His budget line is therefore 80*New+50*Used=400. After the price change, new books cost $88, used books cost $52.5, and he has an income of $440. If he spends all of his income on new books, he can still afford to buy 5 new books, but can now afford to buy 8.4 used books if he buys only used books. The new budget line is 88*New+52.5*Used=440. The budget line has changed its slope and become flatter if we place used books on the horizontal axis.

b. Is Antonio worse or better off after the price change? Explain.

The first year he bought 5 books at a cost of $80 each for a total of $400. The new price of books is $88 and the cost of 5 new books is now $440. The $40 extra income will cover the price increase. Antonio is definitely not worse off since he can still afford the same number of new books. He may in fact be better off if he decides to switch to used books.

11. Consumers in Georgia pay twice as much for avocados as they do for peaches. However, avocados and peaches are equally priced in California. If consumers in both states maximize utility, will the marginal rate of substitution of peaches for avocados be the same for consumers in both states? If not, which will be higher?

The marginal rate of substitution of peaches for avocados is the amount of avocados that a person is willing to give up to obtain one additional peach. When consumers maximize utility, they set their marginal rate of substitution equal to the price ratio, which in this case is $\frac{P_{peach}}{P_{avocado}}$. In Georgia, $P_{avocado} = 2P_{peach}$, which means that when consumers are maximizing utility, $MRS = \frac{P_{peach}}{P_{avocado}} = \frac{1}{2}$. In California, $P_{avocado} = P_{peach}$, which means that when consumers are maximizing utility, $MRS = \frac{P_{peach}}{P_{avocado}} = \frac{1}{1}$. The marginal rate of substitution is therefore not the same in both states, and will be higher in California.

12. Ben allocates his lunch budget between two goods, pizza and burritos.

a. Illustrate Ben's optimal bundle on a graph with pizza on the horizontal axis.

This is the standard graph, where Ben's budget line is linear and he consumes at the point where his indifference curve is tangent to his budget line. This places him on the highest possible indifference curve.

b. Suppose now that pizza is taxed, causing the price to increase by 20%. Illustrate Ben's new optimal bundle.

When the price of pizza increases, the budget line will pivot inwards. This will shrink the size of Ben's budget set and he will no longer be able to afford his old bundle. His new optimal bundle is where the indifference curve is tangent to his new budget line and this indifference curve is below his original indifference curve.

c. **Suppose instead that pizza is rationed at a quantity less than Ben's desired quantity. Illustrate Ben's new optimal bundle.**

Rationing the quantity of pizza that can be purchased will result in Ben not being able to choose his optimal bundle. He will have to choose a bundle on the budget line that is above his original bundle. This new bundle will have a lower level of utility.

13. **Brenda wants to buy a new car and has a budget of $25,000. She has just found a magazine that assigns each car an index for styling and an index for gas mileage. Each index runs from 1-10, with 10 representing either the most styling or the best gas mileage. While looking at the list of cars, Brenda observes that on average, as the style index rises by one unit, the price of the car increases by $5,000. She also observes that as the gas mileage index rises by one unit, the price of the car increases by $2,500.**

a. **Illustrate the various combinations of style (S) and gas mileage (G) that Brenda could select with her $25,000 budget. Place gas mileage on the horizontal axis.**

For every $5,000 she spends on style the index rises by one so the most she can achieve is a car with a style index of 5. For every $2,500 she spends on gas mileage, the index rises by one so the most she can achieve is a car with a gas mileage index of 10. The slope of her "budget line" is -1/2.

b. **Suppose Brenda's preferences are such that she always receives three times as much satisfaction from an extra unit of styling as she does from gas mileage. What type of car will Brenda choose?**

If Brenda always receives three times as much satisfaction from an extra unit of styling as she does from an extra unit of gas mileage then she is willing to trade one unit of styling for three units of gas mileage, and still maintain the same level of satisfaction. This is her MRS or the slope of her indifference curves, which is constant. Since the MRS is 1/3 and the slope of her budget line is -1/2, Brenda will choose all styling. You can also compute the marginal utility per dollar for styling and gas mileage and note that styling will be higher. In the graph below, she will move up to the highest possible indifference curve where she chooses all styling and no gas mileage.

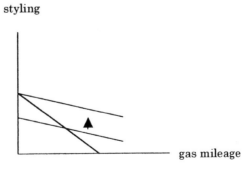

c.   **Suppose that Brenda's marginal rate of substitution (of gas mileage for styling) was equal to $\dfrac{S}{4G}$. What value of each index would she like to have in her car?**

To find the optimal value of each index, set MRS equal to the price ratio of 1/2 and cross multiply to get S=2G. Now substitute into the budget 5000S+2500G=25000 to get G=2 and S=4.

d.   **Suppose that Brenda's marginal rate of substitution (of gas mileage for styling) was equal to $\dfrac{3S}{G}$. What value of each index would she like to have in her car?**

To find the optimal value of each index set MRS equal to the price ratio of 1/2 and cross multiply to get G=6S. Now substitute into the budget 5000S+2500G=25000 to get G=7.5 and S=1.25.

14.   Connie has a monthly income of $200, which she allocates between two goods: meat and potatoes.

a.   **Suppose meat costs $4 per pound and potatoes cost $2 per pound. Draw her budget constraint.**

Let M = meat and P = potatoes. Connie's budget constraint is

$$\$200 = 4M + 2P, \text{ or}$$

$$M = 50 - 0.5P.$$

As shown in the figure below, with M on the vertical axis, the vertical intercept is 50. The horizontal intercept may be found by setting $M = 0$ and solving for P.

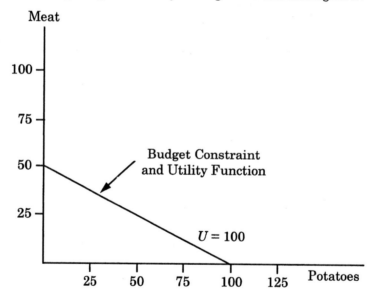

b.   **Suppose also that her utility function is given by the equation u(M, P) = 2M + P. What combination of meat and potatoes should she buy to maximize her utility? (Hint: Meat and potatoes are perfect substitutes.)**

When the two goods are perfect substitutes, the indifference curves are linear. To find the slope of the indifference curve, choose a level of utility and find the equation for a representative indifference curve. Suppose u=50, then 2M+P=50, or M=25-0.5P. Therefore, Connie's budget line and her indifference curves have the same slope. Connie's utility is equal to 100 when she buys 50 pounds of meat and no potatoes or no meat and 100 pounds of potatoes. The indifference curve for $U = 100$ coincides with her budget constraint. Any combination of meat and potatoes along this line will provide her with maximum utility.

c. **Connie's supermarket has a special promotion. If she buys 20 pounds of potatoes (at $2 per pound), she gets the next 10 pounds for free. This offer applies only to the first 20 pounds she buys. All potatoes in excess of the first 20 pounds (excluding bonus potatoes) are still $2 per pound. Draw her budget constraint.**

Assume that potatoes are on the horizontal axis. Connie's budget constraint has a slope of –1/2 until Connie has purchased twenty pounds of potatoes, is then flat from 20 to 30 pounds of potatoes, since the ten next pounds of potatoes are free, and then has a slope of –1/2 until it intercepts the potato axis at 110.

d. **An outbreak of potato rot raises the price of potatoes to $4 per pound. The supermarket ends its promotion. What does her budget constraint look like now? What combination of meat and potatoes maximizes her utility?**

With the price of potatoes at $4, Connie may buy either 50 pounds of meat or 50 pounds of potatoes, or some combination in between. See Figure 3.14.d. She maximizes utility at $U = 100$ at point A when she consumes 50 pounds of meat and no potatoes. *This is a corner solution.*

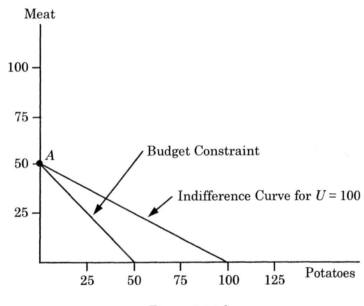

Figure 3.14.d

15. Jane receives utility from days spent traveling on vacation domestically (D) and days spent traveling on vacation in a foreign country (F), as given by the utility function $U(D,F) = 10DF$. In addition, the price of a day spent traveling domestically is $100, the price of a day spent traveling in a foreign country is $400, and Jane's annual travel budget is $4,000.

a. **Illustrate the indifference curve associated with a utility of 800 and the indifference curve associated with a utility of 1200.**

The indifference curve with a utility of 800 has the equation 10DF=800, or DF=80. Choose combinations of D and F whose product is 80 to find a few bundles. The indifference curve with a utility of 1200 has the equation 10DF=1200, or DF=120. Choose combinations of D and F whose product is 120 to find a few bundles.

b. **Graph Jane's budget line on the same graph.**

If Jane spends all of her budget on domestic travel she can afford 40 days. If she spends all of her budget on foreign travel she can afford 10 days.

c.   **Can Jane afford any of the bundles that give her a utility of 800? What about a utility of 1200?**

Yes she can afford some of the bundles that give her a utility of 800 as part of this indifference curve lies below the budget line. She cannot afford any of the bundles that give her a utility of 1200 as this whole indifference curve lies above the budget line.

d.   **Find Jane's utility maximizing choice of days spent traveling domestically and days spent in a foreign country.**

The optimal bundle is where the slope of the indifference curve is equal to the slope of the budget line, and Jane is spending her entire income. The slope of the budget line is

$$-\frac{P_D}{P_F} = -\frac{1}{4}.$$

The slope of the indifference curve is

$$MRS = -\frac{MU_D}{MU_F} = -\frac{10F}{10D} = -\frac{F}{D}.$$

Setting the two equal we get:

$$\frac{F}{D} = \frac{1}{4}$$

$$4F = D.$$

We now have two equations and two unknowns:

$$4F = D$$

$$100D + 400F = 4000.$$

Solving the above two equations gives D=20 and F=5. Utility is 1000.
This bundle is on an indifference curve between the two you had previously drawn.

16. Julio receives utility from consuming food (F) and clothing (C) as given by the utility function $U(F,C) = FC$. In addition, the price of food is \$2 per unit, the price of clothing is \$10 per unit, and Julio's weekly income is \$50.

a.   **What is Julio's marginal rate of substitution of food for clothing when utility is maximized? Explain.**

Utility is maximized when MRS (food for clothing) equals P$_C$/P$_F$, the price ratio. Given that clothing is on the horizontal axis and food is on the vertical axis, then the price ratio is the slope of the budget line, which is price of clothing divided by the price of food or -5.

b.   **Suppose instead that Julio is consuming a bundle with more food and less clothing than his utility maximizing bundle. Would his marginal rate of substitution of food for clothing be greater than or less than your answer in part a? Explain.**

In absolute value terms, the slope of his indifference curve at this non-optimal bundle is greater than the slope of his budget line. He is willing to give up more food than he has to at market prices to obtain one more unit of clothing. He will therefore find it optimal to give up some food in exchange for clothing.

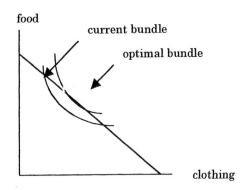

food

current bundle

optimal bundle

clothing

17. The utility that Meredith receives by consuming food F and clothing C is given by u(F,C) = FC. Suppose that Meredith's income in 1990 is $1,200 and the prices of food and clothing are $1 per unit for each. However, by 1995 the price of food has increased to $2 and the price of clothing to $3. Let 100 represent the cost of living index for 1990. Calculate the ideal and the Laspeyres cost-of-living index for Meredith for 1995. (Hint: Meredith will spend equal amounts on food and clothing with these preferences.)

First, we need to calculate F and C, which make up the bundle of food and clothing which maximizes Meredith's utility given 1990 prices and her income in 1990. Use the hint to simplify the problem: Since she spends equal amounts on both goods, $P_F F = P_C C$. Or, you can derive this same equation mathematically: With this utility function, $MU_C = \Delta U/\Delta C = F$, and $MU_F = \Delta U/\Delta F = C$. To maximize utility, Meredith chooses a consumption bundle such that $MU_F/MU_C = P_F/P_C$, which again yields $P_F F = P_C C$.

From the budget constraint, we also know that:

$$P_F F + P_C C = Y.$$

Combining these two equations and substituting the values for the 1990 prices and income yields the system of equations:

$$C = F \text{ and } C + F = 1,200.$$

Solving these two equations, we find that:

$$C = 600 \text{ and } F = 600.$$

Laspeyres Index

The Laspeyres index represents how much more Meredith would have to spend in 1995 versus 1990 if she consumed the same amounts of food and clothing in 1995 as she did in 1990. That is, the Laspeyres index for 1995 (L) is given by:

$$L = 100 \ (Y')/Y$$

where Y' represents the amount Meredith would spend at 1995 prices consuming the same amount of food and clothing as in 1990. In 1995, 600 clothing and 600 food would cost ($3)(600)+($2)(600)=$3000.

Therefore, the Laspeyres cost-of-living index is:

$$L = 100(\$3000/\$1200) = 250.$$

Ideal Index

The ideal index represents how much Meredith would have to spend on food and clothing in 1995 to get the same amount of utility as she had in 1990. That is, the ideal index for 1995 (I) is given by:

$$I = 100(Y'')/Y, \text{ where } Y'' = P'_F F' + P'_C C' = 2F' + 3C'$$

where F' and C' are the amount of food and clothing that give Meredith the same utility as she had in 1990. F' and C' must also be such that Meredith spends the least amount of money at 1995 prices to attain the 1990 utility level.

The bundle (F',C') will be on the same indifference curve as (F,C) so F'C'=FC=360,000 in utility. If Meredith's income is adjusted in 1995 so that the bundle (F',C') is maximizing her utility given her income, then the indifference curve at this point will be tangent to the budget line with slope -(P'$_F$/P'$_C$), where P'$_F$ and P'$_C$ are the prices of food and clothing in 1995. Using MU$_F$/MU$_{C'}$ = P$_F$/P$_{C'}$ we know that 2F' = 3C'.

We now have two equations: F'C'=360,000 and 2F' = 3C'.

Solving for F' yields:

$$F'[(2/3)F'] = 360,000 \text{ or } F' = \sqrt{[(3/2)360,000)]} = 734.8.$$

From this, we obtain C':

$$C' = (2/3)F' = (2/3)734.8 = 489.9.$$

In 1995, the bundle of 734.8 food and 489.9 clothing would cost \$2939.60 and Meredith would still get 360,000 in utility.

We can now calculate the ideal index:

$$I = 100(\$2939.60/\$1200) = 244.9.$$

CHAPTER 4
INDIVIDUAL AND MARKET DEMAND

TEACHING NOTES

Chapter 4 relies on two important ideas from Chapter 3: the influence of price and income changes on the budget line, and how to determine the optimal consumer choice. The chapter focuses on deriving individual demand graphically by changing either price or income, determining the income and substitution effects of a price change, deriving market demand, demand elasticity, and consumer surplus. These concepts are crucial to understanding the application of demand and supply analysis in Chapter 9 as well as the discussion of market failure in Parts III and IV. The analytical tools students learn in this chapter will be important for the discussion of factor supply and demand in Chapter 14.

When discussing the derivation of demand, review how the budget curve pivots around an intercept as price changes and how optimal quantities change as the budget line pivots. Once students understand the effect of price changes on consumer choice, they can grasp the derivation of the price consumption path and the individual demand curve. Remind students that the price a consumer is willing to pay is a measure of the marginal benefit of consuming another unit.

Income and substitution effects are often difficult for the student to understand, and they frequently have trouble remembering which effect is which on the graph. Emphasize that the substitution effect explains the portion of the change in demand caused by the change in relative prices (a pivot of the budget line) and the income effect explains the portion of the change in demand caused by a change in purchasing power (a shift of the budget line). The distinction between normal and inferior goods is used to determine the direction of the income effect. You might point out that the demand curve can only slope upwards if the good is inferior and the income effect is unusually large (a Giffen good). Doing a lot of examples is helpful. You might even skip the topic altogether if you are not prepared to devote some time to it. The labor leisure choice problem and derivation of the labor supply curve is a good illustration of income and substitution effects (see Chapter 14).

When covering the aggregation of individual demand curves, stress that this is equivalent to the summation of the individual demand curves horizontally. To obtain the market demand curve, you must have demand written in the form Q=f(P) as opposed to the inverse demand P=f(Q). The concept of a kink in the market demand curve is often new to students. Emphasize that this is because not all consumers are in the market at all prices.

The concept of elasticity is reintroduced and expanded upon. In particular, the relationship between elasticity and revenue is explained. Many students find elasticity to be a mysterious and puzzling concept. Point out that it is merely a more precise measure than the slope of the curve to measure the response of quantity demanded to a change in price, because it is a unit free measure. One effective teaching method is to use a linear demand curve to show that while the slope is constant, the elasticity changes throughout the range of prices. The text relies on this relationship in the discussion of the monopolist's determination of the profit-maximizing quantity in Chapter 10.

Although this chapter introduces consumer surplus, it is not extensively discussed until Chapter 9; producer surplus is covered in Chapter 8. If you introduce it here, it may be necessary to review it again when you get to Chapter 9.

Finally, there are other special topics in this chapter and its Appendix that you might cover, time and interest permitting. An application of network externalities is given in Example 4.6. The first part of Section 4.6, "Empirical Estimation of Demand," is straightforward, particularly if you have covered the forecasting section of Chapter 2. However, the last part, "The Form of the Demand Relationship," is difficult for students who do not understand logarithms. The Appendix is intended for students with a background in calculus, and contains a brief mathematical treatment of demand theory.

QUESTIONS FOR REVIEW

1. Explain the difference between each of the following terms:

a.   a price consumption curve and a demand curve;

A price consumption curve identifies the utility maximizing combinations of two goods as the price of one of the goods changes. When the price of one of the goods declines, the budget line will pivot outwards, and a new utility maximizing bundle will be chosen. The price consumption curve connects all such bundles. A demand curve is a graphical relationship between the price of a good and the (utility maximizing) quantity demanded of a good, all else the same. Price is plotted on the vertical axis and quantity demanded on the horizontal axis.

b.   an individual demand curve and a market demand curve;

An individual demand curve identifies the (utility maximizing) quantity demanded by one person at any given price of the good. A market demand curve is the sum of the individual demand curves for any given product. At any given price, the market demand curve identifies the quantity demanded by all individuals, all else the same.

c.   an Engel curve and a demand curve;

A demand curve identifies the quantity demanded of a good for any given price, holding income and all else the same. An Engel curve identifies the quantity demanded of a good for any given income, holding prices and all else the same.

d.   an income effect and a substitution effect;

The substitution effect measures the effect of a change in the price of a good on the consumption of the good, utility held constant. This change in price changes the slope of the budget line and causes the consumer to rotate along the current indifference curve. The income effect measures the effect of a change in purchasing power (caused by a change in the price of a good) on the consumption of the good, relative prices held constant. For example, an increase in the price of good 1 (on the horizontal axis) will rotate the budget line down along the indifference curve as the slope of the budget line (the relative price ratio) changes. This is the substitution effect. This new budget line will then shift inwards to reflect the decline in purchasing power caused by the increase in the price of the good. This is the income effect.

2. Suppose that an individual allocates his or her entire budget between two goods, food and clothing. Can both goods be inferior? Explain.

If an individual consumes only food and clothing, then any increase in income must be spent on either food or clothing (recall, we assume there are no savings). If food is an inferior good, then, as income increases, consumption falls. With constant prices, the extra income not spent on food must be spent on clothing. Therefore, as income increases, more is spent on clothing, i.e. clothing is a normal good. For both types of goods, normal and inferior, we still assume that more is preferred to less.

3. Explain whether the following statements are true or false.

a.   The marginal rate of substitution diminishes as an individual moves downward along the demand curve.

This is true. The consumer will maximize his utility by choosing the bundle on his budget line where the price ratio is equal to the MRS. Suppose the consumer chooses the quantity of goods 1 and 2 such that $\frac{P_1}{P_2} = MRS$. As the price of good 1 falls, the price ratio becomes a smaller number and hence the MRS becomes a smaller number.

This means that as the price of good 1 falls, the consumer is willing to give up fewer units of good 2 in exchange for another unit of good 1.

b. **The level of utility increases as an individual moves downward along the demand curve.**

This is true. As the price of a good falls, the budget line pivots outwards and the consumer is able to move to a higher indifference curve.

c. **Engel curves always slope upwards.**

This is false. The Engel curve identifies the relationship between the quantity demanded of a good and income, all else the same. If the good is inferior, then as income increases, quantity demanded will decrease, and the Engel curve will slope downwards.

4. Tickets to a rock concert sell for $10. But at that price, the demand is substantially greater than the available number of tickets. Is the value or marginal benefit of an additional ticket greater than, less than, or equal to $10? How might you determine that value?

If demand exceeds supply at a price of $10, then consumers are willing to bid up the market price to a level where the quantity demanded is equal to the quantity supplied. Since utility-maximizing consumers are willing to pay more than $10, the marginal increase in satisfaction (value) is greater than $10. One way to determine the value of an additional ticket would be to auction it off. The highest bid would equal the marginal benefit of that ticket. If a bid was higher than the marginal benefit, then it would not make sense for the consumer to buy it. If a bid was lower than the marginal benefit, another consumer would bid exactly the marginal benefit, win the ticket, and still be maximizing satisfaction.

5. Which of the following combinations of goods are complements and which are substitutes? Could they be either in different circumstances? Discuss.

a. **a mathematics class and an economics class**

If the math class and the economics class do not conflict in scheduling, then the classes could be either complements or substitutes. The math class may illuminate economics, and the economics class can motivate mathematics. If the classes conflict, they are substitutes.

b. **tennis balls and a tennis racket**

Tennis balls and a tennis racket are both needed to play a game of tennis, thus they are complements.

c. **steak and lobster**

Foods can both complement and substitute for each other. Steak and lobster can compete, i.e., be substitutes, when they are listed as separate items on a menu. However, they can also function as complements because they are often served together.

d. **a plane trip and a train trip to the same destination**

Two modes of transportation between the same two points are substitutes for one another.

e. **bacon and eggs**

Bacon and eggs are often eaten together and are, therefore, complementary goods. By considering them in relation to something else, such as pancakes, bacon and eggs can function as substitutes.

6. Suppose that a consumer spends a fixed amount of income per month on the following pairs of goods:

a.   tortilla chips and salsa;
b.   tortilla chips and potato chips;
c.   movie tickets and gourmet coffee;
d.   travel by bus and travel by subway.

If the price of one of the goods increases, explain the effect on the quantity demanded of each of the goods. In each pair, which are likely to be complements and which are likely to be substitutes?

a. If the price of tortilla chips increases, the demand for both goods will fall, assuming they are complements. The demand curve for salsa will shift to the left.

b. If the price of tortilla chips increases, the demand for tortilla chips will fall and the demand for potato chips will rise, assuming they are substitutes. The demand curve for potato chips will shift to the right.

c. If the price of movie tickets increases, the demand for movie tickets will fall. The demand for coffee is unchanged assuming the goods are unrelated. The demand curve for coffee is unchanged.

d. If the price of bus travel increases then the demand for bus tickets will fall and the demand for subway tickets will rise, assuming they are substitutes. The demand curve for subway tickets will shift to the right.

7. Which of the following events would cause a movement along the demand curve for U.S.-produced clothing, and which would cause a shift in the demand curve?

a.   **the removal of quotas on the importation of foreign clothes**

The removal of quotas will shift the demand curve inward for domestically-produced clothes, because foreign-produced goods are substitutes for domestically-produced goods. Both the equilibrium price and quantity will fall as foreign clothes are traded in a free market environment.

b.   **an increase in the income of U.S. citizens**

When income rises, expenditures on normal goods such as clothing increase, causing the demand curve to shift out. The equilibrium quantity and price will increase.

c.   **a cut in the industry's costs of producing domestic clothes that is passed on to the market in the form of lower clothing prices**

A cut in an industry's costs will shift the supply curve out. The equilibrium price will fall and quantity will increase. There is a movement along the demand curve.

8. For which of the following goods is a price increase likely to lead to a substantial income (as well as substitution) effect?

a.   **salt**

Small income effect, small substitution effect: The amount of income that is spent on salt is relatively small, but since there are few substitutes for salt, consumers will not readily substitute away from it. As the price of salt rises, real income will fall only slightly, thus leading to a small decline in consumption.

b.   **housing**

Large income effect, no substitution effect: The amount of income spent on housing is relatively large for most consumers. If the price of housing were to rise, real income would be reduced substantially, thereby reducing the consumption of all other goods. However, consumers would find it impossible to substitute for housing, in general.

c.   **theater tickets**

Small income effect, large substitution effect: The amount of income that is spent on theater tickets is relatively small, but consumers can substitute away from the theater tickets by choosing other forms of entertainment (e.g., television and movies). As the price of theater tickets rises, real income will fall only slightly, but the substitution effect can be large enough to reduce consumption by a large amount.

d.   **food**

Large income effect, no substitution effect: As with housing, the amount of income spent on food is relatively large for most consumers. Price increases for food will reduce real income substantially, thereby reducing the consumption of all other commodities. Although consumers can substitute out of particular foods, they cannot substitute out of food in general.

9. Suppose that the average household in a state consumes 800 gallons of gasoline per year. A 20-cent gasoline tax is introduced, coupled with a $160 annual tax rebate per household. Will the household be better or worse off under the new program?

If the household does not change its consumption of gasoline, it will be unaffected by the tax-rebate program, because in this case the household pays 0.20*800=$160 in taxes and receives $160 as an annual tax rebate. The two effects would cancel each other out. To the extent that the household reduces its gas consumption through substitution, it must be better off. The new budget line (price change plus rebate) will pass through the old consumption point of 800 gallons of gasoline, and any now affordable bundle that contains less gasoline must be on a higher indifference curve. The household will not choose any bundle with more gasoline because these bundles are all inside the old budget line, and hence are inferior to the bundle with 800 gallons of gas.

10. Which of the following three groups is likely to have the most, and which the least, price-elastic demand for membership in the Association of Business Economists?

a.   **students**

The major difference among the groups is the level of income. We know that if the consumption of a good constitutes a large percentage of an individual's income, then the demand for the good will be relatively elastic. If we assume that a membership in the Association of Business Economists is likely to be a large expenditure for students, we may conclude that the demand will be relatively elastic for this group.

b.   **junior executives**

The level of income for junior executives will be larger than that of students, but smaller than that of senior executives. Therefore, the demand for a membership for this group will be less elastic than that of the students but more elastic than that of the senior executives.

c.   **senior executives**

The high earnings among senior executives will result in a relatively inelastic demand for membership.

11. Explain which of the following items in each pair is more price elastic.

a.   **The demand for a specific brand of toothpaste and the demand for toothpaste in general.**

The demand for a specific brand is more elastic since the consumer can easily switch to another brand if the price goes up.

b. **The demand for gasoline in the short run and the demand for gasoline in the long run.**

Demand in the long run is more elastic since consumers have had more time to adjust to the change in price.

13. **Explain the difference between a positive and a negative network externality, and give an example of each.**

A positive network externality exists if the quantity demanded of a good by one individual increases in response to the purchase of the good by other consumers. Fads are an example of a positive network externality. For example, each individuals demand for baggy pants increases as more other individuals begin to wear baggy pants. This is also called a bandwagon effect. A negative network externality exists if the quantity demanded of a good by one individual decreases in response to the purchase of the good by other consumers. In this case the individual prefers to be different from other individuals. As more people adopt a particular style or purchase a particular type of good, this individual will reduce his demand for the good. Goods like designer clothing can have negative network externalities as some people would not want to wear the same clothes that many other people are wearing.

EXERCISES

1. **An individual sets aside a certain amount of his income per month to spend on his two hobbies, collecting wine and collecting books. Given the information below, illustrate both the price consumption curve associated with changes in the price of wine, and the demand curve for wine.**

Price Wine	Price Book	Quantity Wine	Quantity Book	Budget
$10	$10	7	8	$150
$12	$10	5	9	$150
$15	$10	4	9	$150
$20	$10	2	11	$150

The price consumption curve connects each of the four optimal bundles given in the table above. As the price of wine increases, the budget line will pivot inwards and the optimal bundle will change.

2. **An individual consumes two goods, clothing and food. Given the information below, illustrate the income consumption curve, and the Engel curves for clothing and food.**

Price Clothing	Price Food	Quantity Clothing	Quantity Food	Income
$10	$2	6	20	$100
$10	$2	8	35	$150
$10	$2	11	45	$200
$10	$2	15	50	$250

The income consumption curve connects each of the four optimal bundles given in the table above. As the individual's income increases, the budget line will shift out and the optimal bundle will change. The Engel curves for each good illustrate the relationship between the quantity consumed and income (on the vertical axis). Both Engel curves are upward sloping.

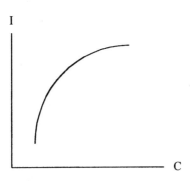

3. Jane always gets twice as much utility from an extra ballet ticket as she does from an extra basketball ticket, regardless of how many tickets of either type she has. Draw Jane's income consumption curve and her Engel curve for ballet tickets.

Jane will consume either all ballet tickets or all basketball tickets, depending on the two prices. As long as ballet tickets are less than twice the price of basketball tickets, she will choose all ballet. If ballet tickets are more than twice the price of basketball tickets then she will choose all basketball. This can be determined by comparing the marginal utility per dollar for each type of ticket, where her marginal utility of another ballet ticket is 2 and her marginal utility of another basketball ticket is 1. Her income consumption curve will then lie along the axis of the good that she chooses. As income increases, and the budget line shifts out, she will stick with the chosen good. The Engel curve is a linear, upward-sloping line. For any given increase in income, she will be able to purchase a fixed amount of extra tickets.

4. a. Orange juice and apple juice are known to be perfect substitutes. Draw the appropriate price-consumption (for a variable price of orange juice) and income-consumption curves.

We know that the indifference curves for perfect substitutes will be straight lines. In this case, the consumer will always purchase the cheaper of the two goods. If the price of orange juice is less than that of apple juice, the consumer will purchase only orange juice and the price consumption curve will be on the "orange juice axis" of the graph (point F). If apple juice is cheaper, the consumer will purchase only apple juice and the price consumption curve will be on the "apple juice axis" (point E). If the two goods have the same price, the consumer will be indifferent between the two; the price consumption curve will coincide with the indifference curve (between E and F). See the figure below.

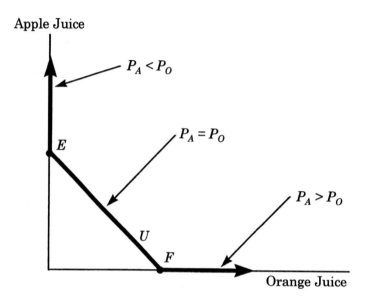

Assuming that the price of orange juice is less than the price of apple juice, the consumer will maximize her utility by consuming only orange juice. As the level of income varies, only the amount of orange juice varies. Thus, the income consumption curve will be the "orange juice axis" in the figure below.

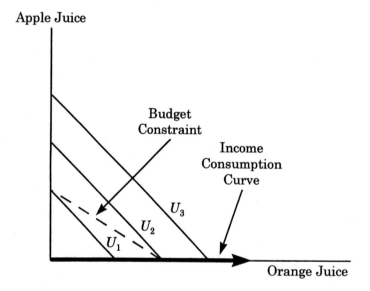

4.b. Left shoes and right shoes are perfect complements. Draw the appropriate price-consumption and income-consumption curves.

For goods that are perfect complements, such as right shoes and left shoes, we know that the indifference curves are L-shaped. The point of utility maximization occurs when the budget constraints, L_1 and L_2 touch the kink of U_1 and U_2. See the following figure.

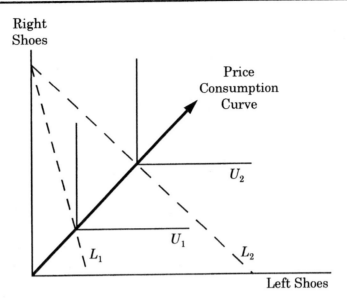

In the case of perfect complements, the income consumption curve is also a line through the corners of the *L*-shaped indifference curves. See the figure below.

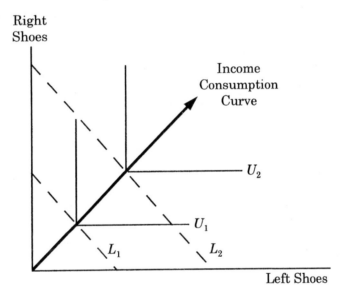

5. Each week, Bill, Mary, and Jane select the quantity of two goods, x_1 and x_2, that they will consume in order to maximize their respective utilities. They each spend their entire weekly income on these two goods.

a.   **Suppose you are given the following information about the choices that Bill makes over a three-week period:**

	x_1	x_2	P_1	P_2	I
Week 1	10	20	2	1	40
Week 2	7	19	3	1	40
Week 3	8	31	3	1	55

Did Bill's utility increase or decrease between week 1 and week 2?   Between week 1 and week 3? Explain using a graph to support your answer.

Bill's utility fell between weeks 1 and 2 since he ended up with less of both goods. In week 2, the price of good 1 rose and his income remained constant. The budget line will pivot inwards and he will have to move to a lower indifference curve. Between week 1 and week 3 his utility rose. The increase in income more than compensated him for the rise in the price of good 1. Since the price of good 1 rose by $1, he would need an extra $10 to afford the same bundle of goods that he chose in week 1. This can be found by multiplying week 1 quantities times week 2 prices. However, his income went up by $15, so his budget line shifted out beyond his week 1 bundle. Therefore, his original bundle lies within his new budget set, and his new week 3 bundle is on a higher indifference curve.

b. **Now consider the following information about the choices that Mary makes:**

	x_1	x_2	P_1	P_2	I
Week 1	10	20	2	1	40
Week 2	6	14	2	2	40
Week 3	20	10	2	2	60

Did Mary's utility increase or decrease between week 1 and week 3? Does Mary consider both goods to be normal goods? Explain.

Mary's utility went up. To afford the week 1 bundle at the new prices, she would need an extra $20, which is exactly what happened to her income. However, since she could have chosen the original bundle at the new prices and income but chose not to, she must have found a bundle that left her slightly better off. In the graph below, the week 1 bundle is at the intersection of the week 1 and week 3 budget lines. The week 3 bundle is somewhere on the line segment that lies above the week 1 indifference curve. This bundle will be on a higher indifference curve. A good is normal if more is chosen when income increases. Good 2 is not normal because when her income went up from week 2 to week 3, she consumed less of the good (holding prices the same).

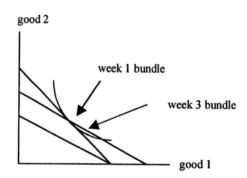

c. **Finally, examine the following information about Jane's choices:**

	x_1	x_2	P_1	P_2	I
Week 1	12	24	2	1	48
Week 2	16	32	1	1	48
Week 3	12	24	1	1	36

Draw a budget line, indifference curve graph that illustrates Jane's three chosen bundles. What can you say about Jane's preferences in this case? Identify the income and substitution effects that result from a change in the price of good 1.

In week 2, the price of good 1 goes down and Jane consumes more of both goods. Her budget line pivots outwards. In week 3 the prices remain at the new level, but Jane's income is reduced. This will shift her budget line inwards, and cause her to consume less of both goods. Notice that Jane always consumes the two goods in a fixed 1:2 ratio. This means that Jane views the two goods as perfect complements, and her indifference curves are L-shaped. Intuitively if the two goods are complements, there is no reason to substitute one for the other during a price change because they have to be consumed in a set ratio. Thus the substitution effect will be zero. When the price ratio changes and utility is kept at the same level, Jane will choose the same point (12,24). The income effect causes her to buy 4 more units of good 1 and 8 more units of good 2.

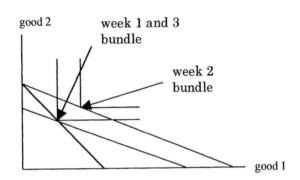

6. Two individuals, Sam and Barb, derive utility from the hours of leisure (L) they consume and from the amount of goods (G) they consume. In order to maximize utility they need to allocate the 24 hours in the day between leisure hours and work hours. Assume that all hours not spent working are leisure hours. The price of a good is equal to $1 and the price of leisure is equal to the hourly wage. We observe the following information about the choices that the two individuals make:

		Sam	Barb	Sam	Barb
Price of G	Price of L	L(hours)	L(hours)	G($)	G($)
1	8	16	14	64	80
1	9	15	14	81	90
1	10	14	15	100	90
1	11	14	16	110	88

Graphically illustrate Sam's leisure demand curve and Barb's leisure demand curve. Place price on the vertical axis and leisure on the horizontal axis. Given that they both maximize utility, how can you explain the difference in their leisure demand curves?

It is important to remember that less leisure implies more hours spent working at the higher wage. Sam's leisure demand curve is downward sloping. As the price of leisure (the wage) rises, he chooses to consume less leisure to spend more time working at a higher wage to buy more goods. Barb's leisure demand curve is upward sloping. As the price of leisure rises, she chooses to consume more leisure since her working hours are generating more income. This difference in demand can be explained by examining the income and substitution effects for the two individuals. The substitution effect measures the effect of the change in the price of leisure, keeping utility constant (the budget line will rotate around the current indifference curve). Since the substitution effect is always negative, a rise in the price of leisure will cause both individuals to consume less leisure. The income effect measures the change in purchasing power caused by the change in the price of leisure. Here, when the price of leisure (the wage) rises, there is an increase in purchasing power (the new budget line will shift outwards). Assuming both individuals consider leisure to be a normal good (this is not a necessary assumption for Sam), then the increase in purchasing power will increase demand for leisure. For Sam, the reduction in leisure demand caused by the substitution effect outweighs the increase in demand for leisure caused by the income effect. For Barb, her income effect is larger than her substitution effect.

7. **The director of a theatre company in a small college town is considering changing the way he prices tickets. He has hired an economic consulting firm to estimate the demand for tickets. The firm has classified people who go the theatre into two groups, and has come up with two demand functions. The demand curves for the general public (Q_{gp}) and students (Q_s) are given below.**

$$Q_{gp} = 500 - 5P$$
$$Q_s = 200 - 4P$$

a. **Graph the two demand curves on one graph, with P on the vertical axis and Q on the horizontal axis. If the current price of tickets is $35, identify the quantity demanded by each group.**

Both demand curves are downward sloping and linear. For the general public, the vertical intercept is 100 and the horizontal intercept is 500. For the students, the vertical intercept is 50 and the horizontal intercept is 200. The general public demands $Q_{gp} = 500 - 5(35) = 325$ tickets and the students demand $Q_s = 200 - 4(35) = 60$ tickets.

b. **Find the price elasticity of demand for each group at the current price and quantity.**

The elasticity for the general public is $\varepsilon_{gp} = \dfrac{-5(35)}{325} = -0.54$ and the elasticity for the students is $\varepsilon_{gp} = \dfrac{-4(35)}{60} = -2.33$. If the price of tickets increases by one percent then the general public will demand .54% fewer tickets and the students will demand 2.33% fewer tickets.

c. **Is the director maximizing the revenue he collects from ticket sales by charging $35 for each ticket? Explain.**

No he is not maximizing revenue since neither one of the calculated elasticities is equal to –1. Since demand by the general public is inelastic at the current price, the director could increase the price and quantity demanded would fall by a smaller amount in percentage terms, causing revenue to increase. Since demand by the students is elastic at the current price, the director could decrease the price and quantity demanded would increase by a larger amount in percentage terms, causing revenue to increase.

d. **What price should he charge each group if he wants to maximize revenue collected from ticket sales?**

To figure this out, find the formula for elasticity, set it equal to –1, and solve for price and quantity. For the general public:

$$\varepsilon_{gp} = \frac{-5P}{Q} = -1$$
$$5P = Q = 500 - 5P$$
$$P = 50$$
$$Q = 250.$$

For the students:

$$\varepsilon_s = \frac{-4P}{Q} = -1$$
$$4P = Q = 200 - 4P$$
$$P = 25$$
$$Q = 100.$$

8. Judy has decided to allocate exactly $500 to textbooks at college every year, even though she knows that the prices are likely to increase by 5 to 10 percent per year and that she will be getting a substantial monetary gift from her grandparents next year. What is Judy's price elasticity of demand for textbooks? Income elasticity?

Price elasticity of demand is percentage change in quantity for a given percentage change in price. Judy knows that prices will go up in the future. Given she is going to spend a fixed amount on books, this must mean that her quantity demanded will decrease as price increases. Since expenditure is constant the percentage change in quantity demanded must be equal to the percentage change in price, and price elasticity is -1. Income elasticity must be zero because although she expects a large monetary gift, she has no plans to purchase more books. Recall that income elasticity is defined as the percentage change in quantity demanded for a given percentage change in income, all else the same.

9. The ACME Corporation determines that at current prices the demand for its computer chips has a price elasticity of -2 in the short run, while the price elasticity for its disk drives is -1.

a.   If the corporation decides to raise the price of both products by 10 percent, what will happen to its sales? To its sales revenue?

We know the formula for the elasticity of demand is:

$$E_P = \frac{\%\Delta Q}{\%\Delta P}.$$

For computer chips, E_P = -2, so a 10 percent increase in price will reduce the quantity sold by 20 percent. For disk drives, E_P = -1, so a 10 percent increase in price will reduce sales by 10 percent.

Sales revenue is equal to price times quantity sold. Let $TR_1 = P_1 Q_1$ be revenue before the price change and $TR_2 = P_2 Q_2$ be revenue after the price change.

For computer chips:
$$\Delta TR_{cc} = P_2 Q_2 - P_1 Q_1$$

$\Delta TR_{cc} = (1.1 P_1)(0.8 Q_1) - P_1 Q_1 = -0.12 P_1 Q_1$, or a 12 percent decline.

For disk drives:
$$\Delta TR_{dd} = P_2 Q_2 - P_1 Q_1$$

$\Delta TR_{dd} = (1.1 P_1)(0.9 Q_1) - P_1 Q_1 = -0.01 P_1 Q_1$, or a 1 percent decline.

Therefore, sales revenue from computer chips decreases substantially, -12 percent, while the sales revenue from disk drives is almost unchanged, -1 percent. Note that at the point on the demand curve where demand is unit elastic, total revenue is maximized.

b.   Can you tell from the available information which product will generate the most revenue for the firm? If yes, why? If not, what additional information do you need?

No. Although we know the responsiveness of demand to changes in price, we need to know both quantities and prices of the products to determine total sales revenue.

10. By observing an individual's behavior in the situations outlined below, determine the relevant income elasticities of demand for each good (i.e., whether the good is normal or inferior). If you cannot determine the income elasticity, what additional information might you need?

a.   **Bill spends all his income on books and coffee. He finds $20 while rummaging through a used paperback bin at the bookstore. He immediately buys a new hardcover book of poetry.**

Books are a normal good since his consumption of books increases with income. Coffee is a normal or neutral good since consumption of coffee did not fall when income increased.

b.   **Bill loses $10 he was going to use to buy a double espresso. He decides to sell his new book at a discount to his friend and use the money to buy coffee.**

Coffee is clearly a normal good.

c.   **Being bohemian becomes the latest teen fad. As a result, coffee and book prices rise by 25 percent. Bill lowers his consumption of both goods by the same percentage.**

Books and coffee are both normal goods since his response to a decline in real income is to decrease consumption of both goods.

d.   **Bill drops out of art school and gets an M.B.A. instead. He stops reading books and drinking coffee. Now he reads *The Wall Street Journal* and drinks bottled mineral water.**

His tastes have changed completely, and we do not know exactly how he would respond to price and income changes. We need more information regarding his new level of income, and relative prices of the goods to determine the income elasticities.

11. Suppose the income elasticity of demand for food is 0.5, and the price elasticity of demand is –1.0. Suppose also that Felicia spends $10,000 a year on food, the price of food is $2, and her income is $25,000.

a.   **If a sales tax on food were to cause the price of food to increase to $2.50, what would happen to her consumption of food? (*Hint*: Since a large price change is involved, you should assume that the price elasticity measures an arc elasticity, rather than a point elasticity.)**

The price of food increases from $2 to $2.50, so arc elasticity should be used:

$$E_P = \left(\frac{\Delta Q}{\Delta P}\right)\left(\frac{\frac{P_1 + P_2}{2}}{\frac{Q_1 + Q_2}{2}}\right).$$

We know that $E_P = -1$, $P = 2$, $\Delta P = 0.5$, and $Q=5000$. We also know that Q_2, the new quantity, is $Q + \Delta Q$. Thus, if there is no change in income, we may solve for ΔQ:

$$-1 = \left(\frac{\Delta Q}{0.5}\right)\left(\frac{\frac{2+2.5}{2}}{\frac{5,000 + (5,000 + \Delta Q)}{2}}\right).$$

By cross-multiplying and rearranging terms, we find that $\Delta Q = -1,000$. This means that she decreases her consumption of food from 5,000 to 4,000 units.

b.   **Suppose that she is given a tax rebate of $2,500 to ease the effect of the sales tax. What would her consumption of food be now?**

A tax rebate of $2,500 implies an income increase of $2,500. To calculate the response of demand to the tax rebate, use the definition of the arc elasticity of income.

$$E_I = \left(\frac{\Delta Q}{\Delta I}\right)\left(\frac{\frac{I_1 + I_2}{2}}{\frac{Q_1 + Q_2}{2}}\right).$$

We know that $E_I = 0.5$, $I = 25,000$, $\Delta I = 2,500$, $Q = 4,000$ (from the answer to 11.a). Assuming no change in price, we solve for ΔQ.

$$0.5 = \left(\frac{\Delta Q}{2,500}\right)\left(\frac{\frac{25,000 + 27,500}{2}}{\frac{4,000 + (4,000 + \Delta Q)}{2}}\right).$$

By cross-multiplying and rearranging terms, we find that $\Delta Q = 195$ (approximately). This means that she increases her consumption of food from 4,000 to 4,195 units.

c.   **Is she better or worse off when given a rebate equal to the sales tax payments? Draw a graph and explain.**

Felicia is likely to be better off after the rebate. The amount of the rebate is enough to allow her to purchase her original bundle of food and other goods. Recall that originally she consumed 5000 units of food. When the price went up by fifty cents per unit, she needed an extra 5000*$0.50=$2,500 to afford the same quantity of food without reducing the quantity of the other goods consumed. This is the exact amount of the rebate. However, she did not choose to return to her original bundle. We can therefore infer that she found a better bundle that gave her a higher level of utility. In the graph below, when the price of food increases, the budget line will pivot inwards. When the rebate is given, this new budget line will shift outwards. The bundle after the rebate is on that part of the new budget line that was previously unaffordable, and that lies above the original indifference curve.

12. **You run a small business and would like to predict what will happen to the quantity demanded for your product if you raise your price. While you do not know the exact demand curve for your product, you do know that in the first year you charged a price of $45 and sold 1200 units and in the second year you charged a price of $30 and sold 1800 units.**

a. **If you plan to raise your price by 10% what would be a reasonable estimate of what might happen to quantity demanded in percentage terms?**

To answer this question, you need to find the elasticity. You can estimate the slope of the demand curve in the following way:

$$\frac{\partial Q}{\partial P} = \frac{\Delta Q}{\Delta P} = \frac{1200 - 1800}{45 - 30} = \frac{600}{-15} = -40.$$

You can now use the elasticity formula and calculate elasticity at each data point, as well as the average point. The elasticities are:

P=45 and Q=1200   elasticity$=\frac{P}{Q}\frac{\Delta Q}{\Delta P} = \frac{-40(45)}{1200} = -1.5.$

P=30 and Q=1800   elasticity$==\frac{P}{Q}\frac{\Delta Q}{\Delta P} = \frac{-40(30)}{1800} = -0.67.$

P=37.5 and Q=1500   elasticity$==\frac{P}{Q}\frac{\Delta Q}{\Delta P} = \frac{-40(37.5)}{1500} = -1.$

Given you are coming up with an estimate based on only two data points, it may be best to go with the average point. If elasticity is -1 then a 10% increase in price will cause quantity demanded to fall by 10%.

b. **If you raise your price by 10%, will revenue increase or decrease?**

If elasticity is really -1 then revenue will fall if price is increased. If elasticity is actually closer to -0.67 (inelastic) then revenue will rise because the effect of the increase in price will outweigh the effect of the decrease in quantity. If elasticity is closer to -1.5 (elastic) then revenue will fall when price is increased.

13. **Suppose you are in charge of a toll bridge that costs essentially nothing to operate. The demand for bridge crossings Q is given by $P = 15 - \frac{1}{2}Q$.**

a. **Draw the demand curve for bridge crossings.**

The demand curve is linear and downward sloping. The vertical intercept is 15 and the horizontal intercept is 30.

b. **How many people would cross the bridge if there were no toll?**

At a price of zero, the quantity demanded would be 30.

c. **What is the loss of consumer surplus associated with a bridge toll of $5?**

If the toll is $5 then the quantity demanded is 20. The lost consumer surplus is the area below the price line of $5 and to the left of the demand curve. The lost consumer surplus can be calculated as (5*20)+0.5(5*10)=$125.

d.   The toll bridge operator is considering an increase in the toll to $7. At this new higher price, how many people would cross the bridge? Would the toll bridge revenue increase or decrease? What does your answer tell you about the elasticity of demand?

At a toll of $7, the quantity demanded would be 16. The initial toll revenue was $5*20=$100. The new toll revenue is $7*16=$112. Since the revenue went up when the toll was increased, demand is inelastic (the increase in price (40%) outweighed the decline in quantity demanded (20%)).

e.   Find the lost consumer surplus associated with the increase in the price of the toll from $5 to $7.

The lost consumer surplus is (7-5)*16+0.5(7-5)(20-16)=$36.

14. Vera has decided to upgrade the operating system on her new PC. She hears that the new Linux operating system is technologically superior to the Windows operating system and substantially lower in price. However, when she asks her friends it turns out they all use PCs with Windows. They agree that Linux is more appealing but add that they see relatively few copies of Linux on sale at the local retail software stores. Based on what she learns and observes, Vera chooses to upgrade her PC with Windows. Can you explain her decision?

Vera is consuming under the influence of a positive network externality (not a bandwagon effect). When she hears that there are limited software choices that are compatible with the Linux operating system, she decides to go with Windows. If she had not been interested in acquiring much software, she may have gone with Linux. See Example 4.6 in the text. In the future, however, there may be a bandwagon effect, i.e., the purchase of Linux because almost everyone else has it. As more people use Linux, manufacturers might introduce more software that is compatible with the Linux operating system. As the Linux based software section at the local computer store gets larger and larger, this prompts more consumers to purchase Linux. Eventually, the Windows section shrinks as the Linux section becomes larger and larger.

16. Suppose that you are the consultant to an agricultural cooperative that is deciding whether members should cut their production of cotton in half next year. The cooperative wants your advice as to whether this will increase the farmers' revenues. Knowing that cotton (C) and watermelons (W) both compete for agricultural land in the South, you estimate the demand for cotton to be $C=3.5-1.0P_C+0.25P_W+0.50I$, where P_C is the price of cotton, P_W the price of watermelon, and I income. Should you support or oppose the plan? Is there any additional information that would help you to provide a definitive answer?

If production of cotton is cut in half, then the price of cotton will increase, given that we see from the equation above that demand is downward sloping. With price increasing and quantity demanded decreasing, revenue could go either way. It depends on whether demand is inelastic or elastic at the current price. If demand is inelastic then a decrease in production and an increase in price could increase revenue. If demand is elastic then a decrease in production and an increase in price will clearly decrease revenue. You need to know the current price and/or quantity demanded to figure out the current level of elasticity.

CHAPTER 4 APPENDIX
DEMAND THEORY – A MATHEMATICAL TREATMENT

EXERCISES

1. Which of the following utility functions are consistent with convex indifference curves, and which are not?

a. $U(X, Y) = 2X + 5Y$

b. $U(X, Y) = (XY)^{0.5}$

c. $U(X, Y) = Min(X, Y)$, where Min is the minimum of the two values of X and Y

The three utility functions are presented in Figures 4A.1.a, 4A.1.b, and 4A.1.c. The first may be represented as a series of straight lines; the second as a series of hyperbolas; and the third as a series of "*L*'s." Only the second utility function meets the definition of a strictly convex shape.

To graph the indifference curves which represent the preferences given by $U(X,Y)=2X+5Y$, set utility to some given level U_0 and solve for Y to get

$$Y = \frac{U_0}{5} - \frac{2}{5}X.$$

Since this is the equation for a straight line, the indifference curves are linear with intercept $\dfrac{U_0}{5}$ and slope $-\dfrac{2}{5}$.

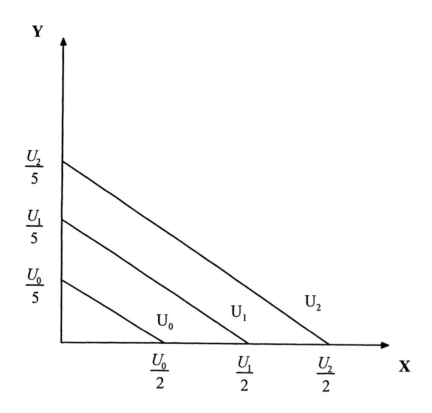

Figure 4A.1.a

58

To graph the indifference curves that represent the preferences given by $U(X,Y) = (XY)^{0.5}$, set utility to some given level U_0 and solve for Y to get

$$Y = \frac{U_0^2}{X}.$$

By plugging in a few values for X and solving for Y, you will be able to graph the indifference curve U_0, which is illustrated in Figure 4A.1.b, along with the indifference curve U_1.

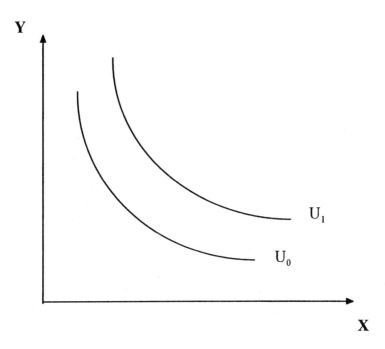

Figure 4A.1.b

To graph the indifference curves which represent the preferences given by $U(X,Y) = Min(X,Y)$, first note that utility functions of this form result in indifference curves which are L-shaped and represent a complementary relationship between X and Y. In this case, for any given level of utility U_0, the value of X and Y will also be equal to U_0. As X increases and Y does not change, utility will also not change. If both X and Y change, then utility will change and we will move to a different indifference curve. See the following table.

X	Y	U
10	10	10
10	11	10
10	9	9
11	10	10
9	10	9
9	9	9

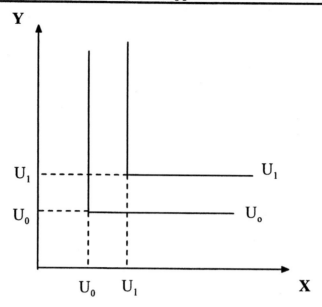

Figure 4A.1.c

2. Show that two utility functions given below generate the identical demand functions for goods X and Y:

a. $U(X, Y) = \log(X) + \log(Y)$

b. $U(X, Y) = (XY)^{0.5}$

The Appendix discusses how to derive demand functions from utility functions. If we show that the two utility functions are equivalent, then we know that the demand functions derived from them are identical. We may show their equivalence by identifying a suitable transformation from one set of numbers into another set without changing their order.

Taking the logarithm of $U(X, Y) = (XY)^{0.5}$ we obtain:

$$\log U(X,\ Y) = 0.5\log(X) + 0.5\log(Y).$$

Now multiply both sides by 2:

$$2(\log U(X,Y) = \log(X) + \log(Y).$$

Therefore, the two utility functions are equivalent and will yield identical demand functions. However, we will solve for the demand functions in both cases to show that they are the same.

a. To find the demand functions for X and Y, corresponding to $U(X,\ Y) = \log(X) + \log(Y)$, given the usual budget constraint, write the Lagrangian:

$$\Phi = \log(X) + \log(Y) - \lambda(P_X X + P_Y Y - I)$$

Differentiating with respect to X, Y, λ, and setting the derivatives equal to zero:

$$\frac{\partial \Phi}{\partial X} = \frac{1}{X} - \lambda P_X = 0$$

$$\frac{\partial \Phi}{\partial Y} = \frac{1}{Y} - \lambda P_Y = 0$$

$$\frac{\partial \Phi}{\partial \lambda} = P_X X + P_Y Y - I = 0.$$

60

The first two conditions imply that $P_X X = \dfrac{1}{\lambda}$ and $P_Y Y = \dfrac{1}{\lambda}$.

The third condition implies that $\dfrac{1}{\lambda} + \dfrac{1}{\lambda} - I = 0$, or $\lambda = \dfrac{2}{I}$.

Substituting this expression into $P_X X = \dfrac{I}{\lambda}$ and $P_Y Y = \dfrac{I}{\lambda}$ gives the demand functions:

$$X = \left(\frac{0.5}{P_X}\right) I \quad \text{and} \quad Y = \left(\frac{0.5}{P_Y}\right) I.$$

Notice that the demand for each good depends only on the price of that good and on income, not on the price of the other good.

b. To find the demand functions for X and Y, corresponding to $U(X, Y) = (XY)^{0.5}$ given the usual budget constraint, first write the Lagrangian:

$$\Phi = 0.5(\log X) + (1 - 0.5)\log Y - \lambda(P_X X + P_Y Y - I)$$

Differentiating with respect to X, Y, λ and setting the derivatives equal to zero:

$$\frac{\partial \Phi}{\partial X} = \frac{0.5}{X} - \lambda P_X = 0$$

$$\frac{\partial \Phi}{\partial Y} = \frac{0.5}{Y} - \lambda P_Y = 0$$

$$\frac{\partial \Phi}{\partial \lambda} = P_X X + P_Y Y - I = 0.$$

The first two conditions imply that $P_X X = \dfrac{0.5}{\lambda}$ and $P_Y Y = \dfrac{0.5}{\lambda}$.

Combining these with the budget constraint gives: $\dfrac{0.5}{\lambda} + \dfrac{0.5}{\lambda} - I = 0$ or $\lambda = \dfrac{1}{I}$.

Now substituting this expression into $P_X X = \dfrac{0.5}{\lambda}$ and $P_Y Y = \dfrac{0.5}{\lambda}$ gives the demand functions:

$$X = \left(\frac{0.5}{P_X}\right) I \quad \text{and} \quad Y = \left(\frac{0.5}{P_Y}\right) I.$$

3. Assume that a utility function is given by Min(X, Y), as in Exercise 1(c). What is the Slutsky equation that decomposes the change in the demand for X in response to a change in its price? What is the income effect? What is the substitution effect?

The Slutsky equation is $\dfrac{\Delta X}{\Delta P_X} = \left.\dfrac{\Delta X}{\Delta P_X}\right|_{U=U^*} - X\left(\dfrac{\Delta X}{\Delta I}\right)$,

where the first term represents the substitution effect and the second term represents the income effect. Because there is no substitution as prices change with this type of utility function, the substitution effect is zero. The income effect is the shift from U_1 to U_2.

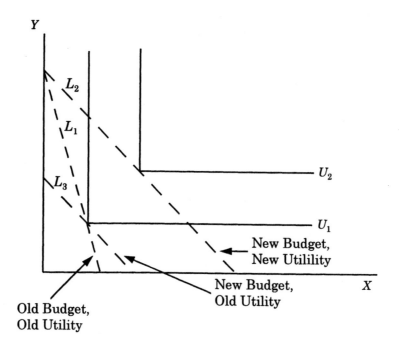

Figure 4A.3

4. Sharon has the following utility function:

$$U(X,Y) = \sqrt{X} + \sqrt{Y}$$

where X is her consumption of candy bars, with price P_X=\$1, and Y is her consumption of espressos, with P_Y=\$3.

a.   Derive Sharon's demand for candy bars and espressos.

Using the Lagrangian method, the Lagrangian equation is

$$\Phi = \sqrt{X} + \sqrt{Y} - \lambda(P_X X + P_Y Y - I).$$

To find the demand functions, we need to maximize the Lagrangian equation with respect to X, Y, and λ, which is the same as maximizing utility subject to the budget constraint. The necessary conditions for a maximum are

(1) $\dfrac{\partial \Phi}{\partial X} = \dfrac{1}{2} X^{-\frac{1}{2}} - P_X \lambda = 0$

(2) $\dfrac{\partial \Phi}{\partial Y} = \dfrac{1}{2} Y^{-\frac{1}{2}} - P_Y \lambda = 0$

(3) $\dfrac{\partial \Phi}{\partial \lambda} = P_X X + P_Y Y - I = 0.$

Combining necessary conditions (1) and (2) results in

$$\lambda = \frac{1}{2 P_X \sqrt{X}} = \frac{1}{2 P_Y \sqrt{Y}}$$

$$P_X X^{\frac{1}{2}} = P_Y Y^{\frac{1}{2}}$$

(4) $X = \left(\dfrac{P_Y^2}{P_X^2} \right) Y.$

You can now substitute (4) into (3) and solve for Y. Once you have solved for Y, you can substitute Y back into (4) and solve for X. Note that algebraically there are several ways to solve this type of problem, and that it does not have to be done exactly as we have done here. The demand functions are

$$Y = \frac{P_X I}{P_Y^2 + P_Y P_X} \text{ or } Y = \frac{I}{12}$$

$$X = \frac{P_Y I}{P_X^2 + P_Y P_X} \text{ or } X = \frac{3I}{4}.$$

b. **Assume that her income I=\$100. How many candy bars and espressos will Sharon consume?**

Substitute the values for the two prices and income into the demand functions to find that she consumes X=75 candy bars and Y=8.3 espressos.

c. **What is the marginal utility of income?**

From part a $\lambda = \frac{1}{2P_X\sqrt{X}} = \frac{1}{2P_Y\sqrt{Y}}$. Substitute into either part of the equation to find that λ=0.058. This is how much utility would increase by if Sharon had one more dollar to spend.

5. Maurice has the following utility function: $U(X,Y) = 20X + 80Y - X^2 - 2Y^2$, **where X is his consumption of CD's, with a price of \$1, and Y is his consumption of movie videos, with a rental price of \$2. He plans to spend \$41 on both forms of entertainment. Determine the number of CD's and video rentals that will maximize Maurice's utility.**

Using the Lagrangian method, the Lagrangian equation is

$$\Phi = 20X + 80Y - X^2 - 2Y^2 - \lambda(X + 2Y - 41).$$

To find the optimal consumption of each good, we need to maximize the Lagrangian equation with respect to X, Y, and λ, which is the same as maximizing utility subject to the budget constraint. The necessary conditions for a maximum are

(1) $\quad \frac{\partial \Phi}{\partial X} = 20 - 2X - \lambda = 0$

(2) $\quad \frac{\partial \Phi}{\partial Y} = 80 - 4Y - 2\lambda = 0$

(3) $\quad \frac{\partial \Phi}{\partial \lambda} = X + 2Y - 41 = 0.$

Combining necessary conditions (1) and (2) results in

$\lambda = 20 - 2X = 40 - 2Y$

(4) $\quad 2Y = 20 + 2X.$

You can now substitute (4) into (3) and solve for X. Once you have solved for X, you can substitute this value back into (4) and solve for Y. Note that algebraically there are several ways to solve this type of problem, and that it does not have to be done exactly as we have done here. The optimal bundle is X=7 and Y=17.

CHAPTER 5
UNCERTAINTY AND CONSUMER BEHAVIOR

TEACHING NOTES

Choice under uncertainty is an important topic in microeconomic theory, but students find the concept difficult. The topic should be covered in business-oriented courses, particularly if you intend to cover the role of risk in capital markets, which is discussed in Chapter 15. The primary purpose of this chapter is to encourage students to think about the influence on behavior of attitudes toward risk. The first three sections of the chapter should be covered in at least two lectures, giving the students time to absorb the basic ideas.

If students have not been previously exposed to probability, expected value, and variance, they will have difficulty with this chapter, particularly with Exercises (1) through (5), which illustrate these concepts. Most students without a background in probability consider risk to be the possibility of loss or injury, instead of the probability of either loss or gain. Make sure they understand this distinction before further discussing uncertainty.

If students have had basic probability theory before and you have covered utility theory, they should easily grasp the definition of expected utility. However, they usually confuse the utility of an expected value with expected utility. Both concepts are needed to explain risk aversion in general and the subtleties of Exercise (7) in particular. For an empirical analysis of gambling, see Selby and Beranek, "Sweepstake Contests: Analysis, Strategies, and Survey," *American Economic Review* (March 1981) and Brunk, "A Test of the Friedman-Savage Gambling Model," *Quarterly Journal of Economics* (May 1981). In a more theoretical class, present the derivation of the Von Neumann-Morgenstern utility function. See Copeland and Weston's discussion of utility theory under uncertainty in Chapter 4, *Financial Theory and Corporate Policy* (Addison-Wesley, 1979).

Even if your students have not fully understood the technical aspects of choice under uncertainty, they should easily comprehend Examples 5.1 and 5.2 (the latter example leads to Exercise (8), which is easier than it looks). This is also true of the topics presented in Section 5.3, i.e., diversification and purchasing insurance and Examples 5.3 and 5.4. Also, you might mention the problems of adverse selection and moral hazard in insurance, to be discussed in Chapter 17.

The last section, 5.4, is more difficult and may be postponed until after the class has completed the discussion of risk and rates of return in Chapter 15.

QUESTIONS FOR REVIEW

1. What does it mean to say that a person is risk averse? Why are some people likely to be risk averse, while others are risk lovers?

A risk-averse person has a diminishing marginal utility of income and prefers a certain income to a gamble with the same expected income. A risk lover has an increasing marginal utility of income and prefers an uncertain income to a certain income. The economic explanation of whether an individual is risk averse or risk loving depends on the shape of the individual's utility function for wealth. Also, a person's risk aversion (or risk loving) depends on the nature of the risk involved and on the person's income.

2. Why is the variance a better measure of variability than the range?

Range is the difference between the highest possible outcome and the lowest possible outcome. Range does not indicate the probabilities of observing these high or low outcomes. Variance weighs the difference of each outcome from the mean outcome by its probability and, thus, is a more useful measure of variability than the range.

3. George has $5,000 to invest in a mutual fund. The expected return on mutual fund A is 15% and the expected return on mutual fund B is 10%. Should George pick mutual fund A or fund B?

George's decision will depend not only on the expected return for each fund, but also on the variability in the expected return on each fund, and on George's preferences. For example, if fund A has a higher standard deviation than fund B, and George is risk averse, then he may prefer fund B even though it has a lower expected return. If George is not particularly risk averse he may choose fund A even if it subject to more variability in its expected return.

4. What does it mean for consumers to maximize expected utility? Can you think of a case where a person might not maximize expected utility?

The expected utility is the sum of the utilities associated with all possible outcomes, weighted by the probability that each outcome will occur. To maximize expected utility means that the individual chooses the option that yields the highest average utility, where average utility is a probability-weighted sum of all utilities. This theory requires that the consumer knows the probability of every outcome. At times, consumers either do not know the relevant probabilities or have difficulty in evaluating low-probability, high-payoff events. In some cases, consumers cannot assign a utility level to these high-payoff events, such as when the payoff is the loss of the consumer's life.

5. Why do people often want to insure fully against uncertain situations even when the premium paid exceeds the expected value of the loss being insured against?

If the cost of insurance is equal to the expected loss, (i.e., if the insurance is actuarially fair), risk-averse individuals will fully insure against monetary loss. The insurance premium assures the individual of having the *same income* regardless of whether or not a loss occurs. Because the insurance is actuarially fair, this certain income is equal to the *expected* income if the individual takes the risky option of not purchasing insurance. This guarantee of the same income, whatever the outcome, generates *more utility* for a risk-averse person than the average utility of a high income when there was no loss and the utility of a low income with a loss (i.e., because of risk aversion, $E[U(x)] \leq U(E[x])$.

6. Why is an insurance company likely to behave *as if* it is risk neutral even if its managers are risk-averse individuals?

Most large companies have opportunities for diversifying risk. Managers acting for the owners of a company choose a portfolio of independent, profitable projects at different levels of risk. Of course, shareholders may diversify their risk by investing in several projects in the same way that the insurance company itself diversifies risk by insuring many people. By operating on a sufficiently large scale, insurance companies can assure themselves that over many outcomes the total premiums paid to the company will be equal to the total amount of money paid out to compensate the losses of the insured. Thus, the insurance company behaves as if it is risk neutral, while the managers, as individuals, might be risk averse.

7. When is it worth paying to obtain more information to reduce uncertainty?

Individuals are willing to pay more for information when the utility of the choice with more information, including the cost of gathering the information, is greater than the expected utility of the choice without the information.

8. How does the diversification of an investor's portfolio avoid risk?

An investor reduces risk by investing in many inversely related assets. For example, a mutual fund is a portfolio of stocks of independent companies. If the variance of the return on one company's stock is inversely related to the variance of the return on another company's stock, a portfolio of both stocks will have a lower variance than either stock held separately. As the number of stocks increases, the variance in the rate of return on the portfolio as a whole decreases. While there is less risk in a portfolio of stocks, risk is not eliminated altogether; there is still some market risk in holding such a portfolio, compared to a low-risk asset, such as a U.S. government savings bond.

9. Why do some investors put a large portion of their portfolios into risky assets, while others invest largely in risk-free alternatives? (Hint: Do the two investors receive exactly the same return on average? Why?)

In a market for risky assets, where investors are risk averse, investors demand a higher return on investments that have a higher level of risk (a higher variance in returns). Although some individuals are willing to accept a higher level of risk in exchange for a higher rate of return, this does not mean that these individuals are less risk averse. On the contrary, they will not invest in risky assets unless they are compensated for the increased risk.

10. What is an endowment effect? Give an example of such an effect.

An endowment effect exists if an individual places a greater value on an item that is in her possession as compared to the value she places on the same item when it is not in her possession. For example, many people would refuse to pay $5 for a simple coffee mug but would also refuse to sell a simple coffee mug they won in a contest for the same price even though they got it for free.

11. Jennifer is shopping and sees an attractive shirt. However, the price of $50 is more than she is willing to pay. A few weeks later she finds the same shirt on sale for $25, and buys it. When a friend offers Jennifer $50 for the shirt, she refuses to sell it. Explain Jennifer's behavior.

To help explain Jennifer's behavior, we need to look at the reference point from which she is making the decision. In the first instance, she does not own the shirt so she is not willing to pay the $50 to buy the shirt. In the second instance, she will not accept $50 for the shirt from her friend because her reference point has changed. Once she owns the shirt, she changed the amount by which she valued the shirt. Individuals often value goods more when they own them than when they do not.

EXERCISES

1. Consider a lottery with three possible outcomes: $125 will be received with probability .2, $100 with probability .3, and $50 with probability .5.

a. What is the expected value of the lottery?

The expected value, *EV*, of the lottery is equal to the sum of the returns weighted by their probabilities:

$$EV = (0.2)(\$125) + (0.3)(\$100) + (0.5)(\$50) = \$80.$$

b. What is the variance of the outcomes of the lottery?

The variance, σ^2, is the sum of the squared deviations from the mean, $80, weighted by their probabilities:

$$\sigma^2 = (0.2)(125 - 80)^2 + (0.3)(100 - 80)^2 + (0.5)(50 - 80)^2 = \$975.$$

c. What would a risk-neutral person pay to play the lottery?

A risk-neutral person would pay the expected value of the lottery: $80.

2. Suppose you have invested in a new computer company whose profitability depends on (1) whether the U.S. Congress passes a tariff that raises the cost of Japanese computers and (2) whether the U.S. economy grows slowly or quickly. What are the four mutually exclusive states of the world that you should be concerned about?

The four mutually exclusive states may be represented as:

	Congress passes tariff	Congress does not pass tariff
Slow growth rate	State 1: Slow growth with tariff	State 2: Slow growth without tariff
Fast growth rate	State 3: Fast growth with tariff	State 4: Fast growth without tariff

3. Richard is deciding whether to buy a state lottery ticket. Each ticket costs $1, and the probability of the following winning payoffs is given as follows:

Probability	Return
0.50	$0.00
0.25	$1.00
0.20	$2.00
0.05	$7.50

a. **What is the expected value of Richard's payoff if he buys a lottery ticket? What is the variance?**

The expected value of the lottery is equal to the sum of the returns weighted by their probabilities:

$$EV = (0.5)(0) + (0.25)(\$1.00) + (0.2)(\$2.00) + (0.05)(\$7.50) = \$1.025$$

The variance is the sum of the squared deviation from the mean, $1.025, weighted by their probabilities:

$$\sigma^2 = (0.5)(0 - 1.025)^2 + (0.25)(1 - 1.025)^2 + (0.2)(2 - 1.025)^2 + (0.05)(7.5 - 1.025)^2,\text{ or}$$

$$\sigma^2 = \$2.812.$$

b. **Richard's nickname is "No-risk Rick." He is an extremely risk-averse individual. Would he buy the ticket?**

An extremely risk-averse individual will probably not buy the ticket, even though the expected outcome is higher than the price, $1.025 > $1.00. The difference in the expected return is not enough to compensate Rick for the risk. For example, if his wealth is $10 and he buys a $1.00 ticket, he would have $9.00, $10.00, $11.00, and $16.50, respectively, under the four possible outcomes. Let us assume that his utility function is $U = W^{0.5}$, where W is his wealth. Then his expected utility is:

$$EU = (0.5)\left(9^{0.5}\right) + (0.25)\left(10^{0.5}\right) + (0.2)\left(11^{0.5}\right) + (0.05)\left(16.5^{0.5}\right) = 3.157.$$

This is less than 3.162, which is the utility associated with not buying the ticket ($U(10) = 10^{0.5} = 3.162$). He would prefer the sure thing, i.e., $10.

c. **Suppose Richard was offered insurance against losing any money. If he buys 1,000 lottery tickets, how much would he be willing to pay to insure his gamble?**

If Richard buys 1,000 tickets, it is likely that he will have $1,025 minus the $1,000 he paid, or $25. He would not buy any insurance, as the expected return, $1,025, is greater than the cost, $1,000. He has insured himself by buying a large number of tickets. Given that Richard is risk averse though, he may still want to buy insurance. The amount he would be willing to pay is equal to the risk premium, which is the amount of money that Richard would pay to avoid the risk. See figure 5.4 in the text. To calculate the risk premium, you need to know the utility function. If the utility function is $U = W^{0.5}$, then his expected utility from the 1,000 lottery tickets is

$$EU = (0.5)(0^{0.5}) + (0.25)(1000^{0.5}) + (0.2)(2000^{0.5}) + (0.05)(7500^{0.5}) = 21.18.$$

This is less than the utility he would get from keeping his $1000 which is $U = 1000^{0.5} = 31.62$. To find the risk premium, find the level of income that would guarantee him a utility of 21.18, which is $448.59. This means he would pay $1000-$448.59=$551.41 to insure his gamble.

d.   In the long run, given the price of the lottery ticket and the probability/return table, what do you think the state would do about the lottery?

In the long run, the state lottery will be bankrupt! Given the price of the ticket and the probabilities, the lottery is a money loser. The state must either raise the price of a ticket or lower the probability of positive payoffs.

4.   Suppose an investor is concerned about a business choice in which there are three prospects, whose probability and returns are given below:

Probability	Return
0.4	$100
0.3	30
0.3	-30

What is the expected value of the uncertain investment? What is the variance?

The expected value of the return on this investment is

$$EV = (0.4)(100) + (0.3)(30) + (0.3)(-30) = \$40.$$

The variance is

$$\sigma^2 = (0.4)(100 - 40)^2 + (0.3)(30 - 40)^2 + (0.3)(-30 - 40)^2 = \$2,940.$$

5.   You are an insurance agent who has to write a policy for a new client named Sam. His company, Society for Creative Alternatives to Mayonnaise (SCAM), is working on a low-fat, low-cholesterol mayonnaise substitute for the sandwich condiment industry. The sandwich industry will pay top dollar to whoever invents such a mayonnaise substitute first. Sam's SCAM seems like a very risky proposition to you. You have calculated his possible returns table as follows.

Probability	Return	
.999	-$1,000,000	(he fails)
.001	$1,000,000,000	(he succeeds and sells the formula)

a.   What is the expected return of his project? What is the variance?

The expected return, ER, of the investment is

$$ER = (0.999)(-1,000,000) + (0.001)(1,000,000,000) = \$1,000.$$

The variance is

$$\sigma^2 = (0.999)(-1,000,000 - 1,000)^2 + (0.001)(1,000,000,000 - 1,000)^2 \text{, or}$$

$$\sigma^2 = 1,000,998,999,000,000.$$

b.   What is the most Sam is willing to pay for insurance? Assume Sam is risk neutral.

Because Sam is risk neutral and because the expected outcome is $1,000, Sam is unwilling to buy insurance.

c.   Suppose you found out that the Japanese are on the verge of introducing their own mayonnaise substitute next month. Sam does not know this and has just turned down your final offer of $1,000 for the insurance. Assume that Sam tells you SCAM is only six months away from perfecting its mayonnaise substitute *and* that you know what you know about the Japanese. Would you raise or lower your policy premium on any subsequent proposal to Sam? Based on his information, would Sam accept?

The entry of the Japanese lowers Sam's probability of a high payoff. For example, assume that the probability of the billion dollar payoff is lowered to zero. Then the expected outcome is:

$$(1.0)(-\$1,000,000) + (0.0)((\$1,000,000,000) = -\$1,000,000.$$

Therefore, you should raise the policy premium substantially. But Sam, not knowing about the Japanese entry, will continue to refuse your offers to insure his losses.

6.   Suppose that Natasha's utility function is given by $u(I) = \sqrt{10I}$, where I represents annual income in thousands of dollars.

a.   Is Natasha risk loving, risk neutral, or risk averse? Explain.

Natasha is risk averse. To show this, assume that she has $10,000 and is offered a gamble of a $1,000 gain with 50 percent probability and a $1,000 loss with 50 percent probability. Her utility of $10,000 is 10, $(u(I) = \sqrt{10*10} = 10)$. Her expected utility is:

$$EU = (0.5)(90^{0.5}) + (0.5)(110^{0.5}) = 9.987 < 10.$$

She would avoid the gamble. If she were risk neutral, she would be indifferent between the $10,000 and the gamble; whereas, if she were risk loving, she would prefer the gamble.

You can also see that she is risk averse by noting that the second derivative is negative, implying diminishing marginal utility.

b.   Suppose that Natasha is currently earning an income of $40,000 ($I = 40$) and can earn that income next year with certainty. She is offered a chance to take a new job that offers a .6 probability of earning $44,000, and a .4 probability of earning $33,000. Should she take the new job?

The utility of her current salary is $400^{0.5}$, which is 20. The expected utility of the new job is

$$EU = (0.6)(440^{0.5}) + (0.4)(330^{0.5}) = 19.85,$$

which is less than 20. Therefore, she should not take the job.

c.   In (b), would Natasha be willing to buy insurance to protect against the variable income associated with the new job? If so, how much would she be willing to pay for that insurance? (Hint: What is the risk premium?)

Assuming that she takes the new job, Natasha would be willing to pay a risk premium equal to the difference between $40,000 and the utility of the gamble so as to ensure that she obtains a level of utility equal to 20. We know the utility of the gamble is equal to 19.85. Substituting into her utility function we have, $19.85 = (10I)^{0.5}$, and solving for I we find the income associated with the gamble to be $39,410. Thus, Natasha would be willing to pay for insurance equal to the risk premium, $40,000 - $39,410 = $590.

7. Suppose that two investments have the same three payoffs, but the probability associated with each payoff differs, as illustrated in the table below:

Payoff	Probabilities for Investment A	Probabilities for Investment B
$300	0.10	0.30
$250	0.80	0.40
$200	0.10	0.30

a. **Find the expected return and standard deviation of each investment.**

The expected value of the return on investment A is

$$EV = (0.1)(300) + (0.8)(250) + (0.1)(200) = \$250.$$

The variance on investment A is

$$\sigma^2 = (0.1)(300 - 250)^2 + (0.8)(250 - 250)^2 + (0.1)(200 - 250)^2 = \$500.$$

The expected value of the return on investment B is

$$EV = (0.3)(300) + (0.4)(250) + (0.3)(200) = \$250.$$

The variance on investment B is

$$\sigma^2 = (0.3)(300 - 250)^2 + (0.4)(250 - 250)^2 + (0.3)(200 - 250)^2 = \$1,500.$$

b. **Jill has the utility function $U = 5I$, where I denotes the payoff. Which investment will she choose?**

Jill's expected utility from investment A is

$$EU = .1*(5*300) + .8*(5*250) + .1*(5*200) = 1,250.$$

Jill's expected utility from investment B is

$$EU = .3*(5*300) + .4*(5*250) + .3*(5*200) = 1,250.$$

Since both investments give Jill the same expected utility she will be indifferent between the two.

c. **Ken has the utility function $U = \sqrt{5I}$. Which investment will he choose?**

Ken's expected utility from investment A is

$$EU = .1*(5*300)^{0.5} + .8*(5*250)^{0.5} + .1*(5*200)^{0.5} = 35.32.$$

Ken's expected utility from investment B is

$$EU = .3*(5*300)^{0.5} + .4*(5*250)^{0.5} + .3*(5*200)^{0.5} = 35.25.$$

Ken will choose investment A since it has a higher expected utility. Notice that since Ken is risk averse, he will prefer the investment with less variability.

d. **Laura has the utility function $U = 5I^2$. Which investment will she choose?**

Laura's expected utility from investment A is

$$EU = .1*(5*300*300) + .8*(5*250*250) + .1*(5*200*200) = 315,000.$$

Laura's expected utility from investment B is

$$EU = .3*(5*300*300) + .4*(5*250*250) + .3*(5*200*200) = 320,000.$$

Laura will choose investment B since it has a higher expected utility.

8. **As the owner of a family farm whose wealth is $250,000, you must choose between sitting this season out and investing last year's earnings ($200,000) in a safe money market fund paying 5.0% or planting summer corn. Planting costs $200,000, with a six-month time to harvest. If there is rain, planting summer corn will yield $500,000 in revenues at harvest. If there is a drought, planting will yield $50,000 in revenues at harvest. As a third choice, you can purchase AgriCorp drought-resistant summer corn at a cost of $250,000 that will yield $500,000 in revenues at harvest if there is rain, and $350,000 in revenues at harvest if there is a drought. You are risk averse and your preferences for family wealth (W) are specified by the relationship $U(W) = \sqrt{W}$. The probability of a summer drought is 0.30 and the probability of summer rain is 0.70. Which of the three options should you choose? Explain.**

> You need to calculate expected utility of wealth under the three options. Wealth is equal to the initial $250,000 plus whatever is earned on growing corn, or investing in the safe financial asset. Expected utility under the safe option allowing for the fact that your initial wealth is $250,000 is:
>
> $$E(U) = (250,000 + 200,000(1 + .05))^{.5} = 678.23.$$
>
> Expected utility with regular corn, again including your initial wealth:
>
> $$E(U) = .7(250,000 + (500,000 - 200,000))^{.5} + .3(250,000 + (50,000 - 200,000))^{.5} = 519.13$$
> $$+ 94.87 = 614.$$
>
> Expected utility with drought-resistant corn, again including your initial wealth:
>
> $$E(U) = .7(250,000 + (500,000 - 250,000))^{.5} + .3(250,000 + (350,000 - 250,000))^{.5} =$$
> $$494.975 + 177.482 = 672.46.$$
>
> You should choose the option with the highest expected utility, which is the safe option of not planting corn.

9. **Draw a utility function over income u(I) that has the property that a man is a risk lover when his income is low but a risk averter when his income is high. Can you explain why such a utility function might reasonably describe a person's preferences?**

> Consider an individual who needs a certain level of income, I^*, in order to stay alive. An increase in income above I^* will have a diminishing marginal utility. Below I^*, the individual will be a risk lover and will take unfair gambles in an effort to make large gains in income. Above I^*, the individual will purchase insurance against losses.

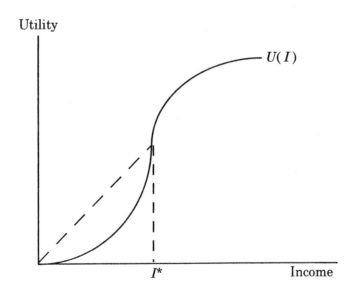

Figure 5.9

10. **A city is considering how much to spend monitoring parking meters. The following information is available to the city manager:**

    i.   **Hiring each meter-monitor costs $10,000 per year.**

    ii.   **With one monitoring person hired, the probability of a driver getting a ticket each time he or she parks illegally is equal to .25.**

    iii.   **With two monitors hired, the probability of getting a ticket is .5, with three monitors the probability is .75, and with four the probability is equal to 1.**

    iv.   **The current fine for overtime parking with two metering persons hired is $?0.**

a. **Assume first that all drivers are risk-neutral. What parking fine would you levy and how many meter monitors would you hire (1, 2, 3, or 4) to achieve the current level of deterrence against illegal parking at the minimum cost?**

If drivers are risk neutral, their behavior is only influenced by the expected fine. With two meter-monitors, the probability of detection is 0.5 and the fine is $20. So, the expected fine is $10 = (0.5)($20). To maintain this expected fine, the city can hire one meter-monitor and increase the fine to $40, or hire three meter-monitors and decrease the fine to $13.33, or hire four meter-monitors and decrease the fine to $10.

If the only cost to be minimized is the cost of hiring meter-monitors, i.e., $10,000 per year, you as the city manager, should minimize the number of meter-monitors. Hire only one monitor and increase the fine to $40 to maintain the current level of deterrence.

b. **Now assume that drivers are highly risk averse. How would your answer to (a) change?**

If drivers are risk averse, their utility of a certain outcome is greater than their utility of an expected value equal to the certain outcome. They will avoid the possibility of paying a parking fine more than would risk-neutral drivers. Therefore, a fine of less than $40 will maintain the current level of deterrence.

c. **(For discussion) What if drivers could insure themselves against the risk of parking fines? Would it make good public policy to permit such insurance?**

Drivers engage in many forms of behavior to insure themselves against the risk of parking fines, such as parking blocks away from their destination in a non-metered spot or taking public transportation. A private insurance firm could offer an insurance policy to pay fines if a ticket is received. Of course, the premium for such insurance would be based on each driver's probability of receiving a parking ticket and on the opportunity cost of providing service. (Note: full insurance leads to moral hazard problems, to be discussed in Chapter 17.)

Public policy should attempt to maximize the difference between the benefits and costs to all parties. Private insurance may not be optimal, because of the increase in transactions costs. Instead, as the city manager, consider offering another form of insurance, e.g., the selling of parking stickers, and give tickets for inappropriately parked cars.

11. A moderately risk-averse investor has 50 percent of her portfolio invested in stocks and 50 percent invested in risk-free Treasury bills. Show how each of the following events will affect the investor's budget line and the proportion of stocks in her portfolio:

a. The standard deviation of the return on the stock market increases, but the expected return on the stock market remains the same.

From section 5.4, the equation for the budget line is

$$R_p = \left[\frac{R_m - R_f}{\sigma_m}\right]\sigma_p + R_f,$$

where R_p is the expected return on the portfolio, R_m is the expected return on the risky asset, R_f is the expected return on the risk-free asset, σ_m is the standard deviation of the return on the risky asset, and σ_p is the standard deviation of the return on the portfolio. The budget line shows the positive relationship between the return on the portfolio, R_p, and the standard deviation of the return on the portfolio, σ_p.

In this case, if the standard deviation of the return on the stock market increases, σ_m, the slope of the budget line will change and the budget line will become flatter. At any given level of portfolio return, there is now a higher standard deviation associated with that level of return. You would expect the proportion of stocks in the portfolio to fall.

b. The expected return on the stock market increases, but the standard deviation of the stock market remains the same.

In this case, if the expected return on the stock market increases, R_m, then the slope of the budget line will change and the budget line will become steeper. At any given level of standard deviation of return, σ_p, there is now a higher level of return, R_p. You would expect the proportion of stocks in the portfolio to rise.

c. The return on risk-free Treasury bills increases.

In this case there is an increase in R_f. The budget line will pivot and shift, or in other words will shift up and become flatter. The proportion of stocks in the portfolio could go either way. On the one hand, Treasury bills now have a higher return and so are more attractive. On the other hand, the investor can now earn a higher return from each Treasury bill so could hold fewer Treasury bills and still maintain the same return in terms of the total flow or payment from the Treasury bills. In this second case, the investor may be willing to place more of his savings into the riskier asset. It will depend on the particular preferences of the investor, as well as the magnitude of the returns to the two assets. An analogy would be to consider what happens to savings when the interest rate increases. On the one hand it goes up because the return is higher, but on the other hand it can go down because a person can save less each period and still come out with the same accumulation of savings at some future date.

CHAPTER 6
PRODUCTION

TEACHING NOTES

Chapter 6 is the first of the three chapters that present the basic theory of supply. It may be beneficial to first review, or summarize, the derivation of demand and present an overview of the theory of competitive supply. The review can be beneficial given the similarities between the theory of demand and the theory of supply. Students often find that the theory of supply is easier to understand because it is less abstract, and the concepts are more familiar. This in turn can improve the students' understanding of the theory of demand when they go back and review it again.

In this chapter it is important to take the time to carefully go through the definitions, as this will be the foundation for what is done in the next two chapters. While the concept of a production function is not difficult, the mathematical and graphical representation can sometimes be confusing. It helps to take the time to do as many examples as you have time for. When describing and graphing the production function with output on the vertical axis and one input on the horizontal axis, point out that the production function is the equation for the boundary of the production set, and hence defines the highest level of output for any given level of inputs. Technical efficiency is assumed throughout the discussion of the theory of supply. At any time you can introduce a discussion of the importance of improving productivity and the concept of learning by doing. Examples 1 and 2 in the text are also good for discussion.

Graphing the production function leads naturally to a discussion of marginal product and diminishing returns. Emphasize that diminishing returns exist because some factors are fixed by definition, and that diminishing returns does not mean negative returns. If you have not discussed marginal utility, now is the time to make sure that the student knows the difference between average and marginal. An example that captures students' attention is the relationship between average and marginal test scores. If their latest mid-term grade is greater than their average grade to date, this will increase their average.

Isoquants are defined and discussed in section 6.3 of the chapter. Rely on the students' understanding of indifference curves when discussing isoquants, and point out that as with indifference curves, isoquants are a two-dimensional representation of a three-dimensional production function. Key concepts in this section of the chapter are the marginal rate of technical substitution and returns to scale. Do as many concrete examples as you have time for to help explain these two important concepts. Examples 6.3 and 6.4 help to give concrete meaning to *MRTS* and returns to scale. Section 6.4 discusses returns to scale.

QUESTIONS FOR REVIEW

1. What is a production function? How does a long-run production function differ from a short-run production function?

A production function represents how inputs are transformed into outputs by a firm. We focus on the firm with one output and aggregate all inputs or factors of production into one of several categories, such as labor, capital, and materials. In the short run, one or more factors of production cannot be changed. As time goes by, the firm has the opportunity to change the levels of all inputs. In the long-run production function, all inputs are variable.

2. Why is the marginal product of labor likely to increase initially in the short run as more of the variable input is hired?

The marginal product of labor is likely to increase initially because when there are more workers, each is able to specialize on an aspect of the production process in which he or she is particularly skilled. For example, think of the typical fast food restaurant. If there is only one worker, he will need to prepare the burgers, fries, and sodas, as well as take the orders. Only so many customers can be served in an hour. With two or three workers, each is able to specialize and the marginal product (number of customers served per hour) is likely to increase as we move from one to two to three workers. Eventually, there will be enough workers and there will be no more gains from specialization. At this point, the marginal product will diminish.

3. Why does production eventually experience diminishing marginal returns to labor in the short run?

The marginal product of labor will eventually diminish because there will be at least one fixed factor of production, such as capital. With capital fixed, the workplace will eventually become so congested, that the productivity of additional workers will decline. Also, with capital fixed, as more workers are added, they will need to share the fixed capital, which will eventually cause the marginal product of labor to diminish as the capital is spread across too many workers. Think for example of an office where there are only three computers. As more and more employees must share the computers, the marginal product of each additional employee will diminish.

4. You are an employer seeking to fill a vacant position on an assembly line. Are you more concerned with the average product of labor or the marginal product of labor for the last person hired? If you observe that your average product is just beginning to decline, should you hire any more workers? What does this situation imply about the marginal product of your last worker hired?

In filling a vacant position, you should be concerned with the marginal product of the last worker hired because the marginal product measures the effect on output, or total product, of hiring another worker. This in turn will help to determine the revenue generated by hiring another worker, which can then be compared to the cost of hiring another worker.

The point at which the average product begins to decline is the point where average product is equal to marginal product. When average product declines, the marginal product of the last worker hired is lower than the average product of previously hired workers.

Although adding more workers results in a further decline in average product, total product continues to increase, so it may still be advantageous to hire another worker.

5. What is the difference between a production function and an isoquant?

A production function describes the maximum output that can be achieved with any given combination of inputs. An isoquant identifies all of the different combinations of the inputs that can be used to produce one particular level of output.

6. Faced with constantly changing conditions, why would a firm ever keep *any* factors fixed? What criteria determine whether a factor is fixed or variable?

Whether a factor is fixed or variable depends on the time horizon in consideration: all factors are fixed in the very short run; all factors are variable in the long run. As stated in the text: "All fixed inputs in the short run represent outcomes of previous long-run decisions based on firms' estimates of what they could profitably produce and sell." Some factors are fixed in the short run, whether the firm likes it or not, simply because it takes time to adjust the level of the variables. For example, the firm may be legally bound by a lease on a building, some employees may have contracts that must be upheld, or construction of a new facility may take some number of months. Recall that the short run is not defined as a specific number of months or years, but as that period of time where some inputs cannot be changed for reasons such as those given above.

7. Isoquants can be convex, linear, or L-shaped. What does each of these shapes tell you about the nature of the production function? What does each of these shapes tell you about the MRTS?

Convex isoquants imply that within some range, some number of units of one input can be substituted for a unit of the other input, and output can be maintained at the same level. In this case, the MRTS is diminishing as we move down along the isoquant. Linear isoquants imply that the slope, or the MRTS, is constant. This means that the same number of units of one input can always be exchanged for a unit of the other input and output can be maintained. The inputs are perfect substitutes. L-shaped isoquants imply that the inputs are perfect complements, or that the firm is producing under a fixed proportions type of technology. In this case the firm cannot give up one input in exchange for the other and still maintain the same level of output. For example, the firm may require exactly 4 units of capital for each unit of labor, in which case one input cannot be substituted for the other.

8. Can an isoquant ever slope upwards? Explain.

No. This would mean that if you increased both inputs then output would stay the same. As a general rule, if the firm has more of all the inputs they can produce more output.

9. Explain the term "marginal rate of technical substitution"? What does a MRTS=4 mean?

MRTS is the amount by which the quantity of one input can be reduced when the other input is increased by one unit, while maintaining the same level of output. If the MRTS is 4 then the one input can be reduced by 4 units as the other is increased by one unit and output will be the same.

10. Explain why the marginal rate of technical substitution is likely to diminish as more and more labor is substituted for capital.

As the quantities of the inputs are changed the marginal product of each input will change. As more and more labor is added, the marginal product of labor is likely to diminish. Because capital has been reduced, each unit of capital remaining is likely to be more productive. Therefore, more units of labor will be required to replace each unit of capital. Alternatively, as we move down and to the right along an isoquant along which the MRTS is diminishing, we have to give up less capital for each unit of labor added to keep output constant.

11. Diminishing returns to a single factor of production and constant returns to scale are not inconsistent. Discuss.

Diminishing returns to a single factor are observable in all production processes at some level of inputs. This fact is so pervasive that economists have named it the "law of diminishing marginal productivity." By definition, the marginal product of an input is the additional output generated by employing one more unit of the input, all other inputs held fixed. The extra output, or returns, to the single input diminish because all other inputs are held fixed. For example, when holding the level of capital constant, each additional unit of labor has less capital to work with.

Unlike the returns to a single factor, returns to scale are proportional increases in *all* inputs. While each factor by itself exhibits diminishing returns, output may more than double, less than double, or exactly double when all the inputs are doubled. The distinction again is that with returns to scale, all inputs are increased in the same proportion and no input is held fixed.

12. Can a firm have a production function that exhibits increasing returns to scale, constant returns to scale, and decreasing returns to scale as output increases? Discuss.

> Most firms have production functions that exhibit first increasing, then constant, and ultimately decreasing returns to scale. At low levels of output, a proportional increase in all inputs may lead to a larger-than-proportional increase in output, based on an increase in the opportunity for each factor to specialize. For example, if there are now two people and two computers, each person can specialize by completing those tasks that they are best at, which allows output to more than double. As the firm grows, the opportunities for specialization may diminish and a doubling of all inputs will lead to only a doubling of output. When there are constant returns to scale, the firm is replicating what it is already doing. At some level of production, the firm will be so large that when inputs are doubled, output will less than double, a situation that can arise from management diseconomies.

13. Give an example of a production process in which the short run involves a day or a week and the long run any period longer than a week.

> Any small business where one input requires more than a week to change would be an example. The process of hiring more labor, which requires announcing the position, interviewing applicants, and negotiating terms of employment, can take a day, if done through a temporary employment agency. Usually, however, the process takes a week or more. Expansion, requiring a larger location, will also take longer than a week.

EXERCISES

1. The menu at Joe's coffee shop consists of a variety of coffee drinks, pastries, and sandwiches. The marginal product of an additional worker can be defined as the number of customers that can be served by that worker in a given time period. Joe has been employing one worker, but is considering hiring a second and a third. Explain why the marginal product of the second and third workers might be higher than the first. Why might you expect the marginal product of additional workers to eventually diminish?

> The marginal product could well increase for the second and third workers, since each of the first 2 or 3 workers would be able to specialize in a different task. If there is only 1 worker, then that worker will have to take orders and prepare all the food. Eventually, however, the marginal product would diminish because there would be too many people behind the counter trying to accomplish a limited number of tasks.

2. Suppose a chair manufacturer is producing in the short run (with its existing plant and equipment). The manufacturer has observed the following levels of production corresponding to different numbers of workers:

Number of chairs	Number of workers
1	10
2	18
3	24
4	28
5	30
6	28
7	25

a. **Calculate the marginal and average product of labor for this production function.**

The average product of labor, AP_L, is equal to $\dfrac{Q}{L}$. The marginal product of labor, MP_L, is equal to $\dfrac{\Delta Q}{\Delta L}$, the change in output divided by the change in labor input. For this production process we have:

L	Q	AP_L	MP_L
0	0	—	—
1	10	10	10
2	18	9	8
3	24	8	6
4	28	7	4
5	30	6	2
6	28	4.7	-2
7	25	3.6	-3

b. **Does this production function exhibit diminishing returns to labor? Explain.**

This production process exhibits diminishing returns to labor. The marginal product of labor, the extra output produced by each additional worker, diminishes as workers are added, and is actually negative for the sixth and seventh workers.

c. **Explain intuitively what might cause the marginal product of labor to become negative.**

Labor's negative marginal product for $L > 5$ may arise from congestion in the chair manufacturer's factory. Since more laborers are using the same, fixed amount of capital, it is possible that they could get in each other's way, decreasing efficiency and the amount of output. Many firms also have to control the quality of output and the high congestion of labor may produce output that is not of a high enough quality to be offered for sale, which can contribute to a negative marginal product.

3. Fill in the gaps in the table below.

Quantity of Variable Input	Total Output	Marginal Product of Variable Input	Average Product of Variable Input
0	0	—	—
1	225		
2			300
3		300	
4	1140		
5		225	
6			225

Quantity of Variable Input	Total Output	Marginal Product of Variable Input	Average Product of Variable Input
0	0	—	—
1	225	225	225
2	600	375	300
3	900	300	300
4	1140	240	285
5	1365	225	273
6	1350	-15	225

4. A political campaign manager has to decide whether to emphasize television advertisements or letters to potential voters in a reelection campaign. Describe the production function for campaign votes. How might information about this function (such as the shape of the isoquants) help the campaign manager to plan strategy?

The output of concern to the campaign manager is the number of votes. The production function uses two inputs, television advertising and direct mail. The use of these inputs requires knowledge of the substitution possibilities between them. If the inputs are perfect substitutes, the resultant isoquants are line segments, and the campaign manager will use only one input based on the relative prices. If the inputs are not perfect substitutes, the isoquants will have a convex shape. The campaign manager will then use a combination of the two inputs.

5. For each of the following examples, draw a representative isoquant. What can you say about the marginal rate of technical substitution in each case?

a. A firm can hire only full-time employees to produce its output, or it can hire some combination of full-time and part-time employees. For each full-time worker let go, the firm must hire an increasing number of temporary employees to maintain the same level of output.

Place part time workers on the vertical axis and full time workers on the horizontal axis. The slope of the isoquant measures the number of part time workers that can be exchanged for a full time worker, while still maintaining output. When we are at the bottom end of the isoquant we have a lot of full time workers and few part time workers. As we move up the isoquant and give up full time workers, we must hire more and more part time workers to replace each full time worker. The slope increases (in absolute value terms) as we move up the isoquant. The isoquant is therefore convex and we have diminishing marginal rate of technical substitution.

b. A firm finds they it can always trade two units of labor for one unit of capital and still keep output constant.

The marginal rate of technical substitution measures the number of units of labor that can be exchanged for a unit of capital while still maintaining output. If the firm can always trade two labor for one capital then the MRTS is constant and the isoquant is linear.

c. A firm requires exactly two full-time workers to operate each piece of machinery in the factory.

This firm operates under a fixed proportions technology, and the isoquants are L-shaped. The firm cannot exchange any labor for capital and still maintain output because it must maintain a fixed 2:1 ratio of labor:capital.

6. A firm has a production process in which the inputs to production are perfectly substitutable in the long run. Can you tell whether the marginal rate of technical substitution is high or low, or is further information necessary? Discuss.

The marginal rate of technical substitution, *MRTS*, is the absolute value of the slope of an isoquant. If the inputs are perfect substitutes, the isoquants will be linear. To calculate the slope of the isoquant, and hence the *MRTS*, we need to know the rate at which one input may be substituted for the other. In this case, we do not know whether the MRTS is high or low. All we know is that it is a constant number. We need to know the marginal product of each input to determine the MRTS.

7. The marginal product of labor in the production of computer chips is 50 chips per hour. The marginal rate of technical substitution of hours of labor for hours of machine-capital is 1/4. What is the marginal product of capital?

The marginal rate of technical substitution is defined at the ratio of the two marginal products. Here, we are given the marginal product of labor and the marginal rate of technical substitution. To determine the marginal product of capital, substitute the given values for the marginal product of labor and the marginal rate of technical substitution into the following formula:

$$\frac{MP_L}{MP_K} = MRTS, \text{ or } \frac{50}{MP_K} = \frac{1}{4}, \text{ or}$$

$MP_K = 200$ computer chips per hour.

8. Do the following functions exhibit increasing, constant, or decreasing returns to scale? What happens to the marginal product of each individual factor as that factor is increased, and the other factor is held constant?

a. $q = 3L + 2K$

This function exhibits constant returns to scale. For example, if L is 2 and K is 2 then q is 10. If L is 4 and K is 4 then q is 20. When the inputs are doubled, output will double. Each marginal product is constant for this production function. When L increases by 1 q will increase by 3. When K increases by 1 q will increase by 2.

b. $q = (2L + 2K)^{\frac{1}{2}}$

This function exhibits decreasing returns to scale. For example, if L is 2 and K is 2 then q is 2.8. If L is 4 and K is 4 then q is 4. When the inputs are doubled, output will less than double. The marginal product of each input is decreasing. This can be determined using calculus by differentiating the production function with respect to either input, while holding the other input constant. For example, the marginal product of labor is

$$\frac{\partial q}{\partial L} = \frac{2}{2(2L + 2K)^{\frac{1}{2}}}.$$

Since L is in the denominator, as L gets bigger, the marginal product gets smaller. If you do not know calculus, then you can choose several values for L, find q (for some fixed value of K), and then find the marginal product. For example, if L=4 and K=4 then q=4. If L=5 and K=4 then q=4.24. If L=6 and K=4 then q= 4.47. Marginal product of labor falls from 0.24 to 0.23.

c. $q = 3LK^2$

This function exhibits increasing returns to scale. For example, if L is 2 and K is 2 then q is 24. If L is 4 and K is 4 then q is 192. When the inputs are doubled, output will more than double. Notice also that if we increase each input by the same factor λ then we get the following:

$$q' = 3(\lambda L)(\lambda K)^2 = \lambda^3 3LK^2 = \lambda^3 q.$$

Since λ is raised to a power greater than 1, we have increasing returns to scale.

The marginal product of labor is constant and the marginal product of capital is increasing. For any given value of K, when L is increased by 1 unit, q will go up by $3K^2$ units, which is a constant number. Using calculus, the marginal product of capital is MPK=2*3*L*K. As K increases, MPK will increase. If you do not know calculus then you can fix the value of L, choose a starting value for K, and find q. Now increase K by 1 unit and find the new q. Do this a few more times and you can calculate marginal product. This was done in part b above, and is done in part d below.

d. $q = L^{\frac{1}{2}}K^{\frac{1}{2}}$

This function exhibits constant returns to scale. For example, if L is 2 and K is 2 then q is 2. If L is 4 and K is 4 then q is 4. When the inputs are doubled, output will exactly double. Notice also that if we increase each input by the same factor λ then we get the following:

$$q' = (\lambda L)^{\frac{1}{2}}(\lambda K)^{\frac{1}{2}} = \lambda L^{\frac{1}{2}}K^{\frac{1}{2}} = \lambda q.$$

Since λ is raised to the power 1, we have constant returns to scale.

The marginal product of labor is decreasing and the marginal product of capital is decreasing. Using calculus, the marginal product of capital is

$$MPK = \frac{L^{\frac{1}{2}}}{2K^{\frac{1}{2}}}.$$

For any given value of L, as K increases, MPK will increase. If you do not know calculus then you can fix the value of L, choose a starting value for K, and find q. Let L=4 for example. If K is 4 then q is 4, if K is 5 then q is 4.47, and if K is 6 then q is 4.89. The marginal product of the 5th unit of K is 4.47-4=0.47, and the marginal product of the 6th unit of K is 4.89-4.47=0.42. Hence we have diminishing marginal product of capital. You can do the same thing for the marginal product of labor.

e. $q = 4L^{\frac{1}{2}} + 4K$

This function exhibits decreasing returns to scale. For example, if L is 2 and K is 2 then q is 13.66. If L is 4 and K is 4 then q is 24. When the inputs are doubled, output will less than double.

The marginal product of labor is decreasing and the marginal product of capital is constant. For any given value of L, when K is increased by 1 unit, q will go up by 4 units, which is a constant number. To see that the marginal product of labor is decreasing, fix K=1 and choose values for L. If L=1 then q=8, if L=2 then q=9.65, and if L=3 then q=10.93. The marginal product of the second unit of labor is 9.65-8=1.65 and the marginal product of the third unit of labor is 10.93-9.65=1.28. Marginal product of labor is diminishing.

9. The production function for the personal computers of DISK, Inc., is given by

$q = 10K^{0.5}L^{0.5}$, **where q is the number of computers produced per day, K is hours of machine time, and L is hours of labor input. DISK's competitor, FLOPPY, Inc., is using the production function** $q = 10K^{0.6}L^{0.4}$.

a. **If both companies use the same amounts of capital and labor, which will generate more output?**

Let Q be the output of DISK, Inc., q_2, be the output of FLOPPY, Inc., and X be the same equal amounts of capital and labor for the two firms. Then, according to their production functions,

$$q = 10X^{0.5}X^{0.5} = 10X^{(0.5 + 0.5)} = 10X$$

and

$$q_2 = 10X^{0.6}X^{0.4} = 10X^{(0.6 + 0.4)} = 10X.$$

Because $q = q_2$, both firms generate the same output with the same inputs. Note that if the two firms both used the same amount of capital and the same amount of labor, but the amount of capital was not equal to the amount of labor, then the two firms would not produce the same level of output. In fact, if K>L then q₂>q.

b. **Assume that capital is limited to 9 machine hours but labor is unlimited in supply. In which company is the marginal product of labor greater? Explain.**

With capital limited to 9 machine units, the production functions become $q = 30L^{0.5}$ and $q_2 = 37.372L^{0.4}$. To determine the production function with the highest marginal productivity of labor, consider the following table:

L	q Firm 1	MP_L Firm 1	q Firm 2	MP_L Firm 2
0	0.0	—	0.00	—
1	30.00	30.00	37.37	37.37
2	42.43	12.43	49.31	11.94
3	51.96	9.53	58.00	8.69
4	60.00	8.04	65.07	7.07

For each unit of labor above 1, the marginal productivity of labor is greater for the first firm, DISK, Inc.

10. In Example 6.3, wheat is produced according to the production function

$q = 100K^{0.8}L^{0.2}$.

a. **Beginning with a capital input of 4 and a labor input of 49, show that the marginal product of labor and the marginal product of capital are both decreasing.**

For fixed labor and variable capital:

$K = 4 \Rightarrow q = (100)(4^{0.8})(49^{0.2}) = 660.22$

$K = 5 \Rightarrow q = (100)(5^{0.8})(49^{0.2}) = 789.25 \Rightarrow MP_K = 129.03$

$K = 6 \Rightarrow q = (100)(6^{0.8})(49^{0.2}) = 913.19 \Rightarrow MP_K = 123.94$

$K = 7 \Rightarrow q = (100)(7^{0.8})(49^{0.2}) = 1,033.04 \Rightarrow MP_K = 119.85.$

For fixed capital and variable labor:

$L = 49 \Rightarrow q = (100)(4^{0.8})(49^{0.2}) = 660.22$

$L = 50 \Rightarrow q = (100)(4^{0.8})(50^{0.2}) = 662.89 \Rightarrow MP_L = 2.67$

$L = 51 \Rightarrow q = (100)(4^{0.8})(51^{0.2}) = 665.52 \Rightarrow MP_L = 2.63$

$L = 52 \Rightarrow q = (100)(4^{0.8})(52^{0.2}) = 668.11 \Rightarrow MP_L = 2.59.$

Notice that the marginal products of both capital and labor are decreasing as the variable input increases.

b. **Does this production function exhibit increasing, decreasing, or constant returns to scale?**

Constant (increasing, decreasing) returns to scale imply that proportionate increases in inputs lead to the same (more than, less than) proportionate increases in output. If we were to increase labor and capital by the same proportionate amount (λ) in this production function, output would change by the same proportionate amount:

$$\lambda q = 100(\lambda K)^{0.8}(\lambda L)^{0.2}, \text{ or}$$

$$\lambda q = 100 K^{0.8} L^{0.2} \lambda^{(0.8 + 0.2)} = q\lambda$$

Therefore, this production function exhibits constant returns to scale.

CHAPTER 7
THE COST OF PRODUCTION

TEACHING NOTES

The key topics in this chapter are

- accounting versus economic costs of production,

- definitions of total, average, and marginal cost in the short run and long run,

- a graphical representation of total, average, and marginal cost, and

- cost minimization, graphically in the chapter, and mathematically in the appendix.

It is important to distinguish between accounting and economic costs so that students will understand that zero (economic) profit is a feasible long run equilibrium. It is important to spend time on the cost curve definitions and graph because they form the foundation for what will be covered in chapter 8 (firm supply). The cost minimization problem is useful for explaining which inputs the firm should use to produce a given quantity of output, and this discussion draws on the discussion of isoquants from chapter 6. It is also possible at this point to discuss the basic concept of hiring inputs until the wage is equal to the marginal revenue product of the input (chapter 14). The chapter also contains three sections that can be covered as special topics (production with two outputs, dynamic changes in costs, and estimating cost), or can be skipped altogether.

Opportunity cost forms the conceptual base of this chapter. While most students think of costs in accounting terms, they must develop an understanding of the distinction between accounting, economic, and opportunity costs. One source of confusion is the opportunity cost of capital, i.e., why the rental rate on capital must be considered explicitly by economists. It is important, for example, to distinguish between the purchase price of capital equipment and the opportunity cost of using the equipment. The opportunity cost of a person's time also leads to some confusion for students.

Following the discussion of opportunity cost, the chapter diverges in two directions: one path introduces types of cost and cost curves, and the other focuses on cost minimization. Both directions converge with the discussion of long-run average cost.

While the definitions of total cost, fixed cost, average cost, and marginal cost and the graphical relationships between them can seem tedious and/or uninteresting to the student, both are important in terms of understanding the derivation of the firm's supply curve in chapter 8. Doing algebraic or numerical examples in table form is helpful for some students in terms of seeing the relationships between the different costs. Explain that each firm has a unique set of cost curves based on its own particular production function and resulting total cost function. Discuss the importance of returns to scale and diminishing returns in explaining the shapes of the cost curves. Point out the clear rules that average cost tends to be u-shaped in the short run and marginal cost will hit average cost and average variable cost at their respective minimum points. Once you have successfully developed the cost curve graph, you can then take it and address the questions of finding the profit maximizing level of output and deriving the firm, and hence industry, supply curve.

The cost minimization problem is useful for addressing a different type of question, namely what quantity of the inputs should the firm use to produce a given level of output. Point out to students that the necessary condition for cost minimization, where the ratio of the marginal products is equal to the ratio of the input costs, is very similar to the necessary condition for profit maximization.

A clear understanding of short-run cost and cost minimization is necessary for the derivation of long-run average cost. With long-run costs, stress that firms are operating on short-run cost curves at each level of the fixed factor and that long-run costs do not exist separately from short-run costs. Exercise (6) illustrates the relationship between long-run cost and cost minimization, with an emphasis on the importance of the expansion path. Stress the connection between the shape of a long-run cost curve and returns to scale.

QUESTIONS FOR REVIEW

1. A firm pays its accountant an annual retainer of $10,000. Is this an economic cost?

Explicit costs are actual outlays. They include all costs that involve a monetary transaction. An implicit cost is an economic cost that does not necessarily involve a monetary transaction, but still involves the use of resources. When a firm pays an annual retainer of $10,000, there is a monetary transaction. The accountant trades his or her time in return for money. Therefore, an annual retainer is an explicit cost.

2. The owner of a small retail store does her own accounting work. How would you measure the opportunity cost of her work?

Opportunity costs are measured by comparing the use of a resource with its alternative uses. The opportunity cost of doing accounting work is the time *not spent in other ways*, i.e., time such as running a small business or participating in leisure activity. The economic, or opportunity, cost of doing accounting work is measured by computing the monetary amount that the owner's time would be worth in its *next best use*.

3. Please explain whether the following statements are true or false.

a. **If the owner of a business pays himself no salary, then the accounting cost is zero, but the economic cost is positive.**

True. Since there is no monetary transaction, there is no accounting, or explicit, cost. However, since the owner of the business could be employed elsewhere, there is an economic cost. The economic cost is positive, reflecting the opportunity cost of the owner's time. The economic cost is the value of the next best alternative, or the amount that the owner would earn if he took the next best job.

b. **A firm that has positive accounting profit does not necessarily have positive economic profit.**

True. Accounting profit considers only the explicit, monetary costs. Since there may be some opportunity costs that were not fully realized as explicit monetary costs, it is possible that when the opportunity costs are added in, economic profit will become negative. This indicates that the firm's resources are not being put to their best use.

c. **If a firm hires a currently unemployed worker, the opportunity cost of utilizing the worker's services is zero.**

False. The opportunity cost measures the value of the worker's time, which is unlikely to be zero. Though the worker was temporarily unemployed, the worker still possesses skills, which have a value and make the opportunity cost of hiring the worker greater than zero. In addition, since opportunity cost is the equivalent of the worker's next best option, it is possible that the worker might have been able to get a better job that utilizes his skills more efficiently. Alternatively, the worker could have been doing unpaid work, such as care of a child or elderly person at home, which would have had a value to those receiving the service.

4. Suppose that labor is the only variable input to the production process. If the marginal cost of production is diminishing as more units of output are produced, what can you say about the marginal product of labor ?

The marginal product of labor must be increasing. The marginal cost of production measures the extra cost of producing one more unit of output. If this cost is diminishing, then it must be taking fewer units of labor to produce the extra unit of output, since the extra cost refers to the extra cost of the labor. If fewer units of labor are required to produce a unit of output, then the marginal product (extra output produced by an extra unit of labor) must be increasing. Note also, that MC=w/MPL, so that if MC is diminishing then MPL must be increasing for any given w.

5. Suppose a chair manufacturer finds that the marginal rate of technical substitution of capital for labor in his production process is substantially greater than the ratio of the rental rate on machinery to the wage rate for assembly-line labor. How should he alter his use of capital and labor to minimize the cost of production?

To minimize cost, the manufacturer should use a combination of capital and labor so the rate at which he can trade capital for labor in his production process is the same as the rate at which he can trade capital for labor in external markets. The manufacturer would be better off if he increased his use of capital and decreased his use of labor, decreasing the marginal rate of technical substitution, *MRTS*. He should continue this substitution until his *MRTS* equals the ratio of the rental rate to the wage rate. The *MRTS* in this case is equal to *MPK/MPL*. As the manufacturer uses more *K* and less *L*, the *MPK* will diminish and the *MPL* will increase, both of which will decrease the *MRTS* until it is equal to the ratio of the input prices (rental rate on capital divided by wage rate).

6. Why are isocost lines straight lines?

The isocost line represents all possible combinations of labor and capital that may be purchased for a given total cost. The slope of the isocost line is the ratio of the input prices of labor and capital. If input prices are fixed, then the ratio of these prices is clearly fixed and the isocost line is straight. Only when the ratio or factor prices change as the quantities of inputs change is the isocost line not straight.

7. Assume the marginal cost of production is increasing. Can you determine whether the average variable cost is increasing or decreasing? Explain.

Marginal cost can be increasing while average variable cost is either increasing or decreasing. If marginal cost is less (greater) than average variable cost, then each additional unit is adding less (more) to total cost than previous units added to the total cost, which implies that the *AVC* declines (increases). Therefore, we need to know whether marginal cost is greater than average variable cost to determine whether the *AVC* is increasing or decreasing.

8. Assume the marginal cost of production is greater than the average variable cost. Can you determine whether the average variable cost is increasing or decreasing? Explain.

If the average variable cost is increasing (decreasing), then the last unit produced is adding more (less) to total variable cost than the previous units did, on average. Therefore, marginal cost is above (below) average variable cost. In fact, the point where marginal cost exceeds average variable cost is also the point where average variable cost starts to rise.

9. If the firm's average cost curves are U-shaped, why does its average variable cost curve achieve its minimum at a lower level of output than the average total cost curve?

Total cost is equal to fixed plus variable cost. Average total cost is equal to average fixed plus average variable cost. When graphed, the difference between the *U*-shaped total cost and average variable cost curves is the average fixed cost curve. Thus, falling average variable cost and average fixed cost sum up to a falling average total cost curve. Since average fixed cost continues to fall as more output is produced, average total cost will continue to fall even after average variable cost has reached its minimum because the drop in average fixed cost exceeds the increase in the average variable cost. Eventually, the fall in average fixed cost becomes small enough so that the rise in average variable cost causes average total cost to begin to rise.

10. If a firm enjoys economies of scale up to a certain output level, and then cost increases proportionately with output, what can you say about the shape of the long-run average cost curve?

When the firm experiences increasing returns to scale, its long-run average cost curve is downward sloping. When the firm experiences constant returns to scale, its long-run average cost curve is horizontal. If the firm experiences increasing returns to scale, then constant returns to scale, its long-run average cost curve falls, then becomes horizontal.

11. How does a change in the price of one input change the firm's long-run expansion path?

The expansion path describes the combination of inputs that the firm chooses to minimize cost for every output level. This combination depends on the ratio of input prices: if the price of one input changes, the price ratio also changes. For example, if the price of an input increases, less of the input can be purchased for the same total cost, and the intercept of the isocost line on that input's axis moves closer to the origin. Also, the slope of the isocost line, the price ratio, changes. As the price ratio changes, the firm substitutes away from the now more expensive input toward the cheaper input. Thus, the expansion path bends toward the axis of the now cheaper input.

12. Distinguish between economies of scale and economies of scope. Why can one be present without the other?

Economies of scale refer to the production of *one* good and occur when proportionate increases in all inputs lead to a more-than-proportionate increase in output. Economies of scope refer to the production of *more than one good* and occur when joint output is less costly than the sum of the costs of producing each good or service separately. There is no direct relationship between increasing returns to scale and economies of scope, so production can exhibit one without the other. See Exercise (14) for a case with constant product-specific returns to scale and multiproduct economies of scope.

13. Is the firm's expansion path always a straight line?

No. If the long run expansion path is a straight line this means that the firm always uses capital and labor in the same proportion. If the capital labor ratio changes as output is increased then the expansion path is not a straight line.

14. What is the difference between economies of scale and returns to scale?

Economies of scale measures the relationship between cost and output, i.e., when output is doubled, does cost double, less then double, or more than double. Returns to scale measures what happens to output when all inputs are doubled.

EXERCISES

1. Joe quits his computer-programming job, where he was earning a salary of $50,000 per year to start his own computer software business in a building that he owns and was previously renting out for $24,000 per year. In his first year of business he has the following expenses: salary paid to himself $40,000, rent, $0, and other expenses $25,000. Find the accounting cost and the economic cost associated with Joe's computer software business.

The accounting cost represents the actual expenses, which are $40,000+$0 + $25,000=$65,000. The economic cost includes accounting cost, but also takes into account opportunity cost. Therefore, economic will include, in addition to accounting cost, an extra $24,000 because Joe gave up $24,000 by not renting the building , and an extra $10,000 because he paid himself a salary $10,000 below market ($50,000-$40,000). Economic cost is then $99,000.

2. a. Fill in the blanks in the following table.

Units of Output	Fixed Cost	Variable Cost	Total Cost	Marginal Cost	Average Fixed Cost	Average Variable Cost	Average Total Cost
0	100	0	100	--	--	0	--
1	100	25	125	25	100	25	125
2	100	45	145	20	50	22.5	72.5
3	100	57	157	12	33.3	19	52.3
4	100	77	177	20	25	19.25	44.25
5	100	102	202	25	20	20.4	40.4
6	100	136	236	34	16.67	22.67	39.3
7	100	170	270	34	14.3	24.3	38.6
8	100	226	326	56	12.5	28.25	40.75
9	100	298	398	72	11.1	33.1	44.2
10	100	390	490	92	10	39	49

b. **Draw a graph that shows marginal cost, average variable cost, and average total cost, with cost on the vertical axis and quantity on the horizontal axis.**

Average total cost is u-shaped and reaches a minimum at an output of 7, based on the above table. Average variable cost is u-shaped also and reaches a minimum at an output of 3. Notice from the table that average variable cost is always below average total cost. The difference between the two costs is the average fixed cost. Marginal cost is first diminishing, to a quantity of 3 based on the table, and then increases as q increases. Marginal cost should intersect average variable cost and average total cost at their respective minimum points, though this is not accurately reflected in the numbers in the table. If the specific functions had been given in the problem instead of just a series of numbers, then it would be possible to find the exact point of intersection between marginal and average total cost and marginal and average variable cost. The curves are likely to intersect at a quantity that is not a whole number, and hence are not listed in the above table.

3. A firm has a fixed production cost of $5,000 and a constant marginal cost of production of $500 per unit produced.

a. **What is the firm's total cost function? Average cost?**

The variable cost of producing an additional unit, marginal cost, is constant at $500, so $VC = \$500q$, and $AVC = \dfrac{VC}{q} = \dfrac{\$500q}{q} = \$500$. Fixed cost is $5,000 and average fixed cost is $\dfrac{\$5,000}{q}$. The total cost function is fixed cost plus variable cost or $TC=\$5,000+\$500q$. Average total cost is the sum of average variable cost and average fixed cost: $ATC = \$500 + \dfrac{\$5,000}{q}$.

b. **If the firm wanted to minimize the average total cost, would it choose to be very large or very small? Explain.**

The firm should choose a very large output because average total cost will continue to decrease as q is increased. As q becomes infinitely large, ATC will equal $500.

4. Suppose a firm must pay an annual tax, which is a fixed sum, independent of whether it produces any output.

a.   **How does this tax affect the firm's fixed, marginal, and average costs?**

Total cost, TC, is equal to fixed cost, FC, plus variable cost, VC. Fixed costs do not vary with the quantity of output. Because the franchise fee, FF, is a fixed sum, the firm's fixed costs increase by this fee. Thus, average cost, equal to $\dfrac{FC + VC}{q}$, and average fixed cost, equal to $\dfrac{FC}{q}$, increase by the average franchise fee $\dfrac{FF}{q}$. Note that the franchise fee does not affect average variable cost. Also, because marginal cost is the *change* in total cost with the production of an additional unit and because the fee is constant, marginal cost is unchanged.

b.   **Now suppose the firm is charged a tax that is proportional to the number of items it produces. Again, how does this tax affect the firm's fixed, marginal, and average costs?**

Let t equal the per unit tax. When a tax is imposed on each unit produced, variable costs increase by tq. Average variable costs increase by t, and because fixed costs are constant, average (total) costs also increase by t. Further, because total cost increases by t with each additional unit, marginal costs increase by t.

5. A recent issue of *Business Week* reported the following:

> During the recent auto sales slump, GM, Ford, and Chrysler decided it was cheaper to sell cars to rental companies at a loss than to lay off workers. That's because closing and reopening plants is expensive, partly because the auto makers' current union contracts obligate them to pay many workers even if they're not working.

When the article discusses selling cars "at a loss," is it referring to accounting profit or economic profit? How will the two differ in this case? Explain briefly.

When the article refers to the car companies selling at a loss, it is referring to accounting profit. The article is stating that the price obtained for the sale of the cars to the rental companies was less than their <u>accounting</u> cost. Economic profit would be measured by the difference of the price with the opportunity cost of the cars. This opportunity cost represents the market value of all the inputs used by the companies to produce the cars. The article mentions that the car companies must pay workers even if they are not working (and thus producing cars). This implies that the wages paid to these workers are sunk and are thus not part of the opportunity cost of production. On the other hand, the wages would still be included in the accounting costs. These accounting costs would then be higher than the opportunity costs and would make the accounting profit lower than the economic profit.

6. Suppose the economy takes a downturn, and that labor costs fall by 50 percent and are expected to stay at that level for a long time. Show graphically how this change in the relative price of labor and capital affects the firm's expansion path.

Figure 7.6 shows a family of isoquants and two isocost curves. Units of capital are on the vertical axis and units of labor are on the horizontal axis. (Note: In drawing this figure we have assumed that the production function underlying the isoquants exhibits constant returns to scale, resulting in linear expansion paths. However, the results do not depend on this assumption.)

If the price of labor decreases while the price of capital is constant, the isocost curve pivots outward around its intersection with the capital axis. Because the expansion path is the set of points where the *MRTS* is equal to the ratio of prices, as the isocost curves pivot outward, the expansion path pivots toward the labor axis. As the price of labor falls relative to capital, the firm uses more labor as output increases.

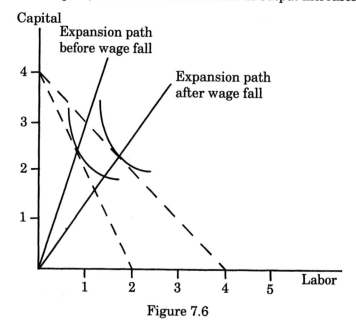

Figure 7.6

7. The cost of flying a passenger plane from point A to point B is $50,000. The airline flies this route four times per day at 7am, 10am, 1pm, and 4pm. The first and last flights are filled to capacity with 240 people. The second and third flights are only half full. Find the average cost per passenger for each flight. Suppose the airline hires you as a marketing consultant and wants to know which type of customer it should try to attract, the off-peak customer (the middle two flights) or the rush-hour customer (the first and last flights). What advice would you offer?

> The average cost per passenger is $50,000/240 for the full flights and $50,000/120 for the half full flights. The airline should focus on attracting more off-peak customers in order to reduce the average cost per passenger on those flights. The average cost per passenger is already minimized for the two peak time flights.

8. You manage a plant that mass produces engines by teams of workers using assembly machines. The technology is summarized by the production function.

$$q = 5\ KL$$

where *q* is the number of engines per week, *K* is the number of assembly machines, and *L* is the number of labor teams. Each assembly machine rents for *r* = $10,000 per week and each team costs *w* = $5,000 per week. Engine costs are given by the cost of labor teams and machines, plus $2,000 per engine for raw materials. Your plant has a fixed installation of 5 assembly machines as part of its design.

a.   **What is the cost function for your plant — namely, how much would it cost to produce *q* engines? What are average and marginal costs for producing *q* engines? How do average costs vary with output?**

> K is fixed at 5. The short-run production function then becomes q = 25L. This implies that for any level of output q, the number of labor teams hired will be
>
> $L = \dfrac{q}{25}$. The total cost function is thus given by the sum of the costs of capital, labor, and raw materials:

$$TC(q) = rK + wL + 2000q = (10,000)(5) + (5,000)(\frac{q}{25}) + 2,000\,q$$

$$TC(q) = 50,000 + 2200q.$$

The average cost function is then given by:

$$AC(q) = \frac{TC(q)}{q} = \frac{50,000 + 2200q}{q}.$$

and the marginal cost function is given by:

$$MC(q) = \frac{\partial TC}{\partial q} = 2200.$$

Marginal costs are constant and average costs will decrease as quantity increases (due to the fixed cost of capital).

b.   **How many teams are required to produce 250 engines? What is the average cost per engine?**

To produce q = 250 engines we need labor teams $L = \frac{q}{25}$ or L=10. Average costs are given by

$$AC(q = 250) = \frac{50,000 + 2200(250)}{250} = 2400.$$

c.   **You are asked to make recommendations for the design of a new production facility. What capital/labor *(K/L)* ratio should the new plant accommodate if it wants to minimize the total cost of producing any level of output q?**

We no longer assume that K is fixed at 5. We need to find the combination of K and L that minimizes costs at any level of output q. The cost-minimization rule is given by

$$\frac{MP_K}{r} = \frac{MP_L}{w}.$$

To find the marginal product of capital, observe that increasing K by 1 unit increases q by 5L, so $MP_K = 5L$. Similarly, observe that increasing L by 1 unit increases Q by 5K, so $MP_L = 5K$. Mathematically,

$$MP_K = \frac{\partial Q}{\partial K} = 5L \text{ and } MP_L = \frac{\partial Q}{\partial L} = 5K.$$

Using these formulas in the cost-minimization rule, we obtain:

$$\frac{5L}{r} = \frac{5K}{w} \Rightarrow \frac{K}{L} = \frac{w}{r} = \frac{5000}{10,000} = \frac{1}{2}.$$

The new plant should accommodate a capital to labor ratio of 1 to 2. Note that the current firm is presently operating at this capital-labor ratio.

9. The short-run cost function of a company is given by the equation TC=200+55q, where TC is the total cost and q is the total quantity of output, both measured in thousands.

a.   **What is the company's fixed cost?**

When q = 0, TC = 200, so fixed cost is equal to 200 (or $200,000).

b. **If the company produced 100,000 units of goods, what is its average variable cost?**

With 100,000 units, $q = 100$. Variable cost is $55q = (55)(100) = 5500$ (or $5,500,000).

Average variable cost is $\dfrac{TVC}{q} = \dfrac{\$5500}{100} = \$55$, or $55,000.

c. **What is its marginal cost *per unit* produced?**

With constant average variable cost, marginal cost is equal to average variable cost, $55 (or $55,000).

d. **What is its average fixed cost?**

At $q = 100$, average fixed cost is $\dfrac{TFC}{q} = \dfrac{\$200}{100} = \$2$ or ($2,000).

e. **Suppose the company borrows money and expands its factory. Its fixed cost rises by $50,000, but its variable cost falls to $45,000 per 1,000 units. The cost of interest (i) also enters into the equation. Each one-point increase in the interest rate raises costs by $3,000. Write the new cost equation.**

Fixed cost changes from 200 to 250, measured in thousands. Variable cost decreases from 55 to 45, also measured in thousands. Fixed cost also includes interest charges: $3i$. The cost equation is

$$C = 250 + 45q + 3i.$$

10. A chair manufacturer hires its assembly-line labor for $30 an hour and calculates that the rental cost of its machinery is $15 per hour. Suppose that a chair can be produced using 4 hours of labor or machinery in any combination. If the firm is currently using 3 hours of labor for each hour of machine time, is it minimizing its costs of production? If so, why? If not, how can it improve the situation? Graphically illustrate the isoquant and the two isocost lines, for the current combination of labor and capital and the optimal combination of labor and capital.

If the firm can produce one chair with either four hours of labor or four hours of capital, machinery, or any combination, then the isoquant is a straight line with a slope of -1 and intercept at $K = 4$ and $L = 4$, as depicted in figure 7.10.

The isocost line, $TC = 30L + 15K$ has a slope of $-\dfrac{30}{15} = -2$ when plotted with capital on the vertical axis and has intercepts at $K = \dfrac{TC}{15}$ and $L = \dfrac{TC}{30}$. The cost minimizing point is a corner solution, where $L = 0$ and $K = 4$. At that point, total cost is $60. Two isocost lines are illustrated on the graph. The first one is further from the origin and represents the higher cost ($105) of using 3 labor and 1 capital. The firm will find it optimal to move to the second isocost line which is closer to the origin, and which represents a lower cost ($60). In general, the firm wants to be on the lowest isocost line possible, which is the lowest isocost line that still intersects the given isoquant.

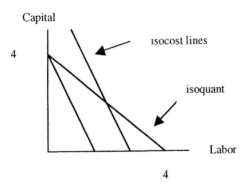

Figure 7.10

11. **Suppose that a firm's production function is** $q = 10L^{\frac{1}{2}}K^{\frac{1}{2}}$**. The cost of a unit of labor is $20 and the cost of a unit of capital is $80.**

a. **The firm is currently producing 100 units of output, and has determined that the cost-minimizing quantities of labor and capital are 20 and 5 respectively. Graphically illustrate this situation on a graph using isoquants and isocost lines.**

The isoquant is convex. The optimal quantities of labor and capital are given by the point where the isocost line is tangent to the isoquant. The isocost line has a slope of 1/4, given labor is on the horizontal axis. The total cost is TC=$20*20+$80*5=$800, so the isocost line has the equation $800=20L+80K. On the graph, the optimal point is point A.

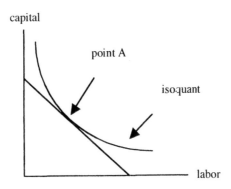

b. **The firm now wants to increase output to 140 units. If capital is fixed in the short run, how much labor will the firm require? Illustrate this point on your graph and find the new cost.**

The new level of labor is 39.2. To find this, use the production function $q = 10L^{\frac{1}{2}}K^{\frac{1}{2}}$ and substitute 140 in for output and 5 in for capital. The new cost is TC=$20*39.2+$80*5=$1184. The new isoquant for an output of 140 is above and to the right of the old isoquant for an output of 100. Since capital is fixed in the short run, the firm will move out horizontally to the new isoquant and new level of labor. This is point B on the graph below. This is not likely to be the cost minimizing point. Given the firm wants to produce more output, they are likely to want to hire more capital in the long run. Notice also that there are points on the new isoquant that are below the new isocost line. These points all involve hiring more capital.

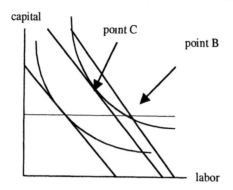

c. **Graphically identify the cost-minimizing level of capital and labor in the long run if the firm wants to produce 140 units.**

This is point C on the graph above. When the firm is at point B they are not minimizing cost. The firm will find it optimal to hire more capital and less labor and move to the new lower isocost line. All three isocost lines above are parallel and have the same slope.

d. **If the marginal rate of technical substitution is $\dfrac{K}{L}$, find the optimal level of capital and labor required to produce the 140 units of output.**

Set the marginal rate of technical substitution equal to the ratio of the input costs so that $\dfrac{K}{L} = \dfrac{20}{80} \Rightarrow K = \dfrac{L}{4}$. Now substitute this into the production function for K, set q equal to 140, and solve for L: $140 = 10L^{\frac{1}{2}}\left(\dfrac{L}{4}\right)^{\frac{1}{2}} \Rightarrow L = 28, K = 7$. The new cost is TC=\$20*28+\$80*7 or \$1120.

12. A computer company's cost function, which relates its average cost of production AC to its cumulative output in thousands of computers Q and its plant size in terms of thousands of computers produced per year q, within the production range of 10,000 to 50,000 computers is given by

$$AC = 10 - 0.1Q + 0.3q.$$

a. **Is there a learning curve effect?**

The learning curve describes the relationship between the cumulative output and the inputs required to produce a unit of output. Average cost measures the input requirements per unit of output. Learning curve effects exist if average cost falls with increases in cumulative output. Here, average cost decreases as cumulative output, Q, increases. Therefore, there are learning curve effects.

b. **Are there economies or diseconomies of scale?**

Economies of scale can be measured by calculating the cost-output elasticity, which measures the percentage change in the cost of production resulting from a one percentage increase in output. There are economies of scale if the firm can double its output for less than double the cost. There are economies of scale because the average cost of production declines as more output is produced, due to the learning effect.

c.   **During its existence, the firm has produced a total of 40,000 computers and is producing 10,000 computers this year. Next year it plans to increase its production to 12,000 computers. Will its average cost of production increase or decrease? Explain.**

First, calculate average cost this year:

$$AC_1 = 10 - 0.1Q + 0.3q = 10 - (0.1)(40) + (0.3)(10) = 9.$$

Second, calculate the average cost next year:

$$AC_2 = 10 - (0.1)(50) + (0.3)(12) = 8.6.$$

(Note: Cumulative output has increased from 40,000 to 50,000.) The average cost will decrease because of the learning effect.

13. **Suppose the long-run total cost function for an industry is given by the cubic equation TC = a + bQ + cQ^2 + dQ^3. Show (using calculus) that this total cost function is consistent with a U-shaped average cost curve for at least some values of a, b, c, d.**

To show that the cubic cost equation implies a *U*-shaped average cost curve, we use algebra, calculus, and economic reasoning to place sign restrictions on the parameters of the equation. These techniques are illustrated by the example below.

First, if output is equal to zero, then $TC = a$, where a represents fixed costs. In the short run, fixed costs are positive, $a > 0$, but in the long run, where all inputs are variable $a = 0$. Therefore, we restrict a to be zero.

Next, we know that average cost must be positive. Dividing TC by Q:

$$AC = b + cQ + dQ^2.$$

This equation is simply a quadratic function. When graphed, it has two basic shapes: a *U* shape and a hill shape. We want the *U* shape, i.e., a curve with a minimum (minimum average cost), rather than a hill shape with a maximum.

At the minimum, the slope should be zero, thus the first derivative of the average cost curve with respect to Q must be equal to zero. For a *U*-shaped AC curve, the second derivative of the average cost curve must be positive.

The first derivative is $c + 2dQ$; the second derivative is $2d$. If the second derivative is to be positive, then $d > 0$. If the first derivative is equal to zero, then solving for c as a function of Q and d yields: $c = -2dQ$. If d and Q are both positive, then c must be negative: $c < 0$.

To restrict b, we know that at its minimum, average cost must be positive. The minimum occurs when $c + 2dQ = 0$. We solve for Q as a function of c and d:

$Q = -\dfrac{c}{2d} > 0$. Next, substituting this value for Q into our expression for average cost, and simplifying the equation:

$$AC = b + cQ + dQ^2 = b + c\left(\frac{-c}{2d}\right) + d\left(\frac{-c}{2d}\right)^2, \text{ or}$$

$$AC = b - \frac{c^2}{2d} + \frac{c^2}{4d} = b - \frac{2c^2}{4d} + \frac{c^2}{4d} = b - \frac{c^2}{4d} > 0.$$

implying $b > \dfrac{c^2}{4d}$. Because $c^2 > 0$ and $d > 0$, b must be positive.

In summary, for *U*-shaped long-run average cost curves, a must be zero, b and d must be positive, c must be negative, and $4db > c^2$. However, the conditions do not insure that marginal cost is positive. To insure that marginal cost has a *U* shape and that its minimum is positive, using the same procedure, i.e., solving for Q at minimum marginal cost $-c/3d$, and substituting into the expression for marginal cost $b + 2cQ + 3dQ^2$, we find that c^2 must be less than $3bd$. Notice that parameter values that satisfy this condition also satisfy $4db > c^2$, but not the reverse.

For example, let $a = 0$, $b = 1$, $c = -1$, $d = 1$. Total cost is $Q - Q^2 + Q^3$; average cost is $1 - Q + Q^2$; and marginal cost is $1 - 2Q + 3Q^2$. Minimum average cost is $Q = 1/2$ and minimum marginal cost is $1/3$ (think of Q as dozens of units, so no fractional units are produced). See Figure 7.13.

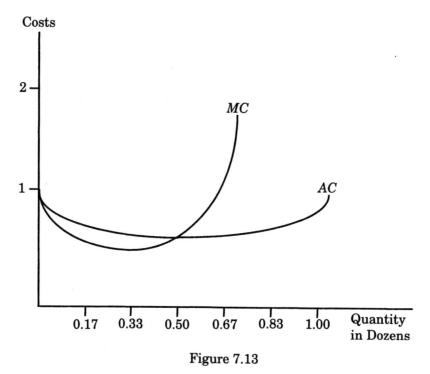

Figure 7.13

*14. A computer company produces hardware and software using the same plant and labor. The total cost of producing computer processing units H and software programs S is given by

TC = aH + bS - cHS,

where a, b, and c are positive. Is this total cost function consistent with the presence of economies or diseconomies of scale? With economies or diseconomies of scope?

There are two types of scale economies to consider: multiproduct economies of scale and product-specific returns to scale. From Section 7.5 we know that multiproduct economies of scale for the two-product case, $S_{H,S}$, are

$$S_{H,S} = \frac{TC(H,S)}{(H)(MC_H) + (S)(MC_S)}$$

where MC_H is the marginal cost of producing hardware and MC_S is the marginal cost of producing software. The product-specific returns to scale are:

$$S_H = \frac{TC(H,S) - TC(0,S)}{(H)(MC_H)} \quad \text{and}$$

$$S_S = \frac{TC(H,S) - TC(H,0)}{(S)(MC_S)}$$

where $TC(0,S)$ implies no hardware production and $TC(H,0)$ implies no software production. We know that the marginal cost of an input is the slope of the total cost with respect to that input. Since

$$TC = (a - cS)H + bS = aH + (b - cH)S,$$

we have $MC_H = a - cS$ and $MC_S = b - cH$.

Substituting these expressions into our formulas for $S_{H,S}$, S_H, and S_S:

$$S_{H,S} = \frac{aH + bS - cHS}{H(a - cS) + S(b - cH)} \quad \text{or}$$

$$S_{H,S} = \frac{aH + bS - cHS}{Ha + Sb - 2cHS} > 1, \text{ because } cHS > 0. \text{ Also,}$$

$$S_H = \frac{(aH + bS - cHS) - bS}{H(a - cS)}, \quad \text{or}$$

$$S_H = \frac{(aH - cHS)}{H(a - cS)} = \frac{(a - cS)}{(a - cS)} = 1 \quad \text{and similarly}$$

$$S_S = \frac{(aH + bS - cHS) - aH}{S(b - cH)} = 1.$$

There are multiproduct economies of scale, $S_{H,S} > 1$, but constant product-specific returns to scale, $S_H = S_C = 1$.

Economies of scope exist if $S_C > 0$, where (from equation (7.8) in the text):

$$S_c = \frac{TC(H,0) + TC(0,S) - TC(H,S)}{TC(H,S)}, \quad \text{or,}$$

$$S_c = \frac{aH + bS - (aH + bS - cHS)}{TC(H,S)}, \quad \text{or}$$

$$S_c = \frac{cHS}{TC(H,S)} > 0.$$

Because cHS and TC are both positive, there are economies of scope.

CHAPTER 7 APPENDIX
PRODUCTION AND COST THEORY—
A MATHEMATICAL TREATMENT

EXERCISES

1. Of the following production functions, which exhibit increasing, constant, or decreasing returns to scale?

a. $F(K, L) = K^2 L$

b. $F(K, L) = 10K + 5L$

c. $F(K, L) = (KL)^{0.5}$

Returns to scale refer to the relationship between output and proportional increases in all inputs. This is represented in the following manner (let $\lambda > 0$):

$F(\lambda K, \lambda L) > \lambda F(K, L)$ implies increasing returns to scale;

$F(\lambda K, \lambda L) = \lambda F(K, L)$ implies constant returns to scale; and

$F(\lambda K, \lambda L) < \lambda F(K, L)$ implies decreasing returns to scale.

a. Applying this to $F(K, L) = K^2 L$,

$$F(\lambda K, \lambda L) = (\lambda K)^2 (\lambda L) = \lambda^3 K^2 L = \lambda^3 F(K, L).$$

This is greater than $\lambda F(K, L)$; therefore, this production function exhibits increasing returns to scale.

b. Applying the same technique to $F(K, L) = 10K + 5L$,

$$F(\lambda K, \lambda L) = 10\lambda K + 5\lambda L = \lambda F(K, L).$$

This production function exhibits constant returns to scale.

c. Applying the same technique to $F(K, L) = (KL)^{0.5}$,

$$F(\lambda K, \lambda L) = (\lambda K \lambda L)^{0.5} = (\lambda^2)^{0.5} (KL)^{0.5} = \lambda (KL)^{0.5} = \lambda F(K, L).$$

This production function exhibits constant returns to scale.

2. The production function for a product is given by q = 100KL. If the price of capital is $120 per day and the price of labor $30 per day, what is the minimum cost of producing 1000 units of output?

The cost-minimizing combination of capital and labor is the one where

$$MRTS = \frac{MP_L}{MP_K} = \frac{w}{r}.$$

The marginal product of labor is $\dfrac{dq}{dL} = 100K$. The marginal product of capital is

$\dfrac{dq}{dK} = 100L$. Therefore, the marginal rate of technical substitution is

$$\frac{100K}{100L} = \frac{K}{L}.$$

To determine the optimal capital-labor ratio set the marginal rate of technical substitution equal to the ratio of the wage rate to the rental rate of capital:

$$\frac{K}{L} = \frac{30}{120}, \text{ or } L = 4K.$$

Substitute for L in the production function and solve where K yields an output of 1,000 units:

$$1,000 = (100)(K)(4K), \text{ or } K = 1.58.$$

Because L equals $4K$ this means L equals 6.32.

With these levels of the two inputs, total cost is:

$$TC = wL + rK, \text{ or}$$

$$TC = (30)(6.32) + (120)(1.58) = \$379.20.$$

To see if $K = 1.58$ and $L = 6.32$ are the cost minimizing levels of inputs, consider small changes in K and L. around 1.58 and 6.32. At $K = 1.6$ and $L = 6.32$, total cost is $381.60, and at $K = 1.58$ and $L = 6.4$, total cost is $381.6, both greater than $379.20. We have found the cost-minimizing levels of K and L.

3. Suppose a production function is given by F(K, L) = KL^2, the price of capital is $10, and the price of labor $15. What combination of labor and capital minimizes the cost of producing any given output?

The cost-minimizing combination of capital and labor is the one where

$$MRTS = \frac{MP_L}{MP_K} = \frac{w}{r}.$$

The marginal product of labor is $\frac{dq}{dL} = 2KL$. The marginal product of capital is

$$\frac{dq}{dK} = L^2.$$

Set the marginal rate of technical substitution equal to the input price ratio to determine the optimal capital-labor ratio:

$$\frac{2KL}{L^2} = \frac{15}{10}, \text{ or } K = 0.75L.$$

Therefore, the capital-labor ratio should be 0.75 to minimize the cost of producing any given output.

4. Suppose the process of producing light-weight parkas by Polly's Parkas is described by the function:

$$q = 10K^8(L - 40)^2$$

where q is the number of parkas produced, K the number of computerized stitching-machine hours, and L the number of person-hours of labor. In addition to capital and labor, $10 worth of raw materials are used in the production of each parka.

We are given the production function: $q = F(K,L) = 10K^8(L - 40)^2$

We also know that the cost of production, in addition to the cost of capital and labor, includes $10 of raw material per unit of output. This yields the following total cost function:

$$TC(q) = wL + rK + 10q$$

a. By minimizing cost subject to the production function, derive the cost-minimizing demands for K and L as a function of output (q), wage rates (w), and rental rates on machines (r). Use these results to derive the total cost function, that is costs as a function of q, r, w, and the constant \$10 per unit materials cost.

We need to find the combinations of K and L that will minimize this cost function for any given level of output q and factor prices r and w. To do this, we set up the Lagrangian:

$$\Phi = wL + rK + 10q - \lambda[10K^{.8}(L-40)^{.2} - q]$$

Differentiating with respect to K, L, and λ, and setting the derivatives equal to zero:

(1) $$\frac{\partial \Phi}{\partial K} = r - 10\lambda(.8)K^{-.2}(L-40)^{.2} = 0$$

(2) $$\frac{\partial \Phi}{\partial L} = w - 10\lambda K^{.8}(.2)(L-40)^{-.8} = 0$$

(3) $$\frac{\partial \Phi}{\partial \lambda} = 10K^{.8}(L-40)^{.2} - q = 0.$$

The first 2 equations imply:

$$r = 10\lambda(.8)K^{-.2}(L-40)^{.2} \quad \text{and} \quad w = 10\lambda K^{.8}(.2)(L-40)^{-.8}.$$

or

$$\frac{r}{w} = \frac{4(L-40)}{K}.$$

This further implies:

$$K = \frac{4w(L-40)}{r} \quad \text{and} \quad L-40 = \frac{rK}{4w}..$$

Substituting the above equations for K and L-40 into equation (3) yields solutions for K and L:

$$q = 10\left(\frac{4w}{r}\right)^{.8}(L-40)^{.8}(L-40)^{.2} \quad \text{and} \quad q = 10K^{.8}\left(\frac{rK}{4w}\right)^{.2}.$$

or

$$L = \frac{r^{.8}q}{30.3w^{.8}} + 40 \quad \text{and} \quad K = \frac{w^{.2}q}{7.6r^{.2}}.$$

We can now obtain the total cost function in terms of only r, w, and Q by substituting these cost-minimizing values for K and L into the total cost function:

$$TC(q) = wL + rK + 10q$$

$$TC(q) = \frac{wr^{.8}q}{30.3w^{.8}} + 40w + \frac{rw^{.2}q}{7.6r^{.2}} + 10q$$

$$TC(q) = \frac{w^{.2}r^{.8}q}{30.3} + 40w + \frac{r^{.8}w^{.2}q}{7.6} + 10q.$$

b. This process requires skilled workers, who earn \$32 per hour. The rental rate on the machines used in the process is \$64 per hour. At these factor prices, what are total costs as a function of q? Does this technology exhibit decreasing, constant, or increasing returns to scale?

Given the values w = 32 and r = 64, the total cost function becomes:

$$TC(q) = 19.2q + 1280.$$

The average cost function is then given by

$$AC(q) = 19.2 + 1280/q.$$

To find returns to scale, choose an input combination and find the level of output, and then double all inputs and compare the new and old output levels. Assume K=50 and L=60. Then $q_1 = 10(50)^{0.8}(60-40)^{0.2} = 416.3$. When K=100 and L=120, $q_2 = 10(100)^{0.8}(120-40)^{0.2} = 956.4$. Since $q_2/q_1 > 2$, the production function exhibits increasing returns to scale.

c. Polly's Parkas plans to produce 2000 parkas per week. At the factor prices given above, how many workers should the firm hire (at 40 hours per week) and how many machines should it rent (at 40 machines-hours per week)? What are the marginal and average costs at this level of production?

Given q = 2,000 per week, we can calculate the required amount of inputs K and L using the formulas derived in part a:

$$L = \frac{r^8 q}{30.3 w^8} + 40 \quad and \quad K = \frac{w^2 q}{7.6 r^2}.$$

Thus L = 154.9 worker hours and K = 229.1 machine hours. Assuming a 40 hour week, L = 154.9/40 = 3.87 workers per week, and K = 229.1/40 = 5.73 machines per week. Polly's Parkas should hire 4 workers and rent 6 machines per week.

We know that the total cost and average cost functions are given by:

$$TC(q) = 19.2q + 1280$$
$$AC(q) = 19.2 + 1280/q,$$

so the marginal cost function is

$$MC(q) = d\,TC(q)\,/\,d\,q = 19.2.$$

Marginal costs are constant at \$19.2 per parka and average costs are 19.2+1280/2000 or \$19.84 per parka.

CHAPTER 8
PROFIT MAXIMIZATION AND COMPETITIVE SUPPLY

TEACHING NOTES

This chapter identifies the behavioral incentives of the profit-maximizing firm and then explores the interaction of these firms in a competitive market. Each section of the chapter is important and builds a solid understanding of the supply side of the competitive market. It is necessary to build this foundation before moving on to the chapters in part III of the text. While the material in the chapter is written in a very clear, easy to understand manner, students still struggle with many of the concepts related to how the firm should choose the optimal quantity to produce, and how to apply the cost curve diagram learned in the previous chapter. One option for lecture is to spend time working with a table similar to the one used in the exercises at the end of the chapter. Working through many examples with this type of a table can help the students understand the different types of cost, as well as the firm's optimal level of production.

Section 8.1 identifies the three basic assumptions of perfect competition and section 8.2 discusses the assumption of profit maximization as the goal of the firm. Both sections are important in building the foundation for deriving the firm's supply curve, which is done in sections 8.3 to 8.5. Section 8.3 derives the general result that the firm should produce where marginal revenue is equal to marginal cost. The section then goes on to identify perfect competition as a special case where price is equal to marginal revenue, which follows directly from the assumption of price taker behavior in section 8.1. If your students have had calculus, it is helpful to derive the marginal revenue equals marginal cost rule by differentiating the profit function with respect to q. If your students have not had calculus then it is helpful to do some more work with the data tables so they understand that profit is maximized when marginal revenue equals marginal cost. Emphasize that the perfectly competitive firm chooses quantity and not price in order to maximize profit.

To put perfect competition in perspective, it can also be helpful to give a brief overview of monopoly, oligopoly, and monopolistic competition before presenting the assumptions of perfect competition. Restrict this discussion to identifying how many firms are in the industry, if there are barriers to entry, product differentiation, and what assumptions does each firm make about how the other firms in the industry will react to their price and quantity decisions. This will stimulate the student's interest about upcoming lectures.

Sections 8.4 and 8.5 further explore the firm's decision to produce where price is equal to marginal cost, and show that the firm's supply curve is its marginal cost curve above its average variable cost curve. Although some students will understand references to second-order conditions, expect to be asked why q_0 in Figure 8.3 is not profit maximizing, although $MR = MC$. Two additional points warrant careful explanation: 1) why the firm would remain in business if the firm sustains a loss in the short run, and 2) that maximizing profit is the same as minimizing loss.

Although the summation of firm supply curves into a market supply curve is straightforward, the analysis of long-run competitive equilibrium is difficult. Difficult concepts include:

- why it may be optimal for the firm to incur losses in the short run but not the long run.

- why free entry and exit will reduce economic profit to zero in the long run.

- why price is equal to minimum average cost in the long run.

It can be helpful to present an example, algebraic and graphical, which starts out with only one firm in the industry that is earning positive economic profit, and then show how the market will converge on its long run equilibrium point. Explore changes in price, quantity produced, and the level of profits, and relate the changes to the firm's behavioral motivations.

This chapter introduces two other important topics that will be elaborated on in Chapter 9: producer surplus and economic rent. Students frequently confuse profit, producer surplus, and economic rent.

REVIEW QUESTIONS

1. Why would a firm that incurs losses choose to produce rather than shut down?

Losses occur when revenues do not cover total costs. Revenues could be greater than variable costs, but not total costs, in which case the firm is better off producing in the short run rather than shutting down, even though they are incurring a loss. The firm should compare the level of loss with no production to the level of loss with positive production, and pick the option that results in the smallest loss. In the short run, losses will be minimized as long as the firm covers its variable costs. In the long run, all costs are variable, and thus, all costs must be covered if the firm is to remain in business.

2. Explain why the industry supply curve is not the long-run industry marginal cost curve.

In the short run, a change in the market price induces the profit-maximizing firm to change its optimal level of output. This optimal output occurs when price is equal to marginal cost, as long as marginal cost exceeds average variable cost. Therefore, the supply curve of the firm is its marginal cost curve, above average variable cost. (When the price falls below average variable cost, the firm will shut down.)

In the long run, the firm adjusts its inputs so that its long-run marginal cost is equal to the market price. At this level of output, it is operating on a short-run marginal cost curve where short-run marginal cost is equal to price. As the long-run price changes, the firm gradually changes its mix of inputs to minimize cost. Thus, the long-run supply response is this adjustment from one set of short-run marginal cost curves to another.

Note also that in the long run there will be entry and the firm will earn zero profit, so that any level of output where MC>AC is not possible.

3. In long-run equilibrium, all firms in the industry earn zero economic profit. Why is this true?

The theory of perfect competition explicitly assumes that there are no entry or exit barriers to new participants in an industry. With free entry, positive economic profits induce new entrants. As these firms enter, the supply curve shifts to the right, causing a fall in the equilibrium price of the product. Entry will stop, and equilibrium will be achieved, when economic profits have fallen to zero.

4. What is the difference between economic profit and producer surplus?

While economic profit is the difference between total revenue and total cost, producer surplus is the difference between total revenue and total variable cost. The difference between economic profit and producer surplus is the fixed cost of production.

5. Why do firms enter an industry when they know that in the long run economic profit will be zero?

Firms enter an industry when they expect to earn economic profit. These short-run profits are enough to encourage entry. Zero economic profits in the long run imply *normal* returns to the factors of production, including the labor and capital of the owners of firms. For example, the owner of a small business might experience positive accounting profits before the foregone wages from running the business are subtracted from these profits. If the revenue minus other costs is just equal to what could be earned elsewhere, then the owner is indifferent to staying in business or exiting.

6. At the beginning of the twentieth century, there were many small American automobile manufacturers. At the end of the century, there are only three large ones. Suppose that this situation is not the result of lax federal enforcement of antimonopoly laws. How do you explain the decrease in the number of manufacturers? (Hint: What is the inherent cost structure of the automobile industry?)

Automobile plants are highly capital-intensive. Assuming there have been no impediments to competition, increasing returns to scale can reduce the number of firms in the long run. As firms grow, their costs decrease with increasing returns to scale. Larger firms are able to sell their product for a lower price and push out smaller firms in the long run. Increasing returns may cease at some level of output, leaving more than one firm in the industry.

7. Industry X is characterized by perfect competition, so every firm in the industry is earning zero economic profit. If the product price falls, no firms can survive. Do you agree or disagree? Discuss.

Disagree. As the market price falls, firms cut their production. If price falls below average total cost, firms continue to produce in the short run and cease production in the long run. If price falls below average variable costs, firms cease production in the short run. Therefore, with a small decrease in price, i.e., less than the difference between the price and average variable cost, the firm can survive. With larger price decrease, i.e., greater than the difference between price and minimum average cost, the firm cannot survive. In general, we would expect that some firms will survive and that just enough firms will leave to bring profit back up to zero.

8. An increase in the demand for video films also increases the salaries of actors and actresses. Is the long-run supply curve for films likely to be horizontal or upward sloping? Explain.

The long-run supply curve depends on the cost structure of the industry. If there is a fixed supply of actors and actresses, as more films are produced, higher salaries must be offered. Therefore, the industry experiences increasing costs. In an increasing-cost industry, the long-run supply curve is upward sloping. Thus, the supply curve for videos would be upward sloping.

9. True or false: A firm should always produce at an output at which long-run average cost is minimized. Explain.

False. In the long run, under perfect competition, firms will produce where long-run average costs are minimized. In the long-run, the firm will have adjusted its mix of capital and labor so that average costs are minimized. In addition, entry and exit will force price to adjust so it is close to minimum average cost. In the short run, however, the firm might not be producing the optimal long-run output. For example, if there are any fixed factors of production, the firm does not always produce where long-run average cost is minimized. Also, in the short run the firm may be producing at a point where price equals marginal cost at a quantity that is different than that which corresponds to minimum long-run average cost.

10. Can there be constant returns to scale in an industry with an upward-sloping supply curve? Explain.

Constant returns to scale imply that proportional increases in all inputs yield the same proportional increase in output. Proportional increases in inputs can induce higher prices if the supply curves for these inputs are upward sloping. For example, production that uses rare or depleting inputs will see higher costs of production as production increases in scale. Doubling inputs will still yield double output, but because of rising costs, the firm cannot offer increasing amounts of the good without higher prices. Therefore, constant returns to scale does not always imply long-run horizontal supply curves.

11. What assumptions are necessary for a market to be perfectly competitive? In light of what you have learned in this chapter, why is each of these assumptions important?

> The two primary assumptions of perfect competition are (1) all firms in the industry are price takers, and (2) there is free entry and exit of firms from the market. This chapter discusses how competitive equilibrium is achieved under these assumptions. The first assumption is important because it means that no firm has any market power. Given no firm has market power, firms will produce where price is equal to marginal cost. In the short run, price could equal marginal cost at a quantity where marginal cost is greater than average cost, implying positive economic profits. With free entry and exit, positive economic profits would encourage other firms to enter. This entry exerts downward pressure on price until price is equal to both marginal cost and minimum average cost.

12. Suppose a competitive industry faces an increase in demand (i.e., the demand curve shifts upward). What are the steps by which a competitive market insures increased output? Will your answer change if the government imposes a price ceiling?

> If demand increases with fixed supply, price and profits increase. The price increase induces the firms in the industry to increase output. Also, with positive profit, firms enter the industry, shifting the supply curve to the right. This results in a new equilibrium with a higher quantity produced and a price that earns all firms zero economic profit. With an effective price ceiling, profit will be lower than without the ceiling, reducing the incentive for firms to enter the industry. With zero economic profit, no firms enter and there is no shift in the supply curve.

13. The government passes a law that allows a substantial subsidy for every acre of land used to grow tobacco. How does this program affect the long-run supply curve for tobacco?

> A subsidy on tobacco production decreases the firm's costs of production. These cost decreases encourage other firms to enter tobacco production, and the supply curve for the industry shifts out to the right

14. A certain brand of vacuum cleaners can be purchased from several local stores as well as from several catalogue or web site sources.

a.   If all sellers charge the same price for the vacuum cleaner, will they all earn zero economic profit in the long run?

> Yes by charging the same price they will all earn zero economic profit in the long run. If economic profit was greater than zero then firms would enter the industry and if economic profit was less than zero firms would exit the industry.

b.   If all sellers charge the same price and one local seller owns the building in which he does business, paying no rent, is this seller earning a positive economic profit?

> No this seller would still earn zero economic profit. If he pays no rent then the accounting cost of using the building is zero, but there is still an opportunity cost, which represents the value of the next best alternative use of the building.

c.   Does the seller who pays no rent have an incentive to lower the price he charges for the vacuum cleaner?

> No he has no incentive to charge a lower price because this will lower his economic profit. Given all firms sell an identical good, they will charge the same price for that good. By charging a lower price, the firm is no longer maximizing profit.

EXERCISES

1. The data in the following table give information about the price (in dollars) for which a firm can sell a unit of output and the total cost of production.

a.   Fill in the blanks in the table.

b.   Show what happens to the firm's output choice and profit if the price of the product falls from $60 to $50.

Q	P	TR P=60	TC	π P=60	MC	MR P=60	TR P=50	MR P=50	π P=50
0	60		100						
1	60		150						
2	60		178						
3	60		198						
4	60		212						
5	60		230						
6	60		250						
7	60		272						
8	60		310						
9	60		355						
10	60		410						
11	60		475						

The table below shows the firm's revenue and cost for the two prices.

Q	P	TR P=60	TC	π P=60	MC	MR P=60	TR P=50	MR P=50	π P=50
0	60	0	100	-100	—	—	0	—	-100
1	60	60	150	-90	50	60	50	50	-100
2	60	120	178	-58	28	60	100	50	-78
3	60	180	198	-18	20	60	150	50	-48
4	60	240	212	28	14	60	200	50	-12
5	60	300	230	70	18	60	250	50	20
6	60	360	250	110	20	60	300	50	50
7	60	420	272	148	22	60	350	50	78
8	60	480	310	170	38	60	400	50	90
9	60	540	355	185	45	60	450	50	95
10	60	600	410	190	55	60	500	50	90
11	60	660	475	185	65	60	550	50	75

At a price of $60, the firm should produce ten units of output to maximize profit because this is the point closest to where price equals marginal cost without having marginal cost exceed price. At a price of $50, the firm should produce nine units to maximize profit. When price falls from $60 to $50, profit falls from $190 to $95.

2. Using the data in the table, show what happens to the firm's output choice and profit if the fixed cost of production increases from $100 to $150, and then to $200. Assume that the price of the output remains at $60 per unit. What general conclusion can you reach about the effects of fixed costs on the firm's output choice?

The table below shows the firm's revenue and cost information for fixed cost, *FC* of 100, 150, and 200.

In all of the given cases, with fixed cost equal to 100, then 150, and then 200, the firm will produce 10 units of output because this is the point closest to where price equals marginal cost without having marginal cost exceed price. Fixed costs do not influence the optimal quantity, because they do not influence marginal cost. Higher fixed costs also result in lower profits.

Q	P	TR	TC FC = 100	π FC = 100	MC	TC FC = 150	π FC = 150	TC FC = 200	π FC = 200
0	60	0	100	-100	—	150	-150	200	-200
1	60	60	150	-90	50	200	-140	250	-190
2	60	120	178	-58	28	228	-108	278	-158
3	60	180	198	-18	20	248	-68	298	-118
4	60	240	212	28	14	262	-22	312	-72
5	60	300	230	70	18	280	20	330	-30
6	60	360	250	110	20	300	60	350	10
7	60	420	272	148	22	322	98	372	48
8	60	480	310	170	38	360	120	410	70
9	60	540	355	185	45	405	135	455	85
10	60	600	410	190	55	460	140	510	90
11	60	660	475	185	65	525	135	575	85

3. Use the same information as in Exercise 1.

a.   Derive the firm's short-run supply curve. (Hint: you may want to plot the appropriate cost curves.)

The firm's short-run supply curve is its marginal cost curve above average variable cost. The table below lists marginal cost, total cost, variable cost, fixed cost, and average variable cost. The firm will produce 8 or more units depending on the market price and will not produce in the 0-7 units of output range because in this range AVC is greater than MC. When AVC is greater than MC, the firm minimizes losses by producing nothing.

Q	TC	MC	TVC	TFC	AVC
0	100	—	0	100	—
1	150	50	50	100	50.0
2	178	28	78	100	39.0
3	198	20	98	100	32.7
4	212	14	112	100	28.0
5	230	18	130	100	26.0
6	250	20	150	100	25.0
7	272	22	172	100	24.6
8	310	38	210	100	26.3
9	355	45	255	100	28.3
10	410	55	310	100	31.0
11	475	65	375	100	34.1

b.   If 100 identical firms are in the market, what is the industry supply curve?

For 100 firms with identical cost structures, the market supply curve is the horizontal summation of each firm's output at each price.

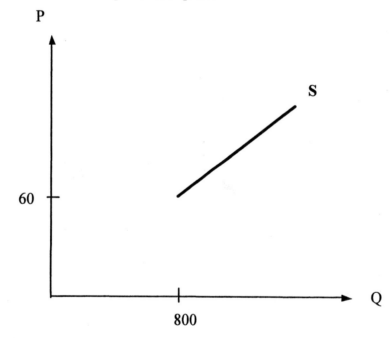

4. **Suppose you are the manager of a watchmaking firm operating in a competitive market. Your cost of production is given by C = 200 +2 q², where q is the level of output and C is total cost. (The marginal cost of production is 4q. The fixed cost of production is $200.)**

a. **If the price of watches is $100, how many watches should you produce to maximize profit?**

Profits are maximized where marginal cost is equal to marginal revenue. Here, marginal revenue is equal to $100; recall that price equals marginal revenue in a competitive market:

$$100 = 4q, \text{ or } q = 25.$$

b. **What will the profit level be?**

Profit is equal to total revenue minus total cost:

$$\pi = (100)(25) - (200 + 2*25^2) = \$1050.$$

c. **At what minimum price will the firm produce a positive output?**

A firm will produce in the short run if the revenues it receives are greater than its variable costs. Remember that the firm's short-run supply curve is its marginal cost curve above the minimum of average variable cost. Here, average variable cost is $\dfrac{VC}{q} = \dfrac{2q^2}{q} = 2q$. Also, MC is equal to $4q$. So, MC is greater than AVC for any quantity greater than 0. This means that the firm produces in the short run as long as price is positive.

5. **Suppose that a competitive firm's marginal cost of producing output q is given by MC(q) = 3 + 2q. Assume that the market price of the firm's product is $9.**

a. **What level of output will the firm produce?**

To maximize profits, the firm should set marginal revenue equal to marginal cost. Given the fact that this firm is operating in a competitive market, the market price it faces is equal to marginal revenue. Thus, the firm should set the market price equal to marginal cost to maximize its profits:

$$9 = 3 + 2q, \text{ or } q = 3.$$

b. **What is the firm's producer surplus?**

Producer surplus is equal to the area below the market price, i.e., $9.00, and above the marginal cost curve, i.e., $3 + 2q$. Because MC is linear, producer surplus is a triangle with a base equal to $6 (9 - 3 = 6). The height of the triangle is 3, where $P = MC$. Therefore, producer surplus is

$$(0.5)(6)(3) = \$9.$$

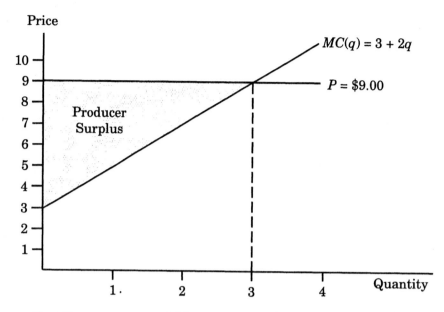

c. Suppose that the average variable cost of the firm is given by AVC(q) = 3 + q. Suppose that the firm's fixed costs are known to be $3. Will the firm be earning a positive, negative, or zero profit in the short run?

Profit is equal to total revenue minus total cost. Total cost is equal to total variable cost plus fixed cost. Total variable cost is equal to $(AVC)(q)$. Therefore, at $q = 3$,

$$TVC = (3 + 3)(3) = \$18.$$

Fixed cost is equal to $3. Therefore, total cost equals TVC plus TFC, or

$$TC = 18 + 3 = \$21.$$

Total revenue is price times quantity:

$$TR = (\$9)(3) = \$27.$$

Profit is total revenue minus total cost:

$$\pi = \$27 - \$21 = \$6.$$

Therefore, the firm is earning positive economic profits. More easily, you might recall that profit equals producer surplus minus fixed cost. Since we found that producer surplus was $9 in part b, profit equals 9-3 or $6.

6. A firm produces a product in a competitive industry and has a total cost function $TC = 50 + 4q + 2q^2$ and a marginal cost function $MC = 4 + 4q$. At the given market price of $20, the firm is producing 5 units of output. Is the firm maximizing profit? What quantity of output should the firm produce in the long run?

If the firm is maximizing profit, then price will be equal to marginal cost. P=MC results in P=20=4+4q=MC, or q=4. The firm is not maximizing profit, since it is producing too much output. The current level of profit is

$$\text{profit} = 20*5-(50+4*5+2*5*5) = -20,$$

and the profit maximizing level is

$$\text{profit} = 20*4-(50+4*4+2*4*4) = -18.$$

Given no change in the price of the product or the cost structure of the firm, the firm should produce q=0 units of output in the long run since at the quantity where price is equal to marginal cost, economic profit is negative. The firm should exit the industry.

7. Suppose the cost function is C(q)=4q²+16.

a. **Find variable cost, fixed cost, average cost, average variable cost, and average fixed cost. Hint: Marginal cost is MC=8q.**

Variable cost is that part of total cost that depends on q ($4q^2$) and fixed cost is that part of total cost that does not depend on q (16).

$$VC = 4q^2$$

$$FC = 16$$

$$AC = \frac{C(q)}{q} = 4q + \frac{16}{q}$$

$$AVC = \frac{VC}{q} = 4q$$

$$AFC = \frac{FC}{q} = \frac{16}{q}$$

b. **Show the average cost, marginal cost, and average variable cost curves on a graph.**

Average cost is u-shaped. Average cost is relatively large at first because the firm is not able to spread the fixed cost over very many units of output. As output increases, average fixed costs will fall relatively rapidly. Average cost will increase at some point because the average fixed cost will become very small and average variable cost is increasing as q increases. Average variable cost will increase because of diminishing returns to the variable factor labor. MC and AVC are linear, and both pass through the origin. Average variable cost is everywhere below average cost. Marginal cost is everywhere above average variable cost. If the average is rising, then the marginal must be above the average. Marginal cost will hit average cost at its minimum point.

c. **Find the output that minimizes average cost.**

The minimum average cost quantity is where MC is equal to AC:

$$AC = 4q + \frac{16}{q} = 8q = MC$$

$$\frac{16}{q} = 4q$$

$$16 = 4q^2$$

$$4 = q^2$$

$$2 = q.$$

d. **At what range of prices will the firm produce a positive output?**

The firm will supply positive levels of output as long as P=MC>AVC, or as long as the firm is covering its variable costs of production. In this case, marginal cost is everywhere above average variable cost so the firm will supply positive output at any positive price.

e. **At what range of prices will the firm earn a negative profit?**

The firm will earn negative profit when P=MC<AC, or at any price below minimum average cost. In part c above we found that the minimum average cost quantity was q=2. Plug q=2 into the average cost function to find AC=16. The firm will therefore earn negative profit if price is below 16.

111

f.   **At what range of prices will the firm earn a positive profit?**

In part e we found that the firm would earn negative profit at any price below 16. The firm therefore earns positive profit as long as price is above 16.

8. A competitive firm has the following short run cost function:

$$C(q) = q^3 - 8q^2 + 30q + 5.$$

a.   **Find MC, AC, and AVC and sketch them on a graph.**

The functions can be calculated as follows:

$$MC = \frac{\partial C}{\partial q} = 3q^2 - 16q + 30$$

$$AC = \frac{C}{q} = q^2 - 8q + 30 + \frac{5}{q}$$

$$AVC = \frac{VC}{q} = q^2 - 8q + 30$$

Graphically, all three cost functions are u-shaped in that cost declines initially as q increases, and then cost increases as q increases. Average variable cost is below average cost. Marginal cost will be initially below AVC and will then increase to hit AVC at its minimum point. MC will be initially below AC and will also hit AC at its minimum point.

b.   **At what range of prices will the firm supply zero output?**

The firm will find it profitable to produce in the short run as long as price is greater than or equal to average variable cost. If price is less than average variable cost then the firm will be better off shutting down in the short run, as it will only lose its fixed cost and not fixed plus some of variable cost. Here we need to find the minimum average variable cost, which can be done in two different ways. You can either set marginal cost equal to average variable cost, or you can differentiate average variable cost with respect to q and set this equal to zero. In both cases, you can solve for q and then plug into AVC to find the minimum AVC. Here we will set AVC equal to MC:

$$AVC = q^2 - 8q + 30 = 3q^2 - 16q + 30 = MC$$

$$2q^2 = 8q$$

$$q = 4$$

$$AVC(q = 4) = 4^2 - 8*4 + 30 = 14.$$

Hence, the firm supplies zero output if P<14.

c.   **Identify the firm's supply curve on your graph.**

The firm supply curve is the MC curve above the point where MC=AVC. The firm will produce at the point where price equals MC as long as MC is greater than or equal to AVC.

d.   **At what price would the firm supply exactly 6 units of output?**

The firm maximizes profit by choosing the level of output such that P=MC. To find the price where the firm would supply 6 units of output, set q equal to 6 and solve for MC:

$$P = MC = 3q^2 - 16q + 30 = 3(6^2) - 16(6) + 30 = 42.$$

9. a. Suppose that a firm's production function is $q = 9x^{\frac{1}{2}}$ in the short run, where there are fixed costs of \$1,000 and x is the variable input, whose cost is \$4,000 per unit. What is the total cost of producing a level of output q. In other words, identify the total cost function C(q).

The total cost function C(x) = fixed cost + variable cost = 1000 + 4000x. Since the variable input costs \$4,000 per unit, the variable cost is 4000 times the number of units, or 4000x. Now rewrite the production function to express x in terms of q so that $x = \dfrac{q^2}{81}$. We can then substitute this into the above cost function to find C(q):

$$C(q) = \frac{4000q^2}{81} + 1000 .$$

b. Write down the equation for the supply curve.

The firm supplies output where P=MC so the marginal cost curve is the supply curve, or $P = \dfrac{8000q}{81}$.

c. If price is \$1000, how many units will the firm produce? What is the level of profit? Illustrate on a cost curve graph.

To figure this out, set price equal to marginal cost to find:

$$P = \frac{8000q}{81} = 1000 \Rightarrow q = 10.125 .$$

Profit is 1000*10.125-(1000+(4000*10.125*10.125)/81) = 4062.5. Graphically, the firm produces where the price line hits the MC curve. Since profit is positive, this will occur at a quantity where price is greater than average cost. To find profit on the graph, take the difference of the revenue box (price times quantity) and the cost box (average cost times quantity). This rectangle is the profit area.

10. Suppose you are given the following information about a particular industry:

$$Q^D = 6500 - 100P \qquad \text{Market demand}$$

$$Q^S = 1200P \qquad \text{Market supply}$$

$$C(q) = 722 + \frac{q^2}{200} \qquad \text{Firm total cost function}$$

$$MC(q) = \frac{2q}{200} \qquad \text{Firm marginal cost function.}$$

Assume that all firms are identical, and that the market is characterized by pure competition.

a. Find the equilibrium price, the equilibrium quantity, the output supplied by the firm, and the profit of the firm.

Equilibrium price and quantity are found by setting market supply equal to market demand, so that 6500-100P=1200P. Solve to find P=5 and substitute into either equation to find Q=6000. To find the output for the firm set price equal to marginal cost so that $5 = \dfrac{2q}{200}$ and q=500. Profit of the firm is total revenue minus total cost

or $\Pi = pq - C(q) = 5(500) - 722 - \dfrac{500^2}{200} = 528$. Notice that since the total output in the market is 6000, and the firm output is 500, there must be 6000/500=12 firms in the industry.

113

b.   **Would you expect to see entry into or exit from the industry in the long-run? Explain. What effect will entry or exit have on market equilibrium?**

Entry because the firms in the industry are making positive profit. As firms enter, the supply curve for the industry will shift down and to the right and the equilibrium price will fall, all else the same. This will reduce each firm's profit down to zero until there is no incentive for further entry.

c.   **What is the lowest price at which each firm would sell its output in the long run? Is profit positive, negative, or zero at this price? Explain.**

In the long run the firm will not sell for a price that is below minimum average cost. At any price below minimum average cost, profit is negative and the firm is better off selling its fixed resources and producing zero output. To find the minimum average cost, set marginal cost equal to average cost and solve for q:

$$\frac{2q}{200} = \frac{722}{q} + \frac{q}{200}$$

$$\frac{q}{200} = \frac{722}{q}$$

$$q^2 = 722(200)$$

$$q = 380$$

$$AC(q = 380) = 3.8.$$

Therefore, the firm will not sell for any price less than 3.8 in the long run.

d.   **What is the lowest price at which each firm would sell its output in the short run? Is profit positive, negative, or zero at this price? Explain.**

The firm will sell for any positive price, because at any positive price marginal cost will be above average variable cost (AVC=q/2000). Profit is negative as long as price is below minimum average cost, or as long as price is below 3.8.

11. Suppose that a competitive firm has a total cost function $C(q) = 450 + 15q + 2q^2$ and a marginal cost function $MC(q) = 15 + 4q$. If the market price is P=\$115 per unit, find the level of output produced by the firm. Find the level of profit and the level of producer surplus.

The firm should produce where price is equal to marginal cost so that P=115=15+4q=MC and q=25. Profit is

$\Pi = 115(25) - 450 - 15(25) - 2(25^2) = 800$. Producer surplus is profit plus fixed cost, which is 1250. Note that producer surplus can also be found graphically by calculating the area below the price line and above the marginal cost (supply) curve, so that PS=0.5*(115-15)*25=1250.

12. A number of stores offer film developing as a service to their customers. Suppose that each store that offers this service has a cost function $C(q) = 50 + 0.5q + 0.08q^2$ and a marginal cost $MC = 0.5 + 0.16q$.

a.   **If the going rate for developing a roll of film is \$8.50, is the industry in long run equilibrium? If not find the price associated with long run equilibrium.**

First find the profit maximizing quantity associated with a price of \$8.50 by setting price equal to marginal cost so that MC=0.5+0.16q=8.5=P, or q=50. Profit is then 8.5*50-(50+0.5*50+0.08*50*50)=\$150. The industry is not in long run equilibrium because profit is greater than zero. In a long run equilibrium, firms produce where price is equal to minimum average cost and there is no incentive for entry or exit. To

114

find the minimum average cost point, set marginal cost equal to average cost and solve for q:

$$MC = 0.5 + 0.16q = \frac{50}{q} + 0.5 + 0.08q = AC$$
$$0.08q^2 = 50$$
$$q = 25.$$

To find the long run price in the market, substitute q=25 into either marginal cost or average cost to get P=$4.50.

b.   **Suppose now that a new technology is developed which will reduce the cost of film developing by 25%. Assuming that the industry is in long run equilibrium, how much would any one store be willing to pay to purchase this new technology?**

The new total cost function and marginal cost function can be found by multiplying the old functions by 0.75 (or 75%) and are as follows:

$$C_{new}(q) = .75(50 + 0.5q + 0.08q^2) = 37.5 + 0.375q + 0.06q^2$$
$$MC_{new}(q) = 0.375 + 0.12q.$$

The firm will set marginal cost equal to price, which is $4.50 in the long run equilibrium. Solve for q to find that the firm will develop approximately 34 rolls of film (rounding down). If q=34 then profit is $33.39. This is the most the firm would be willing to pay for the new technology. Note that if all firms adopt the new technology and produce more output, then price in the market will fall and profit for each firm will be reduced to zero.

13.   Consider a city that has a number of hot dogs stands operating throughout the downtown area. Suppose that each vendor has a marginal cost of $1.50 per hot dog sold, and no fixed cost. Suppose the maximum number of hot dogs any one vendor can sell in a day is 100.

a.   **If the price of a hot dog is $2, how may hot dogs does each vendor want to sell?**

Since marginal cost is equal to 1.5 and the price is equal to 2, the hot dog vendor will want to sell as many hot dogs as possible, or in other words, 100 hot dogs.

b.   **If the industry is perfectly competitive will the price remain at $2 for a hot dog? If not, what will the price be?**

The price should fall to $1.50 so that price is equal to marginal cost. Each hot dog vendor will have an incentive to lower the price of a hot dog below $2 so they can sell more hot dogs than their competitors. No hot dog vendor will sell a hot dog for a price below marginal cost, so the price will fall until it reaches $1.50.

c.   **If each vendor sells exactly 100 hot dogs a day and the demand for hot dogs from vendors in the city is Q=4400-1200P, how many vendors are there?**

If price is 1.50 then Q=4400-1200*1.5=2600 in total. If each vendor sells 100 hot dogs then there are 26 vendors.

d.   **Suppose the city decides to regulate hot dog vendors by issuing permits. If the city issues only 20 permits, and if each vendor continues to sell 100 hot dogs a day, what price will a hot dog sell for?**

If there are 20 vendors selling 100 hot dogs each then the total number sold is 2000. If Q=2000 then P=$2, from the demand curve.

e. **Suppose the city decided to sell the permits. What is the highest price a vendor would pay for a permit?**

At the new price of $2 per hot dog the vendor is making a profit of $0.50 per hot dog, or a total of $50. This is the most they would pay on a per day basis.

14. A sales tax of $1 per unit of output is placed on one firm whose product sells for $5 in a competitive industry.

a. **How will this tax affect the cost curves for the firm?**

With the imposition of a $1 tax on a single firm, all its cost curves shift up by $1. Total cost becomes TC+tq, or TC+q since t=1. Average cost is now AC+1. Marginal cost is now MC+1.

b. **What will happen to the firm's price, output, and profit?**

Since the firm is a price-taker in a competitive market, the imposition of the tax on only one firm does not change the market price. Since the firm's short-run supply curve is its marginal cost curve above average variable cost and that marginal cost curve has shifted up (inward), the firm supplies less to the market at every price. Profits are lower at every quantity.

c. **Will there be entry or exit in the industry?**

If the tax is placed on a single firm, that firm will go out of business. In the long run, price in the market will be below the minimum average cost point of this firm.

15. A sales tax of 10 percent is placed on half the firms (the polluters) in a competitive industry. The revenue is paid to the remaining firms (the nonpolluters) as a 10 percent subsidy on the value of output sold.

a. **Assuming that all firms have identical constant long-run average costs before the sales tax-subsidy policy, what do you expect to happen to the price of the product, the output of each of the firms, and industry output, in the short run and the long run? (Hint: How does price relate to industry input?)**

The price of the product depends on the quantity produced by all firms in the industry. The immediate response to the sales-tax=subsidy policy is a reduction in quantity by polluters and an increase in quantity by non-polluters. If a long-run competitive equilibrium existed before the sales-tax=subsidy policy, price would have been equal to marginal cost and long-run minimum average cost. For the polluters, the price after the sales tax is below long-run average cost; therefore, in the long run, they will exit the industry. Furthermore, after the subsidy, the non-polluters earn economic profits that will encourage the entry of non-polluters. If this is a constant cost industry and the loss of the polluters' output is compensated by an increase in the non-polluters' output, the price will remain constant.

b. **Can such a policy *always* be achieved with a balanced budget in which tax revenues are equal to subsidy payments? Why or why not? Explain.**

As the polluters exit and non-polluters enter the industry, revenues from polluters decrease and the subsidy to the non-polluters increases. This imbalance occurs when the first polluter leaves the industry and persists ever after. If the taxes and subsidies are re-adjusted with every entering firm and exiting firm, then tax revenues from polluting firms will shrink and the non-polluters get smaller and smaller subsidies.

CHAPTER 9
THE ANALYSIS OF COMPETITIVE MARKETS

TEACHING NOTES

With the exception of Chapter 1, Chapter 9 is the most straightforward and easily understood chapter in the text. The chapter begins with a review of consumer and producer surplus in section 9.1. If you have postponed these topics, you should carefully explain the definition of each. Section 9.2 discusses the basic concept of efficiency in competitive markets by comparing competitive outcomes with those under market failure. A more detailed discussion of efficiency is presented in Chapter 16.

Sections 9.3 to 9.6 present examples of government policies that cause the market equilibrium to differ from the competitive, efficient equilibrium. The instructor can pick and choose among sections 9.3 to 9.6 depending on time constraints and personal preference. The presentation in each of these sections follows the same format: there is a general discussion of why market intervention leads to deadweight loss, followed by the presentation of an important policy example. Each section is discussed in one review question and applied in at least one exercise. Exercise (1) focuses on minimum wages presented in Section 9.3. Exercises (4) and (5) reinforce discussion of price supports and production quotas from Section 9.4. The use of tariffs and quotas, presented in Section 9.5, can be found in Exercises (3), (6), (7), (8), (11), and (12). Taxes and subsidies (Section 9.6) are discussed in Exercises (2), (9), and (14). Exercise (10) reviews natural gas price controls in Example 9.1, a continuation of Example 2.7. Exercise (4) may be compared to Example 9.4 and discussed as an extension of Example 2.2.

REVIEW QUESTIONS

1. What is meant by deadweight loss? Why does a price ceiling usually result in a deadweight loss?

Deadweight loss refers to the benefits lost to either consumers or producers when markets do not operate efficiently. The term deadweight denotes that these are benefits unavailable to any party. A price ceiling will tend to result in a deadweight loss because at any price below the market equilibrium price, quantity supplied will be below the market equilibrium quantity supplied, resulting in a loss of surplus to producers. Consumers will purchase less than the market equilibrium quantity, resulting in a loss of surplus to consumers. Consumers will also purchase less than the quantity they demand at the price set by the ceiling. The surplus lost by consumers and producers is not captured by either group, and surplus not captured by market participants is deadweight loss.

2. Suppose the supply curve for a good is completely inelastic. If the government imposed a price ceiling below the market-clearing level, would a deadweight loss result? Explain.

When the supply curve is completely inelastic, the imposition of an effective price ceiling transfers all loss in producer surplus to consumers. Consumer surplus increases by the difference between the market-clearing price and the price ceiling times the market-clearing quantity. Consumers capture all decreases in total revenue. Therefore, no deadweight loss occurs.

3. How can a price ceiling make consumers better off? Under what conditions might it make them worse off?

If the supply curve is perfectly inelastic a price ceiling will increase consumer surplus. If the demand curve is inelastic, price controls may result in a net loss of consumer surplus because consumers willing to pay a higher price are unable to purchase the price-controlled good or service. The loss of consumer surplus is greater than the transfer of producer surplus to consumers. If demand is elastic (and supply is relatively inelastic) consumers in the aggregate will enjoy an increase in consumer surplus.

4. Suppose the government regulates the price of a good to be no lower than some minimum level. Can such a minimum price make producers as a whole worse off? Explain.

Because a higher price increases revenue and decreases demand, some consumer surplus is transferred to producers but some producer revenue is lost because consumers purchase less. The problem with a price floor or minimum price is that it sends the wrong signal to producers. Thinking that more should be produced as the price goes up, producers incur extra cost to produce more than what consumers are willing to purchase at these higher prices. These extra costs can overwhelm gains captured in increased revenues. Thus, unless all producers decrease production, a minimum price can make producers as a whole worse off.

5. How are production limits used in practice to raise the prices of the following goods or services: (a) taxi rides, (b) drinks in a restaurant or bar, (c) wheat or corn?

Municipal authorities usually regulate the number of taxis through the issuance of licenses. When the number of taxis is less than it would be without regulation, those taxis in the market may charge a higher-than-competitive price.

State authorities usually regulate the number of liquor licenses. By requiring that any bar or restaurant that serves alcohol have a liquor license and then limiting the number of licenses available, the State limits entry by new bars and restaurants. This limitation allows those establishments that have a license to charge a higher price for alcoholic beverages.

Federal authorities usually regulate the number of acres of wheat or corn in production by creating acreage limitation programs that give farmers financial incentives to leave some of their acreage idle. This reduces supply, driving up the price of wheat or corn.

6. Suppose the government wants to increase farmers' incomes. Why do price supports or acreage limitation programs cost society more than simply giving farmers money?

Price supports and acreage limitations cost society more than the dollar cost of these programs because the higher price that results in either case will reduce quantity demanded and hence consumer surplus, leading to a deadweight loss because the farmer is not able to capture the lost surplus. Giving the farmers money does not result in any deadweight loss, but is merely a redistribution of surplus from one group to the other.

7. Suppose the government wants to limit imports of a certain good. Is it preferable to use an import quota or a tariff? Why?

Changes in domestic consumer and producer surpluses are the same under import quotas and tariffs. There will be a loss in (domestic) total surplus in either case. However, with a tariff, the government can collect revenue equal to the tariff times the quantity of imports and these revenues can be redistributed in the domestic economy to offset the domestic deadweight loss by, for example, reducing taxes. Thus, there is less of a loss to the domestic society as a whole. With the import quota, foreign producers can capture the difference between the domestic and world price times the quantity of imports. Therefore, with an import quota, there is a loss to the domestic society as a whole. If the national government is trying to increase welfare, it should use a tariff.

8. The burden of a tax is shared by producers and consumers. Under what conditions will consumers pay most of the tax? Under what conditions will producers pay most of it? What determines the share of a subsidy that benefits consumers?

The burden of a tax and the benefits of a subsidy depend on the elasticities of demand and supply. If the ratio of the elasticity of demand to the elasticity of supply is small, the burden of the tax falls mainly on consumers. On the other hand, if the ratio of the elasticity of demand to the elasticity of supply is large, the burden of the tax falls mainly on producers. Similarly, the benefit of a subsidy accrues mostly to consumers (producers) if the ratio of the elasticity of demand to the elasticity of supply is small (large).

9. Why does a tax create a deadweight loss? What determines the size of this loss?

A tax creates deadweight loss by artificially increasing price above the free market level, thus reducing the equilibrium quantity. This reduction in demand reduces consumer as well as producer surplus. The size of the deadweight loss depends on the elasticities of supply and demand. As the elasticity of demand increases and the elasticity of supply decreases, i.e., as supply becomes more inelastic, the deadweight loss becomes larger.

EXERCISES

---

1. In 1996, the U.S. Congress raised the minimum wage from $4.25 per hour to $5.15 per hour. Some people suggested that a government subsidy could help employers finance the higher wage. This exercise examines the economics of a minimum wage and wage subsidies. Suppose the supply of low-skilled labor is given by $L^S = 10w$, where L^S is the quantity of low-skilled labor (in millions of persons employed each year) and w is the wage rate (in dollars per hour). The demand for labor is given by $L^D = 80 - 10w$.

a. What will the free market wage rate and employment level be? Suppose the government sets a minimum wage of $5 per hour. How many people would then be employed?

In a free-market equilibrium, $L^S = L^D$. Solving yields $w = \$4$ and $L^S = L^D = 40$. If the minimum wage is $5, then $L^S = 50$ and $L^D = 30$. The number of people employed will be given by the labor demand, so employers will hire 30 million workers.

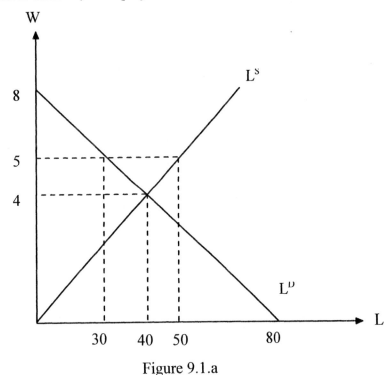

Figure 9.1.a

119

b. **Suppose that instead of a minimum wage, the government pays a subsidy of $1 per hour for each employee. What will the total level of employment be now? What will the equilibrium wage rate be?**

Let w denote the wage received by the employee. Then the employer receiving the $1 subsidy per worker hour only pays w-1 for each worker hour. As shown in Figure 9.1.b, the labor demand curve shifts to:

$$L^D = 80 - 10 \, (w-1) = 90 - 10w,$$

where w represents the wage received by the employee.

The new equilibrium will be given by the intersection of the old supply curve with the new demand curve, and therefore, $90-10_w{}^{**} = 10_w{}^{**}$, or $w^{**} = \$4.5$ per hour and $L^{**} = 10(4.5) = 45$ million persons employed. The real cost to the employer is $3.5 per hour.

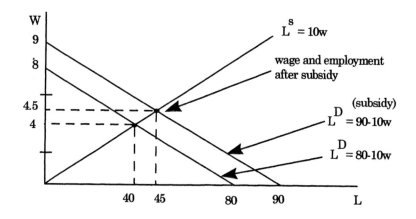

Figure 9.1.b

2. Suppose the market for widgets can be described by the following equations:

Demand: P = 10 - Q	**Supply: P = Q - 4**

where P is the price in dollars per unit and Q is the quantity in thousands of units.

a. **What is the equilibrium price and quantity?**

To find the equilibrium price and quantity, equate supply and demand and solve for Q_{EQ}:

$$10 - Q = Q - 4, \text{ or } Q_{EQ} = 7.$$

Substitute Q_{EQ} into either the demand equation or the supply equation to obtain P_{EQ}.

$$P_{EQ} = 10 - 7 = 3,$$

or

$$P_{EQ} = 7 - 4 = 3.$$

b. **Suppose the government imposes a tax of $1 per unit to reduce widget consumption and raise government revenues. What will the new equilibrium quantity be? What price will the buyer pay? What amount per unit will the seller receive?**

With the imposition of a $1.00 tax per unit, the demand curve for widgets shifts inward. At each price, the consumer wishes to buy less. Algebraically, the new demand function is:

$$P = 9 - Q.$$

The new equilibrium quantity is found in the same way as in (2a):

$$9 - Q = Q - 4, \text{ or } Q^* = 6.5.$$

To determine the price the buyer pays, P_B^*, substitute Q^* into the demand equation:

$$P_B^* = 10 - 6.5 = \$3.50.$$

To determine the price the seller receives, P_S^*, substitute Q^* into the supply equation:

$$P_S^* = 6.5 - 4 = \$2.50.$$

c. **Suppose the government has a change of heart about the importance of widgets to the happiness of the American public. The tax is removed and a subsidy of \$1 per unit is granted to widget producers. What will the equilibrium quantity be? What price will the buyer pay? What amount per unit (including the subsidy) will the seller receive? What will be the total cost to the government?**

The original supply curve for widgets was $P = Q - 4$. With a subsidy of \$1.00 to widget producers, the supply curve for widgets shifts outward. Remember that the supply curve for a firm is its marginal cost curve. With a subsidy, the marginal cost curve shifts down by the amount of the subsidy. The new supply function is:

$$P = Q - 5.$$

To obtain the new equilibrium quantity, set the new supply curve equal to the demand curve:

$$Q - 5 = 10 - Q, \text{ or } Q = 7.5.$$

The buyer pays $P = \$2.50$, and the seller receives that price plus the subsidy, i.e., \$3.50. With quantity of 7,500 and a subsidy of \$1.00, the total cost of the subsidy to the government will be \$7,500.

3. Japanese rice producers have extremely high production costs, in part due to the high opportunity cost of land and to their inability to take advantage of economies of large-scale production. Analyze two policies intended to maintain Japanese rice production: (1) a per-pound subsidy to farmers for each pound of rice produced, or (2) a per-pound tariff on imported rice. Illustrate with supply-and-demand diagrams the equilibrium price and quantity, domestic rice production, government revenue or deficit, and deadweight loss from each policy. Which policy is the Japanese government likely to prefer? Which policy are Japanese farmers likely to prefer?

Figure 9.3.a shows the gains and losses from a per-pound subsidy with domestic supply, S, and domestic demand, D. P_S is the subsidized price, P_B is the price paid by the buyers, and P_{EQ} is the equilibrium price without the subsidy, assuming no imports. With the subsidy, buyers demand Q_1. Farmers gain amounts equivalent to areas A and B. This is the increase in producer surplus. Consumers gain areas C and F. This is the increase in consumer surplus. Deadweight loss is equal to the area E. The government pays a subsidy equal to areas $A + B + C + F + E$.

Figure 9.3.b shows the gains and losses from a per-pound tariff. P_W is the world price, and P_{EQ} is the equilibrium price. With the tariff, assumed to be equal to $P_{EQ} - P_W$, buyers demand Q_T, farmers supply Q_D, and $Q_T - Q_D$ is imported. Farmers gain a surplus equivalent to area A. Consumers lose areas A, B, C; this is the decrease in consumer surplus. Deadweight loss is equal to the areas B and C.

Figure 9.3.a

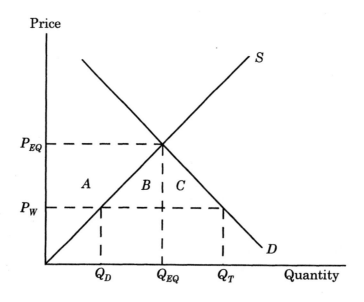

Figure 9.3.b

Without more information regarding the size of the subsidy and the tariff, and the specific equations for supply and demand, it seems sensible to assume that the Japanese government would avoid paying subsidies by choosing a tariff, but the rice farmers would prefer the subsidy.

4. In 1983, the Reagan Administration introduced a new agricultural program called the Payment-in-Kind Program. To see how the program worked, let's consider the wheat market.

a.   Suppose the demand function is $Q^D = 28 - 2P$ and the supply function is $Q^S = 4 + 4P$, where P is the price of wheat in dollars per bushel and Q is the quantity in billions of bushels. Find the free-market equilibrium price and quantity.

Equating demand and supply, $Q^D = Q^S$,

$$28 - 2P = 4 + 4P, \text{ or } P = 4.$$

To determine the equilibrium quantity, substitute $P = 4$ into either the supply equation or the demand equation:

$$Q^S = 4 + 4(4) = 20$$

and

$$Q^D = 28 - 2(4) = 20.$$

b.   **Now suppose the government wants to lower the supply of wheat by 25 percent from the free-market equilibrium by paying farmers to withdraw land from production. However, the payment is made in wheat rather than in dollars—hence the name of the program. The wheat comes from the government's vast reserves that resulted from previous price-support programs. The amount of wheat paid is equal to the amount that could have been harvested on the land withdrawn from production. Farmers are free to sell this wheat on the market. How much is now produced by farmers? How much is indirectly supplied to the market by the government? What is the new market price? How much do the farmers gain? Do consumers gain or lose?**

Because the free market supply by farmers is 20 billion bushels, the 25 percent reduction required by the new Payment-In-Kind (PIK) Program would imply that the farmers now produce 15 billion bushels. To encourage farmers to withdraw their land from cultivation, the government must give them 5 billion bushels, which they sell on the market.

Because the total supply to the market is still 20 billion bushels, the market price does not change; it remains at $4 per bushel. The farmers gain $20 billion, equal to ($4)(5 billion bushels), from the PIK Program, because they incur no costs in supplying the wheat (which they received from the government) to the market. The PIK program does not affect consumers in the wheat market, because they purchase the same amount at the same price as they did in the free market case.

c.   **Had the government not given the wheat back to the farmers, it would have stored or destroyed it. Do taxpayers gain from the program? What potential problems does the program create?**

Taxpayers gain because the government is not required to store the wheat. Although everyone seems to gain from the PIK program, it can only last while there are government wheat reserves. The PIK program assumes that the land removed from production may be restored to production when stockpiles are exhausted. If this cannot be done, consumers may eventually pay more for wheat-based products.

5.   **About 100 million pounds of jelly beans are consumed in the United States each year, and the price has been about 50 cents per pound. However, jelly bean producers feel that their incomes are too low, and they have convinced the government that price supports are in order. The government will therefore buy up as many jelly beans as necessary to keep the price at $1 per pound. However, government economists are worried about the impact of this program, because they have no estimates of the elasticities of jelly bean demand or supply.**

a.   **Could this program cost the government *more* than $50 million per year? Under what conditions? Could it cost *less* than $50 million per year? Under what conditions? Illustrate with a diagram.**

If the quantities demanded and supplied are very responsive to price changes, then a government program that doubles the price of jelly beans could easily cost more than $50 million. In this case, the change in price will cause a large change in quantity supplied, and a large change in quantity demanded. In Figure 9.5.a.i, the cost of the program is $(Q_S - Q_D)*\$1$. Given $Q_S - Q_D$ is larger than 50 million, then the government will pay more than 50 million dollars. If instead supply and demand were relatively price inelastic, then the change in price would result in very small changes in quantity supplied and quantity demanded and (Q$_S$-Q$_D$) would be less than $50 million, as illustrated in figure 9.5.a.ii.

b.   **Could this program cost consumers (in terms of lost consumer surplus) *more* than $50 million per year? Under what conditions? Could it cost consumers *less* than $50 million per year? Under what conditions? Again, use a diagram to illustrate.**

When the demand curve is perfectly inelastic, the loss in consumer surplus is $50 million, equal to ($0.5)(100 million pounds). This represents the highest possible loss in consumer surplus. If the demand curve has any elasticity at all, the loss in consumer surplus would be less then $50 million. In Figure 9.5.b, the loss in consumer surplus is area A plus area B if the demand curve is D and only area A if the demand curve is D'.

Figure 9.5.a.i

Figure 9.5.a.ii

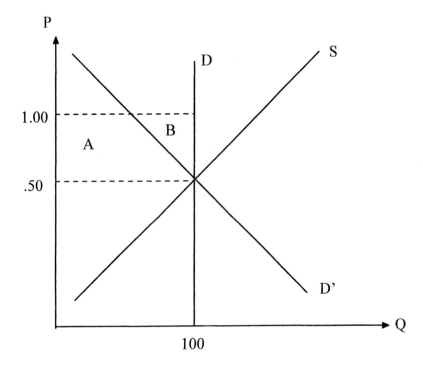

Figure 9.5.b

6. In Exercise 4 of Chapter 2, we examined a vegetable fiber traded in a competitive world market and imported into the United States at a world price of $9 per pound. U.S. domestic supply and demand for various price levels are shown in the following table.

Price	U.S. Supply (million pounds)	U.S. Demand (million pounds)
3	2	34
6	4	28
9	6	22
12	8	16
15	10	10
18	12	4

Answer the following about the U.S. market:

a. **Confirm that the demand curve is given by $Q_D = 40 - 2P$, and that the supply curve is given by $Q_S = \frac{2}{3}P$.**

To find the equation for demand, we need to find a linear function $Q_D = a + bP$ such that the line it represents passes through two of the points in the table such as (15,10) and (12,16). First, the slope, b, is equal to the "rise" divided by the "run,"

$$\frac{\Delta Q}{\Delta P} = \frac{10 - 16}{15 - 12} = -2 = b.$$

Second, we substitute for b and one point, e.g., (15, 10), into our linear function to solve for the constant, a:

$$10 = a - 2(15), \text{ or } a = 40.$$

Therefore, $Q_D = 40 - 2P$.

Similarly, we may solve for the supply equation $Q_S = c + dP$ passing through two points such as (6,4) and (3,2). The slope, d, is

$$\frac{\Delta Q}{\Delta P} = \frac{4 - 2}{6 - 3} = \frac{2}{3}..$$

Solving for c:

$$4 = c + \left(\frac{2}{3}\right)(6), \text{ or } c = 0.$$

Therefore, $Q_S = \left(\frac{2}{3}\right)P$.

b. **Confirm that if there were no restrictions on trade, the U.S. would import 16 million pounds.**

If there are no trade restrictions, the world price of $9.00 will prevail in the U.S. From the table, we see that at $9.00 domestic supply will be 6 million pounds. Similarly, domestic demand will be 22 million pounds. Imports will provide the difference between domestic demand and domestic supply: 22 - 6 = 16 million pounds.

c. **If the United States imposes a tariff of $3 per pound, what will be the U.S. price and level of imports? How much revenue will the government earn from the tariff? How large is the deadweight loss?**

With a $3.00 tariff, the U.S. price will be $12 (the world price plus the tariff). At this price, demand is 16 million pounds and supply is 8 million pounds, so imports are 8 million pounds (16-8). The government will collect $3*8=$24 million. The deadweight loss is equal to

$$0.5(12\text{-}9)(8\text{-}6)+0.5(12\text{-}9)(22\text{-}16)=\$12 \text{ million.}$$

d. **If the United States has no tariff but imposes an import quota of 8 million pounds, what will be the U.S. domestic price? What is the cost of this quota for U.S. consumers of the fiber? What is the gain for U.S. producers?**

With an import quota of 8 million pounds, the domestic price will be $12. At $12, the difference between domestic demand and domestic supply is 8 million pounds, i.e., 16 million pounds minus 8 million pounds. Note you can also find the equilibrium price by setting demand equal to supply plus the quota so that

$$40 - 2P = \frac{2}{3}P + 8.$$

The cost of the quota to consumers is equal to area A+B+C+D in Figure 9.6.d, which is

$$(12 - 9)(16) + (0.5)(12 - 9)(22 - 16) = \$57 \text{ million.}$$

The gain to domestic producers is equal to area A in Figure 9.6.d, which is

$$(12 - 9)(6) + (0.5)(8 - 6)(12 - 9) = \$21 \text{ million.}$$

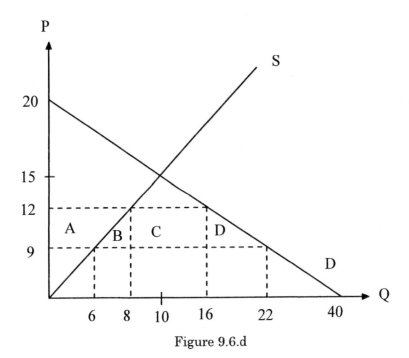

Figure 9.6.d

7. The United States currently imports all of its coffee. The annual demand for coffee by U.S. consumers is given by the demand curve Q = 250 – 10P, where Q is quantity (in millions of pounds) and P is the market price per pound of coffee. World producers can harvest and ship coffee to US distributors at a constant marginal (= average) cost of $8 per pound. U.S. distributors can in turn distribute coffee for a constant $2 per pound. The U.S. coffee market is competitive. Congress is considering imposing a tariff on coffee imports of $2 per pound.

a. If there is no tariff, how much do consumers pay for a pound of coffee? What is the quantity demanded?

If there is no tariff then consumers will pay $10 per pound of coffee, which is found by adding the $8 that it costs to import the coffee plus the $2 that is costs to distribute the coffee in the U.S., per pound. In a competitive market, price is equal to marginal cost. If the price is $10, then demand is 150 million pounds.

b. If the tariff is imposed, how much will consumers pay for a pound of coffee? What is the quantity demanded?

Now we must add $2 per pound to marginal cost, so price will be $12 per pound and demand is Q=250-10(12)=130 million pounds.

b. Calculate the lost consumer surplus.

The lost consumer surplus is (12-10)(130)+0.5(12-10)(150-130)=$280 million.

d. Calculate the tax revenue collected by the government.

The tax revenue is equal to the tax of $2 per pound times the number of pounds imported, which is 130 million pounds. Tax revenue is therefore $260 million.

e. Does the tariff result in a net gain or a net loss to society as a whole?

There is a net loss to society because the gain ($260 million) is less than the loss ($280 million).

8. A particular metal is traded in a highly competitive world market at a world price of $9 per ounce. Unlimited quantities are available for import into the United States at this price. The supply of this metal from domestic U.S. mines and mills can be represented by the equation Q^S = 2/3P, where Q^S is U.S. output in million ounces and P is the domestic price. The demand for the metal in the United States is Q^D = 40 - 2P, where Q^D is the domestic demand in million ounces.

In recent years, the U.S. industry has been protected by a tariff of $9 per ounce. Under pressure from other foreign governments, the United States plans to reduce this tariff to zero. Threatened by this change, the U.S. industry is seeking a Voluntary Restraint Agreement that would limit imports into the United States to 8 million ounces per year.

a. Under the $9 tariff, what was the U.S. domestic price of the metal?

With a $9 tariff, the price of the imported metal on U.S. markets would be $18, the tariff plus the world price of $9. To determine the domestic equilibrium price, equate domestic supply and domestic demand:

$$\frac{2}{3}P = 40 \text{ - } 2P, \text{ or } P = \$15.$$

The equilibrium quantity is found by substituting a price of $15 into either the demand or supply equations:

$$Q^D = 40 - (2)(15) = 10$$

and

$$Q^S = \left(\frac{2}{3}\right)(15) = 10.$$

The equilibrium quantity is 10 million ounces. Because the domestic price of $15 is less than the world price plus the tariff, $18, there will be no imports.

b. **If the United States eliminates the tariff and the Voluntary Restraint Agreement is approved, what will be the U.S. domestic price of the metal?**

With the Voluntary Restraint Agreement, the difference between domestic supply and domestic demand would be limited to 8 million ounces, i.e. Q^D - Q^S = 8. To determine the domestic price of the metal, set Q^D - Q^S = 8 and solve for P:

$$(40 - 2P) - \frac{2}{3}P = 8, \text{ or } P = \$12.$$

At a price of $12, Q^D = 16 and Q^S = 8; the difference of 8 million ounces will be supplied by imports.

9. Among the tax proposals regularly considered by Congress is an additional tax on distilled liquors. The tax would not apply to beer. The price elasticity of supply of liquor is 4.0, and the price elasticity of demand is -0.2. The cross-elasticity of demand for beer with respect to the price of liquor is 0.1.

a. **If the new tax is imposed, who will bear the greater burden, liquor suppliers or liquor consumers? Why?**

Section 9.6 in the text provides a formula for the "pass-through" fraction, i.e., the fraction of the tax borne by the consumer. This fraction is $\dfrac{E_S}{E_S - E_D}$, where E_S is the own-price elasticity of supply and E_D is the own-price elasticity of demand. Substituting for E_S and E_D, the pass-through fraction is

$$\frac{4}{4 - (-0.2)} = \frac{4}{4.2} \approx 0.95.$$

Therefore, 95 percent of the tax is passed through to the consumers because supply is relatively elastic and demand is relatively inelastic.

b. **Assuming that beer supply is infinitely elastic, how will the new tax affect the beer market?**

With an increase in the price of liquor (from the large pass-through of the liquor tax), some consumers will substitute away from liquor to beer, shifting the demand curve for beer outward. With an infinitely elastic supply for beer (a perfectly flat supply curve), there will be no change in the equilibrium price of beer.

10. In Example 9.1, we calculated the gains and losses from price controls on natural gas and found that there was a deadweight loss of $1.4 billion. This calculation was based on a price of oil of $8 per barrel. If the price of oil were $12 per barrel, what would the free market price of gas be? How large a deadweight loss would result if the maximum allowable price of natural gas were $1.00 per thousand cubic feet?

From Example 9.1, we know that the supply and demand curves for natural gas in the 1970s can be approximated as follows:

$$Q_S = 14 + 2P_G + 0.25P_O$$

and

$$Q_D = -5P_G + 3.75P_O,$$

where P_G is the price of gas and P_O is the price of oil.

With the price of oil at $12 per barrel, these curves become,

$$Q_S = 17 + 2P_G$$

and

$$Q_D = 45 - 5P_G.$$

Setting quantity demanded equal to quantity supplied,

$$17 + 2P_G = 45 - 5P_G, \text{ or } P_G = \$4.$$

At this price, the equilibrium quantity is 25 thousand cubic feet (Tcf).

If a ceiling of $1 is imposed, producers would supply 19 Tcf and consumers would demand 40 Tcf. The deadweight loss is the area below the demand curve and above the supply curve, between the quantities of 19 and 25 Tcf. This can be computed as

$$0.5(5.2\text{-}4)(25\text{-}19)+0.5(4\text{-}1)(25\text{-}19)=\$12.6 \text{ billion.}$$

11. Example 9.5 describes the effects of the sugar quota. In 2001, imports were limited to 3 billion pounds, which pushed the domestic price to 21.5 cents per pound. Suppose imports were expanded to 6.5 billion pounds.

a. What would be the new U.S. domestic price?

We are given the equations for the total market demand for sugar in the U.S. and the supply of U.S. producers:

$$Q_D = 26.53 - .285P$$

$$Q_S = -8.70 + 1.214P.$$

The difference between the quantity demanded and supplied, Q_D-Q_S, is the amount of sugar imported that is restricted by the quota. If the quota is increased from 3 billion pounds to 6.5 billion pounds, then we will have $Q_D - Q_S = 6.5$ and we can solve for P:

$$(26.53\text{-}.285P)\text{-}(\text{-}8.70+1.214P)=6.5$$

$$35.23\text{-}1.499P=6.5$$

$$P=19.2 \text{ cents per pound.}$$

At a price of 19.2 cents per pound $Q_S = -8.70 + (1.214)(19.2) = 14.6$ billion pounds and $Q_D = Q_S + 6.5 = 21.1$ billion pounds.

b. **How much would consumers gain and domestic producers lose?**

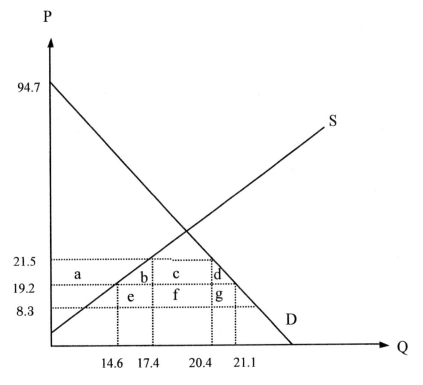

Figure 9.11.b

The gain in consumer surplus is area a+b+c+d in Figure 9.11.b. The loss to domestic producers is equal to area a.

Numerically:

a = (21.5-19.2)(14.6)+(17.4-14.6)(21.5-19.2)(.5)=36.8

b = (17.4-14.6)(21.5-19.2)(.5)=3.22

c = (21.5-19.2)(20.4-17.4)=6.9

d = (21.5-19.2)(21.1-20.5)(.5)=0.69.

These numbers are in billions of cents or tens of millions of dollars.

Thus, consumer surplus increases by \$476.1 million, while domestic producer surplus decreases by \$368 million.

c. **What would be the effect on deadweight loss and foreign producers?**

When the quota was 3 billion pounds, the profit earned by foreign producers is the difference between the domestic price and the world price (21.5-8.3) times the 3 billion units sold, for a total of 39.6, or \$396 million. When the quota is increased to 6.5 billion pounds, domestic price will fall to 19.2 cents per pound and profit earned by foreigners will be (19.2-8.3)*6.5=70.85, or \$708.5 million. Profit earned by foreigners therefore increased by \$312.5 million. On the graph above, this is area (e+f+g)-(c+f)=e+g-c. The deadweight loss of the quota decreases by area b+e+d+g, which is equal to \$420.6 million.

12. The domestic supply and demand curves for hula beans are as follows:

   Supply: P = 50 + Q   Demand: P = 200 - 2Q

where P is the price in cents per pound and Q is the quantity in millions of pounds. The U.S. is a small producer in the world hula bean market, where the current price (which will not be affected by anything we do) is 60 cents per pound. Congress is considering a tariff of 40 cents per pound. Find the domestic price of hula beans that will result if the tariff is imposed. Also compute the dollar gain or loss to domestic consumers, domestic producers, and government revenue from the tariff.

To analyze the influence of a tariff on the domestic hula bean market, start by solving for domestic equilibrium price and quantity. First, equate supply and demand to determine equilibrium quantity:

$$50 + Q = 200 - 2Q, \text{ or } Q_{EQ} = 50.$$

Thus, the equilibrium quantity is 50 million pounds. Substituting Q_{EQ} equals 50 into either the supply or demand equation to determine price, we find:

$$P_S = 50 + 50 = 100 \text{ and } P_D = 200 - (2)(50) = 100.$$

The equilibrium price P is \$1 (100 cents). However, the world market price is 60 cents. At this price, the domestic quantity supplied is $60 = 50 - Q_S$, or $Q_S = 10$, and similarly, domestic demand at the world price is $60 = 200 - 2Q_D$, or $Q_D = 70$. Imports are equal to the difference between domestic demand and supply, or 60 million pounds. If Congress imposes a tariff of 40 cents, the effective price of imports increases to \$1. At \$1, domestic producers satisfy domestic demand and imports fall to zero.

As shown in Figure 9.12, consumer surplus before the imposition of the tariff is equal to area a+b+c, or (0.5)(200 - 60)(70) = 4,900 million cents or \$49 million. After the tariff, the price rises to \$1.00 and consumer surplus falls to area a, or

(0.5)(200 - 100)(50) = \$25 million, a loss of \$24 million. Producer surplus will increase by area b, or (100-60)(10)+(.5)(100-60)(50-10)=\$12 million.

Finally, because domestic production is equal to domestic demand at \$1, no hula beans are imported and the government receives no revenue. The difference between the loss of consumer surplus and the increase in producer surplus is deadweight loss, which in this case is equal to \$12 million. See Figure 9.12.

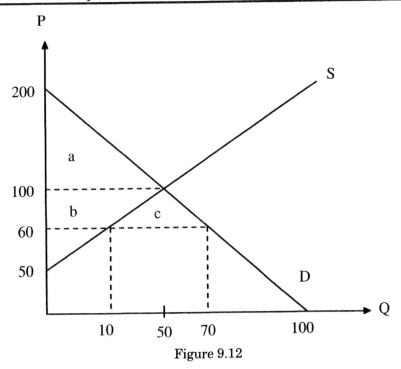

Figure 9.12

13. Currently, the social security payroll tax in the United States is evenly divided between employers and employees. Employers must pay the government a tax of 6.2 percent of the wages they pay, and employees must pay 6.2 percent of the wages they receive. Suppose the tax was changed so that employers paid the full 12.4 percent and employees paid nothing. Would employees then be better off?

If the labor market is competitive, that is, both employers and employees take the wage as given, then shifting an equal tax amount from the employee to the employer will have no effect on the amount of labor employed and on the wage kept by the employee after taxes. The equilibrium amount of labor employed is determined by the total amount of tax paid by both employees and employers. This is represented by the difference between the wage paid by the employer and the wage received by the employee. As long as the total tax doesn't change, the same amount of labor is employed and the wages paid by the employer and received by the employee (after tax) will not change. Hence, employees would be no better or worse off if the employers paid the full amount of the social security tax.

14. You know that if a tax is imposed on a particular product, the burden of the tax is shared by producers and consumers. You also know that the demand for automobiles is characterized by a stock adjustment process. Suppose a special 20 percent sales tax is suddenly imposed on automobiles. Will the share of the tax paid by consumers rise, fall, or stay the same over time? Explain briefly. Repeat for a 50-cents-per-gallon gasoline tax.

For products with demand characterized by a stock adjustment process, the short-run demand curve is more elastic than the long-run demand curve because consumers can delay their purchases of these goods in the short run. For example, when price rises, consumers may continue using the older version of the product, which they currently own. However, in the long run, a new product will be purchased. Thus, the long-run demand curve is more inelastic than the short-run one.

Consider the effect of imposing a 20 percent sales tax on automobiles in the short and long run. To analyze the influence of the tax, we can shift the demand curves because consumers are forced to pay a higher price. Notice that this tax is an ad valorem tax. The demand curve does not shift parallel to the old one, but pivots to reflect the higher tax paid per unit at higher prices.

The burden of the tax shifts from producers to consumers as we move from the short run (Figure 9.15.a) to the long run (Figure 9.15.b). In these figures, P_O is the

133

consumer's price, P_S is the producer's price, and P_O - P_S is the value of the tax. Intuitively, we may assume consumers have a more inelastic demand curve in the long run. They are less able to adjust their demand to price changes and must carry a larger burden of the tax. In both figures, the supply curve is the same in the long and short run. If the supply curve is more elastic in the long run, then even more of the tax burden is shifted to consumers.

Unlike the automobile market, the gasoline demand curve is not characterized by a stock adjustment effect. The long-run demand curve will be more elastic than the short-run one, because in the long run substitutes (e.g., gasohol or propane) will become available for gasoline. We may analyze the effect of the tax on gasoline in the same manner as the tax on automobiles. However, the gasoline tax is a per unit or specific tax, so the demand curves exhibit a parallel shift.

In Figures 9.15.c and 9.15.d, the tax burden shifts from consumers to producers as we move from the short to the long run. Now the elasticity of demand increases from the short run to the long run (the usual case), resulting in less gasoline consumption. Also, if the supply curve is more elastic in the long run, some of the burden would again be shifted back to consumers. Note that we have drawn demand curve shifts in both cases, assuming the consumers pay the tax. The same results may be obtained by shifting the supply curve, assuming the firms pay the tax.

Figure 9.14.a: Short Run

Figure 9.14.b: Long Run

Figure 9.14.c: Short Run

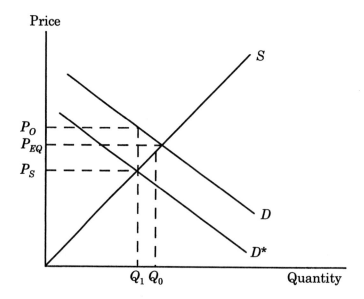

Figure 9.14.d: Long Run

15. In 1998, Americans smoked 23.5 billion packs of cigarettes. They paid an average retail price of $2 per pack.

a. **Given that the elasticity of supply is 0.5 and the elasticity of demand is -0.4, derive linear demand and supply curves for cigarettes.**

Let the demand curve be of the general form Q=a+bP and the supply curve be of the general form Q=c+dP, where a, b, c, and d are the constants that you have to find from the information given above. To begin, recall the formula for the price elasticity of demand

$$E_P^D = \frac{P}{Q}\frac{\Delta Q}{\Delta P}.$$

You are given information about the value of the elasticity, P, and Q, which means that you can solve for the slope, which is b in the above formula for the demand curve.

$$-0.4 = \frac{2}{23.5}\frac{\Delta Q}{\Delta P}$$

$$\frac{\Delta Q}{\Delta P} = -0.4\left(\frac{23.5}{2}\right) = -4.7 = b.$$

To find the constant a, substitute for Q, P, and b into the above formula so that 23.5=a-4.7*2 and a=32.9. The equation for demand is therefore Q=32.9-4.7P. To find the supply curve, recall the formula for the elasticity of supply and follow the same method as above:

$$E_P^S = \frac{P}{Q}\frac{\Delta Q}{\Delta P}$$

$$0.5 = \frac{2}{23.5}\frac{\Delta Q}{\Delta P}$$

$$\frac{\Delta Q}{\Delta P} = 0.5\left(\frac{23.5}{2}\right) = 5.875 = d.$$

To find the constant c, substitute for Q, P, and d into the above formula so that 23.5=c+5.875*2 and c=11.75. The equation for supply is therefore Q=11.75+5.875P.

b. **In November 1998, after settling a lawsuit filed by 46 states, the three major tobacco companies raised the retail price of a pack of cigarettes by 45 cents. What is the new equilibrium price and quantity? How many fewer packs of cigarettes are sold?**

The new price of cigarettes would be $2.45. Plugging $2.45 into the demand curve results in a quantity demanded of 21.39 billion packs, which represents a decrease of 2.11 billion packs of cigarettes. Note that you could also use the formula for elasticity to come up with the answer:

$$\varepsilon_p^D = \frac{\%\Delta Q}{\%\Delta P} = \frac{\%\Delta Q}{22.5\%} \Rightarrow \%\Delta Q = 9\%.$$

The new quantity demanded is then 23.5*.91=21.39 billion packs.

c. **Cigarettes are subject to a Federal tax, which was about 25 cents per pack in 1998. This tax will increase by 15 cents in 2002. What will this increase do to the market-clearing price and quantity?**

The tax of 15 cents will shift the supply curve up by 15 cents. To find the new supply curve, first rewrite the equation for the supply curve as a function of Q instead of P:

$$Q_S = 11.75 + 5.875P \Rightarrow P = \frac{Q_S}{5.875} - \frac{11.75}{5.875}.$$

The new supply curve is now

$$P = \frac{Q_S}{5.875} - \frac{11.75}{5.875} + .15 = 0.17Q_S - 1.85.$$

To equate the new supply with the equation for demand, first rewrite demand as a function of Q instead of P:

$$Q_D = 32.9 - 4.7P \Rightarrow P = 7 - .21Q_D.$$

Now equate supply and demand and solve for the equilibrium quantity:
$$0.17Q - 1.85 = 7 - .21Q \Rightarrow Q = 23.29.$$
Plugging the equilibrium quantity into the equation for demand gives a market price of $2.11.
Note that we assume that part c is independent of part b. If we incorporate information from part b, the supply curve in part c is 60 cents (45+15) higher vertically than the supply curve from part a.

d. **How much of the Federal tax will consumers pay? What part will producers pay?**

Since the price went up by 11 cents, consumers pay 11 of the 15 cents or 73% of the tax, and producers will pay the remaining 27% or 4 cents.

PART III
MARKET STRUCTURE AND COMPETITVE STRATEGY
CHAPTER 10
MARKET POWER: MONOPOLY AND MONOPSONY

TEACHING NOTES

This chapter covers both monopoly and monopsony in order to highlight the similarity between the two types of market power. The chapter begins with a discussion of monopoly in sections 1-4. Section 5 first discusses monopsony, and then offers an instructive comparison of monopoly and monopsony. Section 6 discusses sources of monopsony power and the social costs of monopsony power, while section 7 concludes with a discussion of antitrust law. If you are pressed for time you might choose to only cover the first four sections on monopoly and skip the remainder of the chapter. Section 7 can be covered even if you choose to skip sections 5 and 6. The last part of section 1 on the multiplant firm can also be skipped if you are pressed for time.

Although chapter 8 presented the general rule for profit maximization, you should review marginal revenue and price elasticity of demand through a careful derivation of Equation 10.1. A discussion of the derivation of Equation 10.1 will elucidate the geometry of Figure 10.3. Point out that because marginal revenue is positive at the profit maximizing level of price and quantity for a monopolist, demand at that quantity is elastic. Equation 10.1 also leads directly to the Lerner Index in Section 10.2. This provides fruitful ground for a discussion of a monopolist's market power. For example, if E_d is large (e.g., because of close substitutes), then (1) the demand curve is relatively flat, (2) the marginal revenue curve is relatively flat (although steeper than the demand curve), and (3) the monopolist has little power to raise price above marginal cost. To reinforce these points, introduce a non-linear demand curve by, for example, showing the location of the marginal revenue curve for a unit-elastic demand curve. Once this concept has been clearly presented, the discussion of the effect of an excise tax on a monopolist with non-linear demand (Figure 10.5) will not seem out of place.

The social costs of market power are a good topic for class discussion, and this topic can be introduced by comparing the deadweight loss associated with monopoly with the analysis of market intervention given in Chapter 9. For example, compare Figure 10.10 with Figure 9.5. Given that Exercises (9), (13), and (15) involve "kinked marginal revenue curves," you should present Figure 10.11 if you plan to assign those problems. Although Figure 10.11 is complicated, exposure to it here will help when it reappears in Chapter 12.

REVIEW QUESTIONS

1. A monopolist is producing at a point at which marginal cost exceeds marginal revenue. How should it adjust its output to increase profit?

When marginal cost is greater than marginal revenue, the incremental cost of the last unit produced is greater than incremental revenue. The firm would increase its profit by not producing the last unit. It should continue to reduce production, thereby decreasing marginal cost and increasing marginal revenue, until marginal cost is equal to marginal revenue.

2. We write the percentage markup of prices over marginal cost as (P - MC)/P. For a profit-maximizing monopolist, how does this markup depend on the elasticity of demand? Why can this markup be viewed as a measure of monopoly power?

We can show that this measure of market power is equal to the negative inverse of the price elasticity of demand.

$$\frac{P-MC}{P} = -\frac{1}{E_D}$$

138

The equation implies that, as the elasticity increases (demand becomes more elastic), the inverse of elasticity decreases and the measure of market power decreases. Therefore, as elasticity increases (decreases), the firm has less (more) power to increase price above marginal cost.

3. Why is there no market supply curve under conditions of monopoly?

The monopolist's output decision depends not only on marginal cost, but also on the demand curve. Shifts in demand do not trace out a series of prices and quantities that we can identify as the supply curve for the firm. Instead, shifts in demand lead to changes in price, output, or both. Thus, there is no one-to-one correspondence between the price and the seller's quantity; therefore, a monopolized market lacks a supply curve.

4. Why might a firm have monopoly power even if it is not the only producer in the market?

The degree of monopoly (or market) power enjoyed by a firm depends on the elasticity of the demand curve that it faces. As the elasticity of demand increases, i.e., as the demand curve becomes flatter, the inverse of the elasticity approaches zero and the monopoly power of the firm decreases. Thus, if the firm's demand curve has any elasticity less than infinity, the firm has some monopoly power. It is only the competitive firm that faces a horizontal demand curve who has no market power.

5. What are some of the different types of barriers to entry that give rise to monopoly power? Give an example of each.

The firm's ability to exercise monopoly power depends on how easy it is for other firms to enter the industry. There are several barriers to entry, including exclusive rights (e.g., patents, copyrights, and licenses) and economies of scale. These two barriers to entry are the most common. Exclusive rights are legally granted property rights to produce or distribute a good or service. Positive economies of scale lead to "natural monopolies" because the largest producer can charge a lower price, driving competition from the market. For example, in the production of aluminum, there is evidence to suggest that there are scale economies in the conversion of bauxite to alumina. (See *U.S. v. Aluminum Company of America*, 148 F.2d 416 [1945], discussed in Exercise 8, below.)

6. What factors determine the amount of monopoly power an individual firm is likely to have? Explain each one briefly.

Three factors determine the firm's elasticity of demand: (1) the elasticity of market demand, (2) the number of firms in the market, and (3) interaction among the firms in the market. The elasticity of market demand depends on the uniqueness of the product, i.e., how easy it is for consumers to substitute away from the product. As the number of firms in the market increases, the demand elasticity facing each firm increases because customers may shift to the firm's competitors. The number of firms in the market is determined by how easy it is to enter the industry (the height of barriers to entry). Finally, the ability to raise the price above marginal cost depends on how other firms react to the firm's price changes. If other firms match price changes, customers will have little incentive to switch to another supplier. .

7. Why is there a social cost to monopoly power? If the gains to producers from monopoly power could be redistributed to consumers, would the social cost of monopoly power be eliminated? Explain briefly.

When the firm exploits its monopoly power by charging a price above marginal cost, consumers buy less at the higher price. Consumers enjoy less surplus, the difference between the price they are willing to pay and the market price on each unit consumed. Some of the lost consumer surplus is not captured by the seller and is a deadweight loss to society. Therefore, if the gains to producers were redistributed to consumers, society would still suffer the deadweight loss.

8. Why will a monopolist's output increase if the government forces it to lower its price? If the government wants to set a price ceiling that maximizes the monopolist's output, what price should it set?

By restricting price to be below the monopolist's profit-maximizing price, the government can change the shape of the firm's marginal revenue, *MR*, curve. When a price ceiling is imposed, *MR* is equal to the price ceiling for all quantities lower than the quantity demanded at the price ceiling. If the government wants to maximize output, it should set a price equal to marginal cost, or in other words set price at the point where the demand curve and the marginal cost curve intersect. Prices below this level induce the firm to decrease production, assuming the marginal cost curve is upward sloping. The regulator's problem is to determine the shape of the monopolist's marginal cost curve. This task is difficult given the monopolist's incentive to hide or distort this information.

9. How should a monopsonist decide how much of a product to buy? Will it buy more or less than a competitive buyer? Explain briefly.

The marginal expenditure is the change in the total expenditure as the purchased quantity changes. For a firm competing with many firms for inputs, the marginal expenditure is equal to the average expenditure (price). For a monopsonist, the marginal expenditure curve lies above the average expenditure curve because the decision to buy an extra unit raises the price that must be paid for all units, including the last unit. All firms should buy inputs so that the marginal value of the last unit is equal to the marginal expenditure on that unit. This is true for both the competitive buyer and the monopsonist. However, because the monopsonist's marginal expenditure curve lies above the average expenditure curve and because the marginal value curve is downward sloping, the monopsonist buys less than a firm would buy in a competitive market.

10. What is meant by the term "monopsony power"? Why might a firm have monopsony power even if it is not the only buyer in the market?

Monopsony power refers to the buyer's ability to affect the price of a good. This power enables the buyer to purchase the good for a lower price, as compared to a competitive factor market. Any buyer facing an upward-sloping factor supply curve has some monopsony power. In a competitive market, the seller faces a perfectly-elastic market demand curve and the buyer faces a perfectly-elastic market supply curve. Thus, any characteristic of the market (e.g., when there are a small number of buyers or if buyers engage in collusive behavior) that leads to a less-than-perfectly-elastic supply curve gives the buyer some monopsony power.

11. What are some sources of monopsony power? What determines the amount of monopsony power an individual firm is likely to have?

The individual firm's monopsony power depends on the characteristics of the "buying-side" of the market. There are three characteristics that enhance monopsony power: (1) the elasticity of market supply, (2) the number of buyers, and (3) how the buyers interact. First, if market supply is very inelastic, then the buyer will enjoy more monopsony power. When supply is very elastic, marginal expenditure and average expenditure do not differ by much, so price will be closer to the competitive price. Second, the fewer the number of buyers, the greater the monopsony power. Third, if buyers are able to collude and/or they do not compete very aggressively with each other then each will enjoy more monopsony power.

12. Why is there a social cost to monopsony power? If the gains to buyers from monopsony power could be redistributed to sellers, would the social cost of monopsony power be eliminated? Explain briefly.

With monopsony power, the price is lower and the quantity is less than under competitive buying conditions. Because of the lower price and reduced sales, sellers lose revenue. Only part of this lost revenue is transferred to the buyer as consumer surplus, and the net loss in total surplus is deadweight loss. Even if the consumer surplus could be redistributed to sellers, the deadweight loss persists. This inefficiency will remain because quantity is reduced below the level where price is equal to marginal cost.

13. How do the antitrust laws limit market power in the United States? Give examples of major provisions of the laws.

Antitrust laws, which are subject to interpretation by the courts, limit market power by proscribing a firm's behavior in attempting to maximize profit. Section 1 of the Sherman Act prohibits *every* restraint of trade, including any attempt to fix prices by buyers or sellers. Section 2 of the Sherman Act prohibits behavior that leads to monopolization. The Clayton Act, with the Robinson-Patman Act, prohibits price discrimination and exclusive dealing (sellers prohibiting buyers from buying goods from other sellers). The Clayton Act also limits mergers when they could substantially lessen competition. The Federal Trade Commission Act makes it illegal to use unfair or deceptive practices.

14. Explain briefly how the U.S. antitrust laws are actually enforced.

Antitrust laws are enforced in three ways: (1) through the Antitrust Division of the Justice Department, whenever firms violate federal statutes, (2) through the Federal Trade Commission, whenever firms violate the Federal Trade Commission Act, and (3) through civil suits. The Justice Department can seek to impose fines or jail terms on managers or owners involved or seek to reorganize the firm, as it did in its case against A.T.& T. The FTC can seek a voluntary understanding to comply with the law or a formal Commission order. Individuals or companies can sue in federal court for awards equal to three times the damage arising from the anti-competitive behavior.

EXERCISES

1. Will an increase in the demand for a monopolist's product always result in a higher price? Explain. Will an increase in the supply facing a monopsonist buyer always result in a lower price? Explain.

As illustrated in Figure 10.4b in the textbook, an increase in demand need not *always* result in a higher price. Under the conditions portrayed in Figure 10.4b, the monopolist supplies different quantities at the same price. Similarly, an increase in supply facing the monopsonist need not *always* result in a higher price. Suppose the average expenditure curve shifts from AE_1 to AE_2, as illustrated in Figure 10.1. With the shift in the average expenditure curve, the marginal expenditure curve shifts from ME_1 to ME_2. The ME_1 curve intersects the marginal value curve (demand curve) at Q_1, resulting in a price of P. When the AE curve shifts, the ME_2 curve intersects the marginal value curve at Q_2 resulting in the same price at P.

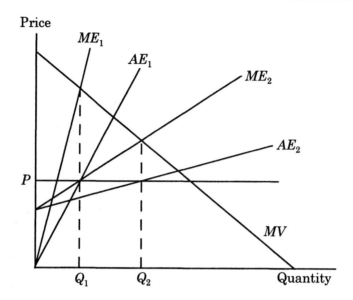

Figure 10.1

2. Caterpillar Tractor, one of the largest producers of farm machinery in the world, has hired you to advise them on pricing policy. One of the things the company would like to know is how much a 5 percent increase in price is likely to reduce sales. What would you need to know to help the company with this problem? Explain why these facts are important.

> As a large producer of farm equipment, Caterpillar Tractor has market power and should consider the entire demand curve when choosing prices for its products. As their advisor, you should focus on the determination of the elasticity of demand for each product. There are three important factors to be considered. First, how similar are the products offered by Caterpillar's competitors? If they are close substitutes, a small increase in price could induce customers to switch to the competition. Secondly, what is the age of the existing stock of tractors? With an older population of tractors, a 5 percent price increase induces a smaller drop in demand. Finally, because farm tractors are a capital input in agricultural production, what is the expected profitability of the agricultural sector? If farm incomes are expected to fall, an increase in tractor prices induces a greater decline in demand than one would estimate with information on only past sales and prices.

3. A monopolist firm faces a demand with constant elasticity of -2.0. It has a constant marginal cost of $20 per unit and sets a price to maximize profit. If marginal cost should increase by 25 percent, would the price charged also rise by 25 percent?

> Yes. The monopolist's pricing rule as a function of the elasticity of demand for its product is:

$$\frac{(P - MC)}{P} = - \frac{1}{E_d}$$

or alternatively,

$$P = \frac{MC}{\left(1 + \left(\dfrac{1}{E_d}\right)\right)}$$

In this example $E_d = -2.0$, so $1/E_d = -1/2$; price should then be set so that:

$$P = \frac{MC}{\left(\frac{1}{2}\right)} = 2MC$$

Therefore, if MC rises by 25 percent, then price will also rise by 25 percent. When MC = \$20, P = \$40. When MC rises to \$20(1.25) = \$25, the price rises to \$50, a 25 percent increase.

4. A firm faces the following average revenue (demand) curve:

$$P = 120 - 0.02Q$$

where Q is weekly production and P is price, measured in cents per unit. The firm's cost function is given by C = 60Q + 25,000. Assume that the firm maximizes profits.

a. **What is the level of production, price, and total profit per week?**

The profit-maximizing output is found by setting marginal revenue equal to marginal cost. Given a linear demand curve in inverse form, $P = 120 - 0.02Q$, we know that the marginal revenue curve will have twice the slope of the demand curve. Thus, the marginal revenue curve for the firm is $MR = 120 - 0.04Q$. Marginal cost is simply the slope of the total cost curve. The slope of $TC = 60Q + 25,000$ is 60, so MC equals 60. Setting $MR = MC$ to determine the profit-maximizing quantity:

$$120 - 0.04Q = 60, \text{ or}$$

$$Q = 1,500.$$

Substituting the profit-maximizing quantity into the inverse demand function to determine the price:

$$P = 120 - (0.02)(1,500) = 90 \text{ cents.}$$

Profit equals total revenue minus total cost:

$$\pi = (90)(1,500) - (25,000 + (60)(1,500)), \text{ or}$$

$$\pi = \$200 \text{ per week.}$$

b. **If the government decides to levy a tax of 14 cents per unit on this product, what will be the new level of production, price, and profit?**

Suppose initially that the consumers must pay the tax to the government. Since the total price (including the tax) consumers would be willing to pay remains unchanged, we know that the demand function is

$$P^* + T = 120 - 0.02Q, \text{ or}$$
$$P^* = 120 - 0.02Q - T,$$

where P^* is the price received by the suppliers. Because the tax increases the price of each unit, total revenue for the monopolist decreases by TQ, and marginal revenue, the revenue on each additional unit, decreases by T:

$$MR = 120 - 0.04Q - T$$

where $T = 14$ cents. To determine the profit-maximizing level of output with the tax, equate marginal revenue with marginal cost:

$$120 - 0.04Q - 14 = 60, \text{ or}$$

$$Q = 1,150 \text{ units.}$$

Substituting Q into the demand function to determine price:

$$P^* = 120 - (0.02)(1,150) - 14 = 83 \text{ cents.}$$

Profit is total revenue minus total cost:

$$\pi = (83)(1{,}150) - ((60)(1{,}150) + 25{,}000) = 1450 \text{ cents, or}$$

$$\$14.50 \text{ per week.}$$

Note: The price facing the consumer after the imposition of the tax is 97 cents. The monopolist receives 83 cents. Therefore, the consumer and the monopolist each pay 7 cents of the tax.

If the monopolist had to pay the tax instead of the consumer, we would arrive at the same result. The monopolist's cost function would then be

$$TC = 60Q + 25{,}000 + TQ = (60 + T)Q + 25{,}000.$$

The slope of the cost function is $(60 + T)$, so $MC = 60 + T$. We set this MC to the marginal revenue function from part (a):

$$120 - 0.04Q = 60 + 14, \text{ or}$$

$$Q = 1{,}150.$$

Thus, it does not matter who sends the tax payment to the government. The burden of the tax is reflected in the price of the good.

5. **The following table shows the demand curve facing a monopolist who produces at a constant marginal cost of \$10.**

Price	Quantity
18	0
16	4
14	8
12	12
10	16
8	20
6	24
4	28
2	32
0	36

a. **Calculate the firm's marginal revenue curve.**

To find the marginal revenue curve, we first derive the inverse demand curve. The intercept of the inverse demand curve on the price axis is 18. The slope of the inverse demand curve is the change in price divided by the change in quantity. For example, a decrease in price from 18 to 16 yields an increase in quantity from 0 to 4. Therefore, the slope is $-\frac{1}{2}$ and the demand curve is

$$P = 18 - 0.5Q.$$

The marginal revenue curve corresponding to a linear demand curve is a line with the same intercept as the inverse demand curve and a slope that is twice as steep. Therefore, the marginal revenue curve is

$$MR = 18 - Q.$$

b.   What are the firm's profit-maximizing output and price? What is its profit?

The monopolist's maximizing output occurs where marginal revenue equals marginal cost. Marginal cost is a constant $10. Setting MR equal to MC to determine the profit-maximizing quantity:

$$18 - Q = 10, \text{ or } Q = 8.$$

To find the profit-maximizing price, substitute this quantity into the demand equation:

$$P = 18 - (0.5)(8) = \$14.$$

Total revenue is price times quantity:

$$TR = (14)(8) = \$112.$$

The profit of the firm is total revenue minus total cost, and total cost is equal to average cost times the level of output produced. Since marginal cost is constant, average variable cost is equal to marginal cost. Ignoring any fixed costs, total cost is $10Q$ or 80, and profit is

$$112 - 80 = \$32.$$

c.   What would the equilibrium price and quantity be in a competitive industry?

For a competitive industry, price would equal marginal cost at equilibrium. Setting the expression for price equal to a marginal cost of 10:

$$18 - 0.5Q = 10 \Rightarrow Q = 16 \Rightarrow P = 10.$$

Note the increase in the equilibrium quantity compared to the monopoly solution.

d.   What would the social gain be if this monopolist were forced to produce and price at the competitive equilibrium? Who would gain and lose as a result?

The social gain arises from the elimination of deadweight loss. Deadweight loss in this case is equal to the triangle above the constant marginal cost curve, below the demand curve, and between the quantities 8 and 16, or numerically

$$(14-10)(16-8)(.5)=\$16.$$

Consumers gain this deadweight loss plus the monopolist's profit of $32. The monopolist's profits are reduced to zero, and the consumer surplus increases by $48.

6. Suppose that an industry is characterized as follows:

$C = 100 + 2Q^2$	Firm total cost function
$MC = 4Q$	Firm marginal cost function
$P = 90 - 2Q$	Industry demand curve
$MR = 90 - 4Q$	Industry marginal revenue curve.

a.   If there is *only one firm* in the industry, find the monopoly price, quantity, and level of profit.

If there is only one firm in the industry, then the firm will act like a monopolist and produce at the point where marginal revenue is equal to marginal cost:

$$MC=4Q=90-4Q=MR$$
$$Q=11.25.$$

For a quantity of 11.25, the firm will charge a price P=90-2*11.25=$67.50. The level of profit is $67.50*11.25-100-2*11.25*11.25=$406.25.

b. **Find the price, quantity, and level of profit if the industry is competitive.**

If the industry is competitive then price is equal to marginal cost, so that 90-2Q=4Q, or Q=15. At a quantity of 15 price is equal to 60. The level of profit is therefore 60*15-100-2*15*15=$350.

c. **Graphically illustrate the demand curve, marginal revenue curve, marginal cost curve, and average cost curve. Identify the difference between the profit level of the monopoly and the profit level of the competitive industry in two different ways. Verify that the two are numerically equivalent.**

The graph below illustrates the demand curve, marginal revenue curve, and marginal cost curve. The average cost curve hits the marginal cost curve at a quantity of approximately 7, and is increasing thereafter (this is not shown in the graph below). The profit that is lost by having the firm produce at the competitive solution as compared to the monopoly solution is given by the difference of the two profit levels as calculated in parts a and b above, or $406.25-$350=$56.25. On the graph below, this difference is represented by the lost profit area, which is the triangle below the marginal cost curve and above the marginal revenue curve, between the quantities of 11.25 and 15. This is lost profit because for each of these 3.75 units extra revenue earned was less than extra cost incurred. This area can be calculated as 0.5*(60-45)*3.75+0.5*(45-30)*3.75=$56.25. The second method of graphically illustrating the difference in the two profit levels is to draw in the average cost curve and identify the two profit boxes. The profit box is the difference between the total revenue box (price times quantity) and the total cost box (average cost times quantity). The monopolist will gain two areas and lose one area as compared to the competitive firm, and these areas will sum to $56.25.

11.25 15

7. Suppose a profit-maximizing monopolist is producing 800 units of output and is charging a price of $40 per unit.

a. **If the elasticity of demand for the product is –2, find the marginal cost of the last unit produced.**

Recall that the monopolist's pricing rule as a function of the elasticity of demand for its product is:

$$\frac{(P - MC)}{P} = -\frac{1}{E_d}$$

or alternatively,

$$P = \frac{MC}{\left(1 + \left(\frac{1}{E_d}\right)\right)}$$

If we then plug in –2 for the elasticity and 40 for price we can solve to find MC=20.

b. **What is the firm's percentage markup of price over marginal cost?**

In percentage terms the mark-up is 50%, since marginal cost is 50% of price.

c. **Suppose that the average cost of the last unit produced is \$15 and the fixed cost is \$2000. Find the firm's profit.**

Total revenue is price times quantity, or \$40*800=\$32,000. Total cost is equal to average cost times quantity, or \$15*800=\$12,000. Profit is then \$20,000. Producer surplus is profit plus fixed cost, or \$22,000.

8. A firm has two factories for which costs are given by:

$$\text{Factory \#1: } C_1(Q_1) = 10Q_1^2$$

$$\text{Factory \#2: } C_2(Q_2) = 20Q_2^2$$

The firm faces the following demand curve:

$$P = 700 - 5Q$$

where Q is total output, i.e. $Q = Q_1 + Q_2$.

a. **On a diagram, draw the marginal cost curves for the two factories, the average and marginal revenue curves, and the total marginal cost curve (i.e., the marginal cost of producing $Q = Q_1 + Q_2$). Indicate the profit-maximizing output for each factory, total output, and price.**

The average revenue curve is the demand curve,

$$P = 700 - 5Q.$$

For a linear demand curve, the marginal revenue curve has the same intercept as the demand curve and a slope that is twice as steep:

$$MR = 700 - 10Q.$$

Next, determine the marginal cost of producing Q. To find the marginal cost of production in Factory 1, take the first derivative of the cost function with respect to Q:

$$\frac{dC_1(Q_1)}{dQ} = 20Q_1.$$

Similarly, the marginal cost in Factory 2 is

$$\frac{dC_2(Q_2)}{dQ} = 40Q_2.$$

Rearranging the marginal cost equations in inverse form and horizontally summing them, we obtain total marginal cost, MC_T:

$$Q = Q_1 + Q_2 = \frac{MC_1}{20} + \frac{MC_2}{40} = \frac{3MC_T}{40}, \text{ or}$$

$$MC_T = \frac{40Q}{3}.$$

Profit maximization occurs where $MC_T = MR$. See Figure 10.8.a for the profit-maximizing output for each factory, total output, and price.

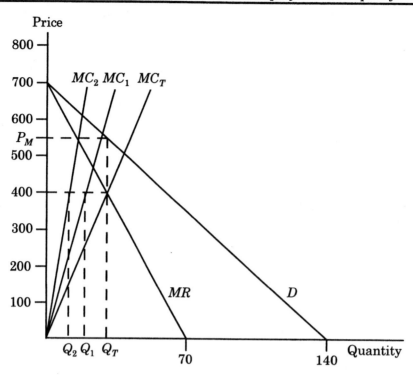

Figure 10.8.a

b.   Calculate the values of Q_1, Q_2, Q, and P that maximize profit.

Calculate the total output that maximizes profit, i.e., Q such that $MC_T = MR$:

$$\frac{40Q}{3} = 700 - 10Q, \ \text{or} \ Q = 30.$$

Next, observe the relationship between MC and MR for multiplant monopolies:

$$MR = MC_T = MC_1 = MC_2.$$

We know that at $Q = 30$, $MR = 700 - (10)(30) = 400$.

Therefore,

$$MC_1 = 400 = 20Q_1, \ \text{or} \ Q_1 = 20 \ \text{and}$$

$$MC_2 = 400 = 40Q_2, \ \text{or} \ Q_2 = 10.$$

To find the monopoly price, P_M, substitute for Q in the demand equation:

$$P_M = 700 - (5)(30), \ \text{or}$$

$$P_M = 550.$$

c.   Suppose labor costs increase in Factory 1 but not in Factory 2. How should the firm adjust the following(i.e., raise, lower, or leave unchanged): Output in Factory 1? Output in Factory 2? Total output? Price?

An increase in labor costs will lead to a horizontal shift to the left in MC_1, causing MC_T to shift to the left as well (since it is the horizontal sum of MC_1 and MC_2). The new MC_T curve intersects the MR curve at a lower quantity and higher marginal revenue. At a higher level of marginal revenue, Q_2 is greater than at the original level for MR. Since Q_T falls and Q_2 rises, Q_1 must fall. Since Q_T falls, price must rise.

9. A drug company has a monopoly on a new patented medicine. The product can be made in either of two plants. The costs of production for the two plants are $MC_1 = 20 + 2Q_1$, and $MC_2 = 10 + 5Q_2$. The firm's estimate of the demand for the product is $P = 20 - 3(Q_1 + Q_2)$. How much should the firm plan to produce in each plant? At what price should it plan to sell the product?

First, notice that *only MC_2* is relevant because the marginal cost curve of the first plant lies above the demand curve.

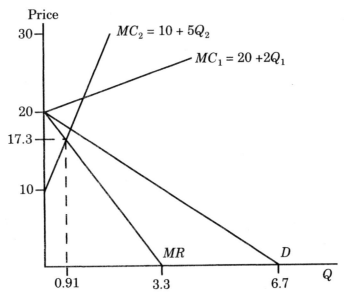

Figure 10.9

This means that the demand curve becomes $P = 20 - 3Q_2$. With an inverse linear demand curve, we know that the marginal revenue curve has the same vertical intercept but twice the slope, or $MR = 20 - 6Q_2$. To determine the profit-maximizing level of output, equate MR and MC_2:

$$20 - 6Q_2 = 10 + 5Q_2, \text{ or}$$

$$Q = Q_2 = 0.91.$$

Price is determined by substituting the profit-maximizing quantity into the demand equation:

$$P = 20 - 3(0.91) = 17.3.$$

10. One of the more important antitrust cases of this century involved the Aluminum Company of America (Alcoa) in 1945. At that time, Alcoa controlled about 90 percent of primary aluminum production in the United States, and the company had been accused of monopolizing the aluminum market. In its defense, Alcoa argued that although it indeed controlled a large fraction of the primary market, secondary aluminum (i.e., aluminum produced from the recycling of scrap) accounted for roughly 30 percent of the total supply of aluminum, and many competitive firms were engaged in recycling. Therefore, Alcoa argued, it did not have much monopoly power.

a.   Provide a clear argument *in favor* of Alcoa's position.

Although Alcoa controlled about 90 percent of primary aluminum production in the United States, secondary aluminum production by recyclers accounted for 30 percent of the total aluminum supply. Therefore, with a higher price, a much larger proportion of aluminum supply could come from secondary sources. This assertion is true because there is a large stock of potential supply in the economy. Therefore, the price elasticity of demand for Alcoa's primary aluminum is much higher (in absolute value) than we would expect, given Alcoa's dominant position in primary aluminum production. In many applications, other metals such as copper and steel are feasible substitutes for aluminum. Again, the demand elasticity Alcoa faces might be higher than we would otherwise expect.

b.   Provide a clear argument *against* Alcoa's position.

While Alcoa could not raise its price by very much at any one time, the stock of potential aluminum supply is limited. Therefore, by keeping a stable high price, Alcoa could reap monopoly profits. Also, since Alcoa had originally produced the metal reappearing as recycled scrap, it would have considered the effect of scrap reclamation on future prices. Therefore, it exerted effective monopolistic control over the secondary metal supply.

c.   The 1945 decision by Judge Learned Hand has been called "one of the most celebrated judicial opinions of our time." Do you know what Judge Hand's ruling was?

Judge Hand ruled against Alcoa but did not order it to divest itself of any of its United States production facilities. The two remedies imposed by the court were (1) that Alcoa was barred from bidding for two primary aluminum plants constructed by the government during World War II (they were sold to Reynolds and Kaiser) and (2) that it divest itself of its Canadian subsidiary, which became Alcan.

11. A monopolist faces the demand curve P = 11 - Q, where P is measured in dollars per unit and Q in thousands of units. The monopolist has a constant average cost of $6 per unit.

a.   Draw the average and marginal revenue curves and the average and marginal cost curves. What are the monopolist's profit-maximizing price and quantity? What is the resulting profit? Calculate the firm's degree of monopoly power using the Lerner index.

Because demand (average revenue) may be described as $P = 11 - Q$, we know that the marginal revenue function is $MR = 11 - 2Q$. We also know that if average cost is constant, then marginal cost is constant and equal to average cost: $MC = 6$.

To find the profit-maximizing level of output, set marginal revenue equal to marginal cost:

$$11 - 2Q = 6, \text{ or } Q = 2.5.$$

That is, the profit-maximizing quantity equals 2,500 units. Substitute the profit-maximizing quantity into the demand equation to determine the price:

$$P = 11 - 2.5 = \$8.50.$$

Profits are equal to total revenue minus total cost,

$$\pi = TR - TC = (AR)(Q) - (AC)(Q), \text{ or}$$

$$\pi = (8.5)(2.5) - (6)(2.5) = 6.25, \text{ or } \$6,250.$$

The degree of monopoly power is given by the Lerner Index:

$$\frac{P - MC}{P} = \frac{8.5 - 6}{8.5} = 0.294.$$

Figure 10.11.a

b.　**A government regulatory agency sets a price ceiling of $7 per unit. What quantity will be produced, and what will the firm's profit be? What happens to the degree of monopoly power?**

To determine the effect of the price ceiling on the quantity produced, substitute the ceiling price into the demand equation.

$$7 = 11 - Q, \text{ or}$$

$$Q = 4{,}000.$$

The monopolist will pick the price of $7 because it is the highest price that it can charge, and this price is still greater than the constant marginal cost of $6, resulting in positive monopoly profit.

Profits are equal to total revenue minus total cost:

$$\pi = (7)(4{,}000) - (6)(4{,}000) = \$4{,}000.$$

The degree of monopoly power is:

$$\frac{P - MC}{P} = \frac{7 - 6}{7} = 0.143.$$

c.　**What price ceiling yields the largest level of output? What is that level of output? What is the firm's degree of monopoly power at this price?**

If the regulatory authority sets a price below $6, the monopolist would prefer to go out of business instead of produce because it cannot cover its average costs. At any price above $6, the monopolist would produce less than the 5,000 units that would be produced in a competitive industry. Therefore, the regulatory agency should set a price ceiling of $6, thus making the monopolist face a horizontal effective demand curve up to $Q = 5{,}000$. To ensure a positive output (so that the monopolist is not indifferent between producing 5,000 units and shutting down), the price ceiling should be set at $6 + δ, where δ is small.

Thus, 5,000 is the maximum output that the regulatory agency can extract from the monopolist by using a price ceiling. The degree of monopoly power is

$$\frac{P - MC}{P} = \frac{6 + \delta - 6}{6} = \frac{\delta}{6} \to 0 \text{ as } \delta \to 0.$$

12. **Michelle's Monopoly Mutant Turtles (MMMT) has the exclusive right to sell Mutant Turtle t-shirts in the United States. The demand for these t-shirts is Q = 10,000/P². The firm's short-run cost is SRTC = 2,000 + 5Q, and its long-run cost is LRTC = 6Q.**

a. **What price should MMMT charge to maximize profit in the short run? What quantity does it sell, and how much profit does it make? Would it be better off shutting down in the short run?**

MMMT should offer enough t-shirts such that $MR = MC$. In the short run, marginal cost is the change in $SRTC$ as the result of the production of another t-shirt, i.e., $SRMC = 5$, the slope of the $SRTC$ curve. Demand is:

$$Q = \frac{10,000}{P^2},$$

or, in inverse form,

$$P = 100Q^{-1/2}.$$

Total revenue (PQ) is $100Q^{1/2}$. Taking the derivative of TR with respect to Q, $MR = 50Q^{-1/2}$. Equating MR and MC to determine the profit-maximizing quantity:

$$5 = 50Q^{-1/2}, \text{ or } Q = 100.$$

Substituting $Q = 100$ into the demand function to determine price:

$$P = (100)(100^{-1/2}) = 10.$$

The profit at this price and quantity is equal to total revenue minus total cost:

$$\pi = (10)(100) - (2000 + (5)(100)) = -\$1,500.$$

Although profit is negative, price is above the average variable cost of 5 and therefore, the firm should not shut down in the short run. Since most of the firm's costs are fixed, the firm loses $2,000 if nothing is produced. If the profit-maximizing quantity is produced, the firm loses only $1,500.

b. **What price should MMMT charge in the long run? What quantity does it sell and how much profit does it make? Would it be better off shutting down in the long run?**

In the long run, marginal cost is equal to the slope of the $LRTC$ curve, which is 6.

Equating marginal revenue and long run marginal cost to determine the profit-maximizing quantity:

$$50Q^{-1/2} = 6 \text{ or } Q = 69.44$$

Substituting $Q = 69.44$ into the demand equation to determine price:

$$P = (100)[(50/6)^2]^{-1/2} = (100)(6/50) = 12$$

Therefore, total revenue is $833.33 and total cost is $416.67. Profit is $416.67. The firm should remain in business.

c. **Can we expect MMMT to have lower marginal cost in the short run than in the long run? Explain why.**

In the long run, MMMT must replace all fixed factors. Therefore, we can expect $LRMC$ to be higher than $SRMC$.

13. **You produce widgets to sell in a perfectly competitive market at a market price of $10 per widget. Your widgets are manufactured in two plants, one in Massachusetts and the other in Connecticut. Because of labor problems in Connecticut, you are forced to raise wages there, so marginal costs in that plant increase. In response to this, should you shift production and produce more in the Massachusetts plant?**

No, production should not shift to the Massachusetts plant, although production in the Connecticut plant should be reduced. In order to maximize profits, a multiplant firm will schedule production at all plants so that the following two conditions are met:

- Marginal costs of production at each plant are equal.

- Marginal revenue of the total amount produced is equal to the marginal cost at each plant.

These two rules can be summarized as $MR=MC_1=MC_2= MC_T$, where the subscript indicates the plant.

The firm in this example has two plants and is in a perfectly competitive market. In a perfectly competitive market $P = MR$. To maximize profits, production among the plants should be allocated such that:

$$P = MC_c(Q_c) = MC_m(Q_m),$$

where the subscripts denote plant locations (c for Connecticut, etc.). The marginal costs of production have increased in Connecticut but have not changed in Massachusetts. Since costs have not changed in Massachusetts, the level of Q_m that sets $MC_m(Q_m) = P$, has not changed.

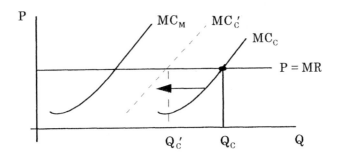

Figure 10.13

14. The employment of teaching assistants (TAs) by major universities can be characterized as a monopsony. Suppose the demand for TAs is W = 30,000 - 125n, where W is the wage (as an annual salary), and n is the number of TAs hired. The supply of TAs is given by W = 1,000 + 75n.

a.   **If the university takes advantage of its monopsonist position, how many TAs will it hire? What wage will it pay?**

The supply curve is equivalent to the average expenditure curve. With a supply curve of $W = 1,000 + 75n$, the total expenditure is $Wn = 1,000n + 75n^2$. Taking the derivative of the total expenditure function with respect to the number of TAs, the marginal expenditure curve is $1,000 + 150n$. As a monopsonist, the university would equate marginal value (demand) with marginal expenditure to determine the number of TAs to hire:

$$30,000 - 125n = 1,000 + 150n, \text{ or}$$

$$n = 105.5.$$

Substituting $n = 105.5$ into the supply curve to determine the wage:

$$1,000 + (75)(105.5) = \$8,909 \text{ annually.}$$

b. **If, instead, the university faced an infinite supply of TAs at the annual wage level of $10,000, how many TAs would it hire?**

With an infinite number of TAs at $10,000, the supply curve is horizontal at $10,000. Total expenditure is $(10,000)(n)$, and marginal expenditure is 10,000. Equating marginal value and marginal expenditure:

$$30,000 - 125n = 10,000, \text{ or}$$

$$n = 160.$$

15. Dayna's Doorstops, Inc. (DD), is a monopolist in the doorstop industry. Its cost is $C = 100 - 5Q + Q^2$, and demand is $P = 55 - 2Q$.

a. **What price should DD set to maximize profit? What output does the firm produce? How much profit and consumer surplus does DD generate?**

To maximize profits, DD should equate marginal revenue and marginal cost. Given a demand of $P = 55 - 2Q$, we know that total revenue, PQ, is $55Q - 2Q^2$. Marginal revenue is found by taking the first derivative of total revenue with respect to Q or:

$$MR = \frac{dTR}{dQ} = 55 - 4Q.$$

Similarly, marginal cost is determined by taking the first derivative of the total cost function with respect to Q or:

$$MC = \frac{dTC}{dQ} = 2Q - 5.$$

Equating MC and MR to determine the profit-maximizing quantity,

$$55 - 4Q = 2Q - 5, \text{ or}$$

$$Q = 10.$$

Substituting $Q = 10$ into the demand equation to determine the profit-maximizing price:

$$P = 55 - (2)(10) = \$35.$$

Profits are equal to total revenue minus total cost:

$$\pi = (35)(10) - (100 - (5)(10) + 10^2) = \$200.$$

Consumer surplus is equal to one-half times the profit-maximizing quantity, 10, times the difference between the demand intercept (the maximum price anyone is willing to pay) and the monopoly price:

$$CS = (0.5)(10)(55 - 35) = \$100.$$

b. **What would output be if DD acted like a perfect competitor and set MC = P? What profit and consumer surplus would then be generated?**

In competition, profits are maximized at the point where price equals marginal cost, where price is given by the demand curve:

$$55 - 2Q = -5 + 2Q, \text{ or}$$

$$Q = 15.$$

Substituting $Q = 15$ into the demand equation to determine the price:

$$P = 55 - (2)(15) = \$25.$$

Profits are total revenue minus total cost or:

$$\pi = (25)(15) - (100 - (5)(15) + 15^2) = \$125.$$

Consumer surplus is

$$CS = (0.5)(55 - 25)(15) = \$225.$$

c. **What is the deadweight loss from monopoly power in part (a)?**

The deadweight loss is equal to the area below the demand curve, above the marginal cost curve, and between the quantities of 10 and 15, or numerically

$$DWL = (0.5)(35 - 15)(15 - 10) = \$50.$$

d. **Suppose the government, concerned about the high price of doorstops, sets a maximum price at \$27. How does this affect price, quantity, consumer surplus, and DD's profit? What is the resulting deadweight loss?**

With the imposition of a price ceiling, the maximum price that DD may charge is \$27.00. Note that when a ceiling price is set above the competitive price the ceiling price is equal to marginal revenue for all levels of output sold up to the competitive level of output.

Substitute the ceiling price of \$27.00 into the demand equation to determine the effect on the equilibrium quantity sold:
$$27 = 55 - 2Q, \text{ or } Q = 14.$$
Consumer surplus is
$$CS = (0.5)(55 - 27)(14) = \$196.$$
Profits are
$$\pi = (27)(14) - (100 - (5)(14) + 14^2) = \$152.$$

The deadweight loss is \$2.00 This is equivalent to a triangle of

$$(0.5)(15 - 14)(27 - 23) = \$2$$

e. **Now suppose the government sets the maximum price at \$23. How does this affect price, quantity, consumer surplus, DD's profit, and deadweight loss?**

With a ceiling price set below the competitive price, DD will decrease its output. Equate marginal revenue and marginal cost to determine the profit-maximizing level of output:

$$23 = -5 + 2Q, \text{ or } Q = 14.$$

With the government-imposed maximum price of \$23, profits are

$$\pi = (23)(14) - (100 - (5)(14) + 14^2) = \$96.$$

Consumer surplus is realized on only 14 doorsteps. Therefore, it is equal to the consumer surplus in part *d.*, i.e. \$196, plus the savings on each doorstep, i.e.,

$$CS = (27 - 23)(14) = \$56.$$

Therefore, consumer surplus is \$252. Deadweight loss is the same as before, \$2.00.

f. **Finally, consider a maximum price of \$12. What will this do to quantity, consumer surplus, profit, and deadweight loss?**

With a maximum price of only \$12, output decreases even further:

$$12 = -5 + 2Q, \text{ or } Q = 8.5.$$
Profits are
$$\pi = (12)(8.5) - (100 - (5)(8.5) + 8.5^2) = -\$27.75.$$

Consumer surplus is realized on only 8.5 units, which is equivalent to the consumer surplus associated with a price of \$38 ($38 = 55 - 2(8.5)$), i.e.,

$$(0.5)(55 - 38)(8.5) = \$72.25$$

plus the savings on each doorstep, i.e.,

$$(38 - 12)(8.5) = \$221.$$

Therefore, consumer surplus is $293.25. Total surplus is $265.50, and deadweight loss is $84.50.

*16. There are 10 households in Lake Wobegon, Minnesota, each with a demand for electricity of Q = 50 - P. Lake Wobegon Electric's (LWE) cost of producing electricity is TC = 500 + Q.

a.   **If the regulators of LWE want to make sure that there is no deadweight loss in this market, what price will they force LWE to charge? What will output be in that case? Calculate consumer surplus and LWE's profit with that price.**

The first step in solving the regulator's problem is to determine the market demand for electricity in Lake Wobegon. The quantity demanded in the market is the sum of the quantity demanded by each individual at any given price. Graphically, we horizontally sum each household's demand for electricity to arrive at market demand, and mathematically

$$Q_M = \sum_{i=1}^{10} Q_i = 10(50 - P) = 500 - 10P \Rightarrow P = 50 - .1Q.$$

To avoid deadweight loss, the regulators will set price equal to marginal cost. Given

$TC = 500 + Q$, $MC = 1$ (the slope of the total cost curve). Setting price equal to marginal cost, and solving for quantity:

$$50 - 0.1Q = 1, \text{ or}$$

$$Q = 490.$$

Profits are equal to total revenue minus total costs:

$$\pi = (1)(490) - (500+490), = -\$500.$$

Total consumer surplus is:

$$CS = (0.5)(50 - 1)(490) = 12{,}005, \text{ or } \$1{,}200.50 \text{ per household.}$$

b.   **If regulators want to ensure that LWE doesn't lose money, what is the lowest price they can impose? Calculate output, consumer surplus, and profit. Is there any deadweight loss?**

To guarantee that LWE does not lose money, regulators will allow LWE to charge the average cost of production, where

$$AC = \frac{TC}{Q} = \frac{500}{Q} + 1.$$

To determine the equilibrium price and quantity under average cost pricing, set price equal to average cost:

$$50 - 0.1Q = \frac{500}{Q} + 1.$$

Solving for Q yields the following quadratic equation:

$$0.1Q^2 - 49Q + 500 = 0.$$

Note: if $Q^2 + bQ + c = 0$, then

$$Q = \frac{-b \pm \sqrt{b^2 - 4ac}}{2a}.$$

Using the quadratic formula:

$$Q = \frac{49 \pm \sqrt{49^2 - (4)(0.1)(500)}}{(2)(0.1)},$$

there are two solutions: 10.4 and 479.6. Note that at a quantity of 10.4, marginal revenue is greater than marginal cost, and the firm will gain by producing more output. Also, note that the larger quantity results in a lower price and hence a larger consumer surplus. Therefore, Q=479.6 and P=$2.04. At this quantity and price, profit is zero (given some slight rounding error). Consumer surplus is

$$CS = (0.5)(50 - 2.04)(479.6) = \$11,500.$$

Deadweight loss is

$$DWL = (2.04 - 1)(490 - 479.6)(0.5) = \$5.40.$$

c.   **Kristina knows that deadweight loss is something that this small town can do without. She suggests that each household be required to pay a fixed amount just to receive any electricity at all, and then a per-unit charge for electricity. Then LWE can break even while charging the price you calculated in part (a). What fixed amount would each household have to pay for Kristina's plan to work? Why can you be sure that no household will choose instead to refuse the payment and go without electricity?**

Fixed costs are $500. If each household pays $50, the fixed costs are covered and the utility can charge marginal cost for electricity. Because consumer surplus per household under marginal cost pricing is $1200.50, each would be willing to pay the $50.

17. A certain town in the Midwest obtains all of its electricity from one company, Northstar Electric. Although the company is a monopoly, it is owned by the citizens of the town, all of whom split the profits equally at the end of each year. The CEO of the company claims that because all of the profits will be given back to the citizens, it makes economic sense to charge a monopoly price for electricity. True or false? Explain.

The CEO's claim is false. If the company charges the monopoly price then it will be producing a smaller quantity than the competitive equilibrium. Therefore, even though all of the monopoly profits are given back to the citizens, there is still a deadweight loss associated with the fact that too little electricity is produced and consumed.

18. A monopolist faces the following demand curve:

$$Q = 144/P^2$$

where Q is the quantity demanded and P is price. Its *average variable* cost is

$$AVC = Q^{1/2},$$

and its *fixed cost* is 5.

a.   **What are its profit-maximizing price and quantity? What is the resulting profit?**

The monopolist wants to choose the level of output to maximize its profits, and it does this by setting marginal revenue equal to marginal cost. To find marginal revenue, first rewrite the demand function as a function of Q so that you can then express total revenue as a function of Q, and calculate marginal revenue:

$$Q = \frac{144}{P^2} \implies P^2 = \frac{144}{Q} \implies P = \sqrt{\frac{144}{Q}} = \frac{12}{\sqrt{Q}}$$

$$R = P * Q = \frac{12}{\sqrt{Q}} * Q = 12\sqrt{Q}$$

$$MR = \frac{\Delta R}{\Delta Q} = 0.5 * \frac{12}{\sqrt{Q}} = \frac{6}{\sqrt{Q}}.$$

To find marginal cost, first find total cost, which is equal to fixed cost plus variable cost. You are given fixed cost of 5. Variable cost is equal to average variable cost times Q so that total cost and marginal cost are:

$$TC = 5 + Q * Q^{\frac{1}{2}} = 5 + Q^{\frac{3}{2}}$$

$$MC = \frac{\Delta TC}{\Delta Q} = \frac{3\sqrt{Q}}{2}.$$

To find the profit-maximizing level of output, we set marginal revenue equal to marginal cost:

$$\frac{6}{\sqrt{Q}} = \frac{3\sqrt{Q}}{2} \implies Q = 4.$$

You can now find price and profit:

$$P = \frac{12}{\sqrt{Q}} = \frac{12}{\sqrt{4}} = \$6$$

$$\Pi = PQ - TC = 6 * 4 - (5 + 4^{\frac{3}{2}}) = \$11.$$

b. **Suppose the government regulates the price to be no greater than \$4 per unit. How much will the monopolist produce? What will its profit be?**

The price ceiling truncates the demand curve that the monopolist faces at $P=4$ or $Q = \frac{144}{16} = 9$. Therefore, if the monopolist produces 9 units or less, the price must be \$4. Because of the regulation, the demand curve now has two parts:

$$P = \begin{cases} \$4, & \text{if } Q \le 9 \\ 12Q^{-1/2}, & \text{if } Q > 9. \end{cases}$$

Thus, total revenue and marginal revenue also should be considered in two parts

$$TR = \begin{cases} 4Q, & \text{if } Q \le 9 \\ 12Q^{1/2}, & \text{if } Q > 9 \end{cases} \quad \text{and}$$

$$MR = \begin{cases} \$4, & \text{if } Q \le 9 \\ 6Q^{-1/2}, & \text{if } Q > 9. \end{cases}$$

To find the profit-maximizing level of output, set marginal revenue equal to marginal cost, so that for $P = 4$,

$$4 = \frac{3}{2}\sqrt{Q}, \text{ or } \sqrt{Q} = \frac{8}{3}, \text{ or } Q = 7.11.$$

If the monopolist produces an integer number of units, the profit-maximizing production level is 7 units, price is \$4, revenue is \$28, total cost is \$23.52, and profit is \$4.48. There is a shortage of two units, since the quantity demanded at the price of \$4 is 9 units.

c. **Suppose the government wants to set a ceiling price that induces the monopolist to produce the largest possible output. What price will accomplish this goal?**

To maximize output, the regulated price should be set so that demand equals marginal cost, which implies;

$$\frac{12}{\sqrt{Q}} = \frac{3\sqrt{Q}}{2} \quad \Rightarrow \quad Q = 8 \text{ and } P = \$4.24.$$

The regulated price becomes the monopolist's marginal revenue curve, which is a horizontal line with an intercept at the regulated price. To maximize profit, the firm produces where marginal cost is equal to marginal revenue, which results in a quantity of 8 units.

CHAPTER 11
PRICING WITH MARKET POWER

TEACHING NOTES

The chapter begins with a discussion of the basic objective of every pricing strategy, which is to capture as much consumer surplus as possible and convert it into additional profit for the firm. The remainder of the chapter explores different methods of capturing the surplus. Section 11.2 discusses first, second, and third degree price discrimination, section 11.3 discusses intertemporal price discrimination and peak load pricing, section 11.4 discusses the two-part tariff, section 11.5 discusses bundling, and section 11.6 discusses advertising. If you are pressed for time you can pick and choose between sections 11.3 to 11.6. The chapter contains an excellent array of examples of how price discrimination is applied in different types of markets, not only in the formal examples but also in the body of the text. Although the graphs can seem very complicated to students, the challenge of figuring out how to price discriminate in a specific case can be quite stimulating and can promote many interesting class discussions. The Appendix to the chapter can be difficult for most students and should not be covered in class unless you are teaching a mathematical or business-oriented course. Should you choose to include the Appendix, make sure students have an intuitive feel for the model before presenting the algebra or geometry.

When introducing this chapter, highlight the requirements for profitable price discrimination: (1) supply-side market power, (2) the ability to separate customers, and (3) differing demand elasticities for different classes of customers. The discussion of first-degree price discrimination begins with the concept of a reservation price. The text uses reservation prices throughout the chapter. Since the discussion of Figure 11.2 may be confusing to students, an alternative presentation could begin with a diagram similar to Figure 9.1, with the addition of information from Figure 10.10. Show that with first-degree price discrimination the monopolist captures deadweight loss and all consumer surplus. Also, stress that with perfect price discrimination the marginal revenue curve coincides with the demand curve.

First-degree price discrimination is best followed by the discussion on third-degree, rather than second-degree, price discrimination. When you do cover second-degree price discrimination, note that many utilities currently charge higher prices for larger blocks. (Use your own electricity bill as an example.) The geometry of third-degree price discrimination is too difficult for most students; therefore, they need a careful explanation of the intuition behind the model. Slowly introduce the algebra so that students can see that the profit-maximizing quantities in each market are those where marginal revenue equals marginal cost. This section concludes with Examples 11.1 and 11.2. Because of the prevalence of coupons, rebates, and airline travel, all students will be able to relate to these examples.

When presenting intertemporal price discrimination and peak-load pricing, begin by comparing the similarities in the analysis with third-degree price discrimination. Discuss the difference between these forms of exploiting monopoly power and third-degree price discrimination. Here, marginal revenue and cost are equal within customer class but need not be equal across classes.

Students easily grasp the case of a two-part tariff with a single customer. Fewer will understand the case for two customers. Fewer still will understand the case of many different customers. Instead of moving directly into a discussion of more than one customer, you could introduce Example 11.4 to give concrete meaning to entry and usage fees. Then return to the cases dealing with more than one customer.

When discussing bundling, point out that in Figure 11.12 prices are on both axes. To introduce bundling, consider starting with Example 11.6 and a menu from a local restaurant. Make sure students understand when bundling is profitable (when demands are negatively correlated) and that mixed bundling can be more profitable than either selling separately or pure bundling (demands are only somewhat negatively correlated and/or when marginal production costs are significant). To distinguish tying, from bundling, point out that with tying the first product is useless without the second product.

REVIEW QUESTIONS

1. Suppose a firm can practice perfect, first-degree price discrimination. What is the lowest price it will charge, and what will its total output be?

When the firm is able to practice perfect first-degree price discrimination, each unit is sold at the reservation price of each consumer, assuming each consumer purchases one unit. Because each unit is sold at the consumer's reservation price, marginal revenue is simply the price of the last unit. We know that firms maximize profits by producing an output such that marginal revenue is equal to marginal cost. For the perfect price discriminator, that point is where the marginal cost curve intersects the demand curve. Increasing output beyond that point would imply that $MR < MC$, and the firm would lose money on each unit sold. For lower quantities, $MR > MC$, and the firm should increase its output.

2. How does a car salesperson practice price discrimination? How does the ability to discriminate correctly affect his or her earnings?

The relevant range of the demand curve facing the car salesperson is bounded above by the manufacturer's suggested retail price plus the dealer's markup and bounded below by the dealer's price plus administrative and inventory overhead. By sizing up the customer, the salesperson determines the customer's reservation price. Through a process of bargaining, a sales price is determined. If the salesperson has misjudged the reservation price of the customer, either the sale is lost because the customer's reservation price is lower than the salesperson's guess or profit is lost because the customer's reservation price is higher than the salesperson's guess. Thus, the salesperson's commission is positively correlated to his or her ability to determine the reservation price of each customer.

3. Electric utilities often practice second-degree price discrimination. Why might this improve consumer welfare?

Consumer surplus is higher under block pricing than under monopoly pricing because more output is produced. For example, assume there are two prices P_1 and P_2, with P_1 greater than P_2. Customers with reservation prices above P_1 pay P_1, capturing surplus equal to the area bounded by the demand curve and P_1. This also would occur with monopoly pricing. Under block pricing, customers with reservation prices between P_1 and P_2 capture surplus equal to the area bounded by the demand curve, the difference between P_1 and P_2, and the difference between Q_1 and Q_2. This quantity is greater than the surplus captured under monopoly, hence block pricing, under these assumptions, improves consumer welfare.

Figure 11.3

4. Give some examples of third-degree price discrimination. Can third-degree price discrimination be effective if the different groups of consumers have different levels of demand but the same price elasticities?

> To engage in third-degree price discrimination, the producer must separate customers into distinct markets (sorting) and prevent the reselling of the product from customers in one market to customers in another market (arbitrage). While examples in this chapter stress the techniques for separating customers, there are also techniques for preventing resale. For example, airlines restrict the use of their tickets by printing the name of the passenger on the ticket. Other examples include dividing markets by age and gender, e.g., charging different prices for movie tickets to different age groups. If customers in the separate markets have the same price elasticities, then from equation 11.2 we know that the prices are the same in all markets. While the producer can effectively separate the markets, there is little profit incentive to do so.

5. Show why optimal, third-degree price discrimination requires that marginal revenue for each group of consumers equals marginal cost. Use this condition to explain how a firm should change its prices and total output if the demand curve for one group of consumers shifted outward, so that marginal revenue for that group increased.

> We know that firms maximize profits by choosing output so marginal revenue is equal to marginal cost. If *MR* for one market is greater than *MC*, then the firm should increase sales to maximize profit, thus lowering the price on the last unit and raising the cost of producing the last unit. Similarly, if *MR* for one market is less than *MC*, the firm should decrease sales to maximize profit, thereby raising the price on the last unit and lowering the cost of producing the last unit. By equating *MR* and *MC* in each market, marginal revenue is equal in all markets.

> If the quantity demanded increased, the marginal revenue at each price would also increase. If *MR* = *MC* before the demand shift, *MR* would be greater than *MC* after the demand shift. To lower *MR* and raise *MC*, the producer should increase sales to this market by lowering price, thus increasing output. This increase in output would increase *MC* of the last unit sold. To maximize profit, the producer must increase the *MR* on units sold in other markets, i.e., increase price in these other markets. The firm shifts sales to the market experiencing the increase in demand and away from other markets.

6. When pricing automobiles, American car companies typically charge a much higher percentage markup over cost for "luxury option" items (such as leather trim, etc.) than for the car itself or for more "basic" options such as power steering and automatic transmission. Explain why.

This can be explained as an instance of third-degree price discrimination. In order to use the model of third-degree price discrimination presented in the text, we need to assume that the costs of producing car options is a function of the total number of options produced and the production of each type of options affects costs in the same way. For simplicity, we can assume that there are two types of option packages, "luxury" and "basic," and that these two types of packages are purchased by two different types of consumers. In this case, the relationship across product types $MR_1 = MR_2$ must hold, which implies that:

$$P_1/P_2 = (1+1/E_2) / (1+1/E_1)$$

where 1 and 2 denote the luxury and basic products types. This means that the higher price is charged for the package with the lower elasticity of demand. Thus the pricing of automobiles can be explained if the "luxury" options are purchased by consumers with low elasticities of demand relative to consumers of more "basic" packages.

7. How is peak-load pricing a form of price discrimination? Can it make consumers better off? Give an example.

Price discrimination involves separating customers into distinct markets. There are several ways of segmenting markets: by customer characteristics, by geography, and by time. In peak-load pricing, sellers charge different prices to customers at different times. When there is a higher quantity demanded at each price, a higher price is charged. Peak-load pricing can increase total consumer surplus by charging a lower price to customers with elasticities greater than the average elasticity of the market as a whole. Most telephone companies charge a different price during normal business hours, evening hours, and night and weekend hours. Callers with more elastic demand wait until the period when the charge is closest to their reservation price.

8. How can a firm determine an optimal two-part tariff if it has two customers with different demand curves? (Assume that it knows the demand curves.)

If all customers had the same demand curve, the firm would set a price equal to marginal cost and a fee equal to consumer surplus. When consumers have different demand curves and, therefore, different levels of consumer surplus, the firm is faced with the following problem. If it sets the user fee equal to the larger consumer surplus, the firm will earn profits only from the consumers with the larger consumer surplus because the second group of consumers will not purchase any of the good. On the other hand, if the firm sets the fee equal to the smaller consumer surplus, the firm will earn revenues from both types of consumers.

9. Why is the pricing of a Gillette safety razor a form of a two-part tariff? Must Gillette be a monopoly producer of its blades as well as its razors? Suppose you were advising Gillette on how to determine the two parts of the tariff. What procedure would you suggest?

By selling the razor and the blades separately, the pricing of a Gillette safety razor can be thought of as a two-part tariff, where the entry fee is the cost of the razor and the usage fee is the cost of the blades. Gillette does not need to be a monopoly producer of its blades. In the simplest case where all consumers have identical demand curves, Gillette should set the blade price to marginal cost, and the razor cost to total consumer surplus for each consumer. Since blade price is set to marginal cost it does not matter if Gillette has a monopoly or not. The determination of the two parts of the tariff becomes more complicated the greater the variety of consumers with different demands, and there is no simple formula to calculate the optimal two part tariff. The key point to consider is that as the entry fee becomes smaller, the number of entrants will rise, and the profit from the entry fee will fall. Arriving at the optimal two part tariff might involve some amount of iteration over different entry and usage fees.

10. In the town of Woodland, California there are many dentists but only one eye doctor. Are senior citizens more likely to be offered discount prices for dental exams or for eye exams? Why.

The dental market is competitive, whereas the eye doctor is a local monopolist. Only firms with market power can practice price discrimination, which implies senior citizens are more likely to be offered discount prices from the eye doctor. Each dentist is already charging a price equal to marginal cost so they are not able to offer a discount.

11. Why did MGM bundle *Gone with the Wind* and *Getting Gertie's Garter*? What characteristic of demands is needed for bundling to increase profits?

Loews bundled its film *Gone with the Wind* and *Getting Gertie's Garter* to maximize revenues. Because Loews could not price discriminate by charging a different price to each customer according to the customer's price elasticity, it chose to bundle the two films and charge theaters for showing both films. The price would have been the combined reservation prices of the last theater that Loews wanted to attract. Of course, this tactic would only maximize revenues if demands for the two films were negatively correlated, as discussed in the chapter.

12. How does mixed bundling differ from pure bundling? Under what conditions is mixed bundling preferable to pure bundling? Why do many restaurants practice mixed bundling (by offering complete dinners as well as an à la carte menu) instead of pure bundling?

Pure bundling involves selling products only as a package. Mixed bundling allows the consumer to purchase the products either separately or together. Mixed bundling yields higher profits than pure bundling when demands for the individual products do not have a strong negative correlation, marginal costs are high, or both. Restaurants can maximize profits with mixed bundling by offering both à la carte and full dinners by charging higher prices for individual items to capture the consumers' willingness to pay and lower prices for full dinners to induce customers with lower reservation prices to purchase more dinners.

13. How does tying differ from bundling? Why might a firm want to practice tying?

Tying involves the sale of two or more goods or services that must be used as complements. Bundling can involve complements or substitutes. Tying allows the firm to monitor customer demand and more effectively determine profit-maximizing prices for the tied products. For example, a microcomputer firm might sell its computer, the tying product, with minimum memory and a unique architecture, then sell extra memory, the tied product, above marginal cost.

14. Why is it incorrect to advertise up to the point that the last dollar of advertising expenditures generates another dollar of sales? What is the correct rule for the marginal advertising dollar?

If the firm increases advertising expenditures to the point that the last dollar of advertising generates another dollar of sales, it will not be maximizing profits, because the firm is ignoring additional advertising costs. The correct rule is to advertise so that the marginal revenue of an additional dollar of advertising equals the additional dollars spent on advertising plus the marginal production cost of the increased sales.

15. How can a firm check that its advertising-to-sales ratio is not too high or too low? What information does it need?

The firm can check whether its advertising-to-sales ratio is profit maximizing by comparing it with the negative of the ratio of the advertising elasticity of demand to the price elasticity of demand. The firm must know both the advertising elasticity of demand and the price elasticity of demand.

EXERCISES

1. **Price discrimination requires the ability to sort customers and the ability to prevent arbitrage. Explain how the following can function as price discrimination schemes and discuss both sorting and arbitrage:**

a. **Requiring airline travelers to spend at least one Saturday night away from home to qualify for a low fare.**

The requirement of staying over Saturday night separates business travelers, who prefer to return for the weekend, from tourists, who travel on the weekend. Arbitrage is not possible when the ticket specifies the name of the traveler.

b. **Insisting on delivering cement to buyers and basing prices on buyers' locations.**

By basing prices on the buyer's location, customers are sorted by geography. Prices may then include transportation charges. These costs vary from customer to customer. The customer pays for these transportation charges whether delivery is received at the buyer's location or at the cement plant. Since cement is heavy and bulky, transportation charges may be large. This pricing strategy leads to "based-point-price systems," where all cement producers use the same base point and calculate transportation charges from this base point. Individual customers are then quoted the same price. For example, in *FTC v. Cement Institute*, 333 U.S. 683 [1948], the Court found that sealed bids by eleven companies for a 6,000-barrel government order in 1936 all quoted $3.286854 per barrel.

c. **Selling food processors along with coupons that can be sent to the manufacturer to obtain a $10 rebate.**

Rebate coupons with food processors separate consumers into two groups: (1) customers who are less price sensitive, i.e., those who have a lower elasticity of demand and do not request the rebate; and (2) customers who are more price sensitive, i.e., those who have a higher demand elasticity and do request the rebate. The latter group could buy the food processors, send in the rebate coupons, and resell the processors at a price just below the retail price without the rebate. To prevent this type of arbitrage, sellers could limit the number of rebates per household.

d. **Offering temporary price cuts on bathroom tissue.**

A temporary price cut on bathroom tissue is a form of intertemporal price discrimination. During the price cut, price-sensitive consumers buy greater quantities of tissue than they would otherwise. Non-price-sensitive consumers buy the same amount of tissue that they would buy without the price cut. Arbitrage is possible, but the profits on reselling bathroom tissue probably cannot compensate for the cost of storage, transportation, and resale.

e. **Charging high-income patients more than low-income patients for plastic surgery.**

The plastic surgeon might not be able to separate high-income patients from low-income patients, but he or she can guess. One strategy is to quote a high price initially, observe the patient's reaction, and then negotiate the final price. Many medical insurance policies do not cover elective plastic surgery. Since plastic surgery cannot be transferred from low-income patients to high-income patients, arbitrage does not present a problem.

2. If the demand for drive-in movies is more elastic for couples than for single individuals, it will be optimal for theaters to charge one admission fee for the driver of the car and an extra fee for passengers. True or False? Explain.

True. Approach this question as a two-part tariff problem where the entry fee is a charge for the car plus the driver and the usage fee is a charge for each additional passenger other than the driver. Assume that the marginal cost of showing the movie is zero, i.e., all costs are fixed and do not vary with the number of cars. The theater should set its entry fee to capture the consumer surplus of the driver, a single viewer, and should charge a positive price for each passenger.

3. In Example 11.1, we saw how producers of processed foods and related consumer goods use coupons as a means of price discrimination. Although coupons are widely used in the United States, that is not the case in other countries. In Germany, coupons are illegal.

a.   Does prohibiting the use of coupons in Germany make German *consumers* better off or worse off?

In general, we cannot tell whether consumers will be better off or worse off. Total consumer surplus can increase or decrease with price discrimination, depending on the number of different prices charged and the distribution of consumer demand. Note, for example, that the use of coupons can increase the market size and therefore increase the total surplus of the market. Depending on the relative demand curves of the consumer groups and the producer's marginal cost curve, the increase in total surplus can be big enough to increase both producer surplus and consumer surplus. Consider the simple example depicted in Figure 11.3.a.

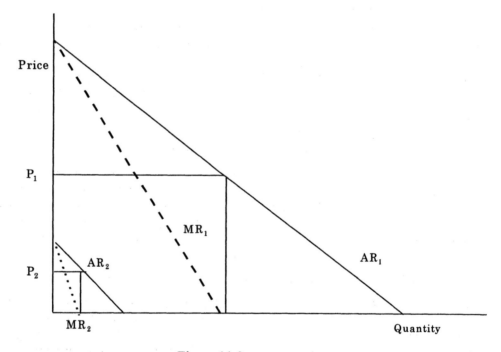

Figure 11.3.a

In this case there are two consumer groups with two different demand curves. Assuming marginal cost is zero, without price discrimination, consumer group 2 is left out of the market and thus has no consumer surplus. With price discrimination, consumer 2 is included in the market and collects some consumer surplus. At the same time, consumer 1 pays the same price under discrimination in this example, and therefore enjoys the same consumer surplus. The use of coupons (price discrimination) thus increases total consumer surplus in this example. Furthermore, although the net change in consumer surplus is ambiguous in general, there is a transfer of consumer surplus from price-insensitive to price-sensitive consumers.

166

Thus, price-sensitive consumers will benefit from coupons, even though on net consumers as a whole can be worse off.

b. **Does prohibiting the use of coupons make German *producers* better off or worse off?**

Prohibiting the use of coupons will make the German producers worse off, or at least not better off. If firms can successfully price discriminate (i.e. they can prevent resale, there are barriers to entry, etc.), price discrimination can never make a firm worse off.

4. Suppose that BMW can produce any quantity of cars at a constant marginal cost equal to $20,000 and a fixed cost of $10 billion. You are asked to advise the CEO as to what prices and quantities BMW should set for sales in Europe and in the U.S. The demand for BMWs in each market is given by:

$$Q_E = 4{,}000{,}000 - 100\ P_E \ \text{ and }\ Q_U = 1{,}000{,}000 - 20P_U$$

where the subscript *E* denotes Europe and the subscript *U* denotes the United States. Assume that BMW can restrict U.S. sales to authorized BMW dealers only.

a. **What quantity of BMWs should the firm sell in each market, and what will the price be in each market? What will the total profit be?**

With separate markets, BMW chooses the appropriate levels of Q_E and Q_U to maximize profits, where profits are:

$$\pi = TR - TC = \left(Q_E P_E + Q_U P_U\right) - \left\{\left(Q_E + Q_U\right)20{,}000 + 10{,}000{,}000{,}000\right\}.$$

Solve for P_E and P_U using the demand equations, and substitute the expressions into the profit equation:

$$\pi = Q_E\left(40{,}000 - \frac{Q_E}{100}\right) + Q_U\left(50{,}000 - \frac{Q_U}{20}\right) - \left\{\left(Q_E + Q_U\right)20{,}000 + 10{,}000{,}000{,}000\right\}.$$

Differentiating and setting each derivative to zero to determine the profit-maximizing quantities:

$$\frac{\partial \pi}{\partial Q_E} = 40{,}000 - \frac{Q_E}{50} - 20{,}000 = 0,\ or\ Q_E = 1{,}000{,}000\ cars$$

and

$$\frac{\partial \pi}{\partial Q_U} = 50{,}000 - \frac{Q_U}{10} - 20{,}000 = 0,\ or\ Q_U = 300{,}000\ cars.$$

Substituting Q_E and Q_U into their respective demand equations, we may determine the price of cars in each market:

$$1{,}000{,}000 = 4{,}000{,}000 - 100P_E,\ or\ P_E = \$30{,}000\ \text{ and}$$

$$300{,}000 = 1{,}000{,}000 - 20P_U,\ or\ P_U = \$35{,}000.$$

Substituting the values for Q_E, Q_U, P_E, and P_U into the profit equation, we have

$$\pi = \{(1{,}000{,}000)(\$30{,}000) + (300{,}000)(\$35{,}000)\} - \{(1{,}300{,}000)(20{,}000)) + 10{,}000{,}000{,}000\},\ or$$

$$\pi = \$4.5\ \text{billion}.$$

b. **If BMW were forced to charge the same price in each market, what would be the quantity sold in each market, the equilibrium price, and the company's profit?**

If BMW charged the same price in both markets, we substitute $Q = Q_E + Q_U$ into the demand equation and write the new demand curve as

$$Q = 5{,}000{,}000 - 120P,\ \text{or in inverse for as }\ P = \frac{5{,}000{,}000}{120} - \frac{Q}{120}.$$

Since the marginal revenue curve has twice the slope of the demand curve:

$$MR = \frac{5,000,000}{120} - \frac{Q}{60}.$$

To find the profit-maximizing quantity, set marginal revenue equal to marginal cost:

$$\frac{5,000,000}{120} - \frac{Q}{60} = 20,000, \text{ or } Q^* = 1,300,000.$$

Substituting Q^* into the demand equation to determine price:

$$P = \frac{5,000,000}{120} - \left(\frac{1,300,000}{120}\right) = \$30,833.33.$$

Substituting into the demand equations for the European and American markets to find the quantity sold

$$Q_E = 4,000,000 - (100)(30,833.3), \text{ or } Q_E = 916,667 \text{ and}$$

$$Q_U = 1,000,000 - (20)(30,833.3), \text{ or } Q_U = 383,333.$$

Substituting the values for Q_E, Q_U, and P into the profit equation, we find

$$\pi = \{1,300,000*\$30,833.33\} - \{(1,300,000)(20,000)) + 10,000,000,000\}, \text{ or}$$

$$\pi = \$4,083,333,330.$$

5. A monopolist is deciding how to allocate output between two geographically separated markets (East Coast and Midwest). Demand and marginal revenue for the two markets are:

$$P_1 = 15 - Q_1 \qquad\qquad MR_1 = 15 - 2Q_1$$

$$P_2 = 25 - 2Q_2 \qquad\qquad MR_2 = 25 - 4Q_2.$$

The monopolist's total cost is C = 5 + 3(Q_1 + Q_2). What are price, output, profits, marginal revenues, and deadweight loss (i) if the monopolist can price discriminate? (ii) if the law prohibits charging different prices in the two regions?

With price discrimination, the monopolist chooses quantities in each market such that the marginal revenue in each market is equal to marginal cost. The marginal cost is equal to 3 (the slope of the total cost curve).

In the first market

$$15 - 2Q_1 = 3, \text{ or } Q_1 = 6.$$

In the second market

$$25 - 4Q_2 = 3, \text{ or } Q_2 = 5.5.$$

Substituting into the respective demand equations, we find the following prices for the two markets:

$$P_1 = 15 - 6 = \$9 \text{ and}$$
$$P_2 = 25 - 2(5.5) = \$14.$$

Noting that the total quantity produced is 11.5, then

$$\pi = ((6)(9) + (5.5)(14)) - (5 + (3)(11.5)) = \$91.5.$$

The monopoly deadweight loss in general is equal to

$$DWL = (0.5)(Q_C - Q_M)(P_M - P_C).$$

Here,

$$DWL_1 = (0.5)(12 - 6)(9 - 3) = \$18 \text{ and}$$
$$DWL_2 = (0.5)(11 - 5.5)(14 - 3) = \$30.25.$$

Therefore, the total deadweight loss is $48.25.

Without price discrimination, the monopolist must charge a single price for the entire market. To maximize profit, we find quantity such that marginal revenue is equal to marginal cost. Adding demand equations, we find that the total demand curve has a kink at $Q = 5$:

$$P = \begin{cases} 25 - 2Q, & \text{if } Q \le 5 \\ 18.33 - 0.67Q, & \text{if } Q > 5. \end{cases}$$

This implies marginal revenue equations of

$$MR = \begin{cases} 25 - 4Q, & \text{if } Q \le 5 \\ 18.33 - 1.33Q, & \text{if } Q > 5. \end{cases}$$

With marginal cost equal to 3, $MR = 18.33 - 1.33Q$ is relevant here because the marginal revenue curve "kinks" when $P = \$15$. To determine the profit-maximizing quantity, equate marginal revenue and marginal cost:

$$18.33 - 1.33Q = 3, \text{ or } Q = 11.5.$$

Substituting the profit-maximizing quantity into the demand equation to determine price:

$$P = 18.33 - (0.67)(11.5) = \$10.6.$$

With this price, $Q_1 = 4.3$ and $Q_2 = 7.2$. (Note that at these quantities $MR_1 = 6.3$ and $MR_2 = -3.7$).

Profit is

$$(11.5)(10.6) - (5 + (3)(11.5)) = \$83.2.$$

Deadweight loss in the first market is

$$DWL_1 = (0.5)(10.6-3)(12-4.3) = \$29.26.$$

Deadweight loss in the second market is

$$DWL_2 = (0.5)(10.6-3)(11-7.2) = \$14.44.$$

Total deadweight loss is $43.7. Note it is always possible to observe slight rounding error. With price discrimination, profit is higher, deadweight loss is smaller, and total output is unchanged. This difference occurs because the quantities in each market change depending on whether the monopolist is engaging in price discrimination.

*6. Elizabeth Airlines (EA) flies only one route: Chicago-Honolulu. The demand for each flight on this route is Q = 500 - P. Elizabeth's cost of running each flight is $30,000 plus $100 per passenger.

a. **What is the profit-maximizing price EA will charge? How many people will be on each flight? What is EA's profit for each flight?**

To find the profit-maximizing price, first find the demand curve in inverse form:

$$P = 500 - Q.$$

We know that the marginal revenue curve for a linear demand curve will have twice the slope, or

$$MR = 500 - 2Q.$$

The marginal cost of carrying one more passenger is $100, so $MC = 100$. Setting marginal revenue equal to marginal cost to determine the profit-maximizing quantity, we have:

$$500 - 2Q = 100, \text{ or } Q = 200 \text{ people per flight.}$$

Substituting Q equals 200 into the demand equation to find the profit-maximizing price for each ticket,

$$P = 500 - 200, \text{ or } P = \$300.$$

Profit equals total revenue minus total costs,

$$\pi = (300)(200) - \{30,000 + (200)(100)\} = \$10,000.$$

Therefore, profit is $10,000 per flight.

b. **Elizabeth learns that the fixed costs per flight are in fact $41,000 instead of $30,000. Will she stay in this business long? Illustrate your answer using a graph of the demand curve that EA faces, EA's average cost curve when fixed costs are $30,000, and EA's average cost curve when fixed costs are $41,000.**

An increase in fixed costs will not change the profit-maximizing price and quantity. If the fixed cost per flight is $41,000, EA will lose $1,000 on each flight. The revenue generated, $60,000, would now be less than total cost, $61,000. Elizabeth would shut down as soon as the fixed cost of $41,000 came due.

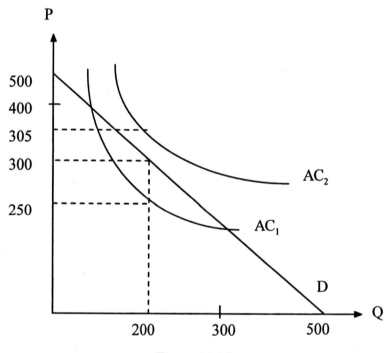

Figure 11.6.b

c. **Wait! EA finds out that two different types of people fly to Honolulu. Type A is business people with a demand of $Q_A = 260 - 0.4P$. Type B is students whose total demand is $Q_B = 240 - 0.6P$. The students are easy to spot, so EA decides to charge them different prices. Graph each of these demand curves and their horizontal sum. What price does EA charge the students? What price does EA charge other customers? How many of each type are on each flight?**

Writing the demand curves in inverse form, we find the following for the two markets:

$$P_A = 650 - 2.5Q_A \text{ and}$$
$$P_B = 400 - 1.67Q_B.$$

Using the fact that the marginal revenue curves have twice the slope of a linear demand curve, we have:

$$MR_A = 650 - 5Q_A \quad \text{and}$$
$$MR_B = 400 - 3.34Q_B.$$

To determine the profit-maximizing quantities, set marginal revenue equal to marginal cost in each market:

$$650 - 5Q_A = 100, \text{ or } Q_A = 110 \text{ and}$$
$$400 - 3.34Q_B = 100, \text{ or } Q_B = 90.$$

Substitute the profit-maximizing quantities into the respective demand curve to determine the appropriate price in each sub-market:

$$P_A = 650 - (2.5)(110) = \$375 \text{ and}$$
$$P_B = 400 - (1.67)(90) = \$250.$$

When she is able to distinguish the two groups, Elizabeth finds it profit-maximizing to charge a higher price to the Type A travelers, i.e., those who have a less elastic demand at any price.

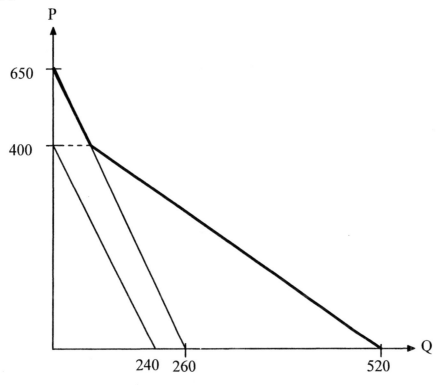

Figure 11.6.c

d. **What would EA's profit be for each flight? Would she stay in business? Calculate the consumer surplus of each consumer group. What is the total consumer surplus?**

With price discrimination, total revenue is

$$(90)(250) + (110)(375) = \$63,750.$$

Total cost is

$$41,000 + (90 + 110)(100) = \$61,000.$$

Profits per flight are

$$\pi = 63,750 - 61,000 = \$2,750.$$

171

Consumer surplus for Type A travelers is

$$(0.5)(650 - 375)(110) = \$15,125.$$

Consumer surplus for Type B travelers is

$$(0.5)(400 - 250)(90) = \$6,750$$

Total consumer surplus is $21,875.

e. **Before EA started price discriminating, how much consumer surplus was the Type A demand getting from air travel to Honolulu? Type B? Why did total surplus decline with price discrimination, even though the total quantity sold was unchanged?**

When price was $300, Type A travelers demanded 140 seats; consumer surplus was

$$(0.5)(650 - 300)(140) = \$24,500.$$

Type B travelers demanded 60 seats at P = $300; consumer surplus was

$$(0.5)(400 - 300)(60) = \$3,000.$$

Consumer surplus was therefore $27,500, which is greater than consumer surplus of $21,875 with price discrimination. Although the total quantity is unchanged by price discrimination, price discrimination has allowed EA to extract consumer surplus from those passengers who value the travel most.

7. Many retail video stores offer two alternative plans for renting films:

- **A *two-part tariff*: Pay an annual membership fee (e.g., $40) and then pay a small fee for the daily rental of each film (e.g., $2 per film per day).**

- **A *straight rental fee*: Pay no membership fee, but pay a higher daily rental fee (e.g., $4 per film per day).**

What is the logic behind the two-part tariff in this case? Why offer the customer a choice of two plans rather than simply a two-part tariff?

By employing this strategy, the firm allows consumers to sort themselves into two groups, or markets (assuming that subscribers do not rent to non-subscribers): high-volume consumers who rent many movies per year (here, more than 20) and low-volume consumers who rent only a few movies per year (less than 20). If only a two-part tariff is offered, the firm has the problem of determining the profit-maximizing entry and rental fees with many different consumers. A high entry fee with a low rental fee discourages low-volume consumers from subscribing. A low entry fee with a high rental fee encourages membership, but discourages high-volume customers from renting. Instead of forcing customers to pay both an entry and rental fee, the firm effectively charges two different prices to two types of customers.

8. Sal's satellite company broadcasts TV to subscribers in Los Angeles and New York. The demand functions for each of these two groups are

$$Q_{NY} = 60 - 0.25P_{NY} \qquad\qquad Q_{LA} = 100 - 0.50P_{LA}$$

where Q is in thousands of subscriptions per year and P is the subscription price per year. The cost of providing Q units of service is given by

$$C = 1,000 + 40Q$$

where $Q = Q_{NY} + Q_{LA}$.

a. **What are the profit-maximizing prices and quantities for the New York and Los Angeles markets?**

We know that a monopolist with two markets should pick quantities in each market so that the marginal revenues in both markets are equal to one another and equal to marginal cost. Marginal cost is \$40 (the slope of the total cost curve). To determine marginal revenues in each market, we first solve for price as a function of quantity:

$$P_{NY} = 240 - 4Q_{NY} \text{ and}$$
$$P_{LA} = 200 - 2Q_{LA}.$$

Since the marginal revenue curve has twice the slope of the demand curve, the marginal revenue curves for the respective markets are:

$$MR_{NY} = 240 - 8Q_{NY} \text{ and}$$
$$MR_{LA} = 200 - 4Q_{LA}.$$

Set each marginal revenue equal to marginal cost, and determine the profit-maximizing quantity in each submarket:

$$40 = 240 - 8Q_{NY}, \text{ or } Q_{NY} = 25 \text{ and}$$
$$40 = 200 - 4Q_{LA}, \text{ or } Q_{LA} = 40.$$

Determine the price in each submarket by substituting the profit-maximizing quantity into the respective demand equation:

$$P_{NY} = 240 - (4)(25) = \$140 \text{ and}$$
$$P_{LA} = 200 - (2)(40) = \$120.$$

b.   **As a consequence of a new satellite that the Pentagon recently deployed, people in Los Angeles receive Sal's New York broadcasts, and people in New York receive Sal's Los Angeles broadcasts. As a result, anyone in New York or Los Angeles can receive Sal's broadcasts by subscribing in either city. Thus Sal can charge only a single price. What price should he charge, and what quantities will he sell in New York and Los Angeles?**

Given this new satellite, Sal can no longer separate the two markets, so he now needs to consider the total demand function, which is the horizontal summation of the LA and NY demand functions. Above a price of 200 (the vertical intercept of the demand function for Los Angeles viewers), the total demand is just the New York demand function, whereas below a price of 200, we add the two demands:

$$Q_T = 60 - 0.25P + 100 - 0.50P, \text{ or } Q_T = 160 - 0.75P.$$

Rewriting the demand function results in

$$P = \frac{160}{0.75} - \frac{1}{0.75}Q.$$

Now total revenue $= PQ = (213.3 - 1.3Q)Q$, or $213.3Q - 1.3Q^2$, and therefore,

$$MR = 213.3 - 2.6Q.$$

Setting marginal revenue equal to marginal cost to determine the profit-maximizing quantity:

$$213.3 - 2.6Q = 40, \text{ or } Q = 65.$$

Substitute the profit-maximizing quantity into the demand equation to determine price:

$$65 = 160 - 0.75P, \text{ or } P = \$126.67.$$

Although a price of \$126.67 is charged in both markets, different quantities are purchased in each market.

$$Q_{NY} = 60 - 0.25(126.67) = 28.3 \text{ and}$$
$$Q_{LA} = 100 - 0.50(126.67) = 36.7.$$

Together, 65 units are purchased at a price of \$126.67 each.

c.　**In which of the above situations, (a) or (b), is Sal better off? In terms of consumer surplus, which situation do people in New York prefer and which do people in Los Angeles prefer? Why?**

Sal is better off in the situation with the highest profit. Under the market condition in 8a, profit is equal to:

$$\pi = Q_{NY}P_{NY} + Q_{LA}P_{LA} - (1{,}000 + 40(Q_{NY} + Q_{LA})), \text{ or}$$

$$\pi = (25)(\$140) + (40)(\$120) - (1{,}000 + 40(25 + 40)) = \$4{,}700.$$

Under the market conditions in 8b, profit is equal to:

$$\pi = Q_TP - (1{,}000 + 40Q_T), \text{ or}$$

$$\pi = (126.67)(65) - (1{,}000 + (40)(65)) = \$4633.33.$$

Therefore, Sal is better off when the two markets are separated.

Consumer surplus is the area under the demand curve above price. Under the market conditions in 8a, consumer surpluses in New York and Los Angeles are:

$$CS_{NY} = (0.5)(240 - 140)(25) = \$1250 \text{ and}$$
$$CS_{LA} = (0.5)(200 - 120)(40) = \$1600.$$

Under the market conditions in 8b the respective consumer surpluses are:

$$CS_{NY} = (0.5)(240 - 126.67)(28.3) = \$1603.67 \text{ and}$$
$$CS_{LA} = (0.5)(200 - 126.67)(36.7) = \$1345.67.$$

The New Yorkers prefer 8b because the equilibrium price is $126.67 instead of $140, thus giving them a higher consumer surplus. The customers in Los Angeles prefer 8a because the equilibrium price is $120 instead of $126.67.

*9. You are an executive for Super Computer, Inc. (SC), which rents out super computers. SC receives a fixed rental payment per time period in exchange for the right to unlimited computing at a rate of P cents per second. SC has two types of potential customers of equal number–10 businesses and 10 academic institutions. Each business customer has the demand function Q = 10 - P, where Q is in millions of seconds per month; each academic institution has the demand Q = 8 - P. The marginal cost to SC of additional computing is 2 cents per second, regardless of the volume.

a.　**Suppose that you could separate business and academic customers. What rental fee and usage fee would you charge each group? What would be your profits?**

For academic customers, consumer surplus at a price equal to marginal cost is

(0.5)(8 - 2)(6) = 18 million cents per month or $180,000 per month.

Therefore, charge $180,000 per month in rental fees and two cents per second in usage fees, i.e., the marginal cost. Each academic customer will yield a profit of $180,000 per month for total profits of $1,800,000 per month.

For business customers, consumer surplus is

(0.5)(10 - 2)(8) = 32 million cents or $320,000 per month.

Therefore, charge $320,000 per month in rental fees and two cents per second in usage fees. Each business customer will yield a profit of $320,000 per month for total profits of $3,200,000 per month.

Total profits will be $5 million per month minus any fixed costs.

b. **Suppose you were unable to keep the two types of customers separate and charged a zero rental fee. What usage fee maximizes your profits? What are your profits?**

Total demand for the two types of customers with ten customers per type is

$$Q = (10)(10 - P) + (10)(8 - P) = 180 - 20P.$$

Solving for price as a function of quantity:

$$P = 9 - \frac{Q}{20}, \text{ which implies } MR = 9 - \frac{Q}{10}.$$

To maximize profits, set marginal revenue equal to marginal cost,

$$9 - \frac{Q}{10} = 2, \text{ or } Q = 70.$$

At this quantity, the profit-maximizing price, or usage fee, is 5.5 cents per second.

$$\pi = (5.5 - 2)(70) = \$2.45 \text{ million cents per month, or } \$24,500.$$

c. **Suppose you set up one two-part tariff- that is, you set one rental and one usage fee that both business and academic customers pay. What usage and rental fees would you set? What would be your profits? Explain why price would not be equal to marginal cost.**

With a two-part tariff and no price discrimination, set the rental fee (RENT) to be equal to the consumer surplus of the academic institution (if the rental fee were set equal to that of business, academic institutions would not purchase any computer time):

$$\text{RENT} = CS_A = (0.5)(8 - P^*)(8 - P^*) = (0.5)(8 - P^*)^2.$$

Total revenue and total costs are:

$$TR = (20)(\text{RENT}) + (Q_A + Q_B)(P^*)$$

$$TC = 2(Q_A + Q_B).$$

Substituting for quantities in the profit equation with total quantity in the demand equation:

$$\pi = (20)(\text{RENT}) + (Q_A + Q_B)(P^*) - (2)(Q_A + Q_B), \text{ or}$$

$$\pi = (10)(8 - P^*)^2 + (P^* - 2)(180 - 20P^*).$$

Differentiating with respect to price and setting it equal to zero:

$$\frac{d\pi}{dP^*} = -20P^* + 60 = 0.$$

Solving for price, $P^* = 3$ cent per second. At this price, the rental fee is

$$(0.5)(8 - 3)^2 = 12.5 \text{ million cents or } \$125,000 \text{ per month.}$$

At this price

$$Q_A = (10)(8 - 3) = 50$$

$$Q_B = (10)(10 - 3) = 70.$$

The total quantity is 120 million seconds. Profits are rental fees plus usage fees minus total cost, i.e., (12.5)(20) plus (120)(3) minus 240, or 370 million cents, or $3.7 million per month. Price does not equal marginal cost, because SC can make greater profits by charging a rental fee and a higher-than-marginal-cost usage fee.

10. **As the owner of the only tennis club in an isolated wealthy community, you must decide on membership dues and fees for court time. There are two types of tennis players. "Serious" players have demand**

$$Q_1 = 10 - P$$

where Q_1 is court hours per week and P is the fee per hour for each individual player. There are also "occasional" players with demand

$$Q_2 = 4 - (1/4)P.$$

Assume that there are 1,000 players of each type. Because you have plenty of courts, the marginal cost of court time is zero. You have fixed costs of $10,000 per week. Serious and occasional players look alike, so you must charge them the same prices.

a. Suppose that to maintain a "professional" atmosphere, you want to limit membership to serious players. How should you set the *annual* membership dues and court fees (assume 52 weeks per year) to maximize profits, keeping in mind the constraint that only serious players choose to join? What would profits be (per week)?

In order to limit membership to serious players, the club owner should charge an entry fee, *T*, equal to the total consumer surplus of serious players. With individual demands of $Q_1 = 10 - P$, individual consumer surplus is equal to:

$$(0.5)(10 - 0)(10 - 0) = \$50, \text{ or}$$

$$(50)(52) = \$2600 \text{ per year.}$$

An entry fee of $2600 maximizes profits by capturing all consumer surplus. The profit-maximizing court fee is set to zero, because marginal cost is equal to zero. The entry fee of $2600 is higher than the occasional players are willing to pay (higher than their consumer surplus at a court fee of zero); therefore, this strategy will limit membership to the serious player. Weekly profits would be

$$\pi = (50)(1,000) - 10,000 = \$40,000.$$

b. A friend tells you that you could make greater profits by encouraging both types of players to join. Is the friend right? What annual dues and court fees would maximize weekly profits? What would these profits be?

When there are two classes of customers, serious and occasional players, the club owner maximizes profits by charging court fees above marginal cost and by setting the entry fee (annual dues) equal to the remaining consumer surplus of the consumer with the lesser demand, in this case, the occasional player. The entry fee, *T*, is equal to the consumer surplus remaining after the court fee is assessed:

$$T = (0.5)(Q_2)(10 - P),$$

where

$$Q_2 = 4 - \left(\frac{1}{4}\right)P, \text{ or}$$

$$T = (0.5)\left(4.0 - \frac{1}{4}P\right)(10 - P) = 20 - \frac{26P}{8} + \frac{P^2}{8}.$$

The entry fees generated by all of the 2,000 players would be

$$(2,000)\left(20 - \frac{26P}{8} + \frac{P^2}{8}\right) = 40,000 - 6,500P + 250P^2.$$

On the other hand, revenues from court fees are equal to

$$P(Q_1 + Q_2).$$

We can substitute demand as a function of price for Q_1 and Q_2:

$$P\left[(10 - P)(1,000) + \left(4 - \frac{P}{4}\right)(1,000)\right] = 14,000P - 1,250P^2.$$

Then total revenue from both entry and user fees is equal to

$$TR = 40,000 + 7,500P - 1,000P^2.$$

To maximize profits, the club owner should choose a price such that marginal revenue is equal to marginal cost, which in this case is zero. Marginal revenue is given by the slope of the total revenue curve:

$$MR = 7,500 - 2,000P.$$

Equating marginal revenue and marginal cost to maximize profits:

$$7,500 - 2,000P = 0, \text{ or } P = \$3.75.$$

Total revenue can be found by substituting into the total revenue function above, or:

$$TR = 40,000 + 7,500*3.75 - 1,000*3.75*3.75 = \$54,062.5.$$

Total cost is equal to fixed costs of $10,000. Profit with a two-part tariff is $44,062.5 per week, which is greater than the $40,000 per week generated when only professional players are recruited to be members.

c.   **Suppose that over the years young, upwardly mobile professionals move to your community, all of whom are serious players. You believe there are now 3,000 serious players and 1,000 occasional players. Would it still be profitable to cater to the occasional player? What would be the profit-maximizing annual dues and court fees? What would profits be per week?**

An entry fee of $50 per week would attract only serious players. With 3,000 serious players, total revenues would be $150,000 and profits would be $140,000 per week. With both serious and occasional players, we may follow the same procedure as in 10b. Entry fees would be equal to 4,000 times the consumer surplus of the occasional player:

$$T = 4,000\left(20 - \frac{26P}{8} + \frac{P^2}{8}\right).$$

Court fees are:

$$P\left[(10 - P)(3,000) + \left(4 - \frac{P}{4}\right)(1,000)\right] = 7000P - 3250P^2.$$

Total revenue from both entry and user fees is equal to

$$TR = 80,000 + 21,000P - 2750P^2.$$

This implies

$$MR = 21,000 - 5,500P.$$

Equate marginal revenue to marginal cost, which is zero, to determine the profit-maximizing price:

$$21,000 - 5,500P = 0, \text{ or } P = \$3.82.$$

Total revenue is equal to $120,090.90. Total cost is equal to fixed costs of $10,000. Profit with a two-part tariff is $110,090.90 per week, which is less than the $140,000 per week with only serious players. The club owner should set annual dues at $2600 and earn profits of $7.79 million per year.

11. Look again at Figure 11.12, which shows the reservation prices of three consumers for two goods. Assuming that the marginal production cost is zero for both goods, can the producer make the most money by selling the goods separately, by bundling, or by using "mixed" bundling (i.e., offering the goods separately or as a bundle)? What prices should be charged?

The following tables summarize the reservation prices of the three consumers and the profits from the three strategies as shown in Figure 11.12 in the text:

Reservation Price

	For 1	For 2	Total
Consumer A	$ 3.25	$ 6.00	$ 9.25
Consumer B	$ 8.25	$ 3.25	$11.50
Consumer C	$10.00	$10.00	$20.00

	Price 1	Price 2	Bundled	Profit
Sell Separately	$ 8.25	$6.00	___	$28.50
Pure Bundling	___	___	$ 9.25	$27.75
Mixed Bundling	$10.00	$6.00	$11.50	$29.00

The profit-maximizing strategy is to use mixed bundling. When each item is sold separately, two of Product 1 are sold at $8.25, and two of Product 2 are sold at $6.00. In the pure bundling case, three bundles are purchased at a price of $9.25. The bundle price is determined by the lowest reservation price. With mixed bundling, one Product 2 is sold at $6.00 and two bundles at $11.50. Mixed bundling is often the ideal strategy when demands are only somewhat negatively correlated and/or when marginal production costs are significant.

12. Look again at Figure 11.17. Suppose that the marginal costs c_1 and c_2 were zero. Show that in this case, pure bundling and not mixed bundling, is the most profitable pricing strategy. What price should be charged for the bundle? What will the firm's profit be?

Figure 11.17 in the text is reproduced as Figure 11.12 here. With marginal costs both equal to zero, the firm wants to sell as many units as possible to maximize profit. Here, revenue maximization is the same as profit maximization. The firm should set the bundle price at $100, since this is the sum of the reservation prices for all consumers. At this price all customers purchase the bundle, and the firm's revenues are $400. This revenue is greater than setting $P_1 = P_2 = \$89.95$ and setting $P_B = \$100$ with the mixed bundling strategy. With mixed bundling, the firm sells one unit of Product 1, one unit of Product 2, and two bundles. Total revenue is $379.90, which is less than $400. Since marginal cost is zero, and demands are negatively correlated, pure bundling is the best strategy.

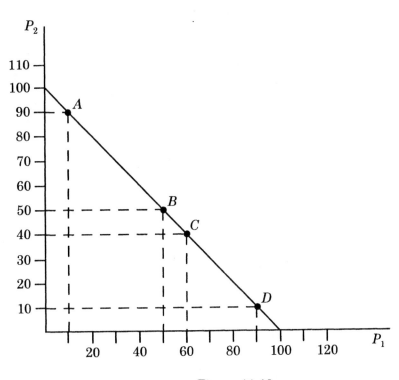

Figure 11.12

13. Some years ago, an article appeared in *The New York Times* about IBM's pricing policy. The previous day IBM had announced major price cuts on most of its small and medium-sized computers. The article said:

> "IBM probably has no choice but to cut prices periodically to get its customers to purchase more and lease less. If they succeed, this could make life more difficult for IBM's major competitors. Outright purchases of computers are needed for ever larger IBM revenues and profits, says Morgan Stanley's Ulric Weil in his new book, *Information Systems in the '80's.* Mr. Weil declares that IBM cannot revert to an emphasis on leasing."

a. Provide a brief but clear argument *in support* of the claim that IBM should try "to get its customers to purchase more and lease less."

If we assume there is no resale market, there are at least three arguments that could be made in support of the claim that IBM should try to "get its customers to purchase more and lease less." First, when customers purchase computers, they are "locked into" the product. They do not have the option of not renewing the lease when it expires. Second, by getting customers to purchase a computer instead of leasing it, IBM leads customers to make a stronger economic decision for IBM and against its competitors. Thus, it would be easier for IBM to eliminate its competitors if all its customers purchased, rather than leased, computers. Third, computers have a high obsolescence rate. If IBM believes that this rate is higher than what their customers perceive it is, the lease charges would be higher than what the customers would be willing to pay and it would be more profitable to sell the computers instead.

b. Provide a brief but clear argument *against* this claim.

The primary argument for leasing computers to customers, instead of selling the computers, is that because IBM has monopoly power on computers, it might be able to charge a two-part tariff and therefore extract some of the consumer surplus and increase its profits. For example, IBM could charge a fixed leasing fee plus a charge per unit of computing time used. Such a scheme would not be possible if the computers were sold outright.

c. **What factors determine whether leasing or selling is preferable for a company like IBM? Explain briefly.**

There are at least three factors that could determine whether leasing or selling is preferable for IBM. The first factor is the amount of consumer surplus that IBM could extract if the computer were leased and a two-part tariff scheme were applied. The second factor is the relative discount rates on cash flows: if IBM has a higher discount rate than its customers, it might prefer to sell; if IBM has a lower discount rate than its customers, it might prefer to lease. A third factor is the vulnerability of IBM's competitors. Selling computers would force customers to make more of a financial commitment to one company over the rest, while with a leasing arrangement the customers have more flexibility. Thus, if IBM feels it has the requisite market power, it should prefer to sell computers instead of lease them.

14. **You are selling two goods, 1 and 2, to a market consisting of three consumers with reservation prices as follows:**

Reservation Price ($)

Consumer	For 1	For 2
A	20	100
B	60	60
C	100	20

The unit cost of each product is $30.

a. **Compute the optimal prices and profits for (i) selling the goods separately, (ii) pure bundling, and (iii) mixed bundling.**

The prices and profits for each strategy are

	Price 1	Price 2	Bundled Price	Profit
Sell Separately	$100.00	$100.00	—	$140.00
Pure Bundling	—	—	$120.00	$180.00
Mixed Bundling	$99.95	$99.95	$120.00	$199.90

You can try other prices to confirm that these are the best. For example, if you charge $60 for good 1 and $60 for good 2 then B and C will buy good 1 and A and B will buy good 2. Since marginal cost for each unit is $30, profit for each unit is $60-$30=$30 for a total of $120.

b. **Which strategy would be most profitable? Why?**

Mixed bundling is best because, for each good, marginal production cost ($30) exceeds the reservation price for one consumer. Consumer A has a reservation price of $100 for good 2 and only $20 for good 1. The firm responds by offering good 2 at a price just below Consumer A's reservation price and by charging a price for the bundle, so that the difference between the bundle price and the price of good 2 is above Consumer A's reservation price of good 1 ($20.05). Consumer C's choice is symmetric to Consumer A's choice. Consumer B chooses the bundle because the bundle's price is equal to the reservation price and the separate prices for the goods are both above the reservation price for either good.

15. **Your firm produces two products, the demands for which are independent. Both products are produced at zero marginal cost. You face four consumers (or groups of consumers) with the following reservation prices:**

Consumer	Good 1 ($)	Good 2 ($)
A	25	100
B	40	80
C	80	40
D	100	25

a. **Consider three alternative pricing strategies: (i) selling the goods separately; (ii) pure bundling; (iii) mixed bundling. For *each strategy*, determine the optimal prices to be charged and the resulting profits. Which strategy would be best?**

For each strategy, the optimal prices and profits are

	Price 1	Price 2	Bundled Price	Profit
Sell Separately	$80.00	$80.00	—	$320.00
Pure Bundling	—	—	$120.00	$480.00
Mixed Bundling	$94.95	$94.95	$120.00	$429.90

You can try other prices to verify that $80 for each good is optimal. For example if each good is $100 then only two units are sold and profit is $100. If one is $100 and one is $80, then one is sold for $100 and two for $80 for a total of $260. Note that in the case of mixed bundling, the price of each good must be set at $94.95 and not $99.95 since the bundle is $5 cheaper than the sum of the reservation prices for consumers A and D. If the price of each good is set at $99.95 then neither consumer A nor D will buy the individual good because they only save five cents off of their reservation price, as opposed to $5 for the bundle. Also the difference between the bundle price and the unit price (120-94.95) is above the reservation price of the other good for each person. Pure bundling dominates mixed bundling, because with marginal costs of zero there is no reason to exclude purchases of both goods by all consumers.

b. **Now suppose that the production of each good entails a marginal cost of $30. How does this information change your answers to (a)? Why is the optimal strategy now different?**

With marginal cost of $30, the optimal prices and profits are:

	Price 1	Price 2	Bundled Price	Profit
Sell Separately	$80.00	$80.00	—	$200.00
Pure Bundling	—	—	$120.00	$240.00
Mixed Bundling	$94.95	$94.95	$120.00	$249.90

Mixed bundling is the best strategy. Since the marginal cost is above the reservation price of consumer's A and D, the firm can benefit by using mixed bundling to encourage them to only buy the one good.

16. **A cable TV company offers, in addition to its basic service, two products: a Sports Channel (Product 1) and a Movie Channel (Product 2). Subscribers to the basic service can subscribe to these additional services individually at the monthly prices P_1 and P_2, respectively, or they can buy the two as a bundle for the price P_B, where $P_B < P_1 + P_2$. (They can also forego the additional services and simply buy the basic service.) The company's marginal cost for these additional services is *zero*. Through market research, the cable company has estimated the reservation prices for these two services for a representative group of consumers in the company's service area. These reservation prices are plotted (as x's) in Figure 11.16, as are the prices P_1, P_2, and P_B that the cable company is currently charging. The graph is divided into regions, I, II, III, and IV.**

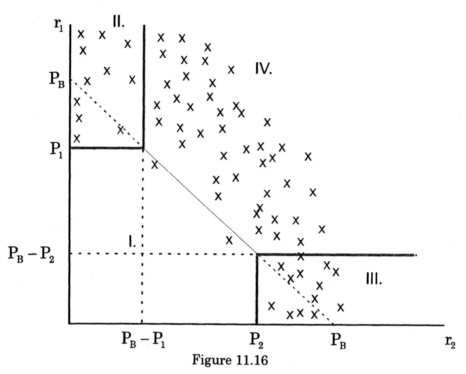

Figure 11.16

a.   **Which products, if any, will be purchased by the consumers in region I? In region II? In region III? In region IV? Explain briefly.**

Product 1 = sports channel. Product 2 = movie channel.

Region	Purchase	Reservation Prices
I	nothing	$r_1 < P_1$, $r_2 < P_2$, $r_1 + r_2 < P_B$
II	sports channel	$r_1 > P_1$, $r_2 < P_B - P_1$
III	movie channel	$r_2 > P_2$, $r_1 < P_B - P_2$
IV	both channels	$r_1 > P_B - P_2$, $r_2 > P_B - P_1$, $r_1 + r_2 > P_B$

To see why consumers in regions II and III do not buy the bundle, reason as follows: For region II, $r_1 > P_1$, so the consumer will buy product 1. If she bought the bundle, she would pay an additional $P_B - P_1$. Since her reservation price for product 2 is less than $P_B - P_1$, she will choose only to buy product 1. Similar reasoning applies to region III.

182

Consumers in region I purchase nothing because the sum of their reservation values are less than the bundling price and each reservation value is lower than the respective price.

In region IV the sum of the reservation values for the consumers are higher than the bundle price, so these consumers would rather purchase the bundle than nothing. To see why the consumers in this region cannot do better than purchase either of the products separately, reason as follows: since $r_1 > P_B - P_2$ the consumer is better off purchasing both products than just product 2, likewise since $r_2 > P_B - P_1$, the consumer is better off purchasing both products rather than just product 1.

b. **Note that the reservation prices for the Sports Channel and the Movie Channel, as drawn in the figure, are negatively correlated. Why would you, or would you not, expect consumers' reservation prices for cable TV channels to be negatively correlated?**

Prices may be negatively correlated if people's tastes differ in the following way: the more avidly a person likes sports, the less he or she will care for movies, and vice versa. Reservation prices would not be negatively correlated if people who were willing to pay a lot of money to watch sports were also willing to pay a lot of money to watch movies.

c. **The company's vice president has said: "Because the marginal cost of providing an additional channel is zero, mixed bundling offers no advantage over pure bundling. Our profits would be just as high if we offered the Sports Channel and the Movie Channel together as a bundle, and only as a bundle." Do you agree or disagree? Explain why.**

It depends. By offering only the bundled product, the company would lose customers below the bundle price in regions II and III. At the same time, those consumers above the bundling price line in these regions would only buy one service, rather than the bundled service. The net effect on revenues is indeterminate. The exact solution depends on the distribution of consumers in those regions.

d. **Suppose the cable company continues to use mixed bundling as a way of selling these two services. Based on the distribution of reservation prices shown in Figure 11.21, do you think the cable company should alter any of the prices it is now charging? If so, how?**

The cable company could raise P_B, P_1, and P_2 slightly without losing any customers. Alternatively, it could raise prices even past the point of losing customers as long as the additional revenue from the remaining customers made up for the revenue loss from the lost customers.

17. Consider a firm with monopoly power that faces the demand curve

$$P = 100 - 3Q + 4A^{1/2}$$

and has the total cost function

$$C = 4Q^2 + 10Q + A,$$

where A is the level of advertising expenditures, and P and Q are price and output.

a. **Find the values of A, Q, and P that maximize the firm's profit.**

Profit (π) is equal to total revenue, TR, minus total cost, TC. Here,

$$TR = PQ = (100 - 3Q + 4A^{1/2})Q = 100Q - 3Q^2 + 4QA^{1/2} \text{ and}$$

$$TC = 4Q^2 + 10Q + A.$$

Therefore,

$$\pi = 100Q - 3Q^2 + 4QA^{1/2} - 4Q^2 - 10Q - A, \text{ or}$$

$$\pi = 90Q - 7Q^2 + 4QA^{1/2} - A.$$

The firm wants to choose its level of output and advertising expenditures to maximize its profits:

$$\text{Max } \pi = 90Q - 7Q^2 + 4QA^{1/2} - A$$

The necessary conditions for an optimum are:

(1) $\qquad \dfrac{\partial \pi}{\partial Q} = 90 - 14Q + 4A^{1/2} = 0,$ and

(2) $\qquad \dfrac{\partial \pi}{\partial A} = 2QA^{-1/2} - 1 = 0.$

From equation (2), we obtain

$$A^{1/2} = 2Q.$$

Substituting this into equation (1), we obtain

$$90 - 14Q + 4(2Q) = 0, \text{ or } Q^* = 15.$$

Then,

$$A^* = (4)(15^2) = 900,$$

which implies

$$P^* = 100 - (3)(15) + (4)(900^{1/2}) = \$175.$$

b. **Calculate the Lerner index, L = (P - MC)/P, for this firm at its profit-maximizing levels of A, Q, and P.**

The degree of monopoly power is given by the formula $\dfrac{P - MC}{P}$. Marginal cost is $8Q + 10$ (the derivative of total cost with respect to quantity). At the optimum, where $Q = 15$, $MC = (8)(15) + 10 = 130$. Therefore, the Lerner index is

$$L = \frac{175 - 130}{175} = 0.257.$$

CHAPTER 11 APPENDIX
TRANSFER PRICING IN THE INTEGRATED FIRM

EXERCISES

1. Review the numerical example about Race Car Motors. Calculate the profit earned by the upstream division, the downstream division, and the firm as a whole in each of the three cases examined: (a) no outside market for engines; (b) a competitive market for engines in which the market price is $6,000; and (c) the firm is a monopoly supplier of engines to an outside market. In which case does Race Car Motors earn the most profit? In which case does the upstream division earn the most? the downstream division?

We shall examine each case, then compare profits. We are given the following information about Race Car Motors:

The demand for its automobiles is

$$P = 20,000 - Q.$$

Therefore its marginal revenue is

$$MR = 20,000 - 2Q.$$

The downstream division's cost of assembling cars is

$$C_A(Q) = 8,000Q,$$

so the division's marginal cost is $MC_A = 8,000$. The upstream division's cost of producing engines is

$$C_E(Q_E) = 2Q_E^2,$$

so division's marginal cost is $MC_E(Q_E) = 4Q_E$.

Case (a): To determine the profit-maximizing quantity of output, set the net marginal revenue for engines equal to the marginal cost of producing engines. Because each car has one engine, Q_E equals Q, and the net marginal revenue of engines is

$$NMR_E = MR - MC_A, \text{ or}$$

$$NMR_E = (20,000 - 2Q) - 8,000 = 12,000 - 2Q_E.$$

Setting NMR_E equal to MC_E:

$$12,000 - 2Q_E = 4Q_E, \text{ or } Q_E = 2,000.$$

The firm should produce 2,000 engines and 2,000 cars. The optimal transfer price is the marginal cost of the 2,000 engines:

$$MC_E = 4Q_E = (4)(2,000) = \$8,000.$$

The profit-maximizing price of the cars is found by substituting the profit-maximizing quantity into the demand function:

$$P = 20,000 - Q, \text{ or } P - 20,000 - 2,000 = \$18,000.$$

The profits for each division are equal to

$$\pi_E = (8,000)(2,000) - (2)(2,000)^2 = \$8,000,000,$$

and

$$\pi_C = (18,000)(2,000) - ((8,000)(2,000) + 16,000,000) = \$4,000,000.$$

Total profits are equal to $\pi_E + \pi_C = \$12,000,000$.

Case (b): To determine the profit-maximizing level of output when an outside market for engines exists, first note that the competitive price for engines on the outside market is $6,000, which is less than the transfer price of $8,000. With the market price less than the transfer price, this means that the firm will buy some of its engines on the outside market. To determine how many cars the firm should produce, set the market price of engines equal to net marginal revenue. We use the market price, since it is now the marginal cost of engines, and the optimal transfer price

$$6,000 = 12,000 - 2Q_E, \text{ or } Q_E = 3,000.$$

The total quantity of engines and automobiles is 3,000. The price of the cars is determined by substituting Q_E into the demand function for cars:

$$P = 20,000 - 3,000, \text{ or } P = \$17,000.$$

The company now produces more cars and sells them at a lower price. To determine the number of engines that the firm will produce and how many the firm will buy on the market, set the marginal cost of engine production equal to 6,000, solve for Q_E, and then find the difference between this number and the 3,000 cars to be produced:

$$MC_E = 4Q_E = 6,000, \text{ or } Q_E = 1,500.$$

Thus, 1,500 engines will be bought on the external market.

For the engine-building division, profits are found by subtracting total costs from total revenue:

$$\pi_E = TR_E - TC_E = (\$6,000)(1,500) - (2)(1,500)^2 = \$4,500,000.$$

For the automobile-assembly division, profits are found by subtracting total costs from total revenue:

$$\pi_A = TR_A - TC_A = (\$17,000)(3,000) - (8,000 + 6,000)(3,000) = \$9,000,000.$$

Total profits for the firm are the sum of the two divisions,

$$\pi_T = \$13,500,000.$$

Case (c): In the case where the firm is a monopoly supplier of engines to the outside market, the demand in the outside market for engines is:

$$P_{E,M} = 10,000 - Q_E,$$

which means that the marginal revenue curve for engines in the outside market is:

$$MR_{E,M} = 10,000 - 2Q_E.$$

To determine the optimal transfer price, find the *total* net marginal revenue by horizontally summing $MR_{E,M}$ with the net marginal revenue from "sales" to the downstream division, $12,000 - 2Q_E$. For output of Q_E greater than 1,000, this is:

$$NMR_{E,\ Total} = 11,000 - Q_E.$$

Set $NMR_{E,\ Total}$ equal to the marginal cost of producing engines to determine the optimal quantity of engines:

$$11,000 - Q_E = 4Q_E, \text{ or } Q_E = 2,200.$$

Now we must determine how many of the 2,200 engines produced will be sold to the downstream division and how may will be sold on the external market. First, note that the marginal cost of producing these 2,200 engines, and therefore the optimal transfer price, is $4Q_E = \$8,800$. Set the optimal transfer price equal to the marginal revenue from sales in the outside market:

$$8,800 = 10,000 - 2Q_E, \text{ or } Q_E = 600.$$

Therefore, 600 engines should be sold in the external market.

To determine the price at which these engines should be sold, substitute 600 into demand in the outside market for engines and solve for P:

$$P_{E,M} = 10,000 - 600 = \$9,400.$$

Finally, set the \$8,800 transfer price equal to the net marginal revenue from the "sales" to the downstream division:

$$8,800 = 12,000 - 2Q_E, \text{ or } Q_E = 1,600.$$

Thus, 1,600 engines should be sold to the downstream division for use in the production of 1,600 cars.

To determine the sale price of the cars, substitute 1,600 into the demand curve for automobiles:

$$P = 20,000 - 1,600 = \$18,400.$$

To determine the level of profits for each division, subtract total costs from total revenue:

$$\pi_E = \{(\$8,800)(1,600) + (\$9,400)(600)\} - (2)(2,200)^2 = \$10,040,000,$$

and

$$\pi_A = (\$18,400)(1,600) - [(8,000 + 8,800)(1,600)] = \$2,560,000.$$

Total profits are equal to the sum of the profits from the two divisions, or

$$\pi_T = \$12,600,000.$$

The table gives profits earned by each division and the firm for each case.

Profits with	Upstream Division	Downstream Division	Total
(a) No outside market	8,000,000	4,000,000	12,000,000
(b) Competitive market	4,500,000	9,000,000	13,500,000
(c) Monopolized market	10,000,000	2,600,000	12,600,000

The upstream division, building engines, earns the most profit when it has a monopoly on engines. The downstream division, building automobiles, earns the most when there is a competitive market for engines. Because of the high cost of engines, the firm does best when engines are produced at the lowest cost by an outside, competitive market.

2. Ajax Computer makes a computer for climate control in office buildings. The company uses a microprocessor, produced by its upstream division, along with other parts bought in outside competitive markets. The microprocessor is produced at a constant marginal cost of \$500, and the marginal cost of assembling the computer (including the cost of the other parts) by the downstream division is a constant \$700. The firm has been selling the computer for \$2,000, and until now there has been no outside market for the microprocessor.

a. **Suppose an outside market for the microprocessor develops and Ajax has monopoly power in that market, selling microprocessors for \$1,000 each. Assuming that demand for the microprocessor is unrelated to the demand for the Ajax computer, what transfer price should Ajax apply to the microprocessor for its use by the downstream division? Should its production of computers be increased, decreased, or left unchanged? Explain briefly.**

Ajax should exploit its monopoly power in the processor market by charging its downstream firm a transfer price equal to the marginal cost of \$500. Although its production of processors will be greater than when there was no outside market, this will not affect the production of computers, because the extra production of processors does not increase their marginal cost.

b.   **How would your answer to (a) change if the demands for the computer and the microprocessors were competitive; i.e., some of the people who buy the microprocessors use them to make climate control systems of their own?**

Suppose that the demand for processors comes from a firm that produces a competing computer. Extra processors sold imply a reduced demand for computers, which means that *fewer* computers will be sold. However, the firm should still charge an efficient transfer price of $500, and it would probably want to raise the price that it charges on microprocessors to the outside firm and lower the price that it charges for its computer.

3. Reebok produces and sells running shoes. It faces a market demand schedule P = 11 - 1.5Q$_S$, where Q$_S$ is the number of pairs of shoes sold (in thousands) and P is the price in dollars per thousand pairs of shoes. Production of each pair of shoes requires 1 square yard of leather. The leather is shaped and cut by the Form Division of Reebok. The cost function for leather is

$$TC_L = 1 + Q_L + 0.5Q_L^2,$$

where Q$_L$ is the quantity of leather (in thousands of square yards) produced. The cost function for running shoes is (excluding the leather)

$$TC_S = 2Q_S.$$

a.   **What is the optimal transfer price?**

With demand of $P = 11 - 1.5Q_S$, we have $TR = 11Q_S - 1.5Q_S^2$; therefore $MR = 11 - 3Q_S$. With total cost for shoes equal to $2Q_S$, the marginal cost of shoe production is 2. The marginal product of leather is 1; i.e., 1,000 square yards of leather makes 1,000 pairs of shoes. Therefore, the net marginal revenue is

$$(MR_S - MC_S)(MP_L) = (11 - 3Q_S - 2)(1) = 9 - 3Q_L.$$

For the optimal transfer price, choose the quantity so that

$$NMR_L = MC_L = P_L.$$

With the total cost for leather equal to $1 + Q_L + 0.5Q_L^2$, the marginal cost is $1 + Q_L$.

Therefore, set

$$MC_L = NMR_L,$$

$$1 + Q_L = 9 - 3Q_L, \text{ or } Q_L = 2 \text{ yards.}$$

With this quantity, the optimal transfer price is equal to $MC_L = 1 + 2 = \$3$ per square yard.

b.   **Leather can be bought and sold in a competitive market at the price of P$_F$ = 1.5. In this case, how much leather should the Form Division supply internally? How much should it supply to the outside market? Will Reebok buy any leather in the outside market? Find the optimal transfer price.**

If the transfer price is $1.5, the leather producer sets price equal to marginal cost: i.e.,

$$1.5 = 1 + Q_L, \text{ or } Q_L = 0.5 \text{ square yards.}$$

For the optimal transfer quantity, set

$$NMR_L = P_L,$$

$1.5 = 9 - 3Q$, or $Q = 2.5$ square yards.

Therefore, the shoe division should buy $2.5 - 0.5 = 2.0$ square yards from the outside market, and the leather division should sell nothing to the outside market.

c.   **Now suppose the leather is unique and of extremely high quality. Therefore, the Form Division may act as a monopoly supplier to the outside market as well as a supplier to the downstream division. Suppose the outside demand for leather is given by $P = 32 - Q_L$. What is the optimal transfer price for the use of leather by the downstream division? At what price, if any, should leather be sold to the outside market? What quantity, if any, will be sold to the outside market?**

For the outside market, the leather division can determine the optimal amount of leather to produce by setting marginal cost equal to marginal revenue,

$$1 + Q_L = 32 - 2Q_L, \text{ or } Q_L = 10.67.$$

At that quantity, $MC_L = \$11.67$ per square yard. At this marginal cost, the shoe division would optimally demand a negative amount; i.e., the shoe division should stop making shoes and the firm should confine itself to selling leather. At this quantity, the outside market is willing to pay

$$P_L = 32 - Q_L, \text{ or } P_L = \$21.33 \text{ per square yard.}$$

4. The House Products Division of Acme Corporation manufactures and sells digital clock radios. A major component for these is supplied by the Electronic Division of Acme. The cost functions for the radio and the electronic component divisions are, respectively,

$$TC_r = 30 + 2Q_r$$

$$TC_C = 70 + 6Q_C + Q_C^2$$

(Note that TC_r does not include the cost of the component.) Manufacture of one radio set requires the use of one electronic component. Market studies show that the firm's demand curve for the digital clock radio is given by:

$$P_r = 108 - Q_r$$

a.   **Assuming no outside market for the components, how many of them should be produced in order to maximize profits for Acme on a whole? What is the optimal transfer price?**

Radios require exactly one component and assembly.

      radio assembly cost: $TC_r = 30 + 2Q_r$

      component cost: $TC_c = 70 + 6Q_c + Q_c^2$

      radio demand: $P_r = 108 - Q_r$

First we must solve for the profit-maximizing number of radios to produce. We must then set the transfer price that induces the internal supplier of components to provide the profit-maximizing level of components.

Profits are given by: $p = (108 - Q_c)Q_c - (30 + 2Q_c) - (70 + 6Q_c + Q_c^2)$.

Since one and only one component is used in each radio, we can set $Q_c = Q_r$:

$$\pi = (108 - Q_c)Q_c - (30 + 2Q_c) - (70 + 6Q_c + Q_c^2).$$

Profit maximization implies: $\partial\pi/\partial Qc = 108 - 2Q_c - 2 - 6 - 2Q_c = 0$ or $Q_c = 25$.

We must now calculate the transfer price that will induce the internal supplier to supply exactly 25 components. This will be the price for which $MC_c(Q_c = 25) = P_t$ or

$$MC_c(Q_c = 25) = 6 + 2Q_c = \$56.$$

We can check our solution as follows:

Component division: $Max\ \pi_c = 56Q_c - 70 - 6Q_c - Q_c^2$

$$d\pi_c/dQ_c = 0 \Leftrightarrow 56 - 6 - 2Q_c = 0 \Leftrightarrow Q_c = 25.$$

Radio assembly division: $Max\ \pi = (108 - Q_r)Q_r - (30 + 2Q_r) - 56Q_r$

$$d\pi/dQ_r = 0 \Leftrightarrow 108 - 2Q_r - 2 - 56 = 0 \Leftrightarrow Q_r = 25.$$

b. **If other firms are willing to purchase in the outside market the component manufactured by the electronics division (which is the only supplier of this product), what is the optimal transfer price? Why? What price should be charged in the outside market? Why? How many units will the electronics division supply internally and to the outside market? Why? (Note: The demand for components in the outside market is: $P_c = 72 - 1.5Q_c$.)**

We now assume there is an outside market for components; the firm has market power in this outside market with market demand:

$$P_c = 72 - 3(Q_c/2)$$

First we solve for the profit-maximizing level of outside and internal sales. Then, we set the transfer price that induces the component division to supply the total output (sum of internal and external supply). We define Q_c as the outside sales of components and Q_i as components used inside.

Profits are given by:

$$\pi = (108 - Q_i)Q_i + (72 - (3/2)Q_c)Q_c - (30 + 2Q_i) - (70 + 6(Q_i + Q_c) + (Q_i + Q_c)^2).$$

Profit maximization implies:

$$\partial\pi/\partial Q_i = 108 - 2Q_c - 2 - 6 - 2(Q_i + Q_c) = 0$$

$$\partial\pi/\partial Q_{ic} = 72 - 3Q_c - 6 - 2(Q_i + Q_c) = 0$$

which yields:

$$Q_i + Q_c/2 = 25$$

$$5Q_c + 2Q_i = 66$$

and

$$Q_c = 4$$

$$Q_i = 23.$$

Thus, total components will be $23 + 4$, or 27.

As in part a, we solve for the transfer price by finding the marginal cost of the component division of producing the profit-maximizing level of output:

$$P_t = MC_c(Q_i^* + Q_c^*) = \$60.$$

The outside price will be: $P_c = 72 - (3/2)Q_c = \$66$ (this should actually be greater than the internal price since the firm has market power in the external price and, therefore, $MR_c < P_c$).

CHAPTER 12
MONOPOLISTIC COMPETITION AND OLIGOPOLY

TEACHING NOTES

Students viewing this material for the first time can be overwhelmed because of the number of models presented. Chapter 12 discusses seven models: monopolistic competition, Cournot-Nash, Stackelberg, Bertrand, non-cooperative game, kinked demand, and price leadership. You might want to concentrate your attention in class on the more basic models, e.g., monopolistic competition, Cournot-Nash, non-cooperative game, and price leadership. You can otherwise pick and choose among the models as time permits.

When introducing the material in this chapter, start by reviewing the basic results of the models of competition and monopoly. When presenting monopolistic competition, focus on why positive profits encourage entry and on the similarities and differences of this model with competition and monopoly. The example of brand competition in cola and coffee markets presented at the end of Section 12.2 facilitates a class discussion of the costs and benefits of freedom of choice among a vast array of brand names and trademarks. The chapter ends with two topics that invoke opinions from almost every student: an application on OPEC and Example 12.5, "The Cartelizaton of Intercollegiate Athletics."

Students may find the Cournot-Nash duopoly model to be a drastic change from the worlds of competition and monopoly. The key to understanding Cournot-Nash is a grasp of reaction functions. Stress that reaction functions are being graphed on axes that represent quantities (see Figure 12.4). Once they understand reaction functions, they will be able to follow the assumptions, reasoning, and results of the Cournot-Nash, Stackelberg, and Bertrand models. Although they might not comprehend the algebraic derivation of the Cournot-Nash equilibrium, point out the representations in Figure 12.5 of the competitive, Cournot-Nash, and collusive (monopoly) equilibria. Figure 12.5 gives the impression that the duopolists always have symmetric reaction curves. Exercise (2) shows that if the cost structures are not identical, the reaction curves are asymmetric.

While the Nash equilibrium, payoff matrices, and the Prisoners' Dilemma are introduced in this chapter, more attention is allotted to them in Chapter 13. If you will be covering Chapter 13, you can postpone discussion of Section 12.5, using it as a bridge between oligopoly theory and game theory. The discussion of a non-cooperative game is intuitive, but some students find payoff matrices difficult to read quickly. Example 12.3, "Procter & Gamble in a Prisoners' Dilemma," is an excellent representation of the pricing problems facing U.S. firms in foreign markets.

Sections 12.6 and 12.7 discuss price rigidity and price leadership. Students who have understood kinked marginal revenue curves in previous chapters will find the analysis of price rigidity easy. Those who have not mastered this concept will find Figure 12.7 difficult unless it is derived slowly. It is best to proceed as follows: (1) discuss a kinked demand curve; (2) add a kinked *MR* curve; (3) add a *MC* curve; and (4) derive profit-maximizing output.

REVIEW QUESTIONS

1. What are the characteristics of a monopolistically competitive market? What happens to the equilibrium price and quantity in such a market if one firm introduces a new, improved product?

The two primary characteristics of a monopolistically competitive market are (1) that firms compete by selling differentiated products which are highly, but not perfectly, substitutable and (2) that there is free entry and exit from the market. When a new firm enters a monopolistically competitive market (seeking positive profits), the demand curve for each of the incumbent firms shifts inward, thus reducing the price and quantity received by the incumbents. Thus, the introduction of a new product by a firm will reduce the price received and quantity sold of existing products.

2. Why is the firm's demand curve flatter than the total market demand curve in monopolistic competition? Suppose a monopolistically competitive firm is making a profit in the short run. What will happen to its demand curve in the long run?

The flatness or steepness of the firm's demand curve is a function of the elasticity of demand for the firm's product. The elasticity of the firm's demand curve is greater than the elasticity of market demand because it is easier for consumers to switch to another firm's highly substitutable product than to switch consumption to an entirely different product. Profit in the short run induces other firms to enter; as firms enter the incumbent firm's demand and marginal revenue curves shift inward, reducing the profit-maximizing quantity. Eventually, profits fall to zero, leaving no incentive for more firms to enter.

3. Some experts have argued that too many brands of breakfast cereal are on the market. Give an argument to support this view. Give an argument against it.

Pro: Too many brands of any single product signals excess capacity, implying an output level smaller than one that would minimize average cost.

Con: Consumers value the freedom to choose among a wide variety of competing products.

(Note: In 1972 the Federal Trade Commission filed suit against Kellogg, General Mills, and General Foods. It charged that these firms attempted to suppress entry into the cereal market by introducing 150 heavily advertised brands between 1950 and 1970, crowding competitors off grocers' shelves. This case was eventually dismissed in 1982.)

4. Why is the Cournot equilibrium stable (i.e., why don't firms have any incentive to change their output levels once in equilibrium)? Even if they can't collude, why don't firms set their outputs at the joint profit-maximizing levels (i.e., the levels they would have chosen had they colluded)?

A Cournot equilibrium is stable because each firm is producing the amount that maximizes its profits, *given what its competitors are producing*. If all firms behave this way, no firm has an incentive to change its output. Without collusion, firms find it difficult to agree tacitly to reduce output. Once one firm reduces its output, other firms have an incentive to increase output and increase profits at the expense of the firm that is limiting its sales.

5. In the Stackelberg model, the firm that sets output first has an advantage. Explain why.

The Stackelberg leader gains the advantage because the second firm must accept the leader's large output as given and produce a smaller output for itself. If the second firm decided to produce a larger quantity, this would reduce price and profit. The first firm knows that the second firm will have no choice but to produce a smaller output in order to maximize profit, and thus, the first firm is able to capture a larger share of industry profits.

6. What do the Cournot and Bertrand models have in common? What is different about the two models?

Both are oligopoly models in which firms produce a homogeneous good. In the Cournot model, each firm assumes its rivals will not change the quantity produced. In the Bertrand model, each firm assumes its rivals will not change the price they charge. In both models, each firm takes some aspect of its rivals behavior (either quantity or price) as fixed when making its own decision. The difference between the two is that in the Bertrand model firms end up producing where price equals marginal cost, whereas in the Cournot model the firms will produce more than the monopoly output but less than the competitive output.

7. Explain the meaning of a Nash equilibrium when firms are competing with respect to price. Why is the equilibrium stable? Why don't the firms raise prices to the level that maximizes joint profits?

A Nash equilibrium in price competition occurs when each firm chooses its price, assuming *its competitor's price as fixed*. In equilibrium, each firm does the best it can, conditional on its competitors' prices. The equilibrium is stable because firms are maximizing profit and no firm has an incentive to raise or lower its price.

Firms do not always collude: a cartel agreement is difficult to enforce because each firm has an incentive to cheat. By lowering price, the cheating firm can increase its market share and profits. A second reason that firms do not collude is that such collusion violates antitrust laws. In particular, price fixing violates Section 1 of the Sherman Act. Of course, there are attempts to circumvent antitrust laws through tacit collusion.

8. The kinked demand curve describes price rigidity. Explain how the model works. What are its limitations? Why does price rigidity arise in oligopolistic markets?

According to the kinked-demand curve model, each firm faces a demand curve that is kinked at the currently prevailing price. If a firm raises its price, most of its customers would shift their purchases to its competitors. This reasoning implies a highly elastic demand for price increases. If the firm lowers its price, however, its competitors would also lower their prices. This implies a demand curve that is more inelastic for price decreases than for price increases. This kink in the demand curve implies a discontinuity in the marginal revenue curve, so only large changes in marginal cost lead to changes in price. However accurate it is in pointing to price rigidity, this model does not explain *how* the rigid price is determined. The origin of the rigid price is explained by other models, such as the firms' desire to avoid mutually destructive price competition.

9. Why does price leadership sometimes evolve in oligopolistic markets? Explain how the price leader determines a profit-maximizing price.

Since firms cannot explicitly coordinate on setting price, they use implicit means. One form of implicit collusion is to follow a price leader. The price leader, often the dominant firm in the industry, determines its profit-maximizing price by calculating the demand curve it faces: it subtracts the quantity supplied at each price by all other firms from the market demand, and the residual is its demand curve. The leader chooses the quantity that equates its marginal revenue with marginal cost. The market price is the price at which the leader's profit-maximizing quantity sells in the market. At that price, the followers supply the remainder of the market.

10. Why has the OPEC oil cartel succeeded in raising prices substantially, while the CIPEC copper cartel has not? What conditions are necessary for successful cartelization? What organizational problems must a cartel overcome?

Successful cartelization requires two characteristics: demand should be inelastic, and the cartel must be able to control most of the supply. OPEC succeeded in the short run because the short-run demand and supply of oil were both inelastic. CIPEC has not been successful because both demand and non-CIPEC supply were highly responsive to price. A cartel faces two organizational problems: agreement on a price and a division of the market among cartel members; and monitoring and enforcing the agreement.

EXERCISES

1. Suppose all firms in a monopolistically competitive industry were merged into one large firm. Would that new firm produce as many different brands? Would it produce only a single brand? Explain.

Monopolistic competition is defined by product differentiation. Each firm earns economic profit by distinguishing its brand from all other brands. This distinction can arise from underlying differences in the product or from differences in advertising. If these competitors merge into a single firm, the resulting monopolist would not produce as many brands, since too much brand competition is internecine (mutually destructive). However, it is unlikely that only one brand would be produced after the merger. Producing several brands with different prices and characteristics is one method of splitting the market into sets of customers with different price elasticities, which may also stimulate overall demand.

2. Consider two firms facing the demand curve $P = 50 - 5Q$, where $Q = Q_1 + Q_2$. The firms' cost functions are $C_1(Q_1) = 20 + 10Q_1$ and $C_2(Q_2) = 10 + 12Q_2$.

a. Suppose both firms have entered the industry. What is the joint profit-maximizing level of output? How much will each firm produce? How would your answer change if the firms have not yet entered the industry?

If both firms enter the market, and they collude, they will face a marginal revenue curve with twice the slope of the demand curve:

$$MR = 50 - 10Q.$$

Setting marginal revenue equal to marginal cost (the marginal cost of Firm 1, since it is lower than that of Firm 2) to determine the profit-maximizing quantity, Q:

$$50 - 10Q = 10, \text{ or } Q = 4.$$

Substituting $Q = 4$ into the demand function to determine price:

$$P = 50 - 5*4 = \$30.$$

The question now is how the firms will divide the total output of 4 among themselves. Since the two firms have different cost functions, it will not be optimal for them to split the output evenly between them. The profit maximizing solution is for firm 1 to produce all of the output so that the profit for Firm 1 will be:

$$\pi_1 = (30)(4) - (20 + (10)(4)) = \$60.$$

The profit for Firm 2 will be:

$$\pi_2 = (30)(0) - (10 + (12)(0)) = -\$10.$$

Total industry profit will be:

$$\pi_T = \pi_1 + \pi_2 = 60 - 10 = \$50.$$

If they split the output evenly between them then total profit would be $46 ($20 for firm 1 and $26 for firm 2). If firm 2 preferred to earn a profit of $26 as opposed to $25 then firm 1 could give $1 to firm 2 and it would still have profit of $24, which is higher than the $20 it would earn if they split output. Note that if firm 2 supplied all the output then it would set marginal revenue equal to its marginal cost or 12 and earn a profit of 62.2. In this case, firm 1 would earn a profit of –20, so that total industry profit would be 42.2.

If Firm 1 were the only entrant, its profits would be $60 and Firm 2's would be 0.

If Firm 2 were the only entrant, then it would equate marginal revenue with its marginal cost to determine its profit-maximizing quantity:

$$50 - 10Q_2 = 12, \text{ or } Q_2 = 3.8.$$

Substituting Q_2 into the demand equation to determine price:

$$P = 50 - 5*3.8 = \$31.$$

The profits for Firm 2 will be:

$$\pi_2 = (31)(3.8) - (10 + (12)(3.8)) = \$62.20.$$

b. **What is each firm's equilibrium output and profit if they behave noncooperatively? Use the Cournot model. Draw the firms' reaction curves and show the equilibrium.**

In the Cournot model, Firm 1 takes Firm 2's output as given and maximizes profits. The profit function derived in 2.a becomes

$$\pi_1 = (50 - 5Q_1 - 5Q_2)Q_1 - (20 + 10Q_1), \text{ or}$$

$$\pi = 40Q_1 - 5Q_1^2 - 5Q_1Q_2 - 20.$$

Setting the derivative of the profit function with respect to Q_1 to zero, we find Firm 1's reaction function:

$$\frac{\partial \pi}{\partial Q_1} = 40 - 10Q_1 - 5Q_2 = 0, \text{ or } Q_1 = 4 - \left(\frac{Q_2}{2}\right).$$

Similarly, Firm 2's reaction function is

$$Q_2 = 3.8 - \left(\frac{Q_1}{2}\right).$$

To find the Cournot equilibrium, we substitute Firm 2's reaction function into Firm 1's reaction function:

$$Q_1 = 4 - \left(\frac{1}{2}\right)\left(3.8 - \frac{Q_1}{2}\right), \text{ or } Q_1 = 2.8.$$

Substituting this value for Q_1 into the reaction function for Firm 2, we find $Q_2 = 2.4$.

Substituting the values for Q_1 and Q_2 into the demand function to determine the equilibrium price:

$$P = 50 - 5(2.8 + 2.4) = \$24.$$

The profits for Firms 1 and 2 are equal to

$$\pi_1 = (24)(2.8) - (20 + (10)(2.8)) = 19.20 \text{ and}$$
$$\pi_2 = (24)(2.4) - (10 + (12)(2.4)) = 18.80.$$

c. **How much should Firm 1 be willing to pay to purchase Firm 2 if collusion is illegal but the takeover is not?**

In order to determine how much Firm 1 will be willing to pay to purchase Firm 2, we must compare Firm 1's profits in the monopoly situation versus those in an oligopoly. The difference between the two will be what Firm 1 is willing to pay for Firm 2. From part a, profit of firm 1 when it set marginal revenue equal to its marginal cost was $60. This is what the firm would earn if it was a monopolist. From part b, profit was $19.20 for firm 1. Firm 1 would therefore be willing to pay up to $40.80 for firm 2.

3. A monopolist can produce at a constant average (and marginal) cost of AC = MC = 5. It faces a market demand curve given by Q = 53 - P.

a. **Calculate the profit-maximizing price and quantity for this monopolist. Also calculate its profits.**

The monopolist wants to choose quantity to maximize its profits:

$$\max \pi = PQ - C(Q),$$

$$\pi = (53 - Q)(Q) - 5Q, \text{ or } \pi = 48Q - Q^2.$$

To determine the profit-maximizing quantity, set the change in π with respect to the change in Q equal to zero and solve for Q:

$$\frac{d\pi}{dQ} = -2Q + 48 = 0, \text{ or } Q = 24.$$

Substitute the profit-maximizing quantity, $Q = 24$, into the demand function to find price:

$$24 = 53 - P, \text{ or } P = \$29.$$

Profits are equal to

$$\pi = TR - TC = (29)(24) - (5)(24) = \$576.$$

b. **Suppose a second firm enters the market. Let Q_1 be the output of the first firm and Q_2 be the output of the second. Market demand is now given by**

$$Q_1 + Q_2 = 53 - P.$$

Assuming that this second firm has the same costs as the first, write the profits of each firm as functions of Q_1 and Q_2.

When the second firm enters, price can be written as a function of the output of two firms: $P = 53 - Q_1 - Q_2$. We may write the profit functions for the two firms:

$$\pi_1 = PQ_1 - C(Q_1) = (53 - Q_1 - Q_2)Q_1 - 5Q_1, \text{ or } \pi_1 = 53Q_1 - Q_1^2 - Q_1Q_2 - 5Q_1$$

and

$$\pi_2 = PQ_2 - C(Q_2) = (53 - Q_1 - Q_2)Q_2 - 5Q_2, \text{ or } \pi_2 = 53Q_2 - Q_2^2 - Q_1Q_2 - 5Q_2.$$

c. **Suppose (as in the Cournot model) that each firm chooses its profit-maximizing level of output on the assumption that its competitor's output is fixed. Find each firm's "reaction curve" (i.e., the rule that gives its desired output in terms of its competitor's output).**

Under the Cournot assumption, Firm 1 treats the output of Firm 2 as a constant in its maximization of profits. Therefore, Firm 1 chooses Q_1 to maximize π_1 in b with Q_2 being treated as a constant. The change in π_1 with respect to a change in Q_1 is

$$\frac{\partial \pi_1}{\partial Q_1} = 53 - 2Q_1 - Q_2 - 5 = 0, \text{ or } Q_1 = 24 - \frac{Q_2}{2}.$$

This equation is the reaction function for Firm 1, which generates the profit-maximizing level of output, given the constant output of Firm 2. Because the problem is symmetric, the reaction function for Firm 2 is

$$Q_2 = 24 - \frac{Q_1}{2}.$$

d.   **Calculate the Cournot equilibrium (i.e., the values of Q_1 and Q_2 for which both firms are doing as well as they can given their competitors' output). What are the resulting market price and profits of each firm?**

To find the level of output for each firm that would result in a stationary equilibrium, we solve for the values of Q_1 and Q_2 that satisfy both reaction functions by substituting the reaction function for Firm 2 into the one for Firm 1:

$$Q_1 = 24 - \left(\frac{1}{2}\right)\left(24 - \frac{Q_1}{2}\right), \text{ or } Q_1 = 16.$$

By symmetry, $Q_2 = 16$.

To determine the price, substitute Q_1 and Q_2 into the demand equation:

$$P = 53 - 16 - 16 = \$21.$$

Profits are given by

$$\pi_i = PQ_i - C(Q_i) = \pi_1 = (21)(16) - (5)(16) = \$256.$$

Total profits in the industry are $\pi_1 + \pi_2 = \$256 + \$256 = \$512$.

*e.   **Suppose there are N firms in the industry, all with the same constant marginal cost, MC = 5. Find the Cournot equilibrium. How much will each firm produce, what will be the market price, and how much profit will each firm earn? Also, show that as N becomes large the market price approaches the price that would prevail under perfect competition.**

If there are N identical firms, then the price in the market will be

$$P = 53 - \left(Q_1 + Q_2 + \cdots + Q_N\right).$$

Profits for the i'th firm are given by

$$\pi_i = PQ_i - C(Q_i),$$

$$\pi_i = 53Q_i - Q_1Q_i - Q_2Q_i - \cdots - Q_i^2 - \cdots - Q_NQ_i - 5Q_i.$$

Differentiating to obtain the necessary first-order condition for profit maximization,

$$\frac{d\pi}{dQ_i} = 53 - Q_1 - \cdots - 2Q_i - \cdots - Q_N - 5 = 0.$$

Solving for Q_i,

$$Q_i = 24 - \frac{1}{2}\left(Q_1 + \cdots + Q_{i-1} + Q_{i+1} + \cdots + Q_N\right).$$

If all firms face the same costs, they will all produce the same level of output, i.e., $Q_i = Q^*$. Therefore,

$$Q^* = 24 - \frac{1}{2}(N-1)Q^*, \text{ or } 2Q^* = 48 - (N-1)Q^*, \text{ or}$$

$$(N+1)Q^* = 48, \text{ or } Q^* = \frac{48}{(N+1)}.$$

We may substitute for $Q = NQ^*$, total output, in the demand function:

$$P = 53 - N\left(\frac{48}{N+1}\right).$$

Total profits are

$$\pi_T = PQ - C(Q) = P(NQ^*) - 5(NQ^*)$$

or

$$\pi_T = \left[53 - N\left(\frac{48}{N+1}\right)\right](N)\left(\frac{48}{N+1}\right) - 5N\left(\frac{48}{N+1}\right) \text{ or}$$

$$\pi_T = \left[48 - (N)\left(\frac{48}{N+1}\right)\right](N)\left(\frac{48}{N+1}\right)$$

or

$$\pi_T = (48)\left(\frac{N+1-N}{N+1}\right)(48)\left(\frac{N}{N+1}\right) = (2,304)\left(\frac{N}{(N+1)^2}\right).$$

Notice that with N firms

$$Q = 48\left(\frac{N}{N+1}\right)$$

and that, as N increases $(N \rightarrow \infty)$

$$Q = 48.$$

Similarly, with

$$P = 53 - 48\left(\frac{N}{N+1}\right),$$

as $N \rightarrow \infty$,

$$P = 53 - 48 = 5.$$

With $P = 5$, $Q = 53 - 5 = 48$.

Finally,

$$\pi_T = 2,304\left(\frac{N}{(N+1)^2}\right),$$

so as $N \rightarrow \infty$,

$$\pi_T = \$0.$$

In perfect competition, we know that profits are zero and price equals marginal cost. Here, $\pi_T = \$0$ and $P = MC = 5$. Thus, when N approaches infinity, this market approaches a perfectly competitive one.

4. This exercise is a continuation of Exercise 3. We return to two firms with the same constant average and marginal cost, AC = MC = 5, facing the market demand curve $Q_1 + Q_2 = 53 - P$. Now we will use the Stackelberg model to analyze what will happen if one of the firms makes its output decision before the other.

a. **Suppose Firm 1 is the Stackelberg leader (i.e., makes its output decisions before Firm 2). Find the reaction curves that tell each firm how much to produce in terms of the output of its competitor.**

Firm 1, the Stackelberg leader, will choose its output, Q_1, to maximize its profits, subject to the reaction function of Firm 2:

$$\max \pi_1 = PQ_1 - C(Q_1),$$

subject to

$$Q_2 = 24 - \left(\frac{Q_1}{2}\right).$$

Substitute for Q_2 in the demand function and, after solving for P, substitute for P in the profit function:

$$\max \pi_1 = \left(53 - Q_1 - \left(24 - \frac{Q_1}{2} \right) \right)(Q_1) - 5Q_1.$$

To determine the profit-maximizing quantity, we find the change in the profit function with respect to a change in Q_1:

$$\frac{d\pi_1}{dQ_1} = 53 - 2Q_1 - 24 + Q_1 - 5.$$

Set this expression equal to 0 to determine the profit-maximizing quantity:

$$53 - 2Q_1 - 24 + Q_1 - 5 = 0, \text{ or } Q_1 = 24.$$

Substituting $Q_1 = 24$ into Firm 2's reaction function gives Q_2:

$$Q_2 = 24 - \frac{24}{2} = 12.$$

Substitute Q_1 and Q_2 into the demand equation to find the price:

$$P = 53 - 24 - 12 = \$17.$$

Profits for each firm are equal to total revenue minus total costs, or

$$\pi_1 = (17)(24) - (5)(24) = \$288 \text{ and}$$
$$\pi_2 = (17)(12) - (5)(12) = \$144.$$

Total industry profit, $\pi_T = \pi_1 + \pi_2 = \$288 + \$144 = \$432.$

Compared to the Cournot equilibrium, total output has increased from 32 to 36, price has fallen from \$21 to \$17, and total profits have fallen from \$512 to \$432. Profits for Firm 1 have risen from \$256 to \$288, while the profits of Firm 2 have declined sharply from \$256 to \$144.

b.   How much will each firm produce, and what will its profit be?

If *each* firm believes that it is the Stackelberg leader, while the other firm is the Cournot follower, they both will initially produce 24 units, so total output will be 48 units. The market price will be driven to \$5, equal to marginal cost. It is impossible to specify exactly where the new equilibrium point will be, because no point is stable when both firms are trying to be the Stackelberg leader.

5. Two firms compete in selling identical widgets. They choose their output levels Q_1 and Q_2 simultaneously and face the demand curve

$$P = 30 - Q,$$

where $Q = Q_1 + Q_2$. Until recently, both firms had *zero marginal costs*. Recent environmental regulations have increased Firm 2's marginal cost to \$15. Firm 1's marginal cost remains constant at zero. True or false: As a result, the market price will rise to the *monopoly* level.

True.

If only one firm were in this market, it would charge a price of \$15 a unit. Marginal revenue for this monopolist would be

$$MR = 30 - 2Q,$$

Profit maximization implies $MR = MC$, or

$$30 - 2Q = 0, \quad Q = 15, \quad (\text{using the demand curve}) \ P = 15.$$

The current situation is a Cournot game where Firm 1's marginal costs are zero and Firm 2's marginal costs are 15. We need to find the best response functions:

Firm 1's revenue is

$$PQ_1 = (30 - Q_1 - Q_2)Q_1 = 30Q_1 - Q_1^2 - Q_1Q_2,$$

and its marginal revenue is given by:

$$MR_1 = 30 - 2Q_1 - Q_2.$$

Profit maximization implies $MR_1 = MC_1$ or

$$30 - 2Q_1 - Q_2 = 0 \Rightarrow Q_1 = 15 - \frac{Q_2}{2},$$

which is Firm 1's best response function.

Firm 2's revenue function is symmetric to that of Firm 1 and hence

$$MR_2 = 30 - Q_1 - 2Q_2.$$

Profit maximization implies $MR_2 = MC_2$, or

$$30 - 2Q_2 - Q_1 = 15 \Rightarrow Q_2 = 7.5 - \frac{Q_1}{2},$$

which is Firm 2's best response function.

Cournot equilibrium occurs at the intersection of best response functions. Substituting for Q_1 in the response function for Firm 2 yields:

$$Q_2 = 7.5 - 0.5(15 - \frac{Q_2}{2}).$$

Thus $Q_2=0$ and $Q_1=15$. $P = 30 - Q_1 + Q_2 = 15$, which is the monopoly price.

6. Suppose that two identical firms produce widgets and that they are the only firms in the market. Their costs are given by $C_1 = 60Q_1$ and $C_2 = 60Q_2$, where Q_1 is the output of Firm 1 and Q_2 the output of Firm 2. Price is determined by the following demand curve:

$$P = 300 - Q$$

where $Q = Q_1 + Q_2$.

a.   **Find the Cournot-Nash equilibrium. Calculate the profit of each firm at this equilibrium.**

To determine the Cournot-Nash equilibrium, we first calculate the reaction function for each firm, then solve for price, quantity, and profit. Profit for Firm 1, $TR_1 - TC_1$, is equal to

$$\pi_1 = 300Q_1 - Q_1^2 - Q_1Q_2 - 60Q_1 = 240Q_1 - Q_1^2 - Q_1Q_2.$$

Therefore,

$$\frac{\partial \pi_1}{\partial Q_1} = 240 - 2Q_1 - Q_2.$$

Setting this equal to zero and solving for Q_1 in terms of Q_2:

$$Q_1 = 120 - 0.5Q_2.$$

This is Firm 1's reaction function. Because Firm 2 has the same cost structure, Firm 2's reaction function is

$$Q_2 = 120 - 0.5Q_1.$$

Substituting for Q_2 in the reaction function for Firm 1, and solving for Q_1, we find

$$Q_1 = 120 - (0.5)(120 - 0.5Q_1), \text{ or } Q_1 = 80.$$

By symmetry, $Q_2 = 80$. Substituting Q_1 and Q_2 into the demand equation to determine the price at profit maximization:

$$P = 300 - 80 - 80 = \$140.$$

Substituting the values for price and quantity into the profit function,

$$\pi_1 = (140)(80) - (60)(80) = \$6,400 \text{ and}$$

$$\pi_2 = (140)(80) - (60)(80) = \$6,400.$$

Therefore, profit is \$6,400 for both firms in Cournot-Nash equilibrium.

b.   **Suppose the two firms form a cartel to maximize joint profits. How many widgets will be produced? Calculate each firm's profit.**

Given the demand curve is $P=300-Q$, the marginal revenue curve is $MR=300-2Q$. Profit will be maximized by finding the level of output such that marginal revenue is equal to marginal cost:

$$300-2Q=60$$

$$Q=120.$$

When output is equal to 120, price will be equal to 180, based on the demand curve. Since both firms have the same marginal cost, they will split the total output evenly between themselves so they each produce 60 units. Profit for each firm is:

$$\pi = 180(60)-60(60)=\$7,200.$$

Note that the other way to solve this problem, and arrive at the same solution is to use the profit function for either firm from part a above and let $Q = Q_1 = Q_2$.

c.   **Suppose Firm 1 were the only firm in the industry. How would the market output and Firm 1's profit differ from that found in part (b) above?**

If Firm 1 were the only firm, it would produce where marginal revenue is equal to marginal cost, as found in part b. In this case firm 1 would produce the entire 120 units of output and earn a profit of \$14,400.

d.   **Returning to the duopoly of part (b), suppose Firm 1 abides by the agreement, but Firm 2 cheats by increasing production. How many widgets will Firm 2 produce? What will be each firm's profits?**

Assuming their agreement is to split the market equally, Firm 1 produces 60 widgets. Firm 2 cheats by producing its profit-maximizing level, given $Q_1 = 60$. Substituting $Q_1 = 60$ into Firm 2's reaction function:

$$Q_2 = 120 - \frac{60}{2} = 90.$$

Total industry output, Q_T, is equal to Q_1 plus Q_2:

$$Q_T = 60 + 90 = 150.$$

Substituting Q_T into the demand equation to determine price:

$$P = 300 - 150 = \$150.$$

Substituting Q_1, Q_2, and P into the profit function:

$$\pi_1 = (150)(60) - (60)(60) = \$5,400 \quad \text{and}$$
$$\pi_2 = (150)(90) - (60)(90) = \$8,100.$$

Firm 2 has increased its profits at the expense of Firm 1 by cheating on the agreement.

7. Suppose that two competing firms, A and B, produce a homogeneous good. Both firms have a marginal cost of MC=\$50. Describe what would happen to output and price in each of the following situations if the firms are at (i) Cournot equilibrium, (ii) collusive equilibrium, and (iii) Bertrand equilibrium.

a.   **Firm A must increase wages and its MC increases to \$80.**

(i) In a Cournot equilibrium you must think about the effect on the reaction functions, as illustrated in figure 12.4 of the text. When firm A experiences an increase in marginal cost, their reaction function will shift inwards. The quantity produced by firm A will decrease and the quantity produced by firm B will increase. Total quantity produced will tend to decrease and price will increase.

(ii) In a collusive equilibrium, the two firms will collectively act like a monopolist. When the marginal cost of firm A increases, firm A will reduce their production. This will increase price and cause firm B to increase production. Price will be higher and total quantity produced will be lower.

(iii) Given that the good is homogeneous, both will produce where price equals marginal cost. Firm A will increase price to \$80 and firm B will keep its price at \$50. Assuming firm B can produce enough output, they will supply the entire market.

b.   **The marginal cost of both firms increases.**

(i) Again refer to figure 12.4. The increase in the marginal cost of both firms will shift both reaction functions inwards. Both firms will decrease quantity produced and price will increase.

(ii) When marginal cost increases, both firms will produce less and price will increase, as in the monopoly case.

(iii) As in the above cases, price will increase and quantity produced will decrease.

c.   **The demand curve shifts to the right.**

(i) This is the opposite of the above case in part b. In this case, both reaction functions will shift outwards and both will produce a higher quantity. Price will tend to increase.

(ii) Both firms will increase the quantity produced as demand and marginal revenue increase. Price will also tend to increase.

(iii) Both firms will supply more output. Given that marginal cost is constant, the price will not change.

8. Suppose the airline industry consisted of only two firms: American and Texas Air Corp. Let the two firms have identical cost functions, C(q) = 40q. Assume the demand curve for the industry is given by P = 100 - Q and that each firm expects the other to behave as a Cournot competitor.

a.   **Calculate the Cournot-Nash equilibrium for each firm, assuming that each chooses the output level that maximizes its profits when taking its rival's output as given. What are the profits of each firm?**

To determine the Cournot-Nash equilibrium, we first calculate the reaction function for each firm, then solve for price, quantity, and profit. Profit for Texas Air, π_1, is equal to total revenue minus total cost:

$$\pi_1 = (100 - Q_1 - Q_2)Q_1 - 40Q_1, \text{ or}$$

$$\pi_1 = 100Q_1 - Q_1^2 - Q_1Q_2 - 40Q_1, \text{ or } \pi_1 = 60Q_1 - Q_1^2 - Q_1Q_2.$$

The change in π_1 with respect to Q_1 is

$$\frac{\partial \pi_1}{\partial Q_1} = 60 - 2Q_1 - Q_2.$$

Setting the derivative to zero and solving for Q_1 in terms of Q_2 will give Texas Air's reaction function:

$$Q_1 = 30 - 0.5Q_2.$$

Because American has the same cost structure, American's reaction function is

$$Q_2 = 30 - 0.5Q_1.$$

Substituting for Q_2 in the reaction function for Texas Air,

$$Q_1 = 30 - 0.5(30 - 0.5Q_1) = 20.$$

By symmetry, $Q_2 = 20$. Industry output, Q_T, is Q_1 plus Q_2, or

$$Q_T = 20 + 20 = 40.$$

Substituting industry output into the demand equation, we find $P = 60$. Substituting Q_1, Q_2, and P into the profit function, we find

$$\pi_1 = \pi_2 = 60(20) - 20^2 - (20)(20) = \$400$$

for both firms in Cournot-Nash equilibrium.

b. **What would be the equilibrium quantity if Texas Air had constant marginal and average costs of \$25, and American had constant marginal and average costs of \$40?**

By solving for the reaction functions under this new cost structure, we find that profit for Texas Air is equal to

$$\pi_1 = 100Q_1 - Q_1^2 - Q_1Q_2 - 25Q_1 = 75Q_1 - Q_1^2 - Q_1Q_2.$$

The change in profit with respect to Q_1 is

$$\frac{\partial \pi_1}{\partial Q_1} = 75 - 2Q_1 - Q_2.$$

Set the derivative to zero, and solving for Q_1 in terms of Q_2,

$$Q_1 = 37.5 - 0.5Q_2.$$

This is Texas Air's reaction function. Since American has the same cost structure as in 8.a., American's reaction function is the same as before:

$$Q_2 = 30 - 0.5Q_1.$$

To determine Q_1, substitute for Q_2 in the reaction function for Texas Air and solve for Q_1:

$$Q_1 = 37.5 - (0.5)(30 - 0.5Q_1) = 30.$$

Texas Air finds it profitable to increase output in response to a decline in its cost structure.

To determine Q_2, substitute for Q_1 in the reaction function for American:

$$Q_2 = 30 - (0.5)(37.5 - 0.5Q_2) = 15.$$

American has cut back slightly in its output in response to the increase in output by Texas Air.

Total quantity, Q_T, is $Q_1 + Q_2$, or

$$Q_T = 30 + 15 = 45.$$

Compared to 8a, the equilibrium quantity has risen slightly.

c. **Assuming that both firms have the original cost function, C(q) = 40q, how much should Texas Air be willing to invest to lower its marginal cost from \$40 to \$25, assuming that American will not follow suit? How much should American be willing to spend to reduce its marginal cost to \$25, assuming that Texas Air will have marginal costs of \$25 regardless of American's actions?**

Recall that profits for both firms were \$400 under the original cost structure. With constant average and marginal costs of 25, Texas Air's profits will be

$$(55)(30) - (25)(30) = \$900.$$

The difference in profit is \$500. Therefore, Texas Air should be willing to invest up to \$500 to *lower costs* from 40 to 25 per unit (assuming American does not follow suit).

To determine how much American would be willing to spend to reduce its average costs, we must calculate the difference in profits, assuming Texas Air's average cost is 25. First, without investment, American's profits would be:

$$(55)(15) - (40)(15) = \$225.$$

Second, with investment by both firms, the reaction functions would be:

$$Q_1 = 37.5 - 0.5Q_2 \text{ and}$$
$$Q_2 = 37.5 - 0.5Q_1.$$

To determine Q_1, substitute for Q_2 in the first reaction function and solve for Q_1:

$$Q_1 = 37.5 - (0.5)(37.5 - 0.5Q_1) = 25.$$

Substituting for Q_1 in the second reaction function to find Q_2:

$$Q_2 = 37.5 - 0.5(37.5 - 0.5Q_2) = 25.$$

Substituting industry output into the demand equation to determine price:

$$P = 100 - 50 = \$50.$$

Therefore, American's profits if $Q_1 = Q_2 = 25$ (when both firms have $MC = AC = 25$) are

$$\pi_2 = (100 - 25 - 25)(25) - (25)(25) = \$625.$$

The difference in profit with and without the cost-saving investment for American is \$400. American would be willing to invest up to \$400 to reduce its marginal cost to 25 if Texas Air also has marginal costs of 25.

*9. Demand for light bulbs can be characterized by Q = 100 - P, where Q is in millions of lights sold, and P is the price per box. There are two producers of lights: Everglow and Dimlit. They have identical cost functions:

$$C_i = 10Q_i + 1/2Q_i^2 \,(i = E, D) \qquad\qquad Q = Q_E + Q_D.$$

a. Unable to recognize the potential for collusion, the two firms act as short-run perfect competitors. What are the equilibrium values of Q_E, Q_D, and P? What are each firm's profits?

Given that the total cost function is $C_i = 10Q_i + 1/2Q_i^2$, the marginal cost curve for each firm is $MC_i = 10 + Q_i$. In the short run, perfectly competitive firms determine the optimal level of output by taking price as given and setting price equal to marginal cost. There are two ways to solve this problem. One way is to set price equal to marginal cost for each firm so that:

$$P = 100 - Q_1 - Q_2 = 10 + Q_1$$
$$P = 100 - Q_1 - Q_2 = 10 + Q_2.$$

Given we now have two equations and two unknowns, we can solve for Q₁ and Q₂. Solve the second equation for Q₂ to get

$$Q_2 = \frac{90 - Q_1}{2},$$

and substitute into the other equation to get

$$100 - Q_1 - \frac{90 - Q_1}{2} = 10 + Q_1.$$

This yields a solution where Q₁=30, Q₂=30, and P=40. You can verify that P=MC for each firm. Profit is total revenue minus total cost or

$$\Pi = 40 * 30 - (10 * 30 + 0.5 * 30 * 30) = \$450 \text{ million.}$$

The other way to solve the problem and arrive at the same solution is to find the market supply curve by summing the marginal cost curves, so that Q_M=2P-20 is the market supply. Setting supply equal to demand results in a quantity of 60 in the market, or 30 per firm since they are identical.

b. Top management in both firms is replaced. Each new manager independently recognizes the oligopolistic nature of the light bulb industry and plays Cournot. What are the equilibrium values of Q_E, Q_D, and P? What are each firm's profits?

To determine the Cournot-Nash equilibrium, we first calculate the reaction function for each firm, then solve for price, quantity, and profit. Profits for Everglow are equal to $TR_E - TC_E$, or

$$\pi_E = (100 - Q_E - Q_D)Q_E - (10Q_E + 0.5Q_E^2) = 90Q_E - 1.5Q_E^2 - Q_EQ_D.$$

The change in profit with respect to Q_E is

$$\frac{\partial \pi_E}{\partial Q_E} = 90 - 3Q_E - Q_D.$$

To determine Everglow's reaction function, set the change in profits with respect to Q_E equal to 0 and solve for Q_E:

$$90 - 3Q_E - Q_D = 0, \text{ or}$$

$$Q_E = \frac{90 - Q_D}{3}.$$

Because Dimlit has the same cost structure, Dimlit's reaction function is

$$Q_D = \frac{90 - Q_E}{3}.$$

Substituting for Q_D in the reaction function for Everglow, and solving for Q_E:

$$Q_E = \frac{90 - \dfrac{90 - Q_E}{3}}{3}$$

$$3Q_E = 90 - 30 + \frac{Q_E}{3}$$

$$Q_E = 22.5.$$

By symmetry, $Q_D = 22.5$, and total industry output is 45.

Substituting industry output into the demand equation gives P:

$$45' = 100 - P, \text{ or } P = \$55.$$

Substituting total industry output and P into the profit function:

$$\Pi_i = 22.5 * 55 - (10 * 22.5 + 0.5 * 22.5 * 22.5) = \$759.375 \text{ million.}$$

c.   **Suppose the Everglow manager guesses correctly that Dimlit has a Cournot conjectural variation, so Everglow plays Stackelberg. What are the equilibrium values of Q_E, Q_D, and P? What are each firm's profits?**

Recall Everglow's profit function:

$$\pi_E = \left(100 - Q_E - Q_D\right)Q_E - \left(10Q_E + 0.5Q_E^2\right)$$

If Everglow sets its quantity first, knowing Dimlit's reaction function $\left(\text{i.e., } Q_D = 30 - \dfrac{Q_E}{3}\right)$, we may determine Everglow's reaction function by substituting for Q_D in its profit function. We find

$$\pi_E = 60Q_E - \frac{7Q_E^2}{6}.$$

To determine the profit-maximizing quantity, differentiate profit with respect to Q_E, set the derivative to zero and solve for Q_E:

$$\frac{\partial \pi_E}{\partial Q_E} = 60 - \frac{7Q_E}{3} = 0, \text{ or } Q_E = 25.7.$$

Substituting this into Dimlit's reaction function, we find $Q_D = 30 - \dfrac{25.7}{3} = 21.4$. Total industry output is 47.1 and $P = \$52.90$. Profit for Everglow is $772.29 million. Profit for Dimlit is $689.08 million.

d.   **If the managers of the two companies collude, what are the equilibrium values of Q_E, Q_D, and P? What are each firm's profits?**

If the firms split the market equally, total cost in the industry is $10Q_T + \dfrac{Q_T^2}{2}$; therefore,

$MC = 10 + Q_T$.   Total revenue is $100Q_T - Q_T^2$; therefore, $MR = 100 - 2Q_T$. To determine the profit-maximizing quantity, set $MR = MC$ and solve for Q_T:

$$100 - 2Q_T = 10 + Q_T, \text{ or } Q_T = 30.$$

This means $Q_E = Q_D = 15$.

Substituting Q_T into the demand equation to determine price:

$$P = 100 - 30 = \$70.$$

The profit for each firm is equal to total revenue minus total cost:

$$\pi_i = (70)(15) - \left((10)(15) + \frac{15^2}{2} \right) = \$787.50 \text{ million.}$$

10. **Two firms produce luxury sheepskin auto seat covers, Western Where (WW) and B.B.B. Sheep (BBBS). Each firm has a cost function given by:**

$$C(q) = 30q + 1.5q^2$$

The market demand for these seat covers is represented by the inverse demand equation:

$$P = 300 - 3Q,$$

where $Q = q_1 + q_2$, total output.

a.   **If each firm acts to maximize its profits, taking its rival's output as given (i.e., the firms behave as Cournot oligopolists), what will be the equilibrium quantities selected by each firm? What is total output, and what is the market price? What are the profits for each firm?**

We are given each firm's cost function $C(q) = 30q + 1.5q^2$ and the market demand function $P = 300 - 3Q$ where total output Q is the sum of each firm's output q_1 and q_2. We find the best response functions for both firms by setting marginal revenue equal to marginal cost (alternatively you can set up the profit function for each firm and differentiate with respect to the quantity produced for that firm):

$$R_1 = P \, q_1 = (300 - 3(q_1 + q_2)) \, q_1 = 300q_1 - 3q_1^2 - 3q_1q_2.$$

$$MR_1 = 300 - 6q_1 - 3q_2$$

$$MC_1 = 30 + 3q_1$$

$$300 - 6q_1 - 3q_2 = 30 + 3q_1$$

$$q_1 = 30 - (1/3)q_2.$$

By symmetry, BBBS's best response function will be:

$$q_2 = 30 - (1/3)q_1.$$

Cournot equilibrium occurs at the intersection of these two best response functions, given by:

$$q_1 = q_2 = 22.5.$$

Thus,

$$Q = q_1 + q_2 = 45$$

$$P = 300 - 3(45) = \$165.$$

Profit for both firms will be equal and given by:

$$R - C = (165)(22.5) - (30(22.5) + 1.5(22.5^2)) = \$2278.13.$$

b. **It occurs to the managers of WW and BBBS that they could do a lot better by colluding. If the two firms collude, what would be the profit-maximizing choice of output? The industry price? The output and the profit for each firm in this case?**

If firms can collude, then in this case they should each produce half the quantity that maximizes total industry profits (i.e. half the monopoly profits). If on the other hand. the two firms had different cost functions, then it would not be optimal for them to split the monopoly output evenly.

Joint profits will be $(300-3Q)Q - 2(30(Q/2) + 1.5(Q/2)^2) = 270Q - 3.75Q^2$ and will be maximized at $Q = 36$. You can find this quantity by differentiating the above profit function with respect to Q, setting the resulting first order condition equal to zero, and then solving for Q.

Thus, we will have $q_1 = q_2 = 36 / 2 = 18$ and $\quad P = 300 - 3(36) = \$192.$

Profit for each firm will be $18(192) - (30(18) + 1.5(18^2)) = \$2,430.$

c. **The managers of these firms realize that explicit agreements to collude are illegal. Each firm must decide on its own whether to produce the Cournot quantity or the cartel quantity. To aid in making the decision, the manager of WW constructs a payoff matrix like the real one below. Fill in each box with the (profit of WW, profit of BBBS). Given this payoff matrix, what output strategy is each firm likely to pursue?**

If WW produces the Cournot level of output (22.5) and BBBS produces the collusive level (18), then:

$$Q = q_1 + q_2 = 22.5 + 18 = 40.5$$

$$P = 300 - 3(40.5) = \$178.5.$$

Profit for WW $= 22.5(178.5) - (30(22.5) + 1.5(22.5^2)) = \$2581.88.$

Profit for BBBS $= 18(178.5) - (30(18) + 1.5(18^2)) = \$2187.$

Both firms producing at the Cournot output levels will be the only Nash Equilibrium in this industry, given the following payoff matrix. Given the firms end up in any other cell in the matrix, one of them will always have an incentive to change their level of production in order to increase profit. For example, if WW is Cournot and BBBS is cartel, then BBBS has an incentive to switch to cartel to increase profit. (Note: not only is this a Nash Equilibrium, but it is an equilibrium in dominant strategies.)

Profit Payoff Matrix (WW profit, BBBS profit)		BBBS	
		Produce Cournot q	Produce Cartel q
WW	Produce Cournot q	2278,2278	2582, 2187
	Produce Cartel q	2187, 2582	2430,2430

d.   **Suppose WW can set its output level *before* BBBS does. How much will WW choose to produce in this case? How much will BBBS produce? What is the market price, and what is the profit for each firm? Is WW better off by choosing its output first? Explain why or why not.**

WW is now able to set quantity first. WW knows that BBBS will choose a quantity q_2 which will be its best response to q_1 or:

$$q_2 = 30 - \frac{1}{3} q_1.$$

WW profits will be:

$$\Pi = P_1 q_1 - C_1 = (300 - 3q_1 - 3q_2)q_1 - (30q_1 + 1.5q_1^2)$$

$$\Pi = 270q_1 - 4.5q_1^2 - 3q_1 q_2$$

$$\Pi = 270q_1 - 4.5q_1^2 - 3q_1(30 - \frac{1}{3} q_1)$$

$$\Pi = 180q_1 - 3.5q_1^2.$$

Profit maximization implies:

$$\frac{\partial \Pi}{\partial q_1} = 180 - 7q_1 = 0.$$

This results in $q_1 = 25.7$ and $q_2 = 21.4$. The equilibrium price and profits will then be:

$$P = 200 - 2(q_1 + q_2) = 200 - 2(25.7 + 21.4) = \$158.57$$

$$\pi_1 = (158.57)(25.7) - (30)(25.7) - 1.5 * 25.7^2 = \$2313.51$$

$$\pi_2 = (158.57)(21.4) - (30)(21.4) - 1.5 * 21.4^2 = \$2064.46.$$

WW is able to benefit from its first mover advantage by committing to a high level of output. Since firm 2 moves after firm 1 has selected its output, firm 2 can only react to the output decision of firm 1. If firm 1 produces its Cournot output as a leader, firm 2 produces its Cournot output as a follower. Hence, firm 1 cannot do worse as a leader than it does in the Cournot game. When firm 1 produces more, firm 2 produces less, raising firm 1's profits.

*11.   **Two firms compete by choosing price. Their demand functions are**

$$Q_1 = 20 - P_1 + P_2 \qquad \text{and} \qquad Q_2 = 20 + P_1 - P_2$$

where P_1 and P_2 are the prices charged by each firm respectively and Q_1 and Q_2 are the resulting demands. Note that the demand for each good depends only on the difference in prices; if the two firms colluded and set the same price, they could make that price as high as they want, and earn infinite profits. Marginal costs are zero.

a.   **Suppose the two firms set their prices at the *same time*. Find the resulting Nash equilibrium. What price will each firm charge, how much will it sell, and what will its profit be? (Hint: Maximize the profit of each firm with respect to its price.)**

To determine the Nash equilibrium, we first calculate the reaction function for each firm, then solve for price. With zero marginal cost, profit for Firm 1 is:

$$\pi_1 = P_1 Q_1 = P_1 (20 - P_1 + P_2) = 20P_1 - P_1^2 + P_2 P_1.$$

The marginal revenue is the slope of the total revenue function (here it is the slope of the profit function because total cost is equal to zero):

$$MR_1 = 20 - 2P_1 + P_2.$$

At the profit-maximizing price, $MR_1 = 0$. Therefore,

$$P_1 = \frac{20 + P_2}{2}.$$

This is Firm 1's reaction function. Because Firm 2 is symmetric to Firm 1, its reaction function is $P_2 = \frac{20 + P_1}{2}$. Substituting Firm 2's reaction function into that of Firm 1:

$$P_1 = \frac{20 + \dfrac{20 + P_1}{2}}{2} = 10 + 5 + \frac{P_1}{4} = \$20.$$

By symmetry, $P_2 = \$20$.

To determine the quantity produced by each firm, substitute P_1 and P_2 into the demand functions:

$$Q_1 = 20 - 20 + 20 = 20 \text{ and}$$
$$Q_2 = 20 + 20 - 20 = 20.$$

Profits for Firm 1 are $P_1 Q_1 = \$400$, and, by symmetry, profits for Firm 2 are also $\$400$.

b. **Suppose Firm 1 sets its price *first* and then Firm 2 sets its price. What price will each firm charge, how much will it sell, and what will its profit be?**

If Firm 1 sets its price first, it takes Firm 2's reaction function into account. Firm 1's profit function is:

$$\pi_1 = P_1\left(20 - P_1 + \frac{20 + P_1}{2}\right) = 30P_1 - \frac{P_1^2}{2}.$$

To determine the profit-maximizing price, find the change in profit with respect to a change in price:

$$\frac{d\pi_1}{dP_1} = 30 - P_1.$$

Set this expression equal to zero to find the profit-maximizing price:

$$30 - P_1 = 0, \text{ or } P_1 = \$30.$$

Substitute P_1 in Firm 2's reaction function to find P_2:

$$P_2 = \frac{20 + 30}{2} = \$25.$$

At these prices,

$$Q_1 = 20 - 30 + 25 = 15 \text{ and}$$

$$Q_2 = 20 + 30 - 25 = 25.$$

Profits are

$$\pi_1 = (30)(15) = \$450 \text{ and}$$
$$\pi_2 = (25)(25) = \$625.$$

If Firm 1 must set its price first, Firm 2 is able to undercut Firm 1 and gain a larger market share.

c. **Suppose you are one of these firms, and there are three ways you could play the game: (i) Both firms set price at the same time. (ii) You set price first. (iii) Your competitor sets price first. If you could choose among these options, which would you prefer? Explain why.**

Your first choice should be (iii), and your second choice should be (ii). (Compare the Nash profits in part 11.a, $400, with profits in part 11.b., $450 and $625.) From the reaction functions, we know that the price leader provokes a price increase in the follower. By being able to move second, however, the follower increases price by less than the leader, and hence undercuts the leader. Both firms enjoy increased profits, but the follower does best.

*12. **The dominant firm model can help us understand the behavior of some cartels. Let's apply this model to the OPEC oil cartel. We shall use isoelastic curves to describe world demand *W* and noncartel (competitive) supply *S*. Reasonable numbers for the price elasticities of world demand and non-cartel supply are -1/2 and 1/2, respectively. Then, expressing *W* and *S* in millions of barrels per day (mb/d), we could write**

$$W = 160P^{-\frac{1}{2}} \qquad \text{and} \qquad S = 3\frac{1}{3}P^{\frac{1}{2}}.$$

Note that OPEC's net demand is D = W - S.

a. **Sketch the world demand curve *W*, the non-OPEC supply curve *S*, OPEC's net demand curve *D*, and OPEC's marginal revenue curve. For purposes of approximation, assume OPEC's production cost is zero. Indicate OPEC's optimal price, OPEC's optimal production, and non-OPEC production on the diagram. Now, show on the diagram how the various curves will shift, and how OPEC's optimal price will change if non-OPEC supply becomes more expensive because reserves of oil start running out.**

OPEC's net demand curve, *D*, is:

$$D = 160P^{-1/2} - 3\frac{1}{3}P^{1/2}.$$

OPEC's marginal revenue curve starts from the same point on the vertical axis as its net demand curve and is twice as steep. OPEC's optimal production occurs where *MR* = 0 (since production cost is assumed to be zero), and OPEC's optimal price in Figure 12.12.a.i is found from the net demand curve at Q_{OPEC}. Non-OPEC production can be read off of the non-OPEC supply curve at a price of *P**. Note that in the two figures below, the demand and supply curves are actually non-linear. They have been drawn in a linear fashion for ease of accuracy.

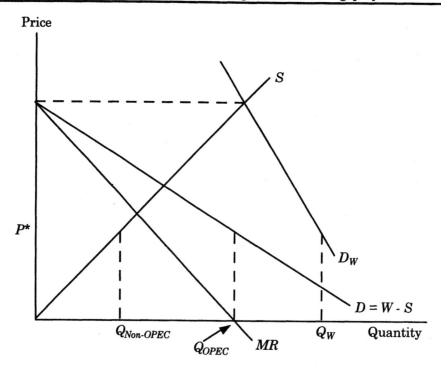

Figure 12.12.a.i

Next, suppose non-OPEC oil becomes more expensive. Then the supply curve S shifts to S^*. This changes OPEC's net demand curve from D to D^*, which in turn creates a new marginal revenue curve, MR^*, and a new optimal OPEC production level of Q_D^*, yielding a new higher price of P^*. At this new price, non-OPEC production is $Q_{Non-OPEC}^*$

. Notice that the curves must be drawn accurately to give this result, and again have been drawn in a linear fashion as opposed to non-linear for ease of accuracy.

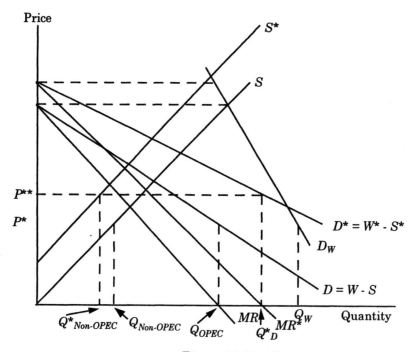

Figure 12.12.a.ii

b. **Calculate OPEC's optimal (profit-maximizing) price. (Hint: Because OPEC's cost is zero, just write the expression for OPEC revenue and find the price that maximizes it.)**

Since costs are zero, OPEC will choose a price that maximizes total revenue:

$$\text{Max } \pi = PQ = P(W - S)$$

$$\pi = P\left(160P^{-1/2} - 3\frac{1}{3}P^{1/2}\right) = 160P^{1/2} - 3\frac{1}{3}P^{3/2}.$$

To determine the profit-maximizing price, we find the change in the profit function with respect to a change in price and set it equal to zero:

$$\frac{\partial \pi}{\partial P} = 80P^{-1/2} - \left(3\frac{1}{3}\right)\left(\frac{3}{2}\right)P^{1/2} = 80P^{-1/2} - 5P^{1/2} = 0.$$

Solving for P,

$$5P^{\frac{1}{2}} = \frac{80}{P^{-\frac{1}{2}}}, \text{ or } P = \$16.$$

c. **Suppose the oil-consuming countries were to unite and form a "buyers' cartel" to gain monopsony power. What can we say, and what can't we say, about the impact this would have on price?**

If the oil-consuming countries unite to form a buyers' cartel, then we have a monopoly (OPEC) facing a monopsony (the buyers' cartel). As a result, there is no well-defined demand or supply curve. We expect that the price will fall below the monopoly price when the buyers also collude, because monopsony power offsets monopoly power. However, economic theory cannot determine the exact price that results from this bilateral monopoly because the price depends on the bargaining skills of the two parties, as well as on other factors, such as the elasticities of supply and demand.

13. Suppose the market for tennis shoes has one dominant firm and five fringe firms. The market demand is Q=400-2P. The dominant firm has a constant marginal cost of 20. The fringe firms each have a marginal cost of MC=20+5q.

a. **Verify that the total supply curve for the five fringe firms is $Q_f = P - 20$.**

The total supply curve for the five firms is found by horizontally summing the five marginal cost curves, or in other words, adding up the quantity supplied by each firm for any given price. Rewrite the marginal cost curve as follows:

$$MC = 20 + 5q = P$$

$$5q = P - 20$$

$$q = \frac{P}{5} - 4$$

Since each firm is identical, the supply curve is five times the supply of one firm for any given price:

$$Q_f = 5(\frac{P}{5} - 4) = P - 20.$$

b. **Find the dominant firm's demand curve.**

The dominant firm's demand curve is given by the difference between the market demand and the fringe total supply curve:

$$Q_D = 400 - 2P - (P - 20) = 420 - 3P.$$

c. **Find the profit-maximizing quantity produced and price charged by the dominant firm, and the quantity produced and price charged by each of the fringe firms.**

The dominant firm will set marginal revenue equal to marginal cost. The marginal revenue curve can be found by recalling that the marginal revenue curve has twice the slope of the linear demand curve, which is shown below:

$$Q_D = 420 - 3P$$

$$P = 140 - \frac{1}{3}Q_D$$

$$MR = 140 - \frac{2}{3}Q_D.$$

We can now set marginal revenue equal to marginal cost in order to find the quantity produced by the dominant firm, and the price charged by the dominant firm:

$$MR = 140 - \frac{2}{3}Q_D = 20 = MC$$

$$Q = 180$$

$$P = 80.$$

Each fringe firm will charge the same price as the dominant firm and the total output produced by the fringe will be $Q_f = P - 20 = 60$. Each fringe firm will produce 12 units.

d. **Suppose there are ten fringe firms instead of five. How does this change your results?**

We need to find the fringe supply curve, the dominant firm demand curve, and the dominant firm marginal revenue curve as was done above. The new total fringe supply curve is $Q_f = 2P - 40$. The new dominant firm demand curve is $Q_D = 440 - 4P$. The new dominant firm marginal revenue curve is $MR = 110 - \frac{Q}{2}$.

The dominant firm will produce where marginal revenue is equal to marginal cost which occurs at 180 units. Substituting a quantity of 180 into the demand curve faced by the dominant firm results in a price of \$65. Substituting the price of \$65 into the total fringe supply curve results in a total fringe quantity supplied of 90, so that each fringe firm will produce 9 units. The market share of the dominant firm drops from 75% to 67%.

e. **Suppose there continue to be five fringe firms but they each manage to reduce their marginal cost to MC=20+2q. How does this change your results?**

Again, we will follow the same method as we did in earlier parts of this problem. Rewrite the fringe marginal cost curve to get $q = \frac{P}{2} - 10$. The new total fringe supply curve is five times the individual fringe supply curve, which is just the marginal cost curve: $Q_f = \frac{5}{2}P - 50$. The new dominant firm demand curve is found by subtracting the fringe supply curve from the market demand curve to get $Q_D = 450 - 4.5P$. The new dominant firm marginal revenue curve is $MR = 100 - \frac{2Q}{4.5}$. The dominant firm will produce 180 units, price will be \$60, and each fringe firm will produce 20 units. The market share of the dominant firm drops from 75% to 64%.

14. **A lemon-growing cartel consists of four orchards. Their total cost functions are:**

$$TC_1 = 20 + 5Q_1^2$$

$$TC_2 = 25 + 3Q_2^2$$

$$TC_3 = 15 + 4Q_3^2$$

$$TC_4 = 20 + 6Q_4^2$$

(TC is in hundreds of dollars, Q is in cartons per month picked and shipped.)

a. **Tabulate total, average, and marginal costs for each firm for output levels between 1 and 5 cartons per month (i.e., for 1, 2, 3, 4, and 5 cartons).**

The following tables give total, average, and marginal costs for each firm.

Units	Firm 1			Firm 2		
	TC	*AC*	*MC*	*TC*	*AC*	*MC*
0	20			25		
1	25	25	5	28	28	3
2	40	20	15	37	18.5	9
3	65	21.67	25	52	17.3	15
4	100	25	35	73	18.25	21
5	145	29	45	100	20	27

Units	Firm 3			Firm 4		
	TC	*AC*	*MC*	*TC*	*AC*	*MC*
0	15			20		
1	19	19	4	26	26	6
2	31	15.5	12	44	22	18
3	51	17	20	74	24.67	30
4	79	19.75	28	116	29	42
5	115	23	36	170	34	54

b. **If the cartel decided to ship 10 cartons per month and set a price of 25 per carton, how should output be allocated among the firms?**

The cartel should assign production such that the lowest marginal cost is achieved for each unit, i.e.,

Cartel Unit Assigned	Firm Assigned	MC
1	2	3
2	3	4
3	1	5
4	4	6
5	2	9
6	3	12
7	1	15
8	2	15
9	4	18
10	3	20

Therefore, Firms 1 and 4 produce 2 units each and Firms 2 and 3 produce 3 units each.

c. **At this shipping level, which firm has the most incentive to cheat? Does any firm *not* have an incentive to cheat?**

At this level of output, Firm 2 has the lowest marginal cost for producing one more unit beyond its allocation, i.e., $MC = 21$ for the fourth unit for Firm 2. In addition, $MC = 21$ is less than the price of $25. For all other firms, the next unit has a marginal cost equal to or greater than $25. Firm 2 has the most incentive to cheat, while Firms 3 and 4 have no incentive to cheat, and Firm 1 is indifferent.

CHAPTER 13
GAME THEORY AND COMPETITIVE STRATEGY

TEACHING NOTES

Chapter 13 continues the discussion of competitive firms in the context of two-player games, with the first three sections covering topics introduced in Chapter 12. If you did not present Section 12.5, you should do so after discussing Sections 13.1 and 13.2. Sections 13.4 through 13.8 introduce advanced topics, as does section 13.9 on auctions, which is new to this edition. The presentation throughout the chapter focuses on the intuition behind each model or strategy. The exercises focus on relating Chapter 13 to Chapter 12 and on behavior in repeated games.

Two concepts pervade this chapter: rationality and equilibrium. Assuming the players are rational means that each player maximizes his or her own payoff whether it hurts or helps other players. Rationality underlies many of the equilibria in the chapter. Underlying all these models is the definition of a Nash equilibrium, which the students will find esoteric. When presenting each model, ask whether a unique Nash equilibrium exists. If there is more than one, discuss the conditions that will favor each equilibrium.

The analysis in the last five sections of the chapter is more demanding, but the examples are more detailed. Section 13.4 examines repeated games, and it will be important to discuss the role of rationality in the achievement of an equilibrium in both finite- and infinite-horizon games. Example 13.2 points out conditions that lead to stability in repeated games, while Example 13.3 presents an unstable case. Sections 13.5, 13.6, and 13.7 introduce strategy in the context of sequential games. To capture the students' attention, discuss the phenomenal success of Wal-Mart in its attempt to preempt the entry of other discount stores in rural areas (see Example 13.4). First, define a strategic move; second, discuss the advantage of moving first; third, present Example 13.4; and fourth, continue with other forms of strategic behavior, including the use of new capacity and R&D to deter entry (see Examples 13.5 and 13.6). You may wish to reintroduce the case of bilateral monopoly during the discussion of strategic behavior in cooperative games.

REVIEW QUESTIONS

1. What is the difference between a cooperative and a noncooperative game? Give an example of each.

In a noncooperative game the players do not formally communicate in an effort to coordinate their actions. They are aware of one another's existence, but act independently. The primary difference between a cooperative and a noncooperative game is that a binding contract, i.e., an agreement between the parties to which both parties must adhere, is possible in the former, but not in the latter. An example of a cooperative game would be a formal cartel agreement, such as OPEC, or a joint venture. An example of a noncooperative game would be a race in research and development to obtain a patent.

2. What is a dominant strategy? Why is an equilibrium stable in dominant strategies?

A dominant strategy is one that is best no matter what action is taken by the other party to the game. When both players have dominant strategies, the outcome is stable because neither party has an incentive to change.

3. Explain the meaning of a Nash equilibrium. How does it differ from an equilibrium in dominant strategies?

A Nash equilibrium is an outcome where both players correctly believe that they are doing the best they can, *given the action of the other player*. A game is in equilibrium if neither player has an incentive to change his or her choice, unless there is a change by the other player. The key feature that distinguishes a Nash equilibrium from an equilibrium in dominant strategies is the *dependence* on the opponent's behavior. An equilibrium in dominant strategies results if each player has a best choice, regardless of the other player's choice. Every dominant strategy equilibrium is a Nash equilibrium but the reverse does not hold.

4. How does a Nash equilibrium differ from a game's maximin solution? In what situations is a maximin solution a more likely outcome than a Nash equilibrium?

A maximin strategy is one in which each player determines the worst outcome for each of the opponent's actions and chooses the option that maximizes the minimum gain that can be earned. Unlike the Nash equilibrium, the maximin solution does not require players to react to an opponent's choice. If no dominant strategy exists (in which case outcomes depend on the opponent's behavior), players can reduce the uncertainty inherent in relying on the opponent's rationality by conservatively following a maximin strategy. The maximin solution is more likely than the Nash solution in cases where there is a higher probability of irrational (non-optimizing) behavior.

5. What is a "tit-for-tat" strategy? Why is it a rational strategy for the infinitely repeated prisoners' dilemma?

A player following a "tit-for-tat" strategy will cooperate as long as his or her opponent is cooperating and will switch to a noncooperative strategy if their opponent switches strategies. When the competitors assume that they will be repeating their interaction in *every* future period, the long-term gains from cooperating will outweigh any short-term gains from not cooperating. Because the "tit-for-tat" strategy encourages cooperation in infinitely repeated games, it is rational.

6. Consider a game in which the prisoners' dilemma is repeated 10 times and both players are rational and fully informed. Is a tit-for-tat strategy optimal in this case? Under what conditions would such a strategy be optimal?

Since cooperation will unravel from the last period back to the first period, the "tit-for-tat" strategy is not optimal when there is a finite number of periods and both players anticipate the competitor's response in *every* period. Given that there is no response possible in the eleventh period for action in the tenth (and last) period, cooperation breaks down in the last period. Then, knowing that there is no cooperation in the last period, players should maximize their self-interest by not cooperating in the second-to-last period. This unraveling occurs because both players assume that the other player has considered *all* consequences in *all* periods. However, if there is some doubt about whether the opponent has fully anticipated the consequences of the "tit-for-tat" strategy in the final period, the game will not unravel and the "tit-for-tat" strategy can be optimal.

7. Suppose you and your competitor are playing the pricing game shown in Table 13.8. Both of you must announce your prices at the same time. Can you improve your outcome by promising your competitor that you will announce a high price?

If the game is to be played only a few times, there is little to gain. If you are Firm 1 and promise to announce a high price, Firm 2 will undercut you and you will end up with a payoff of -50. However, next period you will undercut too, and both firms will earn 10. If the game is played many times, there is a better chance that Firm 2 will realize that if it matches your high price, the long-term payoff of 50 each period is better than 100 at first and 10 thereafter.

8. What is meant by "first-mover advantage"? Give an example of a gaming situation with a first-mover advantage.

A "first-mover" advantage can occur in a game where the first player to act receives the highest payoff. The first-mover signals his or her choice to the opponent, and the opponent must choose a response, *given this signal*. The first-mover goes on the offensive and the second-mover responds defensively. In many recreational games, from chess to football, the first-mover has an advantage. In many markets, the first firm to introduce a product can set the standard for competitors to follow. In some cases, the standard-setting power of the first mover becomes so pervasive in the market that the brand name of the product becomes synonymous with the product, e.g., "Kleenex," the name of Kleenex-brand facial tissue, is used by many consumers to refer to facial tissue of any brand.

9. What is a "strategic move"? How can the development of a certain kind of reputation be a strategic move?

A strategic move involves a commitment to reduce one's options. The strategic move might not seem rational outside the context of the game in which it is played, but it is rational given the anticipated response of the other player. Random responses to an opponent's action may not appear to be rational, but developing a reputation of being unpredictable could lead to higher payoffs in the long run. Another example would be making a promise to give a discount to all previous consumers if you give a discount to one. Such a move makes the firm vulnerable, but the goal of such a strategic move is to signal to rivals that you *won't* be discounting price and hope that your rivals follow suit.

10. Can the threat of a price war deter entry by potential competitors? What actions might a firm take to make this threat credible?

Both the incumbent and the potential entrant know that a price war will leave their firms worse off. Normally, such a threat is not credible. Thus, the incumbent must make his or her threat of a price war believable by signaling to the potential entrant that a price war *will* result if entry occurs. One strategic move is to increase capacity, signaling a lower future price, and another is to engage in apparently irrational behavior. Both types of strategic behavior might deter entry, but for different reasons. While an increase in capacity reduces expected profits by reducing prices, irrational behavior reduces expected profits by increasing uncertainty, hence increasing the rate at which future profits must be discounted into the present.

11. A strategic move limits one's flexibility and yet gives one an advantage. Why? How might a strategic move give one an advantage in bargaining?

A strategic move influences conditional behavior by the opponent. If the game is well understood and the opponent's reaction can be predicted, a strategic move leaves the player better off. Economic transactions involve a bargain, whether implicit or explicit. In every bargain, we assume that both parties attempt to maximize their self-interest. Strategic moves by one player provide signals to which another player reacts. If a bargaining game is played only once (so no reputations are involved), the players might act strategically to maximize their payoffs. If bargaining is repeated, players might act strategically to establish reputations for expected negotiations.

12. Why is the winner's curse potentially a problem for a bidder in a common value auction but not in a private value auction?

The winner's curse states that "The winner of a common value auction is likely to be made worse off (than not winning) because the winner was overly optimistic and, as a consequence, bid more for the item than it was actually worth." In a private value auction, you are aware of your own reservation price, and will bid accordingly. Once the price has escalated above your reservation price, you will no longer bid. If you win, it is because the winning bid was below your reservation price. In a common value auction, you do not know the exact value of the good you are bidding on. The winner will tend to be the person who has most overestimated the value of the good, assuming that some bidders overestimate and some underestimate. If all bids are below the actual value, then there is no winner's curse.

EXERCISES

1. **In many oligopolistic industries, the same firms compete over a long period of time, setting prices and observing each other's behavior repeatedly. Given that the number of repetitions is large, why don't collusive outcomes typically result?**

> If games are repeated indefinitely and all players know all payoffs, rational behavior will lead to apparently collusive outcomes, i.e., the same outcomes that would result if firms were actively colluding. All payoffs, however, might not be known by all players. Sometimes the payoffs of other firms can only be known by engaging in extensive (and costly) information exchanges or by making a move and observing rivals' responses. Also, successful collusion encourages entry. Perhaps the greatest problem in maintaining a collusive outcome is that changes in market conditions change the collusive price and quantity. The firms then have to repeatedly change their agreement on price and quantity, which is costly, and this increases the ability of one firm to cheat without being discovered.

2. **Many industries are often plagued by overcapacity--firms simultaneously make major investments in capacity expansion, so total capacity far exceeds demand. This happens not only in industries in which demand is highly volatile and unpredictable, but also in industries in which demand is fairly stable. What factors lead to overcapacity? Explain each briefly.**

> In Chapter 12, we found that excess capacity may arise in industries with easy entry and differentiated products. In the monopolistic competition model, downward-sloping demand curves for each firm lead to output with average cost above minimum average cost. The difference between the resulting output and the output at minimum long-run average cost is defined as excess capacity. In this chapter, we saw that overcapacity could be used to deter new entry; that is, investments in capacity expansion could convince potential competitors that entry would be unprofitable. (Note that although threats of capacity expansion may deter entry, these threats must be *credible*.)

3. **Two computer firms, A and B, are planning to market network systems for office information management. Each firm can develop either a fast, high-quality system (H), or a slower, low-quality system (L). Market research indicates that the resulting profits to each firm for the alternative strategies are given by the following payoff matrix:**

		Firm B H	Firm B L
Firm A	H	50, 40	60, 45
	L	55, 55	15, 20

a. **If both firms make their decisions at the same time and follow *maximin* (low-risk) strategies, what will the outcome be?**

> With a maximin strategy, a firm determines the worst outcome for each option, then chooses the option that maximizes the payoff among the worst outcomes. If Firm A chooses *H*, the worst payoff would occur if Firm B chooses *H*: A's payoff would be 50. If Firm A chooses *L*, the worst payoff would occur if Firm B chooses *L*: A's payoff would be 15. With a maximin strategy, A therefore chooses *H*. If Firm B chooses *L*, the worst payoff would occur if Firm A chooses *L*: the payoff would be 20. If Firm B chooses *H*, the worst payoff, 40, would occur if Firm A chooses *H*. With a maximin strategy, B therefore chooses *H*. So under maximin, both A and B produce a high-quality system.

b. **Suppose both firms try to maximize profits, but Firm A has a head start in planning, and can commit first. Now what will the outcome be? What will the outcome be if Firm B has a head start in planning and can commit first?**

If Firm A can commit first, it will choose *H*, because it knows that Firm B will rationally choose *L*, since *L* gives a higher payoff to B (45 vs. 40). This gives Firm A a payoff of 60. If Firm A instead committed to L, B would choose H (55 vs. 20), giving A 55 instead of 60. If Firm B can commit first, it will choose *H*, because it knows that Firm A will rationally choose *L*, since *L* gives a higher payoff to A (55 vs. 50). This gives Firm B a payoff of 55.

c. **Getting a head start costs money (you have to gear up a large engineering team). Now consider the *two-stage* game in which *first*, each firm decides how much money to spend to speed up its planning, and *second*, it announces which product (H or L) it will produce. Which firm will spend more to speed up its planning? How much will it spend? Should the other firm spend *anything* to speed up its planning? Explain.**

In this game, there is an apparent advantage to being the first mover. If A moves first, its profit is 60. If it moves second, its profit is 55, a difference of 5. Thus, it would be willing to spend up to 5 for the option of announcing first. On the other hand, if B moves first, its profit is 55. If it moves second, its profit is 45, a difference of 10, and it thus would be willing to spend up to 10 for the option of announcing first.

Once Firm A realizes that Firm B is willing to spend something on the option of announcing first, then the value of the option decreases for Firm A, because if both firms were to invest both firms would choose to produce the high-quality system, which gives them both a lower payoff. Firm A should not spend money to speed up the introduction of its product in any case. If B goes first and chooses high then A can choose low and end up with 55 instead of the 50 it would get if it went high also. This is best for B also because if B goes high and A low, B ends up with 55 instead of 40, so even if it spends the 10 it is still ahead by 5. A should let B go first. Finally, note that even though B is better off if A goes first and chooses high (45 vs. 40), B is still best off if it goes first. Overall, it is worthwhile for B to spend the money and announce but it is not worthwhile for A to spend any money.

4. Two firms are in the chocolate market. Each can choose to go for the high end of the market (high quality) or the low end (low quality). Resulting profits are given by the following payoff matrix:

		Firm 2	
		Low	*High*
	Low	-20, -30	900, 600
Firm 1	*High*	100, 800	50, 50

a. **What outcomes, if any, are Nash equilibria?**

A Nash equilibrium exists when neither party has an incentive to alter its strategy, taking the other's strategy as given. If Firm 2 chooses Low and Firm 1 chooses High, neither will have an incentive to change (100 > -20 for Firm 1 and 800 > 50 for Firm 2). If Firm 2 chooses High and Firm 1 chooses Low, neither will have an incentive to change (900 > 50 for Firm 1 and 600 > -30 for Firm 2). Both outcomes are Nash equilibria. Both firms choosing low is not a Nash equilibrium because, for example, if Firm 1 chooses low then firm 2 is better off by switching to high since 600 is greater than -30.

b. **If the manager of each firm is conservative and each follows a maximin strategy, what will be the outcome?**

If Firm 1 chooses Low, its worst payoff, -20, would occur if Firm 2 chooses Low. If Firm 1 chooses High, its worst payoff, 50, would occur if Firm 2 chooses High. Therefore, with a conservative maximin strategy, Firm 1 chooses High. Similarly, if Firm 2 chooses Low, its worst payoff, -30, would occur if Firm 1 chooses Low. If Firm 2 chooses High, its worst payoff, 50, would occur if Firm 1 chooses High. Therefore, with a maximin strategy, Firm 2 chooses High. Thus, both firms choose High, yielding a payoff of 50 for both.

c. **What is the cooperative outcome?**

The cooperative outcome would maximize *joint* payoffs. This would occur if Firm 1 goes for the low end of the market and Firm 2 goes for the high end of the market. The joint payoff is 1,500 (Firm 1 gets 900 and Firm 2 gets 600).

d. **Which firm benefits most from the cooperative outcome? How much would that firm need to offer the other to persuade it to collude?**

Firm 1 benefits most from cooperation. The difference between its best payoff under cooperation and the next best payoff is 900 - 100 = 800. To persuade Firm 2 to choose Firm 1's best option, Firm 1 must offer at least the difference between Firm 2's payoff under cooperation, 600, and its best payoff, 800, i.e., 200. However, Firm 2 realizes that Firm 1 benefits much more from cooperation and should try to extract as much as it can from Firm 1 (up to 800).

5. Two major networks are competing for viewer ratings in the 8:00-9:00 P.M. and 9:00-10:00 P.M. slots on a given weeknight. Each has two shows to fill this time period and is juggling its lineup. Each can choose to put its "bigger" show first or to place it second in the 9:00-10:00 P.M. slot. The combination of decisions leads to the following "ratings points" results:

		Network 2 First	Network 2 Second
Network 1	First	15, 15	30, 10
	Second	20, 30	18, 18

a. **Find the Nash equilibria for this game, assuming that both networks make their decisions at the same time.**

A Nash equilibrium exists when neither party has an incentive to alter its strategy, taking the other's strategy as given. By inspecting each of the four combinations, we find that (Second, First) is the only Nash equilibrium, yielding a payoff of (20, 30). There is no incentive for either party to change from this outcome. If we pick First for Firm 1 and Second for Firm 2, Firm 2 has an incentive to switch to First, in which case Firm 1 is better switching to Second.

b. **If each network is risk averse and uses a maximin strategy, what will be the resulting equilibrium?**

This conservative strategy of minimizing the maximum loss focuses on limiting the extent of the worst possible outcome, to the exclusion of possible good outcomes. If Network 1 plays First, the worst payoff is 15. If Network 1 plays Second, the worst payoff is 18. Under maximin, Network 1 plays Second. If Network 2 plays First, the worst payoff is 15. If Network 2 plays Second, the worst payoff is 10. Under maximin, Network 2 plays First (This is a dominant strategy). The maximin equilibrium is (Second, First) with a payoff of (20,30).

c.   **What will be the equilibrium if Network 1 can makes its selection first?   If Network 2 goes first?**

If Network 1 plays First, Network 2 will play First, yielding 15 for Network 1.   If Network 1 plays Second, Network 2 will play First, yielding 20 for Network 1. Therefore, if it has the first move, Network 1 will play Second, and the resulting equilibrium will be (Second, First).   If Network 2 plays First, Network 1 will play Second, yielding 30 for Network 2.   If Network 2 plays Second, Network 1 will play First, yielding 10 for Network 2.   If it has the first move, Network 2 will play First, and the equilibrium will again be (Second, First).

d.   **Suppose the network managers meet to coordinate schedules and Network 1 promises to schedule its big show first.   Is this promise credible?   What would be the likely outcome?**

A move is credible if, once declared, *there is no incentive to change.*   If Network 1 goes first, then Network 2 will also want to go first which gives them both 15.   In this case, once Network 1 knows that Network 2 also wants to go first, Network 1 will wants to change its strategy to Second.   In this case, the promise to schedule the bigger show first is not credible.   Network 2 will schedule its bigger show First since this is a dominant strategy and the coordinated outcome is likely to be (Second,First).

6.   Two competing firms are each planning to introduce a new product.   Each will decide whether to produce Product *A*, Product *B*, or Product *C*.   They will make their choices at the same time.   The resulting payoffs are shown below.

We are given the following payoff matrix, which describes a product introduction game:

Firm 2

		A	B	C
	A	-10,-10	0,10	10,20
Firm 1	B	10,0	-20,-20	-5,15
	C	20,10	15,-5	-30,-30

a.   **Are there any Nash equilibria in pure strategies?   If so, what are they?**

There are two Nash equilibria in pure strategies.   Each one involves one firm introducing Product A and the other firm introducing Product C.   We can write these two strategy pairs as (A, C) and (C, A), where the first strategy is for player 1.   The payoff for these two strategies is, respectively, (10,20) and (20,10).

b.   **If both firms use *maximin* strategies, what outcome will result?**

Recall that maximin strategies maximize the minimum payoff for both players.   For each of the players the strategy that maximizes their minimum payoff is A.   Thus (A,A) will result, and payoffs will be (-10,-10).   Each player is much worse off than at either of the pure strategy Nash equilibrium.

c.   **If Firm 1 uses a maximin strategy and Firm 2 knows, what will Firm 2 do?**

If Firm 1 plays its maximin strategy of A, and Firm 2 knows this then Firm 2 would get the highest payoff by playing C.   Notice that when Firm 1 plays conservatively, the Nash equilibrium that results gives Firm 2 the highest payoff of the two Nash equilibria.

7. We can think of the U.S. and Japanese trade policies as a prisoners' dilemma. The two countries are considering policies to open or close their import markets. Suppose the payoff matrix is:

Japan

		Open	Close
	Open	10, 10	5, 5
U.S.	**Close**	-100, 5	1, 1

a. **Assume that each country knows the payoff matrix and believes that the other country will act in its own interest. Does either country have a dominant strategy? What will be the equilibrium policies if each country acts rationally to maximize its welfare?**

Choosing Open is a dominant strategy for both countries. If Japan chooses Open, the U.S. does best by choosing Open. If Japan chooses Close, the U.S. does best by choosing Open. Therefore, the U.S. should choose Open, no matter what Japan does. If the U.S. chooses Open, Japan does best by choosing Open. If the U.S. chooses Close, Japan does best by choosing Open. Therefore, both countries will choose to have Open policies in equilibrium.

b. **Now assume that Japan is not certain that the U.S. will behave rationally. In particular, Japan is concerned that U.S. politicians may want to penalize Japan even if that does not maximize U.S. welfare. How might this affect Japan's choice of strategy? How might this change the equilibrium?**

The irrationality of U.S. politicians could change the equilibrium to (Close, Open). If the U.S. wants to penalize Japan they will choose Close, but Japan's strategy will not be affected since choosing Open is still Japan's dominant strategy.

8. You are a duopolist producer of a homogeneous good. Both you and your competitor have *zero* marginal costs. The market demand curve is

$$P = 30 - Q$$

where $Q = Q_1 + Q_2$. Q_1 is your output and Q_2 your competitor's output. Your competitor has also read this book.

a. **Suppose you will play this game only once. If you and your competitor must announce your output at the same time, how much will you choose to produce? What do you expect your profit to be? Explain.**

These are some of the cells in the payoff matrix:

Firm 2's Output

Firm 1's Output	0	5	10	15	20	25	30
0	0,0	0,125	0,200	0,225	0,200	0,125	0,0
5	125,0	100,100	75,150	50,150	25,100	0,0	0,0
10	200,0	150,75	100,100	50,75	0,0	0,0	0,0
15	225,0	100,50	75,50	0,0	0,0	0,0	0,0
20	200,0	100,25	0,0	0,0	0,0	0,0	0,0
25	125,0	0,0	0,0	0,0	0,0	0,0	0,0
30	0,0	0,0	0,0	0,0	0,0	0,0	0,0

If both firms must announce output at the same time, both firms believe that the other firm is behaving rationally, and each firm treats the output of the other firm as a fixed number, a Cournot equilibrium will result.

For Firm 1, total revenue will be

$$TR_1 = (30 - (Q_1 + Q_2))Q_1, \text{ or } TR_1 = 30Q_1 - Q_1^2 - Q_1Q_2.$$

Marginal revenue for Firm 1 will be the derivative of total revenue with respect to Q_1,

$$\frac{\partial TR}{\partial Q_1} = 30 - 2Q_1 - Q_2.$$

Because the firms share identical demand curves, the solution for Firm 2 will be symmetric to that of Firm 1:

$$\frac{\partial TR}{\partial Q_2} = 30 - 2Q_2 - Q_1.$$

To find the profit-maximizing level of output for both firms, set marginal revenue equal to marginal cost, which is zero:

$$Q_1 = 15 - \frac{Q_2}{2} \quad \text{and}$$

$$Q_2 = 15 - \frac{Q_1}{2}.$$

With two equations and two unknowns, we may solve for Q_1 and Q_2:

$$Q_1 = 15 - (0.5)\left(15 - \frac{Q_1}{2}\right), \text{ or } Q_1 = 10.$$

By symmetry, $Q_2 = 10$.

Substitute Q_1 and Q_2 into the demand equation to determine price:

$$P = 30 - (10 + 10), \text{ or } P = \$10.$$

Since no costs are given, profits for each firm will be equal to total revenue:

$$\pi_1 = TR_1 = (10)(10) = \$100 \quad \text{and}$$
$$\pi_2 = TR_2 = (10)(10) = \$100.$$

Thus, the equilibrium occurs when both firms produce 10 units of output and both firms earn $100. Looking back at the payoff matrix, note that the outcome (100, 100) is indeed a Nash equilibrium: neither firm will have an incentive to deviate, given the other firm's choice.

b.   **Suppose you are told that you must announce your output *before* your competitor does. How much will you produce in this case, and how much do you think your competitor will produce? What do you expect your profit to be? Is announcing first an advantage or disadvantage? Explain briefly. *How much would you pay* to be given the option of announcing either first or second?**

If you must announce first, you would announce an output of 15, knowing that your competitor would announce an output of 7.5. (Note: This is the Stackelberg equilibrium.)

$$TR_1 = \left(30 - (Q_1 + Q_2)\right)Q_1 = 30Q_1 - Q_1^2 - Q_1\left(15 - \frac{Q_1}{2}\right) = 15Q_1 - \frac{Q_1^2}{2}.$$

Therefore, setting $MR = MC = 0$ implies:

$$15 - Q_1 = 0, \text{ or } Q_1 = 15 \quad \text{and}$$
$$Q_2 = 7.5.$$

At that output, your competitor is maximizing profits, given that you are producing 15. At these outputs, price is equal to

$$30 - 15 - 7.5 = \$7.5.$$

Your profit would be

$$(15)(7.5) = \$112.5.$$

Your competitor's profit would be

$$(7.5)(7.5) = \$56.25.$$

Announcing first is an advantage in this game. The difference in profits between announcing first and announcing second is $56.25. You would be willing to pay up to this difference for the option of announcing first.

c.   Suppose instead that you are to play the first round of a *series of 10 rounds* (with the same competitor). In each round, you and your competitor announce your outputs at the same time. You want to maximize the sum of your profits over the 10 rounds. How much will you produce in the *first round*? How much do you expect to produce in the tenth round? In the ninth round? Explain briefly.

Given that your competitor has also read this book, you can assume that he or she will be acting rationally. You should begin with the Cournot output and continue with the Cournot output in each round, including the ninth and tenth rounds. Any deviation from this output will reduce the sum of your profits over the ten rounds.

d.   Once again you will play a series of 10 rounds. This time, however, in each round your competitor will announce its output before you announce yours. How will your answers to (c) change in this case?

If your competitor always announces first, it might be more profitable to behave by reacting "irrationally" in a single period. For example, in the first round your competitor will announce an output of 15, as in Exercise (7.b). Rationally, you would respond with an output of 7.5. If you behave this way in every round, your total profits for all ten rounds will be $562.50. Your competitor's profits will be $1,125. However, if you respond with an output of 15 every time your competitor announces an output of 15, profits will be reduced to zero for both of you in that period. If your competitor fears, or learns, that you will respond in this way, he or she will be better off by choosing the Cournot output of 10, and your profits after that point will be $75 per period. Whether this strategy is profitable depends on your opponent's expectations about your behavior, as well as how you value future profits relative to current profits.

(Note: A problem could develop in the last period, however, because your competitor will know that you realize that there are no more long-term gains to be had from behaving strategically. Thus, your competitor will announce an output of 15, knowing that you will respond with an output of 7.5. Furthermore, knowing that you will not respond strategically in the last period, there are also no long-term gains to be made in the ninth period from behaving strategically. Therefore, in the ninth period, your competitor will announce an output of 15, and you should respond rationally with an output of 7.5, and so on.)

9. You play the following bargaining game. Player A moves first and makes Player B an offer for the division of $100. (For example, Player A could suggest that she take $60 and Player B take $40). Player B can accept or reject the offer. If he rejects it, the amount of money available drops to $90, and he then makes an offer for the division of this amount. If Player A rejects this offer, the amount of money drops to $80 and Player A makes an offer for its division. If Player B rejects this offer, the amount of money drops to 0. Both players are rational, fully informed, and want to maximize their payoffs. Which player will do best in this game?

Solve the game by starting at the end and working backwards. If B rejects A's offer at the 3rd round, B gets 0. When A makes an offer at the 3rd round, B will accept even a minimal amount, such as $1. So A should offer $1 at this stage and take $79 for herself. In the 2nd stage, B knows that A will turn down any offer giving her less than $79, so B must offer $80 to A, leaving $10 for B. At the first stage, A knows B will turn down any offer giving him less than $10. So A can offer $11 to B and keep $89 for herself. B will take that offer, since B can never do any better by rejecting and waiting. The following table summarizes this.

Round	Money Available	Offering Party	Amount to A	Amount to B
1	$100	A	$89	$11
2	$ 90	B	$80	$10
3	$ 80	A	$79	$ 1
End	$ 0		$ 0	$ 0

*10. Defendo has decided to introduce a revolutionary video game. As the first firm in the market, it will have a monopoly position for at least some time. In deciding what type of manufacturing plant to build, it has the choice of two technologies. Technology A is publicly available and will result in annual costs of

$$C^A(q) = 10 + 8q.$$

Technology B is a proprietary technology developed in Defendo's research labs. It involves higher fixed cost of production but lower marginal costs:

$$C^B(q) = 60 + 2q.$$

Defendo must decide which technology to adopt. Market demand for the new product is P = 20 - Q, where Q is total industry output.

a.   Suppose Defendo were certain that it would maintain its monopoly position in the market for the entire product lifespan (about five years) without threat of entry. Which technology would you advise Defendo to adopt? What would be Defendo's profit given this choice?

Defendo has two choices: Technology A with a marginal cost of 8 and Technology B with a marginal cost of 2. Given the inverse demand curve as $P = 20 - Q$, total revenue, PQ, is equal to $20Q - Q^2$ for both technologies. Marginal revenue is $20 - 2Q$. To determine the profits for each technology, equate marginal revenue and marginal cost:

$$20 - 2Q_A = 8, \text{ or } Q_A = 6, \text{ and}$$
$$20 - 2Q_B = 2, \text{ or } Q_B = 9.$$

Substituting the profit-maximizing quantities into the demand equation to determine the profit-maximizing prices, we find:

$$P_A = 20 - 6 = \$14 \text{ and}$$
$$P_B = 20 - 9 = \$11.$$

To determine the profits for each technology, subtract total cost from total revenue:

$$\pi_A = (14)(6) - (10 + (8)(6)) = \$26 \text{ and}$$
$$\pi_B = (11)(9) - (60 + (2)(9)) = \$21.$$

To maximize profits, Defendo should choose technology A.

b. **Suppose Defendo expects its archrival, Offendo, to consider entering the market shortly after Defendo introduces its new product. Offendo will have access only to Technology A. If Offendo does enter the market, the two firms will play a Cournot game (in quantities) and arrive at the Cournot-Nash equilibrium.**

i. If Defendo adopts Technology A and Offendo enters the market, what will be the profit of each firm? Would Offendo choose to enter the market given these profits?

If both firms play Cournot, each will choose its best output, taking the other's strategy as given. Letting D = Defendo and O = Offendo, the demand function will be

$$P = 20 - Q_D - Q_O.$$

Profit for Defendo will be

$$\pi_D = \left(20 - Q_D - Q_O\right)Q_D - \left(10 + 8Q_D\right), \text{ or } \pi_D = 12Q_D - Q_D^2 - Q_D Q_O - 10$$

To determine the profit-maximizing quantity, set the first derivative of profits with respect to Q_D equal to zero and solve for Q_D:

$$\frac{\partial \pi_D}{\partial Q_D} = 12 - 2Q_D - Q_O = 0 \text{, or } Q_D = 6 - 0.5Q_O.$$

This is Defendo's reaction function. Because both firms have access to the same technology, hence the same cost structure, Offendo's reaction function is analogous:

$$Q_O = 6 - 0.5Q_D.$$

Substituting Offendo's reaction function into Defendo's reaction function and solving for Q_D:

$$Q_D = 6 - (0.5)(6 - 0.5Q_D) = 4.$$

Substituting into Defendo's reaction function and solving for Q_O:

$$Q_O = 6 - (0.5)(4) = 4.$$

Total industry output is therefore equal to 8. To determine price, substitute Q_D and Q_O into the demand function:

$$P = 20 - 4 - 4 = \$12.$$

The profits for each firm are equal to total revenue minus total costs:

$$\pi_D = (4)(12) - (10 + (8)(4)) = \$6 \text{ and}$$
$$\pi_O = (4)(12) - (10 + (8)(4)) = \$6.$$

Therefore, Offendo would enter the market.

ii. If Defendo adopts Technology B and Offendo enters the market, what will be the profit of each firm? Would Offendo choose to enter the market given these profits?

Profit for Defendo will be

$$\pi_D = \left(20 - Q_D - Q_O\right)Q_D - \left(60 + 2Q_D\right), \text{ or } \pi_D = 18Q_D - Q_D^2 - Q_D Q_O - 60.$$

The change in profit with respect to Q_D is

$$\frac{\partial \pi_D}{\partial Q_D} = 18 - 2Q_D - Q_O.$$

To determine the profit-maximizing quantity, set this derivative to zero and solve for Q_D:

$$18 - 2Q_D - Q_O = 0, \text{ or } Q_D = 9 - 0.5Q_O.$$

This is Defendo's reaction function. Substituting Offendo's reaction function (from part i above) into Defendo's reaction function and solving for Q_D:

$$Q_D = 9 - 0.5(6 - 0.5Q_D), \text{ or } Q_D = 8.$$

Substituting Q_D into Offendo's reaction function yields

$$Q_O = 6 - (0.5)(8), \text{ or } Q_O = 2.$$

To determine the industry price, substitute the profit-maximizing quantities for Defendo and Offendo into the demand function:

$$P = 20 - 8 - 2 = \$10.$$

The profit for each firm is equal to total revenue minus total cost, or:

$$\pi_D = (10)(8) - (60 + (2)(8)) = \$4 \text{ and}$$
$$\pi_O = (10)(2) - (10 + (8)(2)) = -\$6.$$

With negative profit, Offendo *should not* enter the industry.

iii. Which technology would you advise Defendo to adopt given the threat of possible entry? What will be Defendo's profit given this choice? What will be consumer surplus given this choice?

With Technology A and Offendo's entry, Defendo's profit would be 6. With Technology B and no entry by Defendo, Defendo's profit would be 4. I would advise Defendo to stick with Technology A. Under this advice, total output is 8 and price is 12. Consumer surplus is:

$$(0.5)(20 - 12)(8) = \$32.$$

c. **What happens to social welfare (the sum of consumer surplus and producer profit) as a result of the threat of entry in this market? What happens to equilibrium price? What might this imply about the role of *potential* competition in limiting market power?**

From 10.a we know that, under monopoly, $Q = 6$ and profit is 26. Consumer surplus is

$$(0.5)(20 - 14)(6) = \$18.$$

Social welfare is the sum of consumer surplus plus profits, or

$$18 + 26 = \$44.$$

With entry, social welfare is $32 (consumer surplus) plus $12 (industry profit), or $44. Social welfare does not change with entry, but entry shifts surplus from producers to consumers. The equilibrium price falls with entry, and therefore *potential* competition can *limit* market power.

Note that Defendo has one other option: to increase quantity from the monopoly level of 6 to discourage entry by Offendo. If Defendo increases output from 6 to 8 under Technology A, Offendo is unable to earn a positive profit. With an output of 8, Defendo's profit decreases from $26 to

$$(8)(12) - (10 + (8)(8)) = \$22.$$

As before, with an output of 8, consumer surplus is $32; social welfare is $54. In this case, social welfare rises when output is increased to discourage entry.

11. Three contestants, A, B, and C, each have a balloon and a pistol. From fixed positions, they fire at each other's balloons. When a balloon is hit, its owner is out. When only one balloon remains, its owner is the winner of a $1,000 prize. At the outset, the players decide by lot the order in which they will fire, and each player can choose any remaining balloon as his target. Everyone knows that A is the best shot and always hits the target, that B hits the target with probability .9, and that C hits the target with probability 0.8. Which contestant has the highest probability of winning the $1,000? Explain why.

Intuitively, C has the highest probability of winning, though A has the highest probability of shooting the balloon. Each contestant wants to remove the contestant with the highest probability of success. By following this strategy, each improves his chance of winning the game. A targets B because, by removing B from the game, A's chance of winning becomes much greater. B's probability of success is greater than C's probability of success. C will target A because, if C targets B and hits B, then A will target C and win the game. B will follow a similar strategy, because if B targets C and hits C, then A will target B and will win the game. Therefore, both B and C increase their chance of winning by eliminating A first. Similarly, A increases his chance of winning by eliminating B first. A complete probability tree can be constructed to show that A's chance of winning is 8 percent, B's chance of winning is 32 percent, and C's chance of winning is 60 percent.

12. An antique dealer regularly buys objects at home-town auctions whose bidders are limited to other dealers. Most of her successful bids turn out to be financially worthwhile, because she is able to resell the antiques for a profit. On occasion, however, she travels to a nearby town to bid in an auction that is open to the public. She often finds that on the rare occasions in which she does bid successfully, she is disappointed - the antique cannot be sold at a profit. Can you explain the difference in her success between the two sets of circumstances?

When she bids at the home-town auction that is limited to other dealers, she is bidding against people who are all going to resell the antique if they win the bid. In this case, all of the bidders are limiting their bids to prices that will tend to earn them a profit. A rational dealer will not place a bid which is higher than the price they can expect to resell the antique for. Given that all dealers are rational, the winning bid will tend to be below the expected resale price.

When she bids in the auction that is open to the public she is bidding against the people who are likely to come into her shop. You can assume that local antique lovers will frequent these auctions as well as the local antique shops. In the case where she wins the bid at one of these open auctions, the other participants have decided that the price is too high. In this case, they will not come into her shop and pay any higher price which would earn her a profit. She will only tend to profit in this case if she is able to resell to a customer from out of the area, or who was not at the auction, and who has a sufficiently high reservation price. In any event, the winning bid price will tend to be higher because she was bidding against customers rather than dealers.

13. You are in the market for a new house and have decided to bid for a house at auction. You believe that the value of the house is between $125,000 and $150,000, but you are uncertain as to where in the range it might be. You do know, however, that the seller has reserved the right to withdraw the house from the market if the winning bid is not satisfactory.

a. Should you bid in this auction? Why or why not?

Yes you should bid if you are confident about your estimate of the value of the house and/or if you allow for the possibility of being wrong. To allow for the possibility of being wrong, you reduce your high bid by an amount equal to the expected error of the winning bidder. If you have experience at auction, you will have information on how likely you are to enter a wrong bid and can then adjust your high bid accordingly.

b. Suppose you are a building contractor. You plan to improve the house and then to resell it at a profit. How does this situation affect your answer to (a)? Does it depend on the extent to which your skills are uniquely suitable to improving this particular house?

You need to be aware of the winner's curse which says that the winner is likely to be the person who most overestimated the value of the house. If there are a range of bids, some below the actual value and some above the actual value, the winner will be the person with the largest overestimate of the value. Again, you need to be very confident in your estimate of the value of the house and/or allow for the possibility of being wrong. If you have made many such bids in the past, you will be able to estimate how often you are wrong and adjust accordingly.

CHAPTER 14
MARKETS FOR FACTOR INPUTS

TEACHING NOTES

The following two chapters examine the markets for labor and capital. Although the discussion in this chapter is general, most of the examples refer to labor as the only variable input to production, with the exception of Example 14.1, which discusses "The Demand for Jet Fuel" by airlines. Labor demand and supply are discussed in the first section, and the competitive factor market equilibrium and economic rent are discussed in the second section. Section 14.3 explores the factor market structure for the case where the buyer has monopsony power, and section 14.4 explores the case of monopoly power on the part of the seller of the factor.

An understanding of this chapter relies on concepts from Chapters 4 through 8 and 10. If you have just covered Chapters 11-13, you might begin by reviewing marginal product, marginal revenue, and cost minimization. You should then discuss marginal revenue product and the profit-maximizing condition $MRP_L = w$. Explain why we are only interested in the portion of the MP curve below the average product curve (the downward-sloping portion). The derivation of the firm's demand curve for labor is straightforward when labor is the only factor, but becomes more complicated when there are several variable inputs. In particular, you might explain why the MRP_L curve shifts as the firm substitutes one input for another in production in response to a price change by noting that the MRP_L curve is drawn for a fixed level of the other variable input.

When presenting the market labor demand curve, explain that since the input prices change as more inputs are demanded, the market demand curve is not simply the summation of individual demand curves. You can extend the presentation of price elasticity of input demand (see Example 14.1) by discussing the conditions leading to price sensitivity. Elasticity is greater (1) when the elasticity of demand for the product is higher, (2) when it is easy to substitute one input for another, and (3) when the elasticity of supply is higher for other inputs. Elasticity of supply, which was discussed in Chapter 2, is reintroduced in Example 14.2. You should also distinguish between short-run and long-run elasticity (see Figure 14.6).

If you have already covered substitution and income effects, the students will be ready for the derivation of the backward-bending supply curve for labor. Although Figure 14.9 is a straightforward application of these tools, students are often confused by the plotting of income against leisure. Point out that this is just another type of utility maximization problem where the two goods are leisure and income. Income can be thought of as the consumption of goods other than leisure, in that more income buys more goods. You can also implicitly assume that the price of other goods is $1 and the price of leisure is the wage. The supply of labor curve is derived by changing the wage and finding the new level of hours worked. An individual's supply curve of labor is backward bending only when the income effect dominates the substitution effect and leisure is a normal good. Show typical supply curves for each group in Table 14.2. For an experimental study of the labor-leisure trade-off see Battalio, Green, and Kagel, "Income-Leisure Tradeoff of Animal Workers," *American Economic Review* (September 1981).

Section 14.2 brings together labor demand and supply for both competitive and monopolistic <u>product</u> markets. Although economic rent was presented in Chapter 8, it is reintroduced with more detail here. In Section 14.3, carefully explain why the marginal expenditure curve is above the average expenditure curve for a monopsonist (see Figure 14.14). You can discuss how a monopsonist would price discriminate, e.g., pay a different wage rate to each employee. With perfect price discrimination, the marginal revenue expenditure curve would coincide with the average expenditure curve. Although monopsony exists in some markets, the exercise of monopsony power is rare because of factor mobility. However, the employment of athletes by the owners of professional teams provides a good example (see Example 14.4 "Monopsony Power in the Market for Baseball Players"). On this same topic, see Sommers and Quinton, "Pay and Performance in Major League Baseball: The Case of the First Family of Free Agents," *Journal of Human Resources* (Summer 1982). Section 14.4 discusses the case of unions to explore monopoly power on the part of the seller of the input.

REVIEW QUESTIONS

1. Why is a firm's demand for labor curve more inelastic when the firm has monopoly power in the output market than when the firm is producing competitively?

The firm's demand curve for labor is determined by the incremental revenue from hiring an additional unit of labor known as the marginal revenue product of labor: $MRP_L = (MP_L)(MR)$, the additional output ("product") that the last worker produced, times the additional revenue earned by selling that output. In a competitive industry, the marginal revenue curve is perfectly elastic and equal to price. For a monopolist, marginal revenue is downward sloping. As more labor is hired and more output is produced, the monopolist will charge a lower price and marginal revenue will diminish. All else the same, marginal revenue product will be smaller for the monopolist. This implies that the marginal revenue product for the monopolist is more inelastic than for the competitive firm.

2. Why might a labor supply curve be backward bending?

A backward-bending supply curve for labor may occur when the income effect of an increase in the wage rate dominates the substitution effect. Labor supply decisions are made by individuals choosing the most satisfying combination of work and other (leisure) activities. With a larger income, the individual can afford to work fewer hours: the income effect. As the wage rate increases, the value of leisure time (the opportunity cost of leisure) increases, thus inducing the individual to work longer hours: the substitution effect. Because the two effects work in opposite directions, the shape of an individual's labor supply curve depends on the individual's preferences for income, consumption, and leisure.

3. How is a computer company's demand for computer programmers a derived demand?

A computer company's demand for inputs, including programmers, depends on how many computers it sells. The firm's demand for programming labor depends on (is derived from) the demand it faces in its market for computers. As demand for computers shifts, the demand for programmers shifts.

4. Compare the hiring choices of a monopsonistic and a competitive employer of workers. Which will hire more workers, and which will pay the higher wages? Explain.

Since the decision to hire another worker means the monopsonist must pay a higher wage for *all* workers, and not just the last worker hired, its marginal expenditure curve lies above the input supply curve (the average expenditure curve). The monopsonist's profit-maximizing input demand, where the marginal expenditure curve intersects the marginal revenue product curve, will be less than the competitor's profit-maximizing input choice, where the average expenditure curve intersects the demand curve. The monopsonist hires less labor, and the wage paid will be less than in a competitive market.

5. Rock musicians sometimes earn over $1 million per year. Can you explain such large incomes in terms of economic rent?

Economic rent is the difference between the actual payment to the factor of production and the minimum amount that the factor is willing to accept. In this case, you might assume that there are a limited number of top-quality rock musicians who will continue to play rock music no matter what they are paid. This results in a perfectly inelastic supply curve, or something close to it. Given the high demand for rock music, the wage will be very high and there will be a lot of economic rent. If there was a larger supply of top-quality rock musicians, or a more elastic supply, then the economic rent would be smaller.

6. What happens to the demand for one input when the use of a complementary input increases?

If the demand for the complementary input increases, the demand for the given input will increase as well. When demand for the complementary input increases, there is an increase in the quantity hired and possibly the price paid. Both of these changes will increase the *MRP* of the given input, and hence will increase the quantity hired and possibly the price paid. Whether the prices of the inputs increases depends on the degree of monopsony power on the part of the firm.

7. For a monopsonist, what is the relationship between the supply of an input and the marginal expenditure on it?

The decision to increase employment means the monopsonist must pay *all* units the higher price, and not just the last unit hired. Therefore, its marginal expenditure curve lies above the input supply curve (the average expenditure curve). Hiring more labor will increase the marginal expenditure, which will increase the average expenditure. If the average expenditure is increasing, then the marginal expenditure must be greater than the average expenditure.

8. Currently the National Football League has a system for drafting college players by which each player is picked by only one team. The player must sign with that team or not play in the league. What would happen to the wages of newly drafted and more experienced football players if the draft system were repealed, and all teams could compete for college players?

The National Football League draft and reserve clause (a primary issue in the 1987-1988 season's strike) creates a monopsonist cartel among the owners of NFL teams. If the draft system were repealed, competition among teams would increase wages of football players to the point where the marginal revenue product of each player would be equal to the player's wage.

9. The government wants to encourage individuals on welfare to become employed. It is considering two possible incentive programs for firms.

    A. Give the firm $2 per hour for every individual on welfare who is hired.
    B. Give each firm that hires one or more welfare workers a payment of $1000 per year, irrespective of the number of hires.

To what extent is each of these programs likely to be effective at increasing the employment opportunities for welfare workers?

Firms will hire additional labor as long as the extra benefit is greater than the extra cost of hiring the worker, or until $MRP_L = w$. Option A would be effective because if the firm receives $2 per hour for every welfare worker hired then the effective wage paid, w, will fall and the firm will find it optimal to hire more labor until the benefits (MRP_L) again equal the costs (w) at the margin. Option B would be effective at increasing employment opportunities also in that if the firm hires an individual who has been on welfare they will then receive $1000. However, plan B is not necessarily as effective as plan A given the firm only receives one lump sum payment regardless of the number of welfare workers hired. In this case the firm only has an incentive to hire the one welfare worker, though they may of course choose to hire more than one welfare worker.

10. A small specialty cookie company, whose only variable input is labor, finds that the average worker can produce 50 cookies per day, the cost of the average worker is $64 per day, and the price of a cookie is $1. Is the cookie company maximizing its profit? Explain.

The marginal product of labor is 50 (cookies per day) and the price per cookie is 1 ($ per cookie) so the marginal revenue product is $50/day. Since this is less than the wage of $64 per day the cookie company is not maximizing profit. They are employing too much labor since the cost of labor is greater than the benefit of labor at the margin, and are therefore producing too many cookies.

11. A firm uses both labor and machines in production. Explain why an increase in the average wage rate causes both a movement along the labor demand curve and a shift of the curve.

An increase in the wage rate causes an upward movement along the labor demand curve. For any given marginal revenue product curve, the firm will find that they want to hire fewer workers when the wage increases (an upward movement). However, when the wage increases the marginal cost will increase which will reduce desired output. When output falls, the firm will not need as many machines and the marginal product of labor curve will shift to the left, assuming machines and labor are complementary. This will also reduce the demand for labor.

EXERCISES

1. Suppose that the wage rate is $16 per hour, and the price of the product is $2. Values for output and labor are in units per hour.

q	L
0	0
20	1
35	2
47	3
57	4
65	5
70	6

a.   Find the profit-maximizing quantity of labor.

From the information given above, calculate the marginal product of labor, the extra output produced by hiring one more unit of labor, and then multiply by price to get the marginal revenue product of labor. To find the profit-maximizing quantity of labor, use the rule that the firm wants to hire labor only as long as the marginal revenue product of labor is greater than the nominal wage, or up to the point where the marginal revenue product of labor is equal to the nominal wage. From the table below, the firm will hire 5 units of labor.

q	L	MP_L	MRP_L
0	0	-	-
20	1	20	40
35	2	15	30
47	3	12	24
57	4	10	20
65	5	8	16
70	6	5	10

b.   Suppose that the price of the product remains at $2 but that the wage rate increases to $21. Find the new profit-maximizing quantity of labor.

The above table does not change for this part of the problem. However, the firm no longer wants to hire 5 units of labor because the benefit of the 5th unit ($16 per hour) is less than the cost of the 5th unit ($21 per hour). The firm would only hire 3 units of labor per hour since in this case the benefit still exceeds the cost at the margin. The firm would stick with 3 units instead of 4 unless fractional units are possible. At L=4 the cost is greater than the benefit so you lose profit by hiring the 4th unit of labor.

c. **Suppose the price of the product increases to $3 and the wage remains at $16 per hour. Find the new profit-maximizing quantity of labor.**

A change in the price of the product will not change the marginal product of labor, but it will change the marginal revenue product of labor. The new marginal revenue product of labor is given in the table below. The firm will still want to hire 5 units of labor, as in part a above. It will not hire the 6th unit because the extra benefit is less than the extra cost. Profit will be greater than in part a.

q	L	MP$_L$	MRP$_L$
0	0	-	-
20	1	20	60
35	2	15	45
47	3	12	36
57	4	10	30
65	5	8	24
70	6	5	15

d. **Suppose that the price of the product remains at $2 and the wage remains at $16, but there is a technological breakthrough that increases output by 25% for any given level of labor. Find the new profit-maximizing quantity of labor.**

The technological breakthrough changes the number of units of output produced by a given number of units of labor, and hence changes the marginal product and the marginal revenue product of labor. The new output values are found by multiplying the old values by 1.25. This new information is given in the table below. The firm will still choose to hire 5 units of labor. Profit will be greater than in part a.

q	L	MP$_L$	MRP$_L$
0	0	-	-
25	1	25	50
43.75	2	18.75	37.5
58.75	3	15	30
71.25	4	12.5	25
81.25	5	10	20
87.5	6	6.25	12.5

2. **Assume that workers whose incomes are less than $10,000 currently pay no federal income taxes. Suppose a new government program guarantees each worker $5,000, whether or not he or she earns any income. For all earned income up to $10,000, the worker must pay a 50-percent tax. Draw the budget line facing the workers under this new program. How is the program likely to affect the labor supply curve of workers?**

The budget line for workers under this program is a straight line at $5,000. This line is shown in the figure and table below. Workers earn $5,000 whether they work or not. If workers work only to earn income, i.e., there are no other benefits such as "getting out of the house" or "gaining experience," there is no incentive to work under the new program. Only wages yielding incomes greater than $10,000 will result in a positive labor supply.

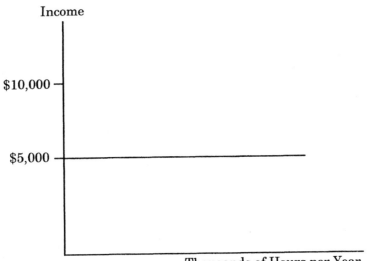

Figure 14.2

Income	After Tax Income	Government Subsidy	Total Income
0	0	5,000	$5,000
$1,000	500	4,500	5,000
2,000	1,000	4,000	5,000
3,000	1,500	3,500	5,000
4,000	2,000	3,000	5,000
5,000	2,500	2,500	5,000
6,000	3,000	2,000	5,000
7,000	3,500	1,500	5,000
8,000	4,000	1,000	5,000
9,000	4,500	500	5,000
10,000	5,000	0	5,000

3. **Using your knowledge of marginal revenue product, explain the following:**

a.   **A famous tennis star is paid $100,000 for appearing in a 30-second television commercial. The actor who plays his doubles partner is paid $500.**

Marginal revenue product of labor, MRP_L, is equal to marginal revenue from an incremental unit of output multiplied by the marginal product from an incremental unit of labor, or in other words, the extra revenue generated by having the tennis star appear in the ad. The famous tennis star is able to help increase revenues far more than the actor, so he is paid much more than the actor. The wage of the actor is determined by the supply and demand of actors willing to play tennis with tennis stars.

b.   **The president of an ailing savings and loan is paid *not* to stay in his job for the last two years of his contract.**

The marginal revenue product of the president of the ailing savings and loan is likely to be negative and therefore, the savings and loan is better off by paying the president not to show up. They have calculated that they will lose less (or gain more) by paying the president off and hiring someone else.

c. **A jumbo jet carrying 400 passengers is priced higher than a 250-passenger model even though both aircraft cost the same to manufacture.**

The ability of the larger jet to generate more revenue increases its value to the airline, and therefore the airline is willing to pay more for it.

4. The demands for the factors of production listed below have increased. What can you conclude about changes in the demand for the related consumer goods? If demands for the consumer goods remain unchanged, what other explanation is there for an increase in derived demands for these items?

a. **Computer memory chips**

In general, an increase in the demand for a good increases the demand for its factor inputs. The converse is not necessarily true; i.e., an increase in the demand for factor inputs does not necessarily imply an increase in the demand for the final product. The demand for an input may increase due to a change in the use of other inputs in the production process. As the price of another input increases, its demand falls and the demand of substitutable inputs rises. In this case, the increase in the demand for computer memory chips must have been caused by an increase in the demand for personal computers given that computer memory chips are used only in computers, and there are no substitutes for computer memory chips.

b. **Jet fuel for passenger planes**

With an increase in the demand for jet travel, the demand for jet fuel will increase. There are no substitutes for jet fuel.

c. **Paper used for newsprint**

Given the paper is being used to print newspapers then there must have been an increase in the circulation of newspapers.

d. **Aluminum used for beverage cans**

With an increase in demand for cold drinks in the summer, the seasonal demand for aluminum increases, so this is one possible explanation. Alternatively, if glass or plastic have become more expensive then this may affect the demand for aluminum. Finally, changes in the market for recycled aluminum may affect the demand for new aluminum.

5. Suppose there are two groups of workers, unionized and nonunionized. Congress passes a law that requires all workers to join the union. What do you expect to happen to the wage rates of formerly nonunionized workers? of those workers who were originally unionized? What have you assumed about the union's behavior?

In general, we expect that nonunionized workers are earning lower wages than unionized workers. If all workers are forced to join the union, it would be reasonable to expect that the nonunionized workers will now receive higher wages and the unionized workers will receive a wage that could go either way. There are a couple of items to consider. First, the union now has more monopoly power in that there are no nonunion workers to act as substitutes for union workers. This gives more power to the union, which means higher wages can in general be negotiated. However, the union now has more members to satisfy. If wages are kept at a high level, there will be fewer jobs, and hence some previously nonunionized workers may end up with no job. The union may wish to trade off some of the wage for a guarantee of more jobs. The average income of all workers will rise if labor demand is inelastic and will fall if labor demand is elastic.

6. Suppose a firm's production function is given by Q = 12L - L², for L = 0 to 6, where L is labor input per day and Q is output per day. Derive and draw the firm's demand for labor curve if the firm's output sells for $10 in a competitive market. How many workers will the firm hire when the wage rate is $30 per day? $60 per day? (Hint: The marginal product of labor is 12 - 2L.)

The demand for labor is given by the marginal revenue product of labor. This is equal to the product of marginal revenue and the marginal product of labor: $MRP_L = (MR)(MP_L)$. In a competitive market, price is equal to marginal revenue, so $MR = 10$. We are given $MP_L = 12 - 2L$ (the slope of the production function).

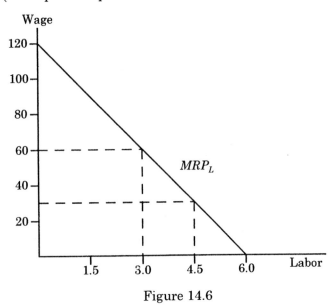

Figure 14.6

Therefore, the $MRP_L = (10)(12 - 2L)$. The firm's profit-maximizing quantity of labor occurs where $MRP_L = w$. If $w = 30$, then $30 = 120 - 20L$ at the optimum. Solving for L yields 4.5 hours per day. Similarly, if $w = 60$, solving for L yields 3 hours per day.

7. The only legal employer of military soldiers in the United States is the federal government. If the government uses its monopsonistic position, what criteria will it employ when figuring how many soldiers to recruit? What happens if a mandatory draft is implemented?

Acting as a monopsonist in hiring soldiers, the federal government would hire soldiers until the marginal value of the last soldier is equal to his or her pay. There are two implications of the government's monopsony power: fewer soldiers are hired, and they are paid less than their marginal product. When a mandatory draft is implemented, even fewer professional soldiers are hired. Wages for volunteer soldiers fall, pushed down by the fact that wages of the draftees can be very low.

8. The demand for labor by an industry is given by the curve L = 1200 - 10w, where L is the labor demanded per day and w is the wage rate. The supply curve is given by L = 20w. What is the equilibrium wage rate and quantity of labor hired? What is the economic rent earned by workers?

The equilibrium wage rate is determined where quantity of labor supplied is equal to the quantity of labor demanded:

$$20w = 1,200 - 10w, \text{ or } w = \$40.$$

Substituting into either the labor supply or labor demand equations, we find the equilibrium quantity of labor is 800:

$$L_S = (20)(40) = 800,$$

and

$$L_D = 1,200 - (10)(40) = 800.$$

Economic rent is the summation of the difference between the equilibrium wage and the wage given by the labor supply curve. Here, it is the area above the labor supply curve up to $L = 800$ and below the equilibrium wage. This triangle's area is $(0.5)(800)(\$40) = \$16,000$.

9. This exercise is a continuation of Exercise 8. Suppose now that the only labor available is controlled by a monopolistic labor union that wishes to maximize the rent earned by union members. What will be the quantity of labor employed and the wage rate? How does your answer compare with your answer to Exercise 8? Discuss. (*Hint*: The union's marginal revenue curve is given by L = 1200 - 20w.)

Recall that the monopolist chooses output by setting marginal revenue equal to the marginal cost of supplying one more unit of output, as opposed to the competitive firm which chooses output by setting price equal to marginal cost, or in other words producing where supply intersects demand. The monopolistic labor union acts in the same way. To maximize rent in this case, the union will choose the number of workers hired so that the marginal revenue to the union (the additional wages earned) is equal to the extra cost of inducing the worker to work. This involves choosing the quantity of labor at the point where the marginal revenue curve crosses the supply curve of labor. Note that the marginal revenue curve has twice the slope of the labor demand curve. Marginal revenue is less than the wage, because when more workers are hired, all workers receive a lower wage.

Setting the marginal revenue curve equal to the supply curve for labor, we find:

$$1200 - 20w = 20w, \text{ or } w^* = 30.$$

At w^*, we may determine the number of workers who are willing to work by substituting w^* into the labor supply equation:

$$L^* = (20)(30) = 600.$$

Therefore, if the union wants to maximize the rent that the union members earn, the union should limit employment to 600 members.

To determine the wage the members will earn, substitute L^* into the labor demand equation:

$$600 = 1,200 - 10w, \text{ or } w = 60.$$

The total rent the employed union members will receive is equal to:

$$\text{Rent} = (60 - 30)(600) + (0.5)(30)(600) = \$27,000.$$

Notice that the wage is higher and the number of workers employed is lower than in Exercise (8).

*10. A firm uses a single input, labor, to produce output q according to the production function $q = 8\sqrt{L}$. The commodity sells for \$150 per unit and the wage rate is \$75 per hour.

a.   Find the profit-maximizing quantity of L.

There are two (equivalent) methods of solving this problem. Most generally, define the profit function, where revenues and costs are expressed in terms of the input, calculate the first order necessary condition (the first derivative of the profit function), and solve for the optimal quantity of the input. Alternatively, use the rule that the firm will hire labor up until the point where the marginal revenue product (p*MP$_L$) equals the wage rate. Using the first method:

$$\pi = TR - TC = pq - wL$$

$$\pi = 150 * 8 * L^{\frac{1}{2}} - 75L$$

$$\frac{\partial \pi}{\partial L} = 600L^{-\frac{1}{2}} - 75 = 0$$

$$L = 64.$$

b.   **Find the profit-maximizing quantity of q.**

From part a, the profit maximizing quantity of labor is 64 so substitute this quantity of labor into the production function to find $q = 8L^{\frac{1}{2}} = 8 * \sqrt{64} = 64$.

c.   **What is the maximum profit?**

Profit is total revenue minus total cost or $\pi = 150 * 64 - 75 * 64 = 4800$.

d.   **Suppose now that the firm is taxed $30 per unit of output and the wage rate is subsidized at a rate of $15 per hour. Assume the firm is a price taker, so that the price of the product remains at $150. Find the new profit-maximizing levels of L, q, and profit.**

After the $30 tax per unit of output is paid, the firm receives 150-30=$120 per unit of output sold. This is the relevant price for the profit maximizing decision. The input cost is now 75-15=$60 per unit labor after the subsidy is received. The profit maximizing values can be found as in parts a-c above:

$$\pi = TR - TC = pq - wL$$

$$\pi = 120 * 8 * L^{\frac{1}{2}} - 60L$$

$$\frac{\partial \pi}{\partial L} = 480L^{-\frac{1}{2}} - 60 = 0$$

$$L = 64$$

$$q = 64$$

$$\pi = 3840.$$

e.   **Now suppose that the firm is required to pay a 20% tax on its profits. Find the new profit-maximizing levels of L, q, and profit.**

The profit maximizing values can be found as in parts a-c above, only here profit is 80% of total revenue minus total cost.

$$\pi = .8(TR - TC) = .8(pq - wL)$$

$$\pi = .8(150 * 8 * L^{\frac{1}{2}} - 75L)$$

$$\frac{\partial \pi}{\partial L} = 480L^{-\frac{1}{2}} - 60 = 0$$

$$L = 64$$

$$q = 64$$

$$\pi = 3840.$$

CHAPTER 15
INVESTMENT, TIME, AND CAPITAL MARKETS

TEACHING NOTES

The primary focus of this chapter is on how firms make capital investment decisions, though the chapter also includes some topical applications of the net present value criterion. The key sections to cover are 15.1, 15.2, and 15.4, which cover stocks and flows, present discounted value, and the net present value criterion respectively. You can then pick and choose between the remaining sections depending on your time constraint and interest in the subject. Each of the special topics is briefly described below.

Students will find *NPV* to be one of the most powerful tools of the course. You will notice that this chapter does not derive the rate of time preference; instead, it introduces students to financial decision-making. Students should have no problem comprehending the trade-off between consumption today and consumption tomorrow, but they may still have problems with $(1 + R)$ as the *price* of today's consumption. Emphasize the opportunity cost interpretation of this price. Human capital theory is a topic that bridges Chapters 14 and 15. Interesting issues for discussion include the relationship between wages and education and the return on education. If students understand present value, mastering the *NPV* criterion is easy. However, applying the *NPV* rule is more difficult.

Section 15.3 extends the discussion of present and future values by exploring the connection between the value of a bond and perpetuities. If students understand the effective yield on a bond, you can introduce the internal rate of return, *IRR*, and then discuss why the net present value, *NPV*, is superior to the *IRR* criterion. For a comparison of *IRR* and *NPV*, see Brealey and Myers, *Principles of Corporate Finance* (McGraw-Hill, 1988).

Section 15.5 discusses risk and the risk-free discount rate. You can motivate the discussion of risk by considering the probability of default by different classes of borrowers (this introduces the discussion of the credit market that will take place in Section 17.1). This section introduces students to the Capital Asset Pricing Model. To understand the *CAPM* model, students need to be familiar with Chapter 5, particularly Section 5.4, "The Demand for Risky Assets." The biggest stumbling block is the definition of β. If students have an intuitive feel for β, they may use Equation (15.7) to calculate a firm's discount rate.

Section 15.6, applies the *NPV* criterion to consumer decisions, leading to a wealth of applications. Example 15.4 presents Hausman's analysis of the decision to purchase an air conditioner. Discuss whether the results of this study are reasonable.

Section 15.7 discusses depletable resources and presents Hotelling's model of exhaustible resources. This example is a particularly good topic for class discussion when oil prices are rising. During other periods, you may need to motivate the analysis. For another example, see the problem of cutting timber in Chiang, *Fundamental Methods of Mathematical Economics* (McGraw-Hill, 1984) pp. 300-301. Note that these problems involve calculus but may be solved geometrically.

Section 15.8 examines the market for loanable funds. If you have introduced students to the marginal rate of time preference, you can complete the analysis by introducing the investment-spending frontier, similar to the production-possibilities frontier in Section 7.5 (see Figure 7.10). The investment frontier shows the rate at which consumption today may be transformed into consumption tomorrow. By superimposing indifference curves onto the frontier, you may show the individual's optimal consumption today and tomorrow. This analysis may be extended by discussing borrowing and lending and will serve as an introduction to the analysis of efficiency in Chapter 16.

REVIEW QUESTIONS

1. A firm uses cloth and labor to produce shirts in a factory that it bought for $10 million. Which of its factor inputs are measured as flows and which as stocks? How would your answer change if the firm had leased a factory instead of buying one? Is its output measured as a flow or a stock? What about profit?

> Inputs that are purchased or used up during a particular time period are flows. Flow variables can be measured in terms of hours, days, weeks, months, or years. Inputs measured at a particular point in time are stocks. All stock variables have an associated flow variable. At any particular time, a firm will have a stock of buildings and machines that it owns. This is the stock variable. During some given time period, the firm may elect to buy a new piece of equipment (this is a flow) or it may depreciate its existing capital resources (this is a flow). In this example, cloth and labor are flows, while the factory is a stock. If the firm instead leases the building, then the factory is still a stock variable that is owned in this case by someone other than the firm. The firm would pay rent during a particular time period, which would be a flow. Output is always a flow variable that is measured over some given time period. Since profit is the difference between the revenues and costs over some given time period, it is also a flow.

2. How do investors calculate the present value of a bond? If the interest rate is 5 percent, what is the present value of a perpetuity that pays $1,000 per year forever?

> The present value of a bond is the sum of discounted values of each payment to the bond holder over the life of the bond. This involves the payment of interest in each period and then the repayment of the principal at the end of the bond's life. A perpetuity involves paying the interest in every future period and no repayment of the principal. The present discounted value of a perpetuity is $PDV = \frac{A}{R}$, where A is the annual payment and R is the annual interest rate. If $A = \$1,000$ and $R = 0.05$,
> $$PDV = \frac{\$1,000}{0.05} = \$20,000 .$$

3. What is the *effective yield* on a bond? How does one calculate it? Why do some corporate bonds have higher effective yields than others?

> The effective yield is the interest rate that equates the present value of a bond's payment stream with the bond's market price. The present discounted value of a payment made in the future is
> $$PDV = FV(1 + R)^{-t},$$
> where t is the length of time before payment. The bond's selling price is its *PDV*. The payments it makes are the future values, *FV*, paid in time *t*. Thus, we must solve for *R*, which is the bond's effective yield. The effective yield is determined by the interaction of buyers and sellers in the bond market. Some corporate bonds have higher effective yields because they are thought to be a more risky investment, and hence buyers must be rewarded with a higher rate of return so that they will be willing to hold the bonds. Higher rates of return imply a lower present discounted value. If bonds have the same coupon payments, the bonds of the riskiest firms will sell for less than the bonds of the less risky firms.

4. What is the Net Present Value (NPV) criterion for investment decisions? How does one calculate the NPV of an investment project? If all cash flows for a project are certain, what discount rate should be used to calculate NPV?

> The Net Present Value criterion for investment decisions is *"invest if the present value of the expected future cash flows from the investment is larger than the cost of the investment"* (Section 15.4). We calculate the *NPV* by (1) determining the present discounted value of all future cash flows and (2) subtracting the discounted value of all

costs, present and future. To discount both income and cost, the firm should use a discount rate that reflects its opportunity cost of capital, the next highest return on an alternative investment of similar riskiness. Therefore, the risk-free interest rate should be used if the cash flows are certain.

5. You are retiring from your job and are given two options. You can accept a lump sum payment from the company, or you can accept a smaller annual payment that will continue for as long as you live. How would you decide which option is best? What information do you need?

The best option is the one that has in the highest present discounted value. The lump sum payment has a present discounted value equal to the amount of the lump sum payment. To calculate the present discounted value of the payment stream you need to know approximately how many years you might live. If you made a guess of 25 years you could then discount each of the 25 payments back to the current year and add them up to see how this sum compares to the lump sum payment. The discount factor would be the average expected interest rate. Alternatively, you could take the average expected interest rate and compute the annual interest that could be earned from the lump sum and see how this interest amount compares to the annual payment. For example, if the sum is $600,000 and the interest rate is 8% then the annual interest is $48,000. This means you could live off of the $48,000 and never touch the principal. The annual payment would need to be greater than $48,000 in this case to make it worthwhile. Finally, you must consider the time and risk involved in managing a lump sum and decide if it is better or easier to just take the smaller annual payment.

6. You have noticed that bond prices have been rising over the past few months. All else equal, what does this suggest has been happening to interest rates? Explain.

This suggests that interest rates have been falling because bond prices and interest rates are inversely related. When the price of a bond (with a fixed coupon payment) rises, then the effective yield on the bond will fall. The only way people will be willing to hold the bond is if interest rates in general are also falling. If interest rates are lower than the effective yield on the bond for example, then people will prefer to hold the bond. When more people move into bonds, the price of the bond will rise and the effective yield will fall. Bond prices therefore adjust to bring the effective yield in line with interest rates.

7. What is the difference between a real discount rate and a nominal discount rate? When should a real discount rate be used in an NPV calculation and when should a nominal rate be used?

The real discount rate is net of inflation, whereas the nominal discount rate includes inflationary expectations. The real discount rate is equal to the nominal discount rate minus the rate of inflation. If cash flows are in real terms, the appropriate discount rate is the real rate. For example, in applying the *NPV* criterion to a manufacturing decision, if future prices of inputs and outputs are not adjusted for inflation (which they often are not), a nominal discount rate should be used to determine whether the *NPV* is positive. In sum, all numbers should either be expressed in real terms or nominal terms, but not a mix.

8. How is a risk premium used to account for risk in NPV calculations? What is the difference between diversifiable and nondiversifiable risk? Why should only nondiversifiable risk enter into the risk premium?

To determine the present discounted value of a cash flow, the discount rate should reflect the riskiness of the project generating the cash flow. The risk premium is the difference between a discount rate that reflects the riskiness of the cash flow and a discount rate on a risk-free flow, e.g., the discount rate associated with a short-term government bond. The higher the riskiness of a project, the higher the risk premium.

Diversifiable risk can be eliminated by investing in many projects. Hence, an efficient capital market will not compensate an investor for taking on risk that can be eliminated costlessly. Nondiversifiable risk is that part of a project's risk that cannot be eliminated by investing in a large number of other projects. It is that part of a project's risk which is correlated with the portfolio of all projects available in the market. Since investors can eliminate diversifiable risk, they cannot expect to earn a risk premium on diversifiable risk.

9. What is meant by the "market return" in the Capital Asset Pricing Model (CAPM)? Why is the market return greater than the risk-free interest rate? What does an asset's "beta" measure in the CAPM? Why should high-beta assets have a higher expected return than low-beta assets?

In the Capital Asset Pricing Model (CAPM), the market return is the rate of return on the portfolio of assets held by the market. The market return reflects nondiversifiable risk.

Since the market portfolio has no diversifiable risk, the market return reflects the risk premium associated with holding one unit of nondiversifiable risk. The market rate of return is greater than the risk-free rate of return, because risk-averse investors must be compensated with higher average returns for holding a risky asset.

An asset's beta reflects the sensitivity (covariance) of the asset's return with the return on the market portfolio. An asset with a high beta will have a greater expected return than a low-beta asset, since the high-beta asset has greater nondiversifiable risk than the low-beta asset.

10. Suppose you are deciding whether to invest $100 million in a steel mill. You know the expected cash flows for the project, but they are risky – steel prices could rise or fall in the future. How would the CAPM help you select a discount rate for an NPV calculation?

To evaluate the net present value of a $100 million investment in a steel mill, you should use the stock market's current evaluation of firms that own steel mills as a guide to selecting the appropriate discount rate. For example, you would (1) identify nondiversified steel firms, those that are primarily involved in steel production, (2) determine the beta associated with stocks issued by those companies (this can be done statistically or by relying on a financial service that publishes stock betas, such as *Value Line*), and (3) take a weighted average of these betas, where the weights are equal to the firm's assets divided by the sum of all diversified steel firms' assets. With an estimate of beta, plus estimates of the expected market and risk-free rates of return, you could infer the discount rate using Equation (15.7) in the text: Discount rate = $r_f + \beta \left(r_m + r_f \right)$.

11. How does a consumer trade off current and future costs when selecting an air conditioner or other major appliance? How could this selection be aided by an NPV calculation?

The *NPV* calculation for a durable good involves discounting to the present all future services from the appliance, as well as any salvage value at the end of the appliance's life, and subtracting its cost and the discounted value of any expenses. Discounting is done at the opportunity cost of money. Of course, this calculation assumes well-defined quantities of future services. If these services are not well defined, the consumer should ask what value of these services would yield an *NPV* of zero. If this value is less than the price that the consumer would be willing to pay in each period, the investment should be made.

12. What is meant by the "user cost" of producing an exhaustible resource? Why does price minus extraction cost rise at the rate of interest in a competitive exhaustible resource market?

In addition to the opportunity cost of extracting the resource and preparing it for sale, there is an additional opportunity cost arising from the depletion of the resource. User cost is the difference between price and the marginal cost of production. User cost rises over time because as reserves of the resource become depleted, the remaining reserves become more valuable.

Given constant demand over time, the price of the resource minus its marginal cost of extraction, P - MC, should rise over time at the rate of interest. If P - MC rises faster than the rate of interest, no extraction should occur in the present period, because holding the resource for another year would earn a higher rate of return than selling the resource now and investing the proceeds for another year. If P - MC rises slower than the rate of interest, current extraction should increase, thus increasing the supply at each price, lowering the equilibrium price, and decreasing the return on producing the resource. In equilibrium, the price of a resource rises at the rate of interest.

13. What determines the supply of loanable funds? The demand for loanable funds? What might cause the supply or demand for loanable funds to shift? How would such a shift affect interest rates?

The supply of loanable funds is determined by the interest rate offered to savers. A higher interest rate induces households to consume less today (save) in favor of greater consumption in the future. The demand for loanable funds comes from consumers who wish to consume more today than tomorrow or from investors who wish to borrow money. Demand depends on the interest rate at which these two groups can borrow. Several factors can shift the demand and supply of loanable funds. On the one hand, for example, a recession decreases demand at all interest rates, shifting the demand curve inward and causing the equilibrium interest rate to fall. On the other hand, the supply of loanable funds will shift out if the Federal Reserve increases the money supply, again causing the interest rate to fall.

EXERCISES

1. Suppose the interest rate is 10 percent. If $100 is invested at this rate today, how much will it be worth after one year? After two years? After five years? What is the value today of $100 paid one year from now? Paid two years from now? Paid five years from now?

We would like to know the future value, FV, of $100 invested today at an interest rate of 10 percent. One year from now our investment will be equal to

$$FV = \$100 + (\$100)(10\%) = \$110.$$

Two years from now we will earn interest on the $100 ($10) *and* we will earn interest on the interest from the first year, i.e., ($10)(10%) = $1. Thus, our investment will be worth $100 + $10 (from the first year) + $10 (from the second year) + $1 (interest on the first year's interest) = $121.

Algebraically, $FV = PDV(1 + R)^t$, where PDV is the present discounted value of the investment, R is the interest rate, and t is the number of years. After two years,

$$FV = PDV(1 + R)^t = (\$100)(1.1)^2 = (\$100)(1.21) = \$121.00.$$

After five years

$$FV = PDV(1 + R)^t = (\$100)(1.1)^5 = (\$100)(1.61051) = \$161.05.$$

To find the present discounted value of $100 paid one year from now, we ask how much is needed to invest today at 10 percent to have $100 one year from now. Using our formula, we solve for PDV as a function of FV:

$$PDV = (FV)(1 + R)^{-t}.$$

With $t = 1$, $R = 0.10$, and $FV = \$100$,

$$PDV = (100)(1.1)^{-1} = \$90.91.$$

With $t = 2$, $PDV = (1.1)^{-2} = \$82.64$,

With $t = 5$, $PDV = (1.1)^{-5} = \$62.09$.

2. You are offered the choice of two payment streams: (a) \$150 paid one year from now and \$150 paid two years from now; (b) \$130 paid one year from now and \$160 paid two years from now. Which payment stream would you prefer if the interest rate is 5 percent? If it is 15 percent?

To compare two income streams, we calculate the present discounted value of each and choose the stream with the highest present discounted value. We use the formula $PDV = FV(1 + R)^{-t}$ for each cash flow. See Exercise (2) above. Stream (a) has two payments:

$$PDV_a = FV_1(1 + R)^{-1} + FV_2(1 + R)^{-2}$$

$$PDV_a = (\$150)(1.05)^{-1} + (\$150)(1.05)^{-2}, \text{ or}$$

$$PDV_a = \$142.86 + 136.05 = \$278.91.$$

Stream (b) has two payments:

$$PDV_b = (\$130)(1.05)^{-1} + (\$160)(1.05)^{-2}, \text{ or}$$

$$PDV_b = \$123.81 + \$145.12 = \$268.93.$$

At an interest rate of 5 percent, you should select (b).

If the interest rate is 15 percent, the present discounted values of the two income streams would be:

$$PDV_a = (\$150)(1.15)^{-1} + (\$150)(1.15)^{-2}, \text{ or}$$

$$PDV_a = \$130.43 + \$113.42 = \$243.85, \text{ and}$$

$$PDV_b = (\$130)(1.15)^{-1} + (\$160)(1.15)^{-2}, \text{ or}$$

$$PDV_b = \$113.04 + \$120.98 = \$234.02.$$

You should still select (b).

3. Suppose the interest rate is 10 percent. What is the value of a coupon bond that pays \$80 per year for each of the next five years and then makes a principal repayment of \$1,000 in the sixth year? Repeat for an interest rate of 15 percent.

We need to determine the present discounted value, PDV, of a stream of payments over the next six years. We translate future values, FV, into the present with the following formula:

$$PDV = \frac{FV}{(1 + R)^t},$$

where R is the interest rate, equal to 10 percent, and t is the number of years in the future. For example, the present value of the first \$80 payment one year from now is

$$PDV = \frac{FV}{(1 + R)^t} = \frac{80}{(1 + 0.10)^1} = \frac{80}{1.1} = \$72.73.$$

The value of all coupon payments over five years can be found the same way:

$$PDV = \frac{80}{(1+R)^1} + \frac{80}{(1+R)^2} + \frac{80}{(1+R)^3} + \frac{80}{(1+R)^4} + \frac{80}{(1+R)^5}, \text{ or}$$

$$PDV = 80\left(\frac{1}{1.1} + \frac{1}{1.21} + \frac{1}{1.331} + \frac{1}{1.4641} + \frac{1}{1.61051}\right) = \$303.26.$$

Finally, we calculate the present value of the final payment of $1,000 in the sixth year:

$$PDV = \frac{\$1,000}{1.1^6} = \frac{\$1,000}{1.771} = \$564.47.$$

Thus, the present value of the bond is $303.26 + $564.47 = $867.73.

With an interest rate of 15 percent, we calculate the value of the bond in the same way:

$$PDV = 80(0.870 + 0.756 + 0.658 + 0.572 + 0.497) + (1,000)(0.432), \text{ or}$$

$$PDV = \$268.17 + \$432.32 = \$700.49.$$

As the interest rate increases, while payments are held constant, the value of the bond decreases.

4. A bond has two years to mature. It makes a coupon payment of $100 after one year and both a coupon payment of $100 and a principal repayment of $1,000 after two years. The bond is selling for $966. What is its effective yield?

We want to know the interest rate that will yield a present value of $966 for an income stream of $100 after one year and $1,100 after two years. Find i such that

$$966 = (100)(1+i)^{-1} + (1,100)(1+i)^{-2}.$$

Algebraic manipulation yields

$$966(1+i)^2 = 100(1+i) + 1,100, \text{ or}$$

$$966 + 1,932i + 966i^2 - 100 - 100i - 1,100 = 0, \text{ or}$$

$$966i^2 + 1,832i - 234 = 0.$$

Using the quadratic formula to solve for i,

$$i = 0.12 \text{ or } -1.068.$$

Since -1.068 does not make economic sense, the effective yield is 12 percent.

5. Equation (15.5) shows the net present value of an investment in an electric motor factory. Half of the $10 million cost is paid initially and the other half after a year. The factory is expected to lose money during its first two years of operation. If the discount rate is 4 percent, what is the NPV? Is the investment worthwhile?

Redefining terms, Equation 15.5 becomes

$$NPV = -5 - \frac{5}{(1.04)} - \frac{1}{(1.04)^2} - \frac{0.5}{(1.04)^3} + \frac{0.96}{(1.04)^4} + \frac{0.96}{(1.04)^5} + \cdots + \frac{0.96}{(1.04)^{20}} + \frac{1}{(1.04)^{20}}.$$

Calculating the *NPV* we find:

$$NPV = -5 - -4.81 - 0.92 - 0.44 + 0.82 + 0.79 + 0.70 + 0.67 + 0.62 + 0.60 + 0.58 + 0.55$$

$$+0.53 + 0.51 + 0.49 + 0.47 + 0.46 + 0.44 + 0.46 = -0.337734.$$

The investment loses $337,734 and is not worthwhile.

6. The market interest rate is 5 percent and is expected to stay at that level. Consumers can borrow and lend all they want at this rate. Explain your choice in each of the following situations:

a. **Would you prefer a $500 gift today or a $540 gift next year?**

The present value of $500 today is $500. The present value of $540 next year is

$$\frac{\$540.00}{1.05} = \$514.29.$$

Therefore, I would prefer the $540 next year.

b. **Would you prefer a $100 gift now or a $500 loan without interest for four years?**

If you take the $500 loan, you can invest it for the four years and then pay back the $500. The future value of the $500 is

$$500 * (1.05)^4 = \$607.75.$$

After you pay back the $500 you will have $107.75 left to keep. The future value of the $100 gift is

$$100(1.05)^4 = \$121.55.$$

You should take the $100 gift.

c. **Would you prefer a $350 rebate on an $8,000 car or one year of financing for the full price of the car at 0 percent interest?**

The interest rate is 0 percent, which is 5 percent less than the current market rate. You save $400 = (0.05)($8,000) one year from now. The present value of this $400 is

$$\frac{\$400}{1.05} = \$380.95.$$

This is greater than $350. Therefore, choose the financing.

d. **You have just won a million dollar lottery and will receive $50,000 a year for the next 20 years. How much is this worth to you today?**

We must find the net present value of $50,000 a year for the next 20 years:

$$NPV = 50,000 + \frac{50,000}{(1.05)^1} + \frac{50,000}{(1.05)^2} + \cdots + \frac{50,000}{(1.05)^{18}} + \frac{50,000}{(1.05)^{19}} = \$.624,613.54$$

e. **You win the "honest million" jackpot. You can have $1 million today or $60,000 per year for eternity (a right that can be passed on to your heirs). Which do you prefer?**

The value of the perpetuity is $1,200,000, which makes it advisable take the $60,000 per year payment.

f. **In the past, adult children had to pay taxes on gifts over $10,000 from their parents, but parents could loan money to their children interest-free. Why did some people call this unfair? To whom were the rules unfair?**

Any gift of $N from parent to child could be made without taxation by loaning the child $\frac{\$N(1+r)}{r}$. For example, to avoid taxes on a $50,000 gift, the parent would loan the child $550,000, assuming a 10 percent interest rate. With that money, the child could earn $55,000 in interest after one year and still have $500,000 to pay back to the parent. The present value of $55,000 one year from now is $50,000. People of more moderate incomes would find these rules unfair: they might only be able to afford to give the child $50,000 directly, but it would not be tax free.

7. **Ralph is trying to decide whether to go to graduate school. If he spends two years in graduate school, paying $15,000 tuition each year, he will get a job that will pay $60,000 per year for the rest of his working life. If he does not go to school, he will go into the work force immediately. He will then make $30,000 per year for the next three years, $45,000 for the following three years, and $60,000 per year every year after that. If the interest rate is 10 percent, is graduate school a good financial investment?**

Consider Ralph's income over the next six years, assuming all payments occur at the end of the year. (After the sixth year, Ralph's income will be the same with or without education.) With graduate school, the present value of income for the next six years is $113,631,

$$-\frac{\$15,000}{(1.1)^1} - \frac{\$15,000}{(1.1)^2} + \frac{\$60,000}{(1.1)^3} + \frac{\$60,000}{(1.1)^4} + \frac{\$60,000}{(1.1)^5} + \frac{\$60,000}{(1.1)^6} = \$131,150.35.$$

Without graduate school, the present value of income for the next six years is

$$\frac{\$30,000}{(1.1)^1} + \frac{\$30,000}{(1.1)^2} + \frac{\$30,000}{(1.1)^3} + \frac{\$45,000}{(1.1)^4} + \frac{\$45,000}{(1.1)^5} + \frac{\$45,000}{(1.1)^6} = \$158,683.95.$$

The payoff from graduate school is not large enough to justify the foregone income and tuition expense while Ralph is in school; he should therefore not go to school.

8. **Suppose your uncle gave you an oil well like the one described in Section 15.8. (Marginal production cost is constant at $10.) The price of oil is currently $20 but is controlled by a cartel that accounts for a large fraction of total production. Should you produce and sell all your oil now or wait to produce? Explain your answer.**

If a cartel accounts for a large fraction of total production, today's price minus marginal cost, $P^t - MC$ will rise at a rate less than the rate of interest. This is because the cartel will choose output such that *marginal revenue* minus MC rises at the rate of interest. Since price exceeds marginal revenue, $P^t - MC$ will rise at a rate less than the rate of interest. So, to maximize net present value, all oil should be sold today. The profits should be invested at the rate of interest.

*9. **You are planning to invest in fine wine. Each case of wine costs $100, and you know from experience that the value of a case of wine held for t years is $(100)t^{1/2}$. One hundred cases of wine are available for sale, and the interest rate is 10 percent.**

a. **How many cases should you buy, how long should you wait to sell them, and how much money will you receive at the time of their sale?**

Buying a case is a good investment if the net present value is positive. If we buy a case and sell it after t years, we pay $100 now and receive $100t^{0.5}$ when it is sold. The *NPV* of this investment is

$$NPV = -100 + e^{-rt}\left(100t^{0.5}\right) = -100 + e^{-0.1t}\left(100t^{0.5}\right)$$

If we do buy a case, we will choose t to maximize the *NPV*. This implies differentiating with respect to t to obtain the necessary condition that

$$\frac{dNPV}{dt} = \left(e^{-0.1t}\right)\left(50t^{-0.5}\right) - \left(0.1e^{-0.1t}\right)\left(100t^{0.5}\right) = 0.$$

By multiplying both sides of the first order condition by $e^{0.1t}$, we obtain

$$50t^{-0.5} - 10t^{0.5} = 0, \text{ or } t = 5.$$

If we held the case for 5 years, the *NPV* is

$$-100 + e^{(-0.1)(5)}(100)(5^{0.5}) = 35.67.$$

Therefore, we should buy a case and hold it for five years, where the value at the time of sale is ($100)($5^{0.5}$). Since each case is a good investment, we should buy all 100 cases.

Another way to get the same answer is to compare holding the wine to putting your $100 in the bank. The bank pays interest of 10 percent, while the wine increases in value at the rate of

$$\frac{\frac{d(value)}{dt}}{value} = \frac{50t^{-0.5}}{100t^{0.5}} = \frac{1}{2t}.$$

As long as $t < 5$, the return on wine is greater than or equal to 10 percent. After $t = 5$, the return on wine drops below 10 percent. Therefore, $t = 5$ is the time to switch your wealth from wine to the bank. As for the issue of whether to buy wine at all, if we put $100 in the bank, we will have $100e^{0.5}$ after five years, whereas if we spend $100 on wine, we will have $100t^{-0.5} = (100)(5^{0.5})$, which is greater than $100e^{0.5}$ in five years.

b. **Suppose that at the time of purchase, someone offers you $130 per case immediately. Should you take the offer?**

You just bought the wine and are offered $130 for resale. You should accept the offer if the *NPV* is positive. You get $130 now, but lose the ($100)($5^{0.5}$) you would get for selling in five years. Thus, the *NPV* of the offer is

$$NPV = 130 - (e^{(-0.1)(5)})(100)(5^{0.5}) = -238 < 0.$$

Therefore, you should not sell.

The other approach to solving this problem is to note that the $130 could be put in the bank and would grow to

$$\$214.33 = (\$130)(e^{0.5}),$$

in five years. This is still less than

$$\$223.61 = (\$100)(5^{0.5}),$$

the value of the wine after five years.

c. **How would your answers change if the interest rate were only 5 percent?**

If the interest rate changes from 10 percent to 5 percent, the *NPV* calculation is

$$NPV = -100 + (e^{-0.05t})(100)(t^{0.5}).$$

As before, we maximize this expression:

$$\frac{dNPV}{dt} = \left(e^{-0.05t}\right)\left(50t^{-0.5}\right) - (0.05)\left(e^{-0.05t}\right)\left(100t^{0.5}\right) = 0.$$

By multiplying both sides of the first order condition by $e^{0.05t}$, it becomes

$$50t^{-0.5} - 5t^{0.5} = 0,$$

or $t = 10$. If we hold the case 10 years, *NPV* is

$$-100 + \left(e^{(-0.05)(10)}\right)\left(100\right)\left(10^{0.5}\right) = \$91.80.$$

With a lower interest rate, it pays to hold onto the wine longer before selling it, because the value of the wine is increasing at the same rate as before. Again, you should buy all the cases.

10. Reexamine the capital investment decision in the disposable diaper industry (Example 15.3) from the point of view of an incumbent firm. If P&G or Kimberly-Clark were to expand capacity by building three new plants, they would not need to spend $60 million on R&D before start-up. How does this advantage affect the NPV calculations in Table 15.5? Is the investment profitable at a discount rate of 12 percent?

If the only change in the cash flow for an incumbent firm is the absence of a $60 million expenditure in the present value, then the *NPV* calculations in Table 15.5 simply increase by $60 million for each discount rate:

Discount Rate:	0.05	0.10	0.15
NPV:	140.50	43.50	-15.10

To determine whether the investment is profitable at a discount rate of 12 percent, we must recalculate the expression for *NPV*. At 12 percent,

$$NPV = -60 - \frac{93.4}{(1.12)} - \frac{56.6}{(1.12)^2} + \frac{40}{(1.12)^3} + \frac{40}{(1.12)^4} + \frac{40}{(1.12)^5} + \frac{40}{(1.12)^6} + \frac{40}{(1.12)^7} +$$

$$\frac{40}{(1.12)^8} + \frac{40}{(1.12)^9} + \frac{40}{(1.12)^{10}} + \frac{40}{(1.12)^{11}} + \frac{40}{(1.12)^{12}} + \frac{40}{(1.12)^{13}} + \frac{40}{(1.12)^{14}} + \frac{40}{(1.12)^{15}} =$$

$16.3 million.

Thus, the incumbent would find it profitable to expand capacity.

11. Suppose you can buy a new Toyota Corolla for $20,000 and sell it for $12,000 after six years. Alternatively, you can lease the car for $300 per month for three years and return it at the end of the three years. For simplification, assume that lease payments are made yearly instead of monthly, i.e., are $3,600 per year for each of three years.

a. **If the interest rate, r, is 4 percent, is it better to lease or buy the car?**

To answer this question, you need to compute the NPV of each option. The NPV of buying the car is:

$$-20,000 + \frac{12,000}{1.04^6} = -10,516.22.$$

The NPV of leasing the car is:

$$-3,600 - \frac{3,600}{1.04} - \frac{3,600}{1.04^2} = -10,389.94.$$

In this case, you are better off leasing the car because the NPV is higher.

b. **Which is better if the interest rate is 12%?**

To answer this question, you need to compute the NPV of each option. The NPV of buying the car is:

$$-20,000 + \frac{12,000}{1.12^6} = -13,920.43.$$

The NPV of leasing the car is:

$$-3,600 - \frac{3,600}{1.12} - \frac{3,600}{1.12^2} = -9,684.18.$$

In this case, you are better off leasing the car because the NPV is higher.

c.   **At what interest rate would you be indifferent between buying and leasing the car?**

You are indifferent between buying and leasing if the two NPV's are equal or:

$$-20,000 + \frac{12,000}{(1+r)^6} = -3,600 - \frac{3,600}{(1+r)} - \frac{3,600}{(1+r)^2} \, .$$

In this case, you need to solve for **r**. The easiest way to do this is to use a spreadsheet and calculate the two NPV's for different values of **r**. Observe first that the interest rate will be something less than 4% given that at 4% the best option was to lease, and as the interest rate rose to 12% leasing became even a better option. The interest rate will be in the neighborhood of 3.8%.

r	NPV Buy	NPV Lease
0.03	-9,950.19	-10,488.49
0.035	-10,237.99	-10,438.90
0.037	-10,350.41	-10,419.24
0.038	-10,406.06	-10,409.44
0.04	-10,516.22	-10,389.94

12. **A consumer faces the following decision: she can buy a computer for $1,000 and pay $10 per month for Internet access for three years, or she can receive a $400 rebate on the computer (so that it costs $600) but agree to pay $25 per month for three years for Internet access. For simplification, assume that the consumer pays the access fees yearly (i.e.,$10 per month = $120 per year).**

a.   **What should the consumer do if the interest rate is 3 percent?**

To figure out the best option, you need to calculate the NPV in each case. The NPV of the first option is:

$$-1,000 - 120 - \frac{120}{1.03} - \frac{120}{1.03^2} = -1,349.62.$$

The NPV of the second option with the rebate is:

$$-600 - 300 - \frac{300}{1.03} - \frac{300}{1.03^2} = -1,474.04.$$

In this case, the first option gives a higher NPV so the consumer should pay the $1000 now and pay $10 per month for Internet access.

b.   **What if the interest rate is 17 percent?**

To figure out the best option, you need to calculate the NPV in each case. The NPV of the first option is:

$$-1,000 - 120 - \frac{120}{1.17} - \frac{120}{1.17^2} = -1,310.23.$$

The NPV of the second option with the rebate is:

$$-600 - 300 - \frac{300}{1.17} - \frac{300}{1.17^2} = -1,375.56.$$

In this case, the first option gives a higher NPV so the consumer should pay the $1000 now and pay $10 per month for Internet access.

c. **At what interest rate is the consumer indifferent between the two options?**

The consumer is indifferent between the two options if the NPV of each option is the same. To find this interest rate set the NPV's equal and solve for r.

$$-1{,}000 - 120 - \frac{120}{1+r} - \frac{120}{(1+r)^2} = -600 - 300 - \frac{300}{1+r} - \frac{300}{(1+r)^2}$$

$$220 = \frac{180}{1+r} + \frac{180}{(1+r)^2}$$

$$220(1+r)^2 = 180(1+r) + 180$$

$$220r^2 + 260r - 140 = 0.$$

Using the quadratic formula to solve for the interest rate r results in r=40.2% (approximately).

PART IV

INFORMATION, MARKET FAILURE, AND THE ROLE OF GOVERNMENT

CHAPTER 16
GENERAL EQUILIBRIUM AND ECONOMIC EFFICIENCY

TEACHING NOTES

This chapter extends the analysis of many of the earlier chapters in the text. Section 16.1 covers general equilibrium analysis and extends supply/demand analysis to situations where more than one market is involved and there is feedback between the markets. Sections 16.2 and 16.4 use the Edgeworth box to explore efficiency in consumption and production, and in this respect extend the analysis of chapters 4 and 7. Section 16.3 looks at the relationship between equity and efficiency and can be skipped if time is short. Sections 16.5 discusses gains from trade and can also be skipped if time is short. Section 16.6 is a nice summary of Sections 16.2 and 16.4 and the efficiency of competitive markets. Section 16.7 introduces types of market failure.

The distinction between partial and general equilibrium is readily accepted by students, but they might find the graphical analysis of Figure 16.1 intimidating. Although this is not a complete discussion of general equilibrium, students can learn to appreciate the limitations of a partial equilibrium analysis and the need to consider interactions among markets. Stress the importance of using a general equilibrium analysis for economy-wide policies, e.g., raising the minimum wage.

To provide a context for the discussion of exchange economies, you might start by discussing two children trading cookies and potato chips at lunchtime. For a more serious example, see Radford, "The Economic Organization of a POW Camp," *Economica* (November 1945). Students find the definition of Pareto optimality (an allocation is Pareto-efficient if goods cannot be reallocated to make someone better off without making someone else worse off) confusing because of its "double negative" expression (i.e., "cannot" and "without" in the same sentence). Try to express the same idea in other ways, e.g., "An allocation is not Pareto-efficient if goods can be traded so that one person is better off and everyone else is just as well off." Pareto efficiency will be particularly important if you are going to cover externalities. Explain why movements toward the contract curve are Pareto-improving, while movements along the contract curve are not Pareto-improving. Point out that all competitive equilibria are Pareto-efficient but not all Pareto-efficient points are in equilibrium. Emphasize that the competitive equilibrium depends on the initial allocation, which will elucidate the distinction between equity and final allocation in a distribution.

You can use the Edgeworth box to show the distinction between efficiency and equity; e.g., a point on the contract curve near one corner might be less preferred because of equity considerations than a point off the curve but nearer to the middle of the box. This conflict introduces the problem of defining equity and incorporating it into an economic analysis. Table 16.2 presents four definitions of equity. After discussing them, ask the class to vote on which definition is closest to their concept of equity. Then ask the students to defend their choices, which should lead to an interesting discussion.

The analysis in Section 16.4 follows from Section 16.2 by introducing students to production in an Edgeworth box. This analysis leads to the definition of input efficiency and the production contract curve. Apply the definition of Pareto optimality to production. Before discussing the geometry of Figure 16.11, make sure that students know the requirements for output efficiency. Unless you have introduced the investment-possibilities frontier and the accompanying analysis in Chapter 15, the geometry will be new. An alternative approach to Figure 16.10 is to draw the Edgeworth box for exchange inside the *PPF* with one of the vertices at point *C*. Show where the marginal rates of substitution are equal for both individuals and also equal to the marginal rate of transformation. Section 16.5 introduces comparative advantage and applies general equilibrium analysis to the gains from international (two-country) trade. Section 16.7 serves as a bridge between Chapter 16 and the following two chapters.

255

QUESTIONS FOR REVIEW

1. Why can feedback effects make a general equilibrium analysis substantially different from a partial equilibrium analysis?

A partial equilibrium analysis focuses on the interaction of supply and demand for *one* market. It ignores the influences that shifts in supply and demand in one market might have on the markets for complements and substitutes. A general equilibrium analysis takes feedback effects into account, where a price or quantity adjustment in one market can cause a price or quantity adjustment in related markets. Ignoring these feedback effects can lead to inaccurate forecasts of the full effect of changes in either supply or demand. An initial shift in demand in one market, for example, can cause a shift in demand in a related market, which can then cause a second shift in demand in the first market. A partial equilibrium analysis will stop at the first initial shift whereas a general equilibrium analysis will continue on and look at possible shifts in demand in related markets. Although analysis should incorporate *all* feedback effects, one task of the economist is to determine the markets that are most closely related to the market of primary concern. Attention is directed toward these markets, thus enabling better forecasts of changes in equilibrium prices and quantities.

2. In the Edgeworth box diagram, explain how one point can simultaneously represent the market baskets owned by two consumers.

The Edgeworth box diagram allows us to represent the distribution of two goods between two individuals. The box is formed by inverting the indifference curves of one individual and superimposing these on the indifference curves of another individual. The sides of the box represent the total amounts of the two goods available to consumers. On the vertical axis, we read off the amount to each individual as the difference between the horizontal axis and the point. For one individual, this is the distance from the bottom of the box to the top, and for the other, this is the distance from the top of the box to the bottom. Similarly, the horizontal axis represents amounts of a second good distributed to the two individuals. Each point in the box represents a different allocation of the two goods between the two individuals.

3. In the analysis of exchange using the Edgeworth box diagram, explain why both consumers' marginal rates of substitution are equal at every point on the contract curve.

The contract curve, in the context of an Edgeworth box diagram, is the set of points where the indifference curves of the two individuals are tangent. We know that the marginal rate of substitution is equal to the (negative) slope of the indifference curves. Also, when two curves are tangent at a point, their slopes are equal at that point. Thus, by defining the contract curve as a set of indifference curve tangencies, the marginal rates of substitution between the two goods are equal for the two individuals given we assume convex indifference curves.

4. "Since all points on a contract curve are efficient, they are all equally desirable from a social point of view." Do you agree with this statement? Explain.

If society is only concerned with efficiency and not with equity, then all points on the contract curve are equally desirable. Since it is impossible to make comparisons of utility between individuals, economics focuses on efficiency. But, if we are also concerned with equity (i.e., whether the final allocation is fair), then all points on the contract curve are not equally desirable.

5. How does the utility possibilities frontier relate to the contract curve?

Since each point in an Edgeworth box can be compared to every other point by each individual, individuals can assign a preference ordering to all points. This preference ordering is the utility function. We can graph these preferences with levels of satisfaction (utility) for one individual on one axis and levels of satisfaction for a second individual on the other axis. (Of course, more than two individuals can be represented with more axes.) The utility-possibility frontier shows the levels of satisfaction achieved by each of two individuals when they have traded to an efficient outcome on the contract curve. While points that lie between the origin and the utility-possibility frontier are feasible they are not efficient because further trading will leave one individual better off without making the other individual worse off. Points outside the frontier are not feasible unless the individuals are given greater amounts of one or both goods.

6. In the Edgeworth production box diagram, what conditions must hold for an allocation to be on the production-contract curve? Why is a competitive equilibrium on the contract curve?

When constructing an Edgeworth box for the production of two goods with two inputs, each point in the box represents an allocation of the two inputs between the two production processes. With production, each point can be ordered according to the total output. These points lie on isoquants instead of on indifference curves. Since each point simultaneously represents the allocation of inputs to two production processes, it lies on two isoquants, one for each production process. The production contract curve represents all combinations of inputs that are technically efficient. Thus, there would be no way to increase the output of one good without decreasing the output of the other good.

A competitive equilibrium is one point on the production-contract curve. It is the intersection of the production-contract curve and a line passing through the initial allocation with a slope equal to the ratio of prices. (The ratio of prices dictates the rates at which inputs can be traded in the market.) For a competitive equilibrium to hold, each producer must use inputs so that the slopes of the isoquants are equal to one another and also equal to the ratio of the prices of the two inputs. Therefore, the competitive equilibrium is efficient in production. (This equilibrium assumes convex indifference curves.)

7. How is the production-possibilities frontier related to the production contract curve?

We can graph the quantities of each good produced (each point in the Edgeworth box) on a two-dimensional graph, where the vertical axis represents the output of one good and the horizontal axis represents the output of the other good. The production-contract curve is represented in this two-dimensional graph as the production possibilities frontier. Points inside this frontier are feasible but inefficient. Points outside the frontier are infeasible and only attainable when more inputs become available or production processes become more efficient. Points on the production-possibilities frontier are the same as those on the production-contract curve. The difference is that the production-contract curve measures inputs on the axes and the production-possibilities frontier measures outputs on the axes.

8. What is the marginal rate of transformation (MRT)? Explain why the MRT of one good for another is equal to the ratio of the marginal costs of producing the two goods.

The marginal rate of transformation, *MRT*, is equal to the absolute value of the slope of the production possibilities frontier, and measures how much of one output must be given up to produce one more unit of the other output. The total cost of all inputs is the same at each point on the production possibilities frontier because we use the same total amount of all inputs, and merely allocate them differently along the frontier. Therefore, when we move down along the frontier, the cost of producing one output is reduced by the same amount that the cost of producing the other output is increased. Suppose the *MRT* is 4 in absolute value terms, then we must give up 4 units of the output on the vertical axis to get one more unit of output on the horizontal axis. This means that the total cost of producing the 4 units is the same as the total cost of producing the one unit, or that the marginal cost of the good on the horizontal axis is 4 times the marginal cost of the good on the vertical axis.

9. Explain why goods will not be distributed efficiently among consumers if the MRT is not equal to the consumers' marginal rate of substitution.

If the marginal rate of transformation, *MRT*, is not equal to the marginal rate of substitution, *MRS*, we could reallocate inputs in producing output to leave the consumers and producers better off. If the *MRS* is greater than the *MRT* then consumers are willing to pay more for another unit of a good than it will cost the producers to produce another unit of the good. Both can therefore be made better off by arranging a trade somewhere between what consumers are willing to pay and what the producers have to pay to produce the extra unit. Note also that when *MRT* ≠ *MRS*, the ratio of marginal cost will not be equal to the ratio of prices. This means that one good is being sold at a price below marginal cost and one good is being sold at a price above marginal cost. We should increase the output of the one good whose price is above marginal cost and reduce the output of the other good whose price is below marginal cost.

10. Why can free trade between two countries make consumers of both countries better off?

Free trade between two countries expands each country's effective production possibilities frontier, and allows each country to consume at a point above its original production possibilities frontier. Assuming each country has a comparative advantage in the production of some good or service, trade allows a country to specialize in the area where it has this advantage. It trades these outputs for those more cheaply produced in another country. Therefore, specialization benefits many consumers in both countries.

11. If Country A has an absolute advantage in the production of both goods compared to Country B, then it is not in Country A's best interest to trade with country B. True or false? Explain.

This statement is false. A country can have an absolute advantage in the production of all goods but they will still only have a comparative advantage in the production of some goods. Suppose Country A requires 4 units of labor to produce good 1 and 8 units of labor to produce good 2, whereas Country B requires 8 units and 12 units respectively. Country A can produce both goods more cheaply so has an absolute advantage in the production of both goods. However, trade is based on comparative advantage, which looks at how much of one good you must give up for one more unit of the other good. Here, Country A must give up 2 units of good 1 for another good 2 whereas Country B must give up only 1.5 units of good 1 for another unit of good 2. Country B therefore has a comparative advantage in producing good 2. Likewise, Country A will have a comparative advantage in producing good 1.

12. Do you agree or disagree with each of the following statements? Explain.

a. **If it is possible to exchange 3 pounds of cheese for 2 bottles of wine, then the price of cheese is 2/3 the price of wine.**

This is a true statement. If 3 pounds of cheese can be exchanged for 2 bottles of wine, then cheese must have a cost that is 2/3 that of wine and the price of cheese will be 2/3 the price of wine.

b. **A country can only gain from trade if it can produce the good at a lower absolute cost than its trading partner.**

This statement is false. Trade is based on comparative advantage and not absolute advantage. A country can be absolutely worse at producing all goods, but will still be comparatively better at producing some good.

c.   **If there are constant marginal and average costs of production, then it is in a country's best interest to completely specialize in the production of some goods, while importing other goods.**

This is a true statement. If Country A has to always give 2 units of good 1 for another good 2 and Country B always has to give 3 units of good 1 for anther unit of good 2, then Country A should produce enough of good 2 to satisfy demand in both countries. Likewise, Country B should produce enough of good 1 to satisfy demand in both countries (its cost is 1/3 vs 1/2 for Country A). Note that in reality, the marginal and average cost will tend to rise after awhile as more resources are devoted to any given industry.

d.   **Assuming that labor is the only input, if the opportunity cost of producing a yard of cloth is 3 bushels of wheat per yard, then wheat must require 3 times as much labor per unit produced as cloth.**

This statement is false. If the country must give up 3 bushels of wheat to produce another yard of cloth then the same labor resources that are producing the 3 bushels of wheat are required to produce the one yard of cloth. Therefore the yard of cloth requires three times as much labor (the only input).

13. What are the four major sources of market failure? In each case, explain briefly why the competitive market does not operate efficiently.

The four major sources of market failure are market power, incomplete information, externalities, and public goods. We know from the study of market structures that *market power* leads to situations where price does not equal marginal cost. In these situations, the producer is producing too little. Consumers could be made better off by redirecting inputs into the production of the good produced under a competitive market structure, thereby lowering price until price is equal to marginal cost. *Incomplete information* implies that prices do not reflect either the marginal cost of production or the change in utility from changes in consumption. Either too much or too little (at the extreme, none) is produced and consumed. *Externalities* occur when a consumption or production activity influences other consumption of production activities, and these effects are not reflected in market prices. *Public goods* are goods that can be consumed at prices below marginal cost (at the extreme, freely) because consumers cannot be excluded. In these four cases, prices do not send the proper signals to either producers or consumers to increase or decrease production or consumption. Thus, the market mechanism cannot equate social marginal costs with social marginal benefits.

EXERCISES

1. Suppose gold (G) and silver (S) are substitutes for each other because both serve as hedges against inflation. Suppose also that the supplies of both are fixed in the short run (Q_G = 75, and Q_S = 300), and that the demands for gold and silver are given by the following equations:

$$P_G = 975 - Q_G + 0.5P_S \qquad \text{and} \qquad P_S = 600 - Q_S + 0.5P_G.$$

a.   **What are the equilibrium prices of gold and silver?**

In the short run, the quantity of gold, Q_G, is fixed at 75. Substitute Q_G into the demand equation for gold:

$$P_G = 975 - 75 + 0.5P_S.$$

In the short run, the quantity of silver, Q_S, is fixed at 300. Substituting Q_S into the demand equation for silver:

$$P_S = 600 - 300 + 0.5P_G.$$

Since we now have two equations and two unknowns, substitute the price of gold into the price of silver demand function and solve for the price of silver:

$$P_S = 600 - 300 + (0.5)(900 + 0.5P_S) = \$1,000.$$

Now substitute the price of silver into the demand for gold function:

$$P_G = 975 - 75 + (0.5)(1,000) = \$1,400.$$

b.   **Suppose a new discovery of gold doubles the quantity supplied to 150. How will this discovery affect the prices of both gold and silver?**

When the quantity of gold increases by 75 units from 75 to 150, we must resolve our system of equations:

$$P_G = 975 - 150 + 0.5P_S, \text{ or } P_G = 825 + (0.5)(300 + 0.5P_G) = \$1,300.$$

The price of silver is equal to:

$$P_S = 600 - 300 + (0.5)(1,300) = \$950.$$

2. Using general equilibrium analysis, and taking into account feedback effects, analyze the following.

a.   **The likely effects of outbreaks of disease on chicken farms on the markets for chicken and pork.**

If consumers are worried about the quality of the chicken then they may choose to consume pork instead. This will shift the demand curve for pork up and to the right and the demand curve for chicken down and to the left. The feedback effects will partially offset these shifts in the two demand curves. As the price of pork rises, some people may switch back to chicken. This will shift the demand curve for chicken back to the right by some amount and the demand curve for pork back to the left by some amount. Overall, we would expect the price of chicken to be lower and the price of pork higher, but not by as much as if there were no feedback effects.

b.   **The effects of increased taxes on airline tickets on travel to major tourist destinations such as Florida and California, and on the hotel rooms in those destinations.**

Given the increase in the airline tax makes it more costly to travel, the demand curve for airline tickets will shift down and to the left, reducing the price of airline tickets. The reduction in the sale of airline tickets will reduce the demand for hotel rooms by out of town visitors, causing the demand curve for hotel rooms to shift down and to the left, reducing the price of a hotel room. For the feedback effects, the lower price for airline tickets and hotel rooms may encourage some consumers to travel more, in which case both demand curves shift back up and to the right by some amount, offsetting the initial decline in the two prices by some amount. We would still expect both prices to be lower, all else the same.

3. Jane has 3 liters of soft drinks and 9 sandwiches. Bob, on the other hand, has 8 liters of soft drinks and 4 sandwiches. With these endowments, Jane's marginal rate of substitution (MRS) of soft drinks for sandwiches is 4 and Bob's MRS is equal to 2. Draw an Edgeworth box diagram to show whether this allocation of resources is efficient. If it is, explain why. If it is not, what exchanges will make both parties better off?

Given that $MRS_{Bob} \neq MRS_{Jane}$, the current allocation of resources is inefficient. Jane and Bob could trade to make one of them better off without making the other worse off. Although we do not know the exact shape of Jane and Bob's indifference curves, we do know the slope of both indifference curves *at the current allocation*, because we know that $MRS_{Jane} = 4$ and $MRS_{Bob} = 2$. At the current allocation point, Jane is willing to trade 4 sandwiches for 1 drink, or she will give up 1 drink in exchange for 4 sandwiches. Bob is willing to trade 2 sandwiches for 1 drink, or he will give up 1 drink in exchange for 2 sandwiches. Jane will give 4 sandwiches for 1 drink while Bob is willing to accept only 2 sandwiches in exchange for 1 drink. If Jane gives Bob 3 sandwiches for 1 drink, she is better off because she was willing to give 4 but only had to give 3. Bob is better off because he was willing to accept 2 sandwiches and actually received 3. Jane ends up with 4 drinks and 6 sandwiches and Bob ends up with 7 drinks and 7 sandwiches. If Jane instead was to trade drinks for sandwiches, she would sell a drink for 4 sandwiches. Bob however would not give her more than 2 sandwiches for a drink. Neither would be willing to make this trade.

4. Jennifer and Drew consume orange juice and coffee. Jennifer's MRS of orange juice for coffee is 1 and Drew's MRS of orange juice for coffee is 3. If the price of orange juice is $2 and the price of coffee is $3, which market is in excess demand? What do you expect to happen to the prices of the two goods?

Jennifer is willing to trade 1 coffee for 1 orange juice. Drew is willing to trade 3 coffee for one orange juice. In the market, it is possible to trade 2/3 of a coffee for an orange juice. Both will find it optimal to trade coffee in exchange for orange juice since they are willing to give up more for orange juice than they have to. There is an excess demand of orange juice and an excess supply of coffee. Price of coffee will go down and price of orange juice will go up. Notice also that at the given rates of MRS and prices, both Jennifer and Drew have a higher marginal utility per dollar for orange juice as compared to coffee.

5. Fill in the missing information in the following tables. For each table, use the information provided to identify a possible trade. Then identify the final allocation and a possible value for the MRS at the efficient solution. (Note: there is more than one correct answer.) Illustrate your results using Edgeworth Box diagrams.

a.   Norman's MRS of food for clothing is 1 and Gina's MRS of food for clothing is 4.

Individual	Initial Allocation	Trade	Final Allocation
Norman	6F,2C	1F for 3C	5F,5C
Gina	1F,8C	3C for 1F	2F,5C

Gina will give 4 clothing for 1 food while Norman is willing to accept only 1 clothing for 1 food. If they settle on 2 or 3 units of clothing for one unit of food they will both be better off. Let's say they settle on 3 units of clothing for 1 unit of food. Gina will give up 3 units of clothing and receive 1 unit of food so her final allocation is 2F and 5C. Norman will give up 1 food and gain 3 clothing so his final allocation is 5F and 5C. Gina's MRS will decrease and Norman's will increase, so given they must be equal in the end, it will be somewhere between 1 and 4, in absolute value terms.

b.   Michael's MRS of food for clothing is 1/2 and Kelly's MRS of food for clothing is 3.

Individual	Initial Allocation	Trade	Final Allocation
Michael	10F,3C	1F for 1C	9F,4C
Kelly	5F,15C	1C for 1F	6F,14C

Michael will give 2 food for 1 clothing while Kelly is willing to accept only 1/3 food for 1 clothing. If they settle on 1 unit of food for 1 unit of clothing they will both be better off. Michael will give up 1 unit of food and receive 1 unit of clothing so his final allocation is 9F and 4C. Kelly will give up 1 clothing and gain 1 food so her final allocation is 6F and 14C. Kelly's MRS will decrease and Michael's will increase, so given they must be equal in the end, it will be somewhere between 3 and 1/2, in absolute value terms.

6. In the analysis of an exchange between two people, suppose both people have identical preferences. Will the contract curve be a straight line? Explain. Can you think of a counterexample?

Given that the contract curve intersects the origin for each individual, a straight line contract curve would be a diagonal line running from one origin to the other. The slope of this line is $\dfrac{Y}{X}$, where Y is the total amount of the good on the vertical axis and X is the total amount of the good on the horizontal axis. (x_1, y_1) are the amounts of the two goods allocated to one individual and $(x_2, y_2) = (X - x_1, Y - y_1)$ are the amounts of the two goods allocated to the other individual; the contract curve may be represented by the equation

$$y_1 = \left(\frac{Y}{X}\right) x_1.$$

We need to show that when the marginal rates of substitution for the two individuals are equal ($MRS^1 = MRS^2$), the allocation lies on the contract curve.

For example, consider the utility function $U = x_i^2 y_i$. Then

$$MRS^i = \frac{MU_x^i}{MU_y^i} = \frac{2x_i y_i}{x_i^2} = \frac{2y_i}{x_i}.$$

If MRS^1 equals MRS^2, then

$$\left(\frac{2y_1}{x_1}\right) = \left(\frac{2y_2}{x_2}\right).$$

Is this point on the contract curve? Yes, because

$$x_2 = X - x_1 \text{ and } y_2 = Y - y_1,$$

$$2\left(\frac{y_1}{x_1}\right) = 2\left(\frac{Y - y_1}{X - x_1}\right).$$

This means that

$$\frac{y_1(X - x_1)}{x_1} = Y - y_1, \text{ or } \frac{y_1 X - y_1 x_1}{x_1} = Y - y_1, \text{and}$$

$$\frac{y_1 X}{x_1} - y_1 = Y - y_1, \text{ or } \frac{y_1 X}{x_1} = Y, \text{ or } y_1 = \left(\frac{Y}{X}\right) x_1.$$

With this utility function we find $MRS^1 = MRS^2$, and the contract curve is a straight line. However, if the two traders have identical preferences but different incomes, the contract curve is not a straight line when one good is inferior.

7. Give an example of conditions when the production possibilities frontier might not be concave.

The production possibilities frontier is concave if at least one of the production functions exhibits decreasing returns to scale. If both production functions exhibit constant returns to scale, then the production possibilities frontier is a straight line. If both production functions exhibit increasing returns to scale, then the production function is convex. The following numerical examples can be used to illustrate this concept. Assume that L is the labor input, and X and Y are the two goods. The first example is the decreasing returns to scale case, the second example is the constant returns to scale case, and the third example is the increasing returns to scale case. Note further that it is not necessary that both products have identical production functions.

Product X		Product Y		PPF	
L	X	L	Y	X	Y
0	0	0	0	0	30
1	10	1	10	10	28
2	18	2	18	18	24
3	24	3	24	24	18
4	28	4	28	28	10
5	30	5	30	30	0

Product X		Product Y		PPF	
L	X	L	Y	X	Y
0	0	0	0	0	50
1	10	1	10	10	40
2	20	2	20	20	30
3	30	3	30	30	20
4	40	4	40	40	10
5	50	5	50	50	0

Product X		Product Y		PPF	
L	X	L	Y	X	Y
0	0	0	0	0	80
1	10	1	10	10	58
2	22	2	22	22	38
3	38	3	38	38	22
4	58	4	58	58	10
5	80	5	80	80	0

8. A monopsonist buys labor for less than the competitive wage. What type of inefficiency will this use of monopsony power cause? How would your answer change if the monopsonist in the labor market were also a monopolist in the output market?

When market power exists, the market will not allocate resources efficiently. If the wage paid by a monopsonist is below the competitive wage, too little labor will be used in the production process. However, output may increase because inputs are generally less costly. If the firm is a monopolist in the output market, output will be such that price is above marginal cost and output will clearly be less. With monopsony, too much may be produced; with monopoly, too little is produced. The incentive to produce too little could be less than, equal to, or greater than the incentive to produce too much. Only in a special configuration of marginal expenditure and marginal revenue would the two incentives be equal.

9. The Acme Corporation produces *x* and *y* units of goods Alpha and Beta, respectively.

a. **Use a production possibility frontier to explain how the willingness to produce more or less Alpha depends on the marginal rate of transformation of Alpha or Beta.**

The production-possibilities frontier shows all efficient combinations of Alpha and Beta. The marginal rate of transformation of Alpha for Beta is the slope of the production-possibilities frontier. The slope measures the marginal cost of producing one good relative to the marginal cost of producing the other. To increase *x*, the units of Alpha, Acme must release inputs in the production of Beta and redirect them to producing Alpha. The rate at which it can efficiently substitute away from Beta to Alpha is given by the marginal rate of transformation.

b. **Consider two cases of production extremes: (i) Acme produces zero units of Alpha initially, or (ii) Acme produces zero units of Beta initially. If Acme always tries to stay on its production-possibility frontier, describe the initial positions of cases (i) and (ii). What happens as the Acme Corporation begins to produce *both* goods?**

The two extremes are corner solutions to the problem of determining efficient output, given market prices. These two solutions are both possible with different price ratios, which could produce tangencies with Acme's end of the frontier. Assuming that the price ratio changes so the firm would find it efficient to produce both goods and, assuming the usual concave shape of the frontier, it is likely that the firm will be able to decrease the production of its primary output by a small amount for a larger gain in the output of the other good. The firm should continue to shift production until the ratio of marginal costs (i.e., the *MRT*) is equal to the ratio of market prices for the two outputs.

10. In the context of our analysis of the Edgeworth production box, suppose a new invention causes a constant-returns-to-scale production process for food to become a sharply-increasing-returns process. How does this change affect the production-contract curve?

In the context of an Edgeworth production box, the production-contract curve is made up of the points of tangency between the isoquants of the two production processes. A change from a constant-returns-to-scale production process to a sharply-increasing-returns-to-scale production process does not necessarily imply a change in the shape of the isoquants. One can simply redefine the quantities associated with each isoquant such that proportional increases in inputs yield greater-than-proportional increases in outputs. Under this assumption, the marginal rate of technical substitution would not change. Thus, there would be no change in the production-contract curve.

If, however, accompanying this change to a sharply-increasing-returns-to-scale technology, there were a change in the trade-off between the two inputs (a change in the shape of the isoquants), then the production-contract curve would change. For example, if the original production function were $Q = LK$ with $MRTS = \dfrac{K}{L}$, the shape of the isoquants would not change if the new production function were $Q = L^2K^2$ with $MRTS = \dfrac{K}{L}$, but the shape would change if the new production function were $Q = L^2K$ with $MRTS = 2\left(\dfrac{K}{L}\right)$. Note that in this case the production possibilities frontier is likely to become convex.

11. **Suppose that country A and country B both produce wine and cheese. Country A has 800 units of available labor, while country B has 600 units. Prior to trade, country A consumes 40 pounds of cheese and 8 bottles of wine, and country B consumes 30 pounds of cheese and 10 bottles of wine.**

	Country A	Country B
labor per pound cheese	10	10
labor per bottle wine	50	30

a. **Which country has a comparative advantage in the production of each good? Explain.**

To produce another bottle of wine, Country A needs 50 units of labor, and must therefore produce five fewer units of cheese. The opportunity cost of a bottle of wine is five pounds of cheese. For Country B the opportunity cost of a bottle of wine is three pounds of cheese. Since Country B has a lower opportunity cost, they should produce the wine and Country A should produce the cheese. The opportunity cost of cheese in Country A is 1/5 of a bottle of wine and in Country B is 1/3 of a bottle of wine.

b. **Determine the production possibilities curve for each country, both graphically and algebraically. (Label the pre-trade production point PT and the post trade production point P.)**

For Country A their production frontier is given by 10C+50W=800, or C=80-5W, and for Country B their production frontier is given by 10C+30W=600, or C=60-3W. The slope of the frontier for Country A is -5 which is the price of wine divided by the price of cheese. Therefore, in Country A the price of wine is 5 and in Country B the price of wine is 3. After trade, the price will settle in the middle somewhere. The post trade production point is on the terms of trade line which has a slope equal to the world price ratio, say –4 in this case. Country A will produce only cheese and Country B will produce only wine. Each can consume at a point on the terms of trade line that lies above and outside the production frontier.

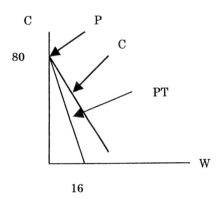

Country A

c. **Given that 36 pounds of cheese and 9 bottles of wine are traded, label the post trade consumption point C.**

See the graph for Country A above. Before trade the country consumed and produced at point PT, which was given as 40 pounds of cheese and 8 bottles of wine. After trade, Country A will completely specialize in the production of cheese and will produce at point P. Given the quantities traded, Country A will consume 80-36=44 pounds of cheese and 0+9 bottles of wine. This is point C on the graph. The graph for Country B is similar except that Country B will produce only wine and the trade line will intersect their production frontier on the wine axis.

d. **Prove that both countries have gained from trade?**

Both countries have gained from trade because they can now both consume more of both goods that they could before trade. Graphically we can see this by noticing that the trade line lies to the left of the production frontier. After trade, the country can consume on the trade line and is able to consume more of both goods. Numerically, Country A consumes 4 more pounds of cheese and 1 more bottle of wine after trade as compared to pre-trade, and Country B consumes 6 more pounds of cheese and 1 more bottle of wine.

e. **What is the slope of the price line at which trade occurs?**

We assumed −4, which is somewhere between the pre-trade prices. All that we can say from the information given is that it will be somewhere between the pre-trade prices, or the slopes of the two production frontiers. We would need more information about demand for the two products in each country to determine the exact post-trade prices.

CHAPTER 17
MARKETS WITH ASYMMETRIC INFORMATION

TEACHING NOTES

This chapter explores different situations in which one party knows more than the other, or in other words, what happens when there is asymmetric information. Section 17.1 discusses the case where the seller has more information than the buyer, and section 17.2 discusses market signaling as a mechanism to deal with the problem of asymmetric information. Section 17.3 discusses the moral hazard problem where one party has more information about their behavior than does the other party. Section 17.4 discusses the principal agent problem and section 17.5 extends the analysis to the case of an integrated firm. Both sections address the issue of differing goals between owners and managers. Section 17.6 examines the efficiency wage theory. There are basically four topics that the instructor can pick and choose between depending on time constraints and general interest.

It is best to introduce asymmetric information by reviewing the cases where microeconomics has assumed perfect information. For example, except for Chapter 5 and sections of Chapter 15, we have assumed perfect knowledge of the future (no uncertainty). In models of uncertainty, consumers and producers play "games against nature." In models of asymmetric information, they are playing games with each other.

Many of your students are likely to have bought or sold a used car and will, therefore, find the lemons model interesting. Start your presentation by asking the sellers of used cars how they determined their asking price. Emphasize the intuition of the model before presenting Figure 17.1. If they have understood the model, they should ask a high price to give the impression to buyers that the car they are selling is of high quality. Class discussion could consider whether the government should pass laws requiring warranties in the sale of used cars.

The market for insurance is also one with which most students are familiar. Although car insurance is required in many states, liability limits may vary from policy to policy. Discuss how risk-averse individuals will want to purchase policies with higher limits and how insurance companies determine the riskiness of the insurance. If you have used the example of buying a house in Chapter 15, you may extend it here by considering how bankers determine whether borrowers will default on their home loans.

When discussing market signaling, point out the dual function of education (as training and as a signal of higher productivity). The "Simple Model of Job Market Signaling," which is presented in Section 17.2, might confuse students unfamiliar with discontinuous functions (see Figure 17.2). Explain how educational degrees lead to discontinuities, and stress the relationship between degrees, guarantees, and warranties of educational quality.

Moral hazard is an easy concept to illustrate with examples, but it is important to draw a clear distinction between adverse selection and moral hazard.

The principal-agent problem is presented in the context of the relationship between employer and employee. It can be generalized to the relationship between a regulator and a regulated firm and to the relationship between voters and elected officials. In discussing the problems of monitoring agents, you can reintroduce the concept of transactions costs (from Section 16.2). The most interesting topic of this section is how to design contracts to provide the proper incentives for agents to perform in the interest of the principal. The starred Section 17.5 extends this topic to managerial incentives in an integrated firm. The model can be applied to government contracts, i.e., defense contracts, for a discussion of cost-plus contracting.

The shirking model of efficiency wages is conceptually difficult. After discussing efficiency in Chapter 16, students might wonder what is so efficient about paying workers a wage that is greater than the value of their marginal product. Stress the role of asymmetric information here: firms have imperfect information about individual worker productivity. If you present this model, first read the references in Footnote 17. While Yellen's article is concise, Stiglitz's is more general, discussing shirking on page 20 and the relationship between efficiency wage theory and unemployment on pages 33-37.

QUESTIONS FOR REVIEW

1. Why can asymmetric information between buyers and sellers lead to a market failure when a market is otherwise perfectly competitive?

Asymmetric information leads to market failure because the transaction price does not reflect either the marginal benefit to the buyer or the marginal cost of the seller. The competitive market fails to achieve an output with a price equal to marginal cost. In some extreme cases, if there is no mechanism to reduce the problem of asymmetric information, the market collapses completely. For example, in the used car case the buyer does not know for sure if they will be getting a high or low quality car, and as a result buyers will tend to be willing to pay less for a car than high quality owners are willing to accept. As a result, not many high quality cars will be offered for sale and this can lead to market failure.

2. If the used car market is a "lemons" market, how would you expect the repair record of used cars that are sold to compare with the repair record of those not sold?

In the market for used cars, the seller has a better idea of the quality of the used car than does the buyer. The repair record of the used car is one indicator of quality. One would expect that, at the margin, cars with good repair records would be kept while cars with poor repair records would be sold. Thus, one would expect the repair records of used cars that are to be sold to be worse than those of used cars not sold.

3. Explain the difference between adverse selection and moral hazard in insurance markets. Can one exist without the other?

In insurance markets, both adverse selection and moral hazard exist. Adverse selection refers to the self-selection of individuals who purchase insurance policies. In other words, people who are less risky than the insured population will, at the margin, choose not to insure, while people more risky than the population will choose to insure. As a result, the insurance company is left with a riskier pool of policy holders. The problem of moral hazard occurs after the insurance is purchased. Once insurance is purchased, less risky individuals might engage in behavior characteristic of more risky individuals. If policy holders are fully insured, they have little incentive to avoid risky situations.

An insurance firm may reduce adverse selection, without reducing moral hazard, and vice versa. Conducting research to determine the riskiness of a *potential* customer helps insurance companies reduce adverse selection. Furthermore, insurance companies reevaluate the premium (sometimes canceling the policy) when claims are made against the policy, thereby reducing moral hazard. Co-payments also reduce moral hazard by creating a disincentive for policyholders to engage in risky behavior.

4. Describe several ways in which sellers can convince buyers that their products are of high quality. Which methods apply in the following products: Maytag washing machines, Burger King hamburgers, large diamonds?

Some sellers signal the quality of their products to buyers through (1) investment in a good reputation, (2) the standardization of products, (3) certification (i.e., the use of educational degrees in the labor market), (4) guarantees, and (5) warranties. Maytag signals the high quality of its washing machines by offering one of the best warranties in the market. Burger King relies on the standardization of its hamburgers, e.g., the Whopper. The sale of a large diamond is accompanied by a certificate that verifies the weight and shape of the stone and discloses any flaws.

5. Why might a seller find it advantageous to signal the quality of a product? How are guarantees and warranties a form of market signaling?

Firms producing high-quality products would like to charge higher prices, but to do this successfully, potential consumers must be made aware of the quality differences among brands. One method of providing product quality information is through guarantees (i.e., the promise to return what has been given in exchange if the product is defective) and warranties (i.e., the promise to repair or replace if defective). Since low-quality producers are unlikely to offer costly signaling devices, consumers can correctly view a guarantee or an extensive warranty as a signal of high quality, thus confirming the effectiveness of these measures as signaling devices.

6. Joe earned a high grade-point average during his four years of college. Is this a strong signal to Joe's future employer that he will be a highly productive worker? Why or why not?

Yes, for the most part a high grade point average is a strong signal to the employer that the employee will perform at an above average level. Regardless of what he actually learned, it indicates that he is able to out-perform the majority of students. On the other hand, Joe could have padded his schedule with easy classes, and/or classes taught by easy professors.

7. Why might managers be able to achieve objectives other than profit maximization, which is the goal of the firm's shareholders?

It is difficult and costly for shareholders to constantly monitor the actions of the firm's managers. The firm's owners are in a better position to engage in monitoring, but a manager's behavior still cannot be scrutinized one hundred percent of the time. Therefore, managers have some leeway to pursue their own objectives.

8. How can the principal-agent model be used to explain why public enterprises, such as post offices, might pursue goals other than profit maximization?

Managers of public enterprises can be expected to act in much the same way as managers of private enterprises, in terms of having an interest in power and other perks, in addition to profit maximization. The problem of overseeing a public enterprise is one of asymmetric information. The manager (agent) is more familiar with the cost structure of the enterprise and the benefits to the customers than the principal, an elected or appointed official, who must elicit cost information controlled by the manager. The costs of eliciting and verifying the information, as well as independently gathering information on the benefits provided by the public enterprise, can be more than the difference between the agency's potential net returns ("profits") and realized returns. This difference provides room for slack, which can be distributed to the management as personal benefits, to the agency's workers as greater-than-efficient job security, or to the agency's customers in the form of greater-than-efficient provision of goods or services.

9. Why are bonus and profit-sharing payment schemes likely to resolve principal-agent problems, whereas a fixed-wage payment will not?

With a fixed wage, the agent-employee has no incentive to maximize productivity. If the agent-employee is hired at a fixed wage equal to the marginal revenue product of the average employee, there is no incentive to work harder than the least productive worker. Bonus and profit-sharing schemes involve a lower fixed wage than fixed-wage schemes, but they include a bonus wage. The bonus can be tied to the profitability of the firm, to the output of the individual employee, or to that of the group in which the employee works. These schemes provide a greater incentive for agents to maximize the objective function of the principal.

10. What is an efficiency wage? Why is it profitable for the firm to pay it when workers have better information about their productivity than firms do?

An efficiency wage, in the context of the shirking model, is the wage at which no shirking occurs. If employers cannot monitor employees' productivity, then employees may shirk (work less productively), which will affect the firm's output and profits. It therefore pays the firm to offer workers a higher-than-market wage, thus reducing the workers' incentive to shirk, because they know that if they are fired and end up working for another firm, their wage will fall. Firms may also pay efficiency wages in order to reduce turnover among employees. If employees are paid a higher wage then, all else the same, they will be happier at their jobs and less likely to leave and find a new job. High turnover rates can be costly for the firm in terms of having to continually train new employees.

EXERCISES

1. Many consumers view a well-known brand name as a signal of quality and will pay more for a brand-name product (e.g., Bayer aspirin instead of generic aspirin, Birds Eye frozen vegetables instead of the supermarket's own brand). Can a brand name provide a useful signal of quality? Why or why not?

A brand name can provide a useful signal of quality for several reasons. First, when information asymmetry is a problem, one solution is to create a "brand-name" product. Standardization of the product produces a reputation for a given level of quality that is signaled by the brand name. Second, if the development of a brand-name reputation is costly (i.e., advertising, warranties, etc.), the brand name is a signal of higher quality. Finally, pioneer products, by virtue of their "first-mover" status, enjoy consumer loyalty if the products are of acceptable quality. The uncertainty surrounding newer products inhibits defection from the pioneering brand-name product.

2. Gary is a recent college graduate. After six months at his new job, he has finally saved enough to buy his first car.

**a.	Gary knows very little about the differences between makes and models. How could he use market signals, reputation, or standardization to make comparisons?**

Gary's problem is one of asymmetric information. As a buyer of a first car, he will be negotiating with sellers who know more about cars than he does. His first choice is to decide between a new or used car. If he buys a used car, he must choose between a professional used-car dealer and an individual seller. Each of these three types of sellers (the new-car dealer, the used-car dealer, and the individual seller) uses different market signals to convey quality information about their products.

The new-car dealer, working with the manufacturer (and relying on the manufacturer's reputation) can offer standard and extended warranties that guarantee the car will perform as advertised. Because few used cars carry a manufacturer's warranty and the used-car dealer is not intimately familiar with the condition of the cars on his or her lot (because of their wide variety and disparate previous usage), it is not in his or her self-interest to offer extensive warranties. The used-car dealer, therefore, must rely on reputation, particularly on a reputation of offering "good values." Since the individual seller neither offers warranties nor relies on reputation, purchasing from such a seller could make it advisable to seek additional information from an independent mechanic or from reading the used-car recommendations in *Consumer Reports*. Given his lack of experience, Gary should gather as much information about these market signals, reputation, and standardization as he can afford.

**b.	You are a loan officer in a bank. After selecting a car, Gary comes to you seeking a loan. Because he has only recently graduated, he does not have a long credit history. Nonetheless, the bank has a long history of financing cars for recent college graduates. Is this information useful in Gary's case? If so, how?**

The bank's problem in loaning money to Gary is also one of asymmetric information. Gary has a much better idea than the bank does about the quality of the car and his ability to pay back the loan. While the bank can learn about the car through the reputation of the manufacturer (if it is a new car) and through inspection (if it is a used car), the bank has little information on Gary's ability to handle credit. Therefore, the bank must infer information about Gary's credit-worthiness from easily available information, such as his recent graduation from college, how much he might have borrowed while in school, and the similarity of his educational and credit profile to that of college graduates currently holding car loans from the bank. If recent graduates have built a good reputation for paying off their loans, Gary can use this reputation to his advantage, but poor repayment patterns by this group will lessen his chances of obtaining a car loan from this bank.

3. A major university bans the assignment of D or F grades. It defends its action by claiming that students tend to perform above average when they are free from the pressures of flunking out. The university states that it wants all its students to get As and Bs. If the goal is to raise overall grades to the B level or above, is this a good policy? Discuss with respect to the problem of moral hazard.

By eliminating the lowest grades, the innovating university creates a moral hazard problem similar to that which is found in insurance markets. Since they are protected from receiving a below-average grade, some students will have little incentive to work at above-average levels. The policy only addresses the pressures facing below-average students, i.e., those who flunk out. Average and above-average students do not face the pressure of failing. For these students, the destructive pressure of earning good grades (instead of learning a subject well) remains. Their problems are not addressed by this policy. Therefore, the policy creates a moral hazard problem primarily for the below-average students who are its intended beneficiaries.

4. Professor Jones has just been hired by the economics department at a major university. The president of the board of regents has stated that the university is committed to providing top-quality education for undergraduates. Two months into the semester, Jones fails to show up for his classes. It seems he is devoting all his time to research rather than to teaching. Jones argues that his research will bring prestige to the department and the university. Should he be allowed to continue exclusively with research? Discuss with reference to the principal-agent problem.

In the university context, the board of regents and its president are the principals, while the agents are the members of the faculty hired by the department with the approval of the president and the board. The dual purpose of most universities is teaching students and producing research; thus, most faculty are hired to perform both tasks. The problem is that teaching effort can be easily monitored (particularly if Jones does not show up for class), while the benefits of establishing a prestigious research reputation are uncertain and are realized only over time. While the quantity of research is easy to calculate, determining research quality is more difficult. The university should not simply take Jones' word regarding the benefits of his research and allow him to continue exclusively with his research without altering his payment scheme. One alternative would be to tell Jones that he does not have to teach if he is willing to accept a lower salary. On the other hand, the university could offer Jones a bonus if, due to his research reputation, he is able to bring a lucrative grant or other donations to the university

5. Faced with a reputation for producing automobiles with poor repair records, a number of American companies have offered extensive guarantees to car purchasers (i.e., a seven-year warranty on all parts and labor associated with mechanical problems).

a.   In light of your knowledge of the lemons market, why is this a reasonable policy?

In the past, American companies enjoyed a reputation for producing high-quality cars. More recently, faced with competition from Japanese car manufacturers, their products appeared to customers to be of lower quality. As this reputation spread, customers were less willing to pay high prices for American cars. To reverse this trend, American companies invested in quality control, improving the repair records of their products. Consumers, however, still considered American cars to be of lower quality (lemons, in some sense), and would not buy them, American companies were forced to signal the improved quality of their products to their customers. One way of providing this information is through improved warranties that directly address the issue of poor repair records. This was a reasonable reaction to the "lemons" problem that they faced.

b.   Is the policy likely to create a moral hazard problem? Explain.

Moral hazard occurs when the insured party (here, the owner of an American automobile with an extensive warranty) can influence the probability of the event that triggers payment (here, the repair of the automobile). The coverage of all parts and labor associated with mechanical problems reduces the incentive to maintain the automobile. Hence, a moral hazard problem is created by the offer of extensive warranties. To avoid this problem, all routine maintenance could be performed as long as the car is under warranty. Note though that manufacturers could stipulate that the warranties will not be honored unless the owner performs and pays for routine maintenance.

6. To promote competition and consumer welfare, the Federal Trade Commission requires firms to advertise truthfully. How does truth in advertising promote competition? Why would a market be less competitive if firms advertised deceptively?

Truth-in-advertising promotes competition by providing the information necessary for consumers to make optimal decisions. "Competitive forces" function properly only if consumers are aware of all prices (and qualities), so comparisons may be made. In the absence of truthful advertising, buyers are unable to make these comparisons because goods priced identically can be of different quality. Hence, there will be a tendency for buyers to "stick" with proven products, reducing competition between existing firms and discouraging entry. Note that monopoly rents may result when consumers stick with proven products.

7. An insurance company is considering issuing three types of fire insurance policies: (i) complete insurance coverage, (ii) complete coverage above and beyond a $10,000 deductible, and (iii) 90 percent coverage of all losses. Which policy is more likely to create moral hazard problems?

Moral hazard problems arise with fire insurance when the insured party can influence the probability of a fire and the magnitude of a loss from a fire. The property owner can engage in behavior that reduces the probability of a fire, for example, by inspecting and replacing faulty wiring. The magnitude of losses can be reduced by the installation of warning systems or the storage of valuables away from areas where fires are likely to start.

After purchasing complete insurance, the insured has little incentive to reduce either the probability or the magnitude of the loss, and the moral hazard problem will be severe. In order to compare a $10,000 deductible and 90 percent coverage, we would need information on the value of the potential loss. Both policies reduce the moral hazard problem of complete coverage. However, if the property is worth less (more) than $100,000, the total loss will be less (more) with 90 percent coverage than with the $10,000 deductible. As the value of the property increases above $100,000, the owner is more likely to engage in fire prevention efforts under the policy that offers 90 percent coverage than under the one that offers the $10,000 deductible.

8. You have seen how asymmetric information can reduce the average quality of products sold in a market as low-quality products drive out the high-quality ones. For those markets in which asymmetric information is prevalent, would you agree or disagree with each of the following? Explain briefly:

a.   The government should subsidize *Consumer Reports*.

Asymmetric information implies an unequal access to information by either buyers or sellers, a problem that leads to inefficient markets or market collapse. Subsidizing the gathering and publishing of information can be advantageous in general because it helps consumers make better decisions and promotes honesty on the part of the firm.

Although *Consumer Reports* provides evaluations for products ranging from hamburgers to washing machines, it refuses to let its name be used as an endorsement of a product. While government support of *Consumer Reports* would be likely to

272

increase the ability of consumers to distinguish between high- and low-quality goods, it is probable that the Consumers Union, publisher of *Consumer Reports,* would reject government subsidization because such subsidization might taint the objectivity of the organization. Note that the government has already provided an indirect subsidy to the publication by granting the Consumers Union nonprofit status.

b. **The government should impose quality standards — e.g., firms should not be allowed to sell low-quality items.**

Option *b* involves a cost of monitoring. After imposing quality standards, the government must either administratively monitor the quality of goods or adjudicate disputes between the public and the manufacturers. Note, however, that low-quality goods may be preferred if they are sufficiently cheaper.

c. **The producer of a high-quality good will probably want to offer an extensive warranty.**

This option provides the least-cost solution to the problems of asymmetric information. It allows the producer to distinguish its products from low-quality goods because it is more costly for the low-quality producer to offer an extensive warranty than for the high-quality producer to offer one.

d. **The government should require *all* firms to offer extensive warranties.**

By requiring *all* firms to offer extensive warranties, the government negates the market signaling value of warranties offered by the producers of high-quality goods.

9. Two used car dealerships compete side by side on a main road. The first, Harry's Cars, always sells high-quality cars that it carefully inspects and, if necessary, services. On average, it costs Harry $8,000 to buy and service each car that it sells. The second dealership, Lew's Motors, always sells lower-quality cars. On average, it costs Lew only $5,000 for each car that it sells. If consumers knew the quality of the used cars they were buying, they would gladly pay $10,000 on average for Harry's cars, but only $7,000 on average for Lew's cars.

Without more information, consumers do not know the quality of each dealership's cars. In this case, consumers would figure that they have a 50-50 chance of ending up with a high-quality car, and are thus willing to pay $8,500 for a car.

Harry has an idea: He will offer a bumper-to-bumper warranty for all cars he sells. He knows that a warranty lasting Y years will cost $500Y on average, and he also knows that if Lew tries to offer the same warranty, it will cost Lew $1000Y on average.

(a) **Suppose Harry offers a one-year warranty on all cars it sells.**

(1) **What is Lew's profit if it does not offer a one-year warranty? If it does offer a one-year warranty?**

(2) **What is Harry's profit if Lew's does not offer a one-year warranty? If it does offer a one-year warranty?**

(3) **Will Lew's match Harry's one-year warranty?**

(4) **Is it a good idea for Harry's to offer a one-year warranty?**

Without offering the warranty, Lew's is able to make $2,000 per car (7000-5000). If it were to offer the warranty, each car will now cost Lew's $6,000, but as consumers will not be able to determine the quality of the cars they will be willing to pay $8,500 for a car, and Lew's will make $2,500 per car (8500-6000).

If Lew's does not offer a one-year warranty then Harry's can buy its cars for $8,000, sell the cars for $10,000, and make a profit of $1,500 per car after the $500 warranty cost. If Lew's does offer a one year warranty then Harry's will only be able to sell its cars for $8,500 and the company will not make any profit.

Lew's will match Harry's warranty because if it does then its profit increases from $2,000 to $2,500 per car.

Harry's should not offer the one-year warranty unless it thinks that Lew's will act irrationally and not offer the one-year warranty. Given Lew's will match the warranty, Harry's is better off not offering the warranty.

(b) **What if Harry offers a two-year warranty? Will this generate a credible signal of quality? What about a three-year warranty?**

If Harry's offers a two-year warranty each car will cost $9,000. It will earn $1,000 per car as consumers will recognize the higher quality of its cars. Lew's will not offer a two year warranty because if they do they will only earn profit of $1,500 per car, which is less than the $2,000 they would earn without offering the warranty. The two year warranty is a credible signal.

With a three-year warranty Harry's would be making $500 per car, the same that it would have made had it not signaled the higher quality of its cars with a warranty. Therefore, Harry's would not offer a three-year warranty.

(c) **If you were advising Harry, how long a warranty would you urge him to offer? Explain why.**

Harry's will need to offer a warranty of sufficient length such that Lew's will not find it profitable to match the warranty. Let t denote the number of years of the warranty, then Lew's will offer a warranty according to the following inequality:

$$7000\text{-}5000 \leq 8500\text{-}5000\text{-}1000t, \text{ or } t \leq 1.5.$$

Therefore, I would advise Harry's to offer a 1.5 year warranty on his cars as Lew's will not find it profitable to match the warranty.

10. As Chairman of the Board of ASP Industries you estimate that your firm's annual profit is given by the table below. Profit (Π) is conditional upon market demand and the effort of your new CEO. The probabilities of each demand condition occurring are also shown in the table.

Market Demand	Low Demand	Medium Demand	High Demand
Market Probabilities	.30	.40	.30
Low Effort	Π=$5 million	Π=$10 million	Π=$15 million
High Effort	Π=$10 million	Π=$15 million	Π=$17 million

You must design a compensation package for the CEO that will maximize the firm's expected profit. While the firm is risk neutral, the CEO is risk averse. The CEO's utility function is:

Utility = $W^{.5}$ when making low effort

Utility = $W^{.5}$ -100, when making high effort,

where W is the CEO's income. (The -100 is the "utility cost" to the CEO of making a high effort.) You know the CEO's utility function, and both you and the CEO know all of the information in the preceding table. You do not know the level of the CEO's effort at time of compensation or the exact state of demand. You do see the firm's profit, however.

Of the three alternative compensation packages below, which do you as Chairman of ASP Industries prefer and why?

PACKAGE 1: Pay the CEO a flat salary of $575,000 per year.

PACKAGE 2: Pay the CEO a fixed 6 percent of yearly firm profits.

PACKAGE 3: Pay the CEO a flat salary of $500,000 per year and then 50 percent of any firm profits *above* $15 million.

The issue here is how to get your CEO to make high effort but not give away the company store – that is, too much in profits. For each package, first calculate whether the executive will make high or low effort. Then calculate firm profits under each effort to decide if the package works to your advantage. Then select that package which maximizes your profits. CEO Utility under the three packages:

PACKAGE 1: the CEO will give low effort to maximize utility:

Low Effort: $E(U) = (\$575,000)^{.5} = 758.29$

High Effort: $E(U) = (\$575,000)^{.5} - 100 = 658.29$.

PACKAGE 2: the CEO will give high effort to maximize utility:

Low Effort: $E(U) = .3(.06\text{x}5,000,000)^{.5} + .4(.06\text{x}10,000,000)^{.5} + .3(.06\text{x}15,000,000)^{.5} = 758.76$

High Effort: $E(U) = .3(.06\text{x}10,000,000)^{.5} + .4(.06\text{x}15,000,000)^{.5} + .3(.06\text{x}17,000,000)^{.5} - 100 = 814.835$

PACKAGE 3: the CEO will give high effort to maximize utility:

Low Effort: $E(U) = .3(500,000)^{.5} + .4(500,000)^{.5} + .3(500,000)^{.5} = 707.11$

High Effort: $E(U) = .3(500,000)^{.5} + .4(500,000)^{.5} + .3(1,500,000)^{.5} - 100 = 762.40$

Now calculate the expected firm profits under each plan net of expected compensation:

PACKAGE 1:

Low Effort: $E(\Pi) = .30\text{x}\$5\text{m} + .40\text{x}\$10\text{m} + .30\text{x}\$15\text{m} - (\$.575\text{m}) = \$9.425\text{million}$

PACKAGE 2:

Low Effort: $E(\Pi) = .30\text{x}\$5\text{m} + .40\text{x}\$10\text{m} + .30\text{x}\$15\text{m} - (.3\text{x}\$.3\text{m} + .4\text{x}\$.6\text{m} + .3\text{x}\$.9\text{m})$
$= \$9.4\text{m}$

High Effort: $E(\Pi) = .30\text{x}\$10\text{m} + .40\text{x}\$15\text{m} + .30\text{x}\$17\text{m} - (.3\text{x}\$.6\text{m} + \$.4\text{x}\$.9\text{m} + .3\text{x}\$1.02\text{m}) = \$13.254\text{m}$

PACKAGE 3:

Low Effort: $E(\Pi) = .30\text{x}\$5\text{m} + .40\text{x}\$10\text{m} + .30\text{x}\$15\text{m} - (.3\text{x}\$.5\text{m} + \$.4\text{x}\$.5\text{m} + .3\text{x}\$.5\text{m})$
$= \$9.5\text{m}$

High Effort: $E(\Pi) = .30\text{x}\$10\text{m} + .40\text{x}\$15\text{m} + .30\text{x}\$17\text{m} - (.3\text{x}\$.5\text{m} + \$.4\text{x}\$.5\text{m} + .3\text{x}\$1.5\text{m}) = \$13.3\text{m}$

To maximize the expected profits of ASP Industries, you recommend compensation PACKAGE 3 which uses a flat salary and then a large bonus when the firm does exceptionally well and makes $17 million. You prefer this package because it maximizes firm expected profits net of compensation – here at a value of $13.30 million.

Notice that if you just gave a very large bonus when the firm did exceptionally well, CEO risk aversion would lead him to make low effort -- or more likely work for someone else. The flat salary offsets the disincentive effects of a risky – but motivating – package. This is the usual form of executive compensation. Notice too that compensation is tied to firm profitability.

When the worker gives high effort, always check that your profits are higher under high effort than under low effort. You might be getting high effort, but you are giving away too much so that you really prefer that the worker be lazy! Well not really, but you a giving away too much of firm profits to motivate your employees. If you find this to be a problem, then reduce compensation while keeping high effort until profits from high effort beat profits from low effort. Then you have a compensation plan that makes some sense.

11. A firm's short-run revenue is given by R = 10e - e^2, where e is the level of effort by a typical worker (all workers are assumed to be identical). A worker chooses his level of effort to maximize his wage net of effort w - e (the per-unit cost of effort is assumed to be 1). Determine the level of effort and the level of profit (revenue less wage paid) for each of the following wage arrangements. Explain why these differing principal-agent relationships generate different outcomes.

a. **w = 2 for e ≥ 1; otherwise w = 0.**

There is no incentive for the worker to provide an effort that exceeds 1, as the wage received by the worker will be 2 if the worker provides one unit of effort but will not increase if the worker provides more effort.

The profit for the firm will be revenue minus the wages paid to the worker:

$$\pi = (10)(1) - 1^2 - 2 = \$7.$$

In this principal-agent relationship there is no incentive for the worker to increase his or her effort as the wage is not related to the revenues of the firm.

b. **w = R/2.**

The worker will attempt to maximize the wage net of the effort required to obtain that wage; that is, the worker will attempt to maximize:

$$w - e = \frac{10e - e^2}{2} - e, \text{ or } 4e - 0.5e^2.$$

To find the maximum effort that the worker is willing to put forth, take the first derivative with respect to effort, set it equal to zero, and solve for effort.

$$\frac{d\left(4e - 0.5e^2\right)}{de} = 4 - e = 0, \text{ or } e = 4.$$

The wage the worker will receive will be

$$w = \frac{R}{2} = \frac{10(4) - 4^2}{2} = 12.$$

The profits for the firm will be

$$\pi = ((10)(4) - 4^2) - 12 = \$12.$$

With this principal-agent relationship, the wage that the individual worker receives is related to the revenue of the firm. Therefore, we see greater effort on the part of the worker and, as a result, greater profits for the firm.

c. **w = R - 12.5.**

Again, the worker will attempt to maximize the wage net of the effort required to obtain that wage; that is, the worker will attempt to maximize:

$$w - e = \left(10e - e^2\right) - 12.50 - e, \text{ or } 9e - e^2 - 12.50.$$

To find the maximum effort that the worker is willing to put forth, take the first derivative with respect to effort, set it equal to zero, and solve for effort:

$$\frac{d\left(9e - e^2 - 12.5\right)}{de} = 9 - 2e = 0, \text{ or } e = 4.5.$$

The wage the worker will receive will be

$$w = R - 12.50 = \left((10)(4.5) - 4.5^2\right) - 12.5 = 12.25.$$

The profits for the firm will be

$$\pi = ((10)(4.5) - 4.5^2) - 12.25 = \$12.50.$$

With this principal-agent relationship, we find that the wage of the worker is more directly related to the performance of the firm than in either *a* or *b*. We find that the worker is willing to supply even more effort resulting in even higher profits for the firm.

CHAPTER 18
EXTERNALITIES AND PUBLIC GOODS

TEACHING NOTES

This chapter discusses the remaining types of market failure which were introduced at the end of Chapter 16, and which were not covered in Chapter 17. Section 18.1 defines the concept of externalities, both positive and negative. Section 18.2 discusses methods of correcting for the market failure that arises in the presence of externalities. These two sections give a good self-contained overview of externalities as a type of market failure. The next two sections, 18.3 and 18.4, explore the relationship between the existence of externalities and property rights. Section 18.5 discusses public goods and section 18.6 offers a brief discussion of determining the optimal level of the public good to provide. Overall the chapter provides a good solid overview of some very interesting problems. Any instructor who had the time and desire to expand upon the presentation in the chapter could find a wealth of information by consulting an environmental or resource economics textbook. There are an abundance of examples related to pollution or natural resource issues that you could choose to talk about. Check your local newspaper for ideas.

The consumption of many goods involves the creation of externalities. Stress the divergence between social and private costs, and the difference between the private (industry competitive) equilibrium and the socially optimal (efficient) equilibrium. You can use the students' knowledge of consumer and producer surplus to explore the welfare gain of moving to the efficient equilibrium. Exercise (5) presents the classic beekeeper/apple-orchard problem, originally popularized in Meade, "External Economies and Diseconomies in a Competitive Situation," *Economic Journal* (March 1952). Empirical research on this example has shown that beekeepers and orchard owners have solved many of their problems: see Cheung, "The Fable of the Bees: An Economic Investigation," *Journal of Law and Economics* (April 1973).

One of the main themes of the law and economics literature since 1969 is the application of Coase's insight on the assignment of property rights. The original article is clear and can be understood by students. Stress the problems posed by transactions costs. For a lively debate, ask students whether non-smokers should be granted the right to smokeless air in public places (see Exercise (4)). For an extended discussion of the Coase Theorem at the undergraduate level, see Polinsky, Chapters 3-6, *An Introduction to Law & Economics* (Little, Brown & Co., 1983).

The last two sections focus on public goods and private choice. Point out the similarities and differences between public goods and other activities with externalities. Since students confuse nonrival and nonexclusive goods, create a table similar to the following and give examples to fill in the cells:

	Exclusive	Nonexclusive
Rival	Most Goods	Air and Water
Nonrival	Congestion	Public Goods

The next stumbling block for students is achieving an understanding of why we add individual demand curves vertically rather than horizontally. Stress that by summing horizontally you are asking the total quantity supplied/demanded at any given price. By summing vertically you are asking the total willingness to pay for a given quantity.

The presentation of public choice is a limited introduction to the subject, but you can easily expand on this material. A logical extension of this chapter is an introduction to cost-benefit analysis. For applications of this analysis, see Part III, "Empirical Analysis of Policies and Programs," in Haveman and Margolis (eds.), *Public Expenditure and Policy Analysis* (Houghton Mifflin, 1983).

QUESTIONS FOR REVIEW

1. Which of the following describes an externality and which does not? Explain the difference.

a. A policy of restricted coffee exports in Brazil causes the U.S. price of coffee to rise, which in turn also causes the price of tea to rise.

Externalities cause market inefficiencies because the price of the good does not reflect the true social value of the good. A policy of restricting coffee exports in Brazil causes the U.S. price of coffee to rise, because supply is reduced. As the price of coffee rises, consumers switch to tea, thereby increasing the demand for tea, and hence, increasing the price of tea. These are market effects, not externalities.

b. An advertising blimp distracts a motorist who then hits a telephone pole.

An advertising blimp is producing information by announcing the availability of some good or service. However, its method of supplying this information can be distracting for some consumers, especially those consumers who happen to be driving near telephone poles. The blimp is creating a negative externality that influences the drivers' safety. Since the price charged by the advertising firm does not incorporate the externality of distracting drivers, too much of this type of advertising is produced from the point of view of society as a whole.

2. Compare and contrast the following three mechanisms for treating pollution externalities when the costs and benefits of abatement are uncertain: (a) an emissions fee, (b) an emissions standard, and (c) a system of transferable emissions permits.

Since pollution creates an external cost that is not reflected in the marginal cost of production, its emission creates an externality. Three policy tools can be used to reduce pollution: an emissions fee, an emissions standard, and a system of transferable permits. The choice between a fee and a standard will depend on the marginal cost and marginal benefit of reducing pollution. If small changes in abatement yield large benefits while adding little to cost, the cost of not reducing emissions is high. Thus, standards should be used. However, if small changes in abatement yield little benefit while adding greatly to cost, the cost of reducing emissions is high. Thus, fees should be used.

A system of transferable emissions permits combines the features of fees and standards to reduce pollution. Under this system, a standard is set and fees are used to transfer permits to the firm that values them the most (i.e., a firm with high abatement costs). However, the total number of permits can be incorrectly chosen. Too few permits will create excess demand, increasing price and inefficiently diverting resources to owners of the permits. Typically, pollution control agencies implement one of three mechanisms, measure the results, reassess the success of their choice, then reset new levels of fees or standards or select a new policy tool.

3. When do externalities require government intervention? When is such intervention unlikely to be necessary?

Economic efficiency can be achieved without government intervention when the externality affects a small number of people and when property rights are well specified. When the number of parties is small, the cost of negotiating an agreement among the parties is small. Further, the amount of required information (i.e., the costs of and benefits to each party) is small. When property rights are not well specified, uncertainty regarding costs and benefits increases and efficient choices might not be made. The costs of coming to an agreement, including the cost of delaying such an agreement, could be greater than the cost of government intervention, including the expected cost of choosing the wrong policy instrument.

4. Consider a market in which a firm has monopoly power. Suppose in addition that the firm produces under the presence of (i) a positive or (ii) a negative externality. Does the externality necessarily lead to a greater misallocation of resources?

In the presence of a negative externality the market will produce too much output, as compared to the socially optimal solution. The monopolist will however produce too little output. It is possible therefore that the monopolist by himself will produce closer to the socially optimal solution than the competitive firms would. For the case of the positive externality the competitive firms will produce too little output, the monopolist will produce even less, and the monopolist is therefore leading to a greater misallocation of resources.

5. Externalities arise solely because individuals are unaware of the consequences of their actions. Agree or disagree? Explain.

This is not a true statement. It is not that people are unaware but that they are not forced to consider and account for all of the consequences of their actions. If a firm dumps waste into a river that affects a swimming area downstream it is generating an externality given it is not forced to consider the cost it is imposing on users of the swimming area. This is true whether the firm is aware of these costs or not.

6. To encourage an industry to produce at the socially optimal level the government should impose a unit tax on output that is equal to the marginal cost of production. True or false? Explain.

This statement is false. While a tax can encourage firms to produce at the socially optimal level, the tax should be set equal to the marginal external cost and not the marginal private cost. Firms will maximize profit by producing at the point where price is equal to marginal cost. When there are external costs involved the marginal cost of the firm is too low from society's point of view, and as a result too much output is produced. By setting a tax equal to the additional cost not being realized by the firm (the marginal external cost) the firm will be encouraged to consider all costs and will reduce output because the tax will increase the overall marginal cost.

7. George and Stan live next door to each other. George likes to plant flowers in his garden, but every time he does, Stan's dog comes over and digs them up. Since it is Stan's dog that is causing the damage, if economic efficiency is to be achieved, it is necessary that Stan pay to put up a fence around his yard to keep the dog in. Agree or disagree? Explain.

If there are leash laws then this would be true. Stan would either need to keep his dog on a leash or put up a fence. In general, it is possible for the two parties to bargain and come up with a solution that will benefit both of them. They could for example split the cost of the fence. Economic efficiency does not require that Stan pay for the fence. It merely requires that Stan and George negotiate over how best to address the problem and come up with a solution that will work for both of them.

8. An emissions fee is paid to the government, whereas an injurer who is sued and held liable pays damages directly to the party harmed by an externality. What differences in the behavior of victims might you expect to arise under these two arrangements?

When victims can receive the damages directly, they are more likely to file a claim, initiate a suit, and try to overstate their damages. When victims are not able to receive the damages directly, they are less likely to report violations and are less likely to overstate their damages. In theory, emissions fees paid to the government require the polluting firm to pay compensation for any damage inflicted and hence to move towards the socially optimal level of production. An individual who is injured by a firm's polluting behavior is again less likely to file a complaint if they do not feel they can directly receive the compensation.

9. Why does free access to a common property resource generate an inefficient outcome?

Free access to a resource means that the marginal cost to the user is less than the social cost because each user has no incentive to consider how his use of the resource will affect the use of the resource by other users. The use of a common property resource by a person or firm excludes others from using it. For example, the use of water by one consumer restricts its use by another. Since private marginal cost is below social marginal cost, too much of the resource is consumed by the individual user, creating an inefficient outcome. Each individual using the common property resource considers only his own actions and does not consider how all of the users collectively are impacting the resource.

10. Public goods are both nonrival and nonexclusive. Explain each of these terms and show clearly how they differ from each other.

A good is *nonrival* if, for any level of production, the marginal cost of providing the good to an additional *consumer* is zero (although the production cost of an additional *unit* could be greater than zero). A good is *nonexclusive* if it is impossible or very expensive to exclude individuals from consuming it. Public goods are *nonrival* and *nonexclusive*. Commodities can be (1) exclusive and rival, (2) exclusive and nonrival, (3) nonexclusive and rival, or (4) nonexclusive and nonrival. Most of the commodities discussed in the text to this point have been of the first type. In this chapter, we focus on commodities of the last type.

Nonrival refers to the *production* of a good or service for one more customer. It usually involves a production process with high fixed costs, such as the cost of building a highway or lighthouse. (Remember that fixed cost depends on the period under consideration: the cost of lighting the lamp at the lighthouse can vary over time, but does not vary with the number of consumers.) Nonexclusive refers to *exchange*, where the cost of charging consumers is prohibitive. Incurring the cost of identifying consumers and collecting from them would result in losses. Some economists focus on the nonexclusion property of public goods because it is this characteristic that poses the most significant problems for efficient provision.

11. A village is located next to 1000 acres of prime grazing land. The village presently owns the land and allows all residents to graze cows freely. Some members of the village council have suggested that the land is being overgrazed. Is this likely to be true? These same members have also suggested that the village should either require grazers to purchase an annual permit, or sell off the land to the grazers. Would either of these be a good idea?

It is true that the common land is likely to be overgrazed since each individual will consider only their own private cost and not the true social cost of grazing. The social cost of grazing is likely to be higher than any one individual's private cost because no one individual has an incentive to take into account how his grazing affects the opportunities of others. For example, one individual could decide to graze only in certain areas during certain times of the year, while preserving other areas for other times of the year. However, the individual will not do this if the resource is common property as any other grazer can come along and freely disrupt the preservation system that the individual has set up. Selling annual permits or selling the land outright would be viable options to the overgrazing problem. By requiring the grazers to buy a permit, their marginal costs will go up and grazing should go down. If an individual purchases the land they will then have an incentive to consider all of the costs associated with using the land, and as a result will use it in such a way that the resource is preserved since they alone capture all of the benefits of preserving the resource.

12. Public television is funded in part by private donations, even though anyone with a television set can watch for free. Can you explain this phenomenon in light of the free rider problem?

The free-rider problem refers to the difficulty of excluding persons from consuming a nonexclusive commodity. Non-paying consumers can "free-ride" on commodities provided by paying customers. Public television is funded in part by contributions. Some viewers contribute, but most watch without paying, hoping that someone else will pay so they will not. To combat this problem these stations (1) ask consumers to assess their true willingness to pay, then (2) ask consumers to contribute up to this amount, and (3) attempt to make everyone else feel guilty for free-riding.

13. Explain why the median voter outcome need not be efficient when majority rule voting determines the level of public spending.

The median voter is the citizen with the middle preference: half the voting population is more strongly in favor of the issue and half is more strongly opposed to the issue. Under majority-rule voting, where each citizen's vote is weighted equally, the preferred spending level on public-goods provision of the *median voter* will win an election against any other alternative. However, majority rule is not necessarily efficient, because it gives each citizen's preferences equal weight. For an efficient outcome, we would need a system that measures and aggregates the willingness to pay of those citizens consuming the public good. Majority rule is not this system. However, as we have seen in previous chapters, majority rule is equitable in the sense that all citizens are treated equally. Thus, we again find a trade-off between equity and efficiency.

EXERCISES

1. A number of firms have located in the western portion of a town after single-family residences took up the eastern portion. Each firm produces the same product and, in the process, emits noxious fumes that adversely affect the residents of the community.

a. Why is there an externality created by the firms?

Noxious fumes created by firms enter the utility function of residents, and the residents have no control over the quantity of the fumes. We can assume that the fumes decrease the utility of the residents (i.e., they are a negative externality) and lower property values.

b. Do you think that private bargaining can resolve the problem? Explain.

If the residents anticipated the location of the firms, housing prices should reflect the disutility of the fumes; the externality would have been internalized by the housing market in housing prices. If the noxious fumes were not anticipated, private bargaining could resolve the problem of the externality only if there are a relatively small number of parties (both firms and families) and property rights are well specified. Private bargaining would rely on each family's willingness to pay for air quality, but truthful revelation might not be possible. All this will be complicated by the adaptability of the production technology known to the firms and the employment relations between the firms and families. It is unlikely that private bargaining will resolve the problem.

c. How might the community determine the efficient level of air quality?

The community could determine the economically efficient level of air quality by aggregating the families' willingness to pay and equating it with the marginal cost of pollution reduction. Both steps involve the acquisition of truthful information.

2. A computer programmer lobbies against copyrighting software, arguing that everyone should benefit from innovative programs written for personal computers and that exposure to a wide variety of computer programs will inspire young programmers to create even more innovative programs. Considering the marginal social benefits possibly gained by this proposal, do you agree with this position?

Computer software as information is a classic example of a public good. Since it can be costlessly copied, the marginal cost of providing software to an additional user is near zero. Therefore, software is nonrival. (The fixed costs of creating software are high, but the variable costs are low.) Furthermore, it is expensive to exclude consumers from copying and using software because copy protection schemes are available only at high cost or high inconvenience to users. Therefore, software is also nonexclusive. As both nonrival and nonexclusive, computer software suffers the problems of public goods provision: the presence of free-riders makes it difficult or impossible for markets to provide the efficient level of software. Rather than regulating this market directly, the legal system guarantees property rights to the creators of software. If copyright protection were not enforced, it is likely that the software market would collapse, or that there would be a significant decrease in the quantity of software developed and supplied, which would reduce the marginal social benefits. Therefore, we do not agree with the computer programmer.

3. Assume that scientific studies provide you with the following information concerning the benefits and costs of sulfur dioxide emissions:

Benefits of abating (reducing) emissions:	**MB=500-20A**
Costs of abating emissions:	**MC=200+5A**

where A is the quantity abated in millions of tons and the benefits and costs are given in dollars per ton.

a.   What is the socially efficient level of emissions abatement?

To find the socially efficient level of emissions abatement, set marginal benefit equal to marginal cost and solve for A:

$$500-20A=200+5A$$

$$A=12.$$

b.   What are the marginal benefit and marginal cost of abatement at the socially efficient level of abatement?

Plug A=12 into the marginal benefit and marginal cost functions to find the benefit and cost:

$$MB=500-20(12)=260$$

$$MC=200+5(12)=260.$$

c.   What happens to net social benefits (benefits minus costs) if you abate 1 million more tons than the efficient level? 1 million fewer?

Net social benefits are the area under the marginal benefit curve minus the area under the marginal cost curve. At the socially efficient level of abatement this is equal to area a+b+c+d in Figure 18.3.c or

$$0.5(500-200)(12)=1800 \text{ million dollars.}$$

If you abate 1 million more tons then the net social benefit is area a+b+c+d-e or

$$1800-0.5(265-240)(1)=1800-12.5=1787.5 \text{ million dollars.}$$

If you abate 1 million less tons then the net social benefit is area a+b or

$$0.5(500-280)(11)+(280-255)(11)+0.5(255-200)(11)=1787.5 \text{ million dollars.}$$

d.   Why is it socially efficient to set marginal benefits equal to marginal costs rather than abating until total benefits equal total costs?

It is socially efficient to set marginal benefit equal to marginal cost rather than total benefit equal to total cost because we want to maximize net benefits, which are total benefit minus total cost. Maximizing total benefit minus total cost means that at the margin, the last unit abated will have an equal cost and benefit. Choosing the point where total benefit is equal to total cost will result in too much abatement, and would be analogous to choosing to produce where total revenue was equal to total cost. If total revenue was always equal to total cost by choice, then there would never be any profit. In the case of abatement, the more we abate, the costlier it is. Given that funds will tend to be scarce, dollars should be allocated to abatement only so long as the benefit of the last unit of abatement is greater than or equal to the cost of the last unit of abatement.

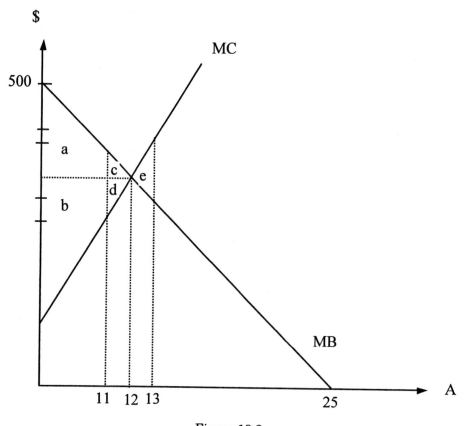

Figure 18.3.c

4. Four firms located at different points on a river dump various quantities of effluent into it. The effluent adversely affects the quality of swimming for homeowners who live downstream. These people can build swimming pools to avoid swimming in the river, and firms can purchase filters that eliminate harmful chemicals in the material dumped in the river. As a policy advisor for a regional planning organization, how would you compare and contrast the following options for dealing with the harmful effect of the effluent:

a.   An equal-rate effluent fee on firms located on the river.

First, one needs to know the value to homeowners of swimming in the river. This information can be difficult to obtain, because homeowners will have an incentive to overstate this value. As an upper boundary, if there are no considerations other than swimming, one could use the cost of building swimming pools, either a pool for each homeowner or a public pool for all homeowners. Next, one needs to know the marginal cost of abatement. If the abatement technology is well understood, this information should be readily obtainable. If the abatement technology is not understood, an estimate based on the firms' knowledge must be used.

The choice of a policy tool will depend on the marginal benefits and costs of abatement. If firms are charged an equal-rate effluent fee, the firms will reduce effluents to the point where the marginal cost of abatement is equal to the fee. If this reduction is not high enough to permit swimming, the fee could be increased. Alternatively, revenue from the fees could be used to provide swimming facilities, reducing the need for effluent reduction.

b.   An equal standard per firm on the level of effluent that each can dump.

Standards will be efficient only if the policy maker has complete information regarding the marginal costs and benefits of abatement, so that the efficient level of the standard can be determined. Moreover, the standard will not encourage firms to reduce effluents further when new filtering technologies become available.

c.   A transferable effluent permit system in which the aggregate level of effluent is fixed and all firms receive identical permits.

A transferable effluent permit system requires the policy maker to determine the efficient effluent standard. Once the permits are distributed and a market develops, firms with a higher cost of abatement will purchase permits from firms with lower abatement costs. However, unless permits are sold initially, rather than merely distributed, no revenue will be generated for the regional organization.

5. Medical research has shown the negative health effects of "secondhand" smoke. Recent social trends point to growing intolerance of smoking in public areas. If you are a smoker and you wish to continue smoking despite tougher anti smoking laws, describe the effect of the following legislative proposals on your behavior. As a result of these programs, do you, the individual smoker, benefit? Does society benefit as a whole?

Since smoking in public areas is similar to polluting the air, the programs proposed here are similar to those examined for air pollution. A bill to lower tar and nicotine levels is similar to an emissions standard, and a tax on cigarettes is similar to an emissions fee. Requiring a smoking permit is similar to a system of emissions permits, assuming that the permits would not be transferable. The individual smoker in all of these programs is being forced to internalize the externality of "second-hand" smoke and will be worse off. Society will be better off if the benefits of a particular proposal outweigh the cost of implementing that proposal. Unfortunately, the benefits of reducing second-hand smoke are uncertain, and assessing those benefits is costly.

a.   A bill is proposed that would lower tar and nicotine levels in all cigarettes.

The smoker will most likely try to maintain a constant level of consumption of nicotine, and will increase his or her consumption of cigarettes. Society may not benefit from this plan if the total amount of tar and nicotine released into the air is the same.

b.   A tax is levied on each pack of cigarettes sold.

Smokers might turn to cigars, pipes, or might start rolling their own cigarettes. The extent of the effect of a tax on cigarette consumption depends on the elasticity of demand for cigarettes. Again, it is questionable whether society will benefit.

c.   Smokers would be required to carry government issued smoking permits at all times.

Smoking permits would effectively transfer property rights to clean air from smokers to non-smokers. The main obstacle to society benefiting from such a proposal would be the high cost of enforcing a smoking permits system. In addition, the cost of the permit raises the effective price of the cigarettes and the resulting affect on quantity smoked will depend on the elasticity of demand.

6. The market for paper in a particular region in the United States is characterized by the following demand and supply curves

$$Q_D = 160,000 - 2000P \text{ and } Q_S = 40,000 + 2000P,$$

where Q_D is the quantity demanded of paper in 100 lb. lots, Q_S is the quantity demanded of paper in 100 lb. lots, and P is the price per 100 lb. lot of paper. Currently there is no attempt to regulate the dumping of effluent into streams and rivers by the paper mills. As a result, dumping is widespread. The marginal external cost (*MEC*) associated with the production of paper is given by the curve $MEC = 0.0006Q_S$.

a. Calculate the output and price of paper if it is produced under competitive conditions and no attempt is made to monitor or regulate the dumping of effluent.

The equilibrium price and output would be where quantity demand is equal to quantity supplied:

$$160,000-2000P=40,000+2000P$$

$$4000P=120,000$$

$$P=\$30 \text{ per } 100 \text{ lb. lot}$$

$$Q=100,000 \text{ lots of } 100 \text{ lb. each.}$$

b. Determine the socially efficient price and output of paper.

To find the socially efficient solution, we need to consider the external costs, as given by $MEC = 0.0006Q_S$, as well as the private costs, as given by $Q_S = 40,000 + 2000P$. Rewriting the supply curve, the private costs are P=0.0005Qs-20=MC. Therefore,

$$MSC=MC+MEC=0.0005Qs-20+0.0006Qs$$

$$MSC=0.0011Qs-20.$$

Setting the marginal social cost equal to the demand curve, or the marginal benefit,

$$0.0011Q-20=80-0.0005Q$$

$$Q=62,500 \text{ lots of } 100 \text{ lb. each.}$$

$$P=\$48.75 \text{ per } 100 \text{ lb. lot.}$$

c. Explain clearly why the answers you calculated in parts a and b differ.

The equilibrium quantity declined and the equilibrium price rose in part b because the external costs were considered. Ignoring some of the costs will result in too much output being produced and sold at too low of a price.

7. In a market for dry cleaning, the inverse market demand function is given by $P = 100 - Q$ and the (private) marginal cost of production for the aggregation of all dry cleaning firms is given by $MC = 10 + Q$. Finally, the pollution generated by the dry cleaning process creates external damages given by the marginal external cost curve $MEC = Q$.

a. Calculate the output and price of dry cleaning if it is produced under competitive conditions absent regulation.

To find the answer, set price equal to marginal cost:

$$100-Q=10+Q,$$
$$Q=45, \text{ and } P=55.$$

b. Determine the socially efficient price and output of dry cleaning.

To find the answer here, we must first calculate the marginal social cost (MSC), which is equal to the marginal external cost plus the private marginal cost. Next, set

MSC equal to the market demand function to solve for price and quantity. When all costs are included, the quantity produced will fall and the price will rise:

$$MSC=MC+MEC=10+2Q=100-Q,$$

Q=30, and P=70.

c. **Determine the tax that would result in a competitive market producing the socially efficient output.**

If there is a unit tax, then the new marginal private cost function is MC'=10+Q+tQ. If we now set this new marginal cost function equal to the price of 70 and substitute in 30 for the quantity, we can solve for t:

$$10+Q+tQ=70$$
$$Q(1+t)=60$$
$$1+t=2$$
$$t=1.$$

The tax should be $1 per unit output. Note that with the tax equal to 1, the new private cost function is the same as the marginal social cost function.

d. **Calculate the output and price of dry cleaning if it is produced under monopolistic conditions without regulation.**

The monopolist will set marginal cost equal to marginal revenue. Recall that the marginal revenue curve has a slope that is twice the slope of the demand curve so MR=100-2Q=MC=10+Q. Therefore, Q=30 and P=70.

e. **Determine the tax that would result in a monopolistic market producing the socially efficient output.**

The tax is equal to zero since the monopolist will produce at the socially efficient output in this case.

f. **Assuming that no attempt is made to monitor or regulate the pollution, which market structure yields higher social welfare? Discuss.**

In this case it is actually the monopolist that yields the higher level of social welfare over the competitive market since the monopolist's profit maximizing price and quantity are the same as the socially efficient solution. Since a monopolist tends to produce less output than the competitive equilibrium, it may end up producing closer to the social equilibrium when a negative externality is present.

8. **A beekeeper lives adjacent to an apple orchard. The orchard owner benefits from the bees because each hive pollinates about one acre of apple trees. The orchard owner pays nothing for this service, however, because the bees come to the orchard without his having to do anything. Because there are not enough bees to pollinate the entire orchard, the orchard owner must complete the pollination by artificial means, at a cost of $10 per acre of trees.**

Beekeeping has a marginal cost of MC = 10 + 5Q, where Q is the number of beehives. Each hive yields $40 worth of honey.

a. **How many beehives will the beekeeper maintain?**

The beekeeper maintains the number of hives that maximizes profits, when marginal revenue is equal to marginal cost. With a constant marginal revenue of $40 (there is no information that would lead us to believe that the beekeeper has any market power) and a marginal cost of 10 + 5Q:

$$40 = 10 + 5Q, \text{ or } Q = 6.$$

b. **Is this the economically efficient number of hives?**

If there are too few bees to pollinate the orchard, the farmer must pay $10 per acre for artificial pollination. Thus, the farmer would be willing to pay up to $10 to the beekeeper to maintain each additional hive. So, the marginal social benefit, *MSB*, of each additional hive is $50, which is greater than the marginal private benefit of $40. Assuming that the private marginal cost is equal to the social marginal cost, we set *MSB* = *MC* to determine the efficient number of hives:

$$50 = 10 + 5Q, \text{ or } Q = 8.$$

Therefore, the beekeeper's private choice of *Q* = 6 is not the socially efficient number of hives.

c. **What changes would lead to the more efficient operation?**

The most radical change that would lead to more efficient operations would be the merger of the farmer's business with the beekeeper's business. This merger would internalize the positive externality of bee pollination. Short of a merger, the farmer and beekeeper should enter into a contract for pollination services.

9. There are three groups in a community. Their demand curves for public television in hours of programming, T, are given respectively by

$$W_1 = \$200 - T,$$

$$W_2 = \$240 - T,$$

$$W_3 = \$320 - 2T.$$

Suppose public television is a pure public good that can be produced at a constant marginal cost of $200 per hour.

a. **What is the efficient number of hours of public television?**

The efficient number of hours is the amount such that the sum of the marginal benefits is equal to marginal cost. Given the demand curves representing the marginal benefits to each individual, we sum these demand curves vertically to determine the sum of all marginal benefits. From the table below one can see that *MSB* = *MC* at *T* = 140 hours of programming.

Willingness to Pay

Time	Group 1	Group 2	Group 3	Vertical Sum
0	200	240	320	760
100	100	140	120	360
120	80	120	80	280
140	60	100	40	200
160	40	80	0	120
180	20	60	0	80

b. **How much public television would a competitive private market provide?**

To find the number of hours that the private market would provide, we add the individual demand curves horizontally. The efficient number of hours is such that the private marginal cost is equal to the private marginal benefit. The demand curve for group 1 lies below *MC* = $200 for all *T* > 0. With marginal cost equal to $200, only groups 2 and 3 would be willing to pay $200. At that price, 100 hours of programming would be provided.

Quantity Demanded

Price	Group 1	Group 2	Group 3	Horizontal Sum
240	0	0	40	40
220	0	20	50	70
200	0	40	60	100
180	20	60	70	150
160	40	80	80	200
140	60	100	90	250

10. Reconsider the common resource problem as given by Example 18.5. Suppose that crawfish popularity continues to increase, and that the demand curve shifts from $C = 0.401 - 0.0064F$ to $C = 0.50 - 0.0064F$. How does this shift in demand affect the actual crawfish catch, the efficient catch, and the social cost of common access? (*Hint*: Use the marginal social cost and private cost curves given in the example.)

The relevant information is now the following:

Demand: $C = 0.50 - 0.0064F$

MSC: $C = -5.645 + 0.6509F$.

With an increase in demand, the demand curve for crawfish shifts upward, intersecting the price axis at $0.50. The private cost curve has a positive slope, so additional effort must be made to increase the catch. Since the social cost curve has a positive slope, the socially efficient catch also increases. We may determine the socially efficient catch by solving the following two equations simultaneously:

$$0.50 - 0.0064F = -5.645 + 0.6509F, \text{ or } F^* = 9.35.$$

To determine the price that consumers are willing to pay for this quantity, substitute F^* into the equation for *marginal social cost* and solve for C:

$$C = -5.645 + (0.6509)(9.35), \text{ or } C = \$0.44.$$

Next, find the actual level of production by solving these equations simultaneously:

Demand: $C = 0.50 - 0.0064F$

MPC: $C = -0.357 + 0.0573F$

$$0.50 - 0.0064F = -0.357 + 0.0573F, \text{ or } F^{**} = 13.45.$$

To determine the price that consumers are willing to pay for this quantity, substitute F^{**} into the equation for *marginal private cost* and solve for C:

$$C = -0.357 + (0.0573)(13.45), \text{ or } C = \$0.41.$$

Notice that the marginal social cost of producing 13.45 units is

$$MSC = -5.645 + (0.6509)(13.45) = \$3.11.$$

With the increase in demand, the social cost is the area of a triangle with a base of 4.1 million pounds (13.45 - 9.35) and a height of $2.70 ($3.11 - 0.41), or $5,535,000 more than the social cost of the original demand.

11. The Georges Bank, a highly productive fishing area off New England, can be divided into two zones in terms of fish population. Zone 1 has the higher population per square mile but is subject to severe diminishing returns to fishing effort. The daily fish catch (in tons) in Zone 1 is

$$F_1 = 200(X_1) - 2(X_1)^2$$

where X_1 is the number of boats fishing there. Zone 2 has fewer fish per mile but is larger, and diminishing returns are less of a problem. Its daily fish catch is

$$F_2 = 100(X_2) - (X_2)^2$$

where X_2 is the number of boats fishing in Zone 2. The marginal fish catch MFC in each zone can be represented as

$$\text{MFC}_1 = 200 - 4(X_1) \qquad\qquad \text{MFC}_2 = 100 - 2(X_2).$$

There are 100 boats now licensed by the U.S. government to fish in these two zones. The fish are sold at \$100 per ton. Total cost (capital and operating) per boat is constant at \$1,000 per day. Answer the following questions about this situation:

a. If the boats are allowed to fish where they want, with no government restriction, how many will fish in each zone? What will be the gross value of the catch?

Without restrictions, the boats will divide themselves so that the average catch (AF_1 and AF_2) for each boat is equal in each zone. (If the average catch in one zone is greater than in the other, boats will leave the zone with the lower catch for the zone with the higher catch.) We solve the following set of equations:

$$AF_1 = AF_2 \text{ and } X_1 + X_2 = 100 \quad \text{where}$$

$$AF_1 = \frac{200X_1 - 2X_1^2}{X_1} = 200 - 2X_1 \quad \text{and}$$

$$AF_2 = \frac{100X_2 - X_2^2}{X_2} = 100 - X_2.$$

Therefore, $AF_1 = AF_2$ implies

$$200 - 2X_1 = 100 - X_2,$$

$$200 - 2(100 - X_2) = 100 - X_2, \text{ or } X_2 = \frac{100}{3} \quad \text{and}$$

$$X_1 = 100 - \left(\frac{100}{3}\right) = \frac{200}{3}.$$

Find the gross catch by substituting the value of X_1 and X_2 into the catch equations:

$$F_1 = (200)\left(\frac{200}{3}\right) - (2)\left(\frac{200}{3}\right)^2 = 13,333 - 8,889 = 4,444, \quad \text{and}$$

$$F_2 = (100)\left(\frac{100}{3}\right) - \left(\frac{100}{3}\right)^2 = 3,333 - 1,111 = 2,222.$$

The total catch is $F_1 + F_2 = 6,666$. At the price of \$100 per ton, the value of the catch is \$666,600. The average catch for each of the 100 boats in the fishing fleet is 66.66 tons.

To determine the profit per boat, subtract total cost from total revenue:

$$\pi = (100)(66.66) - 1,000, \text{ or } \pi = \$5,666.$$

Total profit for the fleet is \$566,600.

b. **If the U.S. government can restrict the boats, how many should be allocated to each zone? What will be the gross value of the catch? Assume the total number of boats remains at 100.**

Assume that the government wishes to maximize the net social value of the fish catch, i.e., the difference between the total social benefit and the total social cost. The government equates the marginal fish catch in both zones, subject to the restriction that the number of boats equals 100:

$$MFC_1 = MFC_2 \text{ and } X_1 + X_2 = 100,$$

$$MFC_1 = 200 - 4X_1 \text{ and } MFC_2 = 100 - 2X_2.$$

Setting $MFC_1 = MFC_2$ implies:

$$200 - 4X_1 = 100 - 2X_2, \text{ or } 200 - 4(100 - X_2) = 100 - 2X_2, \text{ or } X_2 = 50 \text{ and}$$
$$X_1 = 100 - 50 = 50.$$

Find the gross catch by substituting X_1 and X_2 into the catch equations:

$$F_1 = (200)(50) - (2)(50^2) = 10{,}000 - 5{,}000 = 5{,}000 \quad \text{and}$$
$$F_2 = (100)(50) - 50^2 = 5{,}000 - 2{,}500 = 2{,}500.$$

The total catch is equal to $F_1 + F_2 = 7{,}500$. At the market price of $100 per ton, the value of the catch is $750,000. Total profit is $650,000. Notice that the profits are not evenly divided between boats in the two zones. The average catch in Zone A is 100 tons per boat, while the average catch in Zone B is 50 tons per boat. Therefore, fishing in Zone A yields a higher profit for the individual owner of the boat.

c. **If additional fishermen want to buy boats and join the fishing fleet, should a government wishing to maximize the net value of the catch grant them licenses? Why or why not?**

To answer this question, first determine the profit-maximizing number of boats in each zone. Profits in Zone A are

$$\pi_A = (100)\left(200X_1 - 2X_1^2\right) - 1{,}000X, \text{ or } \pi_A = 19{,}000X_1 - 200X_1^2.$$

To determine the change in profit with a change in X_1 take the first derivative of the profit function with respect to X_1:

$$\frac{d\pi_A}{dX_1} = 19{,}000 - 400X_1.$$

To determine the profit-maximizing level of output, set $\dfrac{d\pi_A}{dX_1}$ equal to zero and solve for X_1:

$$19{,}000 - 400X_1 = 0, \text{ or } X_1 = 47.5.$$

Substituting X_1 into the profit equation for Zone A gives:

$$\pi_A = (100)\left((200)(47.5) - (2)\left(47.5^2\right)\right) - (1{,}000)(47.5) = \$451{,}250.$$

For Zone B follow a similar procedure. Profits in Zone B are

$$\pi_B = (100)\left(100X_2 - X_2^2\right) - 1{,}000X_2, \text{ or } \pi_B = 9{,}000X_2 - 100X_2^2.$$

Taking the derivative of the profit function with respect to X_2 gives

$$\frac{d\pi_B}{dX_2} = 9{,}000 - 200X_2.$$

Setting $\dfrac{d\pi_B}{dX_2}$ equal to zero to find the profit-maximizing level of output gives

$$9{,}000 - 200X_2 = 0, \text{ or } X_2 = 45.$$

Substituting X_2 into the profit equation for Zone B gives:

$$\pi_B = (100)((100)(45) - 45^2) - (1{,}000)(45) = \$202{,}500.$$

Total profit from both zones is \$653,750, with 47.5 boats in Zone A and 45 boats in Zone B. Because each additional boat above 92.5 decreases total profit, the government should not grant any more licenses.